Children's Literature from A to Z

Children's Literature
from A *to* Z
a guide for parents and teachers

Jon C. Stott

McGraw-Hill Book Company

New York   St. Louis   San Francisco   Auckland
Bogotá   Hamburg   Johannesburg   London
Madrid   Mexico   Montreal   New Delhi
Panama   São Paulo   Singapore
Sydney   Tokyo   Toronto

Library of Congress Cataloging in Publication Data

Stott, Jon C.
    Children's literature from A to Z.

    Bibliography: p.
    Includes index.
    1. Children's literature, English—History and
criticism.   2. Children's literature, American—History
and criticism.   3. Children's literature—History and
criticism.   4. Illustrated books, Children's—History and
criticism.   I. Title.
PR990.S76 1984   820'.9'9282   84-4425
ISBN 0-07-061791-0

REF.

45,007

1234567890   DOC/DOC   89876543

ISBN 0-07-061791-0

The editors for this book were Thomas Quinn and Michael Hennelly, the
designer was Christine Aulicino, and the production supervisor was Reiko
F. Okamura. It was set in Palatino by Photo-Data, Inc.

Printed and bound by R. R. Donnelley & Sons Company.

To avoid awkward language, the pronoun "he" has been used in this book
to refer to persons of either gender. No sexual bias is implied or intended.

Illustration
Credits

Page 147: Illustration from *Rosie's Walk* by Pat Hutchins, Macmillan, New York, 1968. Copyright 1968, by Pat Hutchins. Reproduced by permission of Macmillan Publishing Co., Inc.

Page 150: Illustration from *Peter's Chair* by Ezra Jack Keats, Harper & Row, New York, 1967. Copyright 1967 by Ezra Jack Keats. Reproduced by permission of Harper & Row, Publishers, Inc.

Page 152: Illustration from *Charley, Charlotte and the Golden Canary* by Charles Keeping, Oxford University Press, London, 1967. Reproduced by permission of Oxford University Press.

Page 163: Illustration by Robert Lawson from *The Story of Ferdinand* by Munro Leaf, Viking, New York, 1936. Illustrations copyright 1936 by Robert Lawson. Copyright renewed 1964 by John W. Boyd. Reproduced by permission of Viking Penguin, Inc.

Page 177: Illustration from *Frederick* by Leo Lionni, Pantheon, New York, 1967. Reproduced by permission of Pantheon.

Page 185: Illustration from *Blueberries for Sal* by Robert McCloskey, Viking, New York, 1948. Copyright 1948, 1976 by Robert McCloskey. Reproduced by permission of Viking Penguin, Inc.

Page 188: Illustration from *Arrow to the Sun* by Gerald McDermott, Viking, New York, 1974. Copyright 1974 by Gerald McDermott. Reproduced by permission of Viking Penguin, Inc.

Page 207: Illustration by Alice Provensen and Martin Provensen from *The Mother Goose Book*, Random House, New York, 1976. Reproduced by permission of Alice Provensen and Martin Provensen.

Page 228: Illustration by Beatrix Potter from *The Tale of Peter Rabbit*, Frederick Warne & Co., London, 1902. Reproduced by permission of Frederick Warne & Co.

Page 232: Illustration by Howard Pyle from *The Merry Adventures of Robin Hood*, Charles Scribner's Sons, New York, 1902. Reproduced by courtesy of Charles Scribner's Sons.

Page 234: Illustration by Arthur Rackham from *Cinderella: Illustrated*, William Heinemann, Ltd., London, 1977. Reproduced by permission of William Heinemann Limited.

Page 246: Illustration from *Where the Wild Things Are* by Maurice Sendak, Harper & Row, New York, 1963. Copyright 1963 by Maurice Sendak. Reproduced by permission of Harper & Row, Publishers, Inc.

Page 250: Illustration from *The Cat in the Hat* by Dr. Seuss, Random House, New York, 1957. Reproduced by permission of Random House.

Page 253: Illustration by Ernest H. Shepard from *When We Were Very Young* by A. A. Milne, McClelland and Stewart, Toronto, 1925. Reproduced by permission of Ernest H. Shepard.

Page 260: Illustration from *Sylvester and the Magic Pebble*, by William Steig, Simon & Schuster, New York, 1969. Copyright 1969 by William Steig. Reproduced by permission of Windmill Books, a division of Simon & Schuster, Inc.

Page 268: Illustration by Sir John Tenniel from *Alice's Adventures in Wonderland*, edited by Donald Rackin, Wadsworth, Belmont, Calif., 1969. Reproduced by permission of Donald Rackin.

Page 278: Illustration from *The Beast of Monsieur Racine* by Tomi Ungerer, Farrar, Straus & Giroux, New York, 1971. Reprinted by permission of Farrar, Straus & Giroux.

Page 280: Illustration from *The Biggest Bear* by Lynd Ward, Houghton Mifflin, Boston, 1952. Copyright 1952 by Lynd Ward. Reproduced by permission of Houghton Mifflin Company.

Page 292: Illustration by Garth Williams from *Charlotte's Web* by E. B. White, Harper & Row, New York, 1952. Illustrations copyright 1952 by Garth Williams; renewed 1980. Reproduced by permission of Harper & Row, Publishers, Inc.

Page 296: From *Duffy and the Devil* by Harve Zemach and Margot Zemach, Farrar, Straus & Giroux, New York, 1973. Reproduced by permission of Farrar, Straus & Giroux.

For Carol,
Andrew,
and Clare

Contents

Introduction

When I first began teaching university courses in children's literature fourteen years ago, many of the students and some of my colleagues used to refer to the field as "kiddie litter," an indication of their low opinion of the course and its subject matter. After all, the implication seemed to be, children's books are simple and cute, they don't usually have a lot of words in them, and any adult who can read simple sentences should have no trouble understanding them. Why would any academic want to teach a serious university course about these books, and why would anyone want to spend considerable time learning about them? And, I must confess, at that time I thought that teaching the course would be merely something that I did to fill out my teaching schedule; my real energies would be directed toward my specialty, nineteenth-century American literature.

My attitudes, and those of my students and colleagues, have certainly changed since then. Children's literature is now viewed as a very important area in the field of English literature. Furthermore, it is now considered essential that adults—parents, teachers, and librarians—be well informed about children's literature so that they can help children to become better readers of all forms of literature. Then too, more and more adults are realizing that the study of children's literature is interesting in and for itself. An increasing number of adults are agreeing with a statement by literary critic and fantasist C. S. Lewis: "a children's story which is enjoyed only by children is a bad children's story."

Children's Literature from A to Z has been written both for adults who work with children and for adults who enjoy reading and studying children's books. Of course, in so vast an area as children's literature, it is not possible to give complete coverage to all authors, illustrators, and subjects. The phrase "A to Z" in the title of this book is intended to indicate its organizational pattern, not its completeness of coverage. However, the facts, analyses, and teaching tips included here will give the reader a broad general introduction to children's literature and ways of introducing it to children.

The articles are of five types: (1) short essays on major authors and illustrators, each one briefly outlining the life and literary career of the subject and indicating certain themes, techniques, and character types found in his or her works; (2) brief notes on a representative sampling of authors and illustrators of the post-World War II era; (3) essays on several of the most widely read folktales and on such heroic figures as Robin Hood; (4) lengthy essays on the major kinds of children's literature; and (5) two essays on the major American children's literature awards, the Newbery and Caldecott medals. Following each article is a short section entitled "Tips for Parents and Teachers." There is no one way of bringing children and books together; the ideas presented in these sections are merely some of the exercises and activities I have found successful in a dozen years of working with teachers and elementary and junior high school children in Canada and the United States. For the reader who wishes to study individual authors or subjects more fully, the bibliographic essay at the conclusion of the book suggests useful reading materials.

No reference book is written in isolation, and this one certainly was not. The bibliographic essay indicates those works to which I am most indebted. In over a decade of reading about children's literature, I have gained valuable insights from dozens of specialists in the field. Here I want specifically to mention my colleagues in the Children's Literature Association, a group of dedicated teachers, librarians, and professors, who, for over a decade, have been giving the field of children's literature the serious analysis it richly deserves.

Many people have generously given me their time while I was writing this book, and I wish to thank them for the help they have provided. At various stages of the writing, these people have read the manuscript and offered suggestions; Ray Jones, A. H. Stott, C. M. Stott, R. F. Tiffin, Rod McGillis, and Libby Smith. The staff and students of the following schools have allowed me to try out my ideas in the classroom: Belgravia, Riverdale, Overlanders, and Holy Family schools in Edmonton, Alberta; Central Elementary School in Lac LaBiche, Alberta; and Bauder Elementary School in Seminole, Florida. I owe a particular debt of gratitude to Norma Youngberg, a teacher in Edmonton who gave me valuable assistance in my early years of working with children. Both Angie Renville of the University of Alberta Library Faculty Lab and Martha Irwin and her staff in the children's room of the St. Petersburg Public Library were extremely helpful in supplying me with books during the writing of this volume. Typists Nancy Fullerton and Terry Diduch were patient and very efficient. Becky Bersagel of the University of Alberta performed great and loyal service in compiling the index. To Bob Rosenbaum, Michael Hennelly, and Tom Quinn, my editors at McGraw-Hill, goes my gratitude for their wisdom, cooperation, and invaluable assistance. The dedication indicates my inestimable debt to my wife and two children. The book has been strengthened by the cooperation of all these people; its deficiencies are all my own responsibility. Finally, I wish to thank the University of Alberta for granting me a study leave in 1979–1980, during which much of the research for this book was performed.

Jon C. Stott
Department of English
University of Alberta
January 14, 1984

John Burningham's ABC, by John Burningham, Jonathan Cape, London, 1964.

🍎ABC Books

   "Knowing your ABCs" is a phrase synonymous with becoming educated, and ABC books, or alphabet books, are among the oldest known children's books, having been used to help children learn to read almost since the beginning of printing. Even today, an alphabet book is often the first book a child is given. One of the most famous of the early alphabet books was *The New England Primer*, which went through countless editions between 1683 and 1830. Not only did it seek to introduce young readers to the letters of the alphabet, but also it attempted to reinforce the doctrines of Protestant Christianity. For example, the opening lines read: *"In Adam's fall/ We sinned all,"* while a later passage notes: *"Time cuts down all/ Both great and small."*

   During the nineteenth century, as books for children proliferated, ABC books grew in popularity. While many of them still contained stern moral advice, more secular ones appeared. One of the most popular themes in ABC books was the "A Apple Pie" motif, in which the fate of a newly baked pie was traced. Of the many "A Apple Pie" alphabets, the most famous was by Kate Greenaway. In the twentieth century, a tremendous variety of ABCs have been published. In addition to very simple volumes in which familiar objects are related to the appropriate letters, books dealing with concepts and specific themes have also appeared. Among these are Fritz Eichenberg's *Ape in a Cape: An Alphabet of Odd Animals* (1952), Helen Oxenbury's *ABC of Things* (1971), and Tom and Muriel Feeling's *Jambo Means Hello: A Swahili Alphabet* (1974). A large majority of the most important modern illustrators have tried their hand at ABC books, including Maurice Sendak (*Alligators All Around*, 1962), Brian Wildsmith (*ABC*, 1962), Ed Emberley (*Ed Emberley's ABC*, 1964), and Tasha Tudor (*A is for Annabelle*, 1954).

While the majority of alphabet books are designed for very young children, there are others for older children. For example, Margaret Musgrove's *From Ashanti to Zulu* (1976), illustrated by Leo and Dianne Dillon, contains detailed discussions of a variety of African tribal customs.

Ed Emberley's ABC, by Ed Emberley, Little, Brown, and Co., Boston, 1978.

On Market Street, by Arnold Lobel; illus. by Anita Lobel, Greenwillow Books, New York, 1981. Three modern illustrators approach the letter "A" in a variety of ways ranging from Burningham's poster style to Lobel's ornate, decorative style.

apples,

In choosing an alphabet book, it is very important to consider carefully the age and background of the intended reader. Young children should be given simply designed books containing familiar objects. They should be able clearly to relate the objects to the letters. Cluttered pages, unknown objects, and unclear relationships between letters and the objects can be confusing. However, as children become older and more at home with the letters of the alphabet, more challenging books can be introduced. Indeed, alphabet books can be used well into the early elementary grades to help children with word recognition and with internal rather than initial sounds.

TIPS FOR PARENTS AND TEACHERS: Before sharing an alphabet book with a child, the adult should carefully study it to make sure that it is appropriate to the child's level of comprehension. Then, child and adult should share the book, with the adult carefully pointing to the letter at first, giving its name and its sound, and then pointing to the objects which relate to the letter. On later readings, the child, now familiar with letters and objects, can tell the adult what he or she sees on the page. At various stages of the child's development, new alphabet books should be introduced; otherwise, the child will merely be responding to a familiar book from memory.

Adams, Richard *(1920 –   )*
English

Born in Newbury, Berkshire, the son of a doctor who read the Doctor Dolittle stories to his children, Richard Adams entered Oxford University in 1938, but interrupted his studies to serve in the British Airborne Forces during World War II. His commanding officer, a quiet man who led by example, served as the model for Hazel in *Watership Down*. The war over, Adams returned to Oxford, receiving a Master of Arts degree in modern history before joining the British Civil Service.

Adams' desire to instill into his children his own love of literature was the indirect reason for his becoming an author himself. While driving to the Shakespeare plays at Stratford-on-Avon, Adams began to tell his children a story about rabbits who left their warren to find a new home. At the urging of one of his daughters, he turned the story into a book, using background materials from R.M. Lockley's *The Private Life of the Rabbit*. *Watership Down* was rejected several times before being published in 1972 by the small firm of Rex Collings. Within a year it had become one of the major publishing successes of the 1970s, and it has since been made into an animated motion picture. His second novel, *Shardik* appeared in 1974, and his third novel, *The Plague Dogs*, in 1977. He has written two short books for younger children: *The Tyger Voyage*(1976), illustrated by Nicola Bayley; and *The Ship's Cat* (1977), illustrated by Alan Aldridge.

Adams' second and third novels did not receive the critical acclaim accorded *Watership Down*. *Shardik* is the story of Kelderek, a simple hunter who is witness to the reincarnation of Shardik, an enormous bear who embodies the power of God. In *The Plague Dogs*, Adams returns to the English countryside, describing the odyssey of two dogs who escape from a laboratory where they have been objects of cruel experimentation.

By usual standards, *Watership Down* is a long children's book, over four hundred pages of small, close-set type, and its length, as well as its quest subject matter, has led many critics to call it an "epic" or "saga" and to compare it to Homer's *Odyssey* or Vergil's *Aeneid*. However, Adams, speaking to interviewer Justin Wintle, has compared it to the works of such traditional English novelists as Henry Fielding, Jane Austen, and Anthony Trollope: "My object was to write something for my children, to give them and say 'This is a novel. It obeys the rules of a novel. It's on the same principles as novels you'll encounter when you get older, like *Vanity Fair* and *Wuthering Heights*.'" He has also related the book to the tradition of the anthropomorphic animal story, which includes traditional folktales, Aesop's *Fables*, medieval beast epics, and the works of such modern writers as Rudyard Kipling (*The Jungle Books* and the *Just So Stories*), Kenneth Grahame (*The Wind in the Willows*), George Orwell (*Animal Farm*), and E. B. White (*Charlotte's Web*). Adams has openly acknowledged his debt to Kipling, noting that Kipling never makes his animals perform feats physically impossible to them. His rabbits, he has remarked, have only three basic motivations: "food, survival, and mating."

From the anthropomorphized animal story came the symbolic elements of *Watership Down*. Adams has stated that the book is about leadership and that using animals as characters gave him the artistic distance necessary to examine a range of social organizations and a variety of leaders. The ideal warren is Watership Down, created under the leadership of Hazel, who is, in a sense, an ordinary hero, becoming chief rabbit because of his ability to recognize the strengths of his followers.

TIPS FOR PARENTS AND TEACHERS: In the upper elementary and junior high grades, *Watership Down* can be treated as a study of social organization and leadership. Students can discuss the personalities of the main characters. A map can be used to show how far the rabbits have progressed toward their destination and how characters and events along the way have helped or hindered this progress. *Watership Down* can also be examined as a criticism of the encroachment of technology into the natural world.

❦ Aiken, Joan *(1924 –   )*
English

Born in Rye, Sussex, Joan Aiken has stated that she is a British citizen by accident only: her father, the American poet and critic Conrad Aiken, neglected to register her birth with the United States Embassy. When she was sixteen, she published a group of poems and a year later one of her stories was dramatized on BBC radio. She began telling her two children stories which were collected in *All You've Ever Wanted* (1953) and *More Than You Bargained For* (1955). Since then, in addition to several adult thrillers, she has written over twenty books for children: novels, short stories, plays, and poems.

Joan Aiken has divided her children's stories into three catagories: short works of fantasy, stories dealing with animals, and novels. In the first group are the tales found in such collections as *More Than You Bargained For* (1955), *Armitage, Armitage, Fly Away Home* (1968), and *Smoke from Cromwell's Time* (1970). The Armitage tales reveal her ability to combine fantasy and humor. A young bride discovers a wishing stone on her honeymoon and hopes that "we'll have two children called Mark and Harriet with cheerful, energetic natures who never mope or sulk or get bored." The best-known of her animal characters is Mortimer of *Arabel's Raven* (1972), an injured bird who, after having been rescued by kindly Ebenezer Jones, causes chaos in the household, devouring the staircase and answering the telephone with the word "nevermore."

Joan Aiken's novels, set in an imaginary nineteenth-century England ruled over by King James III and later Richard IV, show the influence of Charles Dickens, whom Aiken has said possesses "so many of the essential qualities [of a children's writer]: mystery, slapstick, simple emotion, intricate plots, marvelous language." In *The Wolves of Willoughby Chase* (1962), Bonnie Green and her cousin fight to save her absent father's estate from the clutches of the evil Miss Slighcarp, while in *Black Hearts in Battersea* (1964), Bonnie's friend Simon journeys to London to study art, uncovers a plot to destroy the home of eccentric Lord Battersea and depose James III, and learns that he is the missing heir of Battersea. In his adventures he is aided by

Dido Twite, an acerbic street urchin who is apparently drowned while saving Simon's life. One of Aiken's best creations, Dido reappears in *Nightbirds on Nantucket* (1966). Rescued by a whaler whose captain searches for a great pink whale, she learns of a scheme to kill King Richard IV with a huge cannon hidden on Nantucket Island. In *The Cuckoo Tree* (1971), she has returned to England and, astride an elephant, thwarts another plot against the monarchy.

The typical Aiken story is fast paced and filled with danger and excitement. The author is not afraid to employ such stock plot devices as the missing heir and she does not worry about improbabilities of plot. In fact, these do not detract from the stories, for the audacity with which she includes them and the exuberance with which she rushes to describe the next event sweep the reader along. Although they are often very funny, the novels have a serious focus. Aiken has stated that she is "concerned with children tackling the problems of an adult world in which things have gone wrong," and that "children's books should never minimize the fact that life is tough."

Three of Aiken's novels are more explicitly serious. *Night Fall* (1969) analyzes a young woman's confrontation with a recurring dream about a murder she had witnessed as a child. In *Midnight is a Place* (1974), a book Aiken consciously wrote at a deeper level than most of her children's stories, two young children struggle to survive in a Dickensian-type England. *Go Saddle the Sea* (1977) follows the adventures of Felix as he travels from Spain to England in search of answers to the mystery of his birth.

TIPS FOR PARENTS AND TEACHERS: Aiken's mixture of humor and excitement in many of her stories makes them enjoyable reading in the upper elementary grades. Children can discuss the basic moral goodness or evil of her characters.

Alcott, Louisa May *(1832 – 1888)*
American

In 1867, Thomas Niles, the editor of a small Boston publishing firm, asked Louisa May Alcott to write a realistic girl's story to compete with the Oliver Optic adventures which were so popular with boys. At the time, Alcott had achieved a small reputation as the writer of an adult novel, a book of Civil War reminiscences, and several magazine pieces. She claimed that she knew little about writing for children, but began the task, complaining, "I plod away, though I don't enjoy this sort of thing. Never liked girls or knew many, except my sisters; but our queer plays and experiences may prove interesting, though I doubt it." In midsummer of 1868, she submitted over four hundred pages of manuscript to Niles and on October 3, *Little Women; or Meg, Jo, Beth and Amy* was published. The book was an instant success; Alcott began a sequel and was soon on her way to becoming one of America's most popular children's authors.

Although set during the Civil War, *Little Women* draws many of the events from the life of the Alcott family. Born in Germantown, Pennsylvania, Louisa and her three sisters grew up in Boston and Concord, Massachusetts. There they met such famous intellectuals as Ralph Waldo Emerson, Henry David Thoreau, and Margaret Fuller, friends of their father, Bronson, a well-known (but usually poor) educator and philosopher. Louisa, a tomboy, enjoyed taking the boys' roles in the plays the girls often produced and enjoyed listening to her father read from John Bunyan's *Pilgrim's Progress*. Although she decided early in her life to become a writer, she had to work as a teacher, servant, seamstress, travelling companion, and Civil War nurse before being able to devote most of her energies to her career. Even then, she was often called on to take care of the Alcott household and would compose stories in her head while attending to the daily chores.

The success of *Little Women* — it sold over 200,000 copies by 1885 — is easy to understand. The four March sisters, Meg, Jo, Beth, and Amy, are realistically portrayed; they do not engage in fantastic, unbelievable adventures such as were found in contemporary adventure stories. Their escapades, which emerge naturally out of their characters, are those that would be familiar to their readers. Although at times Alcott indulges in sentimentality and, perhaps, overemphasizes the moral lessons to be learned from the stories, she shows the family coping with the harsh realities of life during the Civil War and managing to put on smiling faces. Scholars of children's literature have found one of the most interesting aspects of *Little Women* to be its use of Bunyan's *Pilgrim's Progress*. That novel provides Alcott's book with its underlying structure, as each of the girls consciously tries to see parallels between her own adventures and those in Bunyan's religious allegory. Such chapter titles as "Burdens," "Amy's Valley of Humiliation," "Meg Goes to Vanity Fair," and "Jo Meets Apollyon," as well as the introductory poem, derive from *Pilgrim's Progress*.

Part II of *Little Women*, published in 1869, resumes the story of the March family three years later and focuses on the sisters' growth to adulthood. Generally less popular than Part I, Part II completes the "pilgrim's progress" as three of the girls (Beth has died) find happiness and learn to look realistically at life.

The success of *Little Women* created a great demand for Alcott stories, and in 1870 she wrote a third juvenile novel, *An Old-Fashioned Girl*, about a poor orphan who works in a wealthy home, influencing the family with her goodness and marrying one of the sons. During a trip to Europe with her sister May, Louisa learned that her brother-in-law, John Pratt, had died. Immediately she began writing a novel so that "John's death may not leave Anna and the dear boys in want." *Little Men*, the story of the school run by Jo March and her German husband, was published in 1871, just as she returned from Europe.

During the 1870s and 1880s, Alcott continued her prolific output: travel sketches, children's stories, essays on such issues as temperance and women's rights, and even a melodramatic potboiler, the anonymously published *A Modern Mephistopheles* (1877). In 1874, she made her first contribution to *St. Nicholas*, the most famous and respected nineteenth-century children's magazine. Three of her novels were first serialized here: *Eight Cousins, Under the Lilacs*, and *Jack and Jill*.

Of seven books Alcott published in the 1880s, the most important was *Jo's Boys and How They Turned Out* (1886). It was composed with great difficulty over a four-year period and was, she emphatically stated on the last page, the final book about the March family: "And now, having endeavored to suit everyone by many weddings, few deaths, and as much prosperity as the eternal fitness of things will permit, let the music stop, let the lights die out, and the curtain fall forever on the March family."

Since her death on March 6, 1888, Alcott has been the subject of more biographies (over a dozen) than any other American writer for children. Yet there is little agreement among them about the nature of her character. Cornelia Meigs's Newbery Medal winning *Invincible Louisa* (1933) portrays a dedicated family person who, as a child, "vowed to herself that she would give these beloved ones what each one needed." Madeleine Stern in *Louisa May Alcott* (1950) believes that her subject, who never married, found in writing a means of personal fulfillment. Recently, Martha Saxon, in her feminist biography *Louisa May* (1978), presents Alcott as a woman who, restricted by Victorian attitudes towards women, presents in her stories accepted versions of female behavior.

Although during her lifetime Alcott produced over two dozen volumes for children, nearly as many for adults, and hundreds of magazine pieces, it is only in her realistic family stories for children that she achieved true greatness. Her three books about the March family — *Little Women, Little Men*, and *Jo's Boys* — are justly hailed as pioneering works of the American family novel. Drawing on family memories, but placing her stories at a time contemporary with that of her initial readers, she created believable, universal characters.

Speaking of Alcott, her friend Ralph Waldo Emerson once said, "She is a natural source of stories. . . . She is and is to be, the poet of children. She knows their angels." Although in places her works are dated, the continuing popularity of many of them attests to the fact that she did know the angels of children and how to capture them in stories.

TIPS FOR PARENTS AND TEACHERS: Little Women can be read in the upper elementary grades partly as a war novel, as the Civil War is always in the girls' minds in Part I. Although the novel is dated in places, the character development of the sisters can be examined, and students can notice how the girls learn from their "adventures."

Alexander, Lloyd *(1924 –   )*
American

As a boy growing up in Philadelphia, Lloyd Alexander read tales of King Arthur, Robin Hood, and other heroes, and stories by such authors as Charles Dickens and Mark Twain. When he was fifteen he told his parents that he had decided to become a poet, but after high school graduation he worked as a bank messenger and spent one year at college before joining the Army. While overseas, he visited Wales and was enchanted by the people and scenery. Alexander returned to Philadelphia in the 1950s, working as a cartoonist, layout editor, and assistant editor for a magazine. At the same time he wrote several adult novels, four of them published but none, by the author's own admission, successful. In 1963, with the publication of *Time Cat: The Remarkable Journeys of Jason and Gareth*, a fantasy in which a cat takes his human master into different historical periods, Alexander found that writing for children was what he most wished to do.

While researching Welsh folktales, Alexander decided to create his own fantasy and began to write what became the "Prydain Chronicles," five books centering on the adventures of Taran, the humble pig keeper who becomes a High King. *The Book of Three* (1964) tells of how Taran, who entertains grand notions of heroism, travels to warn Caer Dathyl, the chief city of Prydain, of impending attack by Arawn, Lord of Death. Along the way, the pig keeper befriends several individuals who become his companions in his later adventures: Gurgi, half-human and half-animal, who becomes his devoted servant; Eilonwy, a sharp-tongued princess; Fflewddur

Fflam, a bard whose harp strings break when he stretches the truth; and Doli, one of the Fair Folk, who wishes he could be invisible.

In *The Black Cauldron* (1965), winner of a Newbery Honor Medal, the companions recover the cauldron from which Arawn creates deathless warriors. Princess Eilonwy is the focus of *The Castle of Llyr* (1966). Sent to the Isle of Mona for royal training, she is kidnapped by the evil enchantress Achren and rescued by the companions. In *Taran Wanderer* (1967), the title hero sets out alone to discover the secret of his parentage; while he does not find the answer, he learns much about his inner self. The final book, *The High King* (1968), winner of the Newbery Medal, presents the final struggle between the forces of good and evil and Taran's discovery that he is the High King of Prydain.

While writing the Chronicles, Alexander also wrote two short stories about Prydain, both illustrated by Evaline Ness: *Coll and His White Pig* (1965) and *The Truthful Harp* (1967). More recent stories include *The Marvelous Misadventures of Sebastian* (1970), the winner of a National Book Award; *The Foundling* (1973), several short stories about characters from Prydain; and two stories reflecting Alexander's love of cats: *The Cat Who Wished to be a Man* (1973) and *Town Cats and Other Tales* (1977).

Although drawing on Welsh scenery and folklore, the Prydain Chronicles are Alexander's unique literary creation. He has said that they contain "as much of my own life as there is of ancient legend," and that "a writer of fantasy . . . must find the essential content of his work within himself." The Prydain Chronicles center on two themes: the grand-scale struggle between good and evil, and the growth of the individual through the acquisition of self-knowledge and the making of wise choices. The five books trace the growth to maturity of Taran. Early in *The Book of Three*, he laments, "I don't even know who *I* am." During his adventures, he comes to understand the complexity of existence and the need for friends in his quest. In *Taran Wanderer*, in which he "comes to grips with a merciless opponent: the truth about himself," the hero meets an old shepherd, Craddoc, who falsely claims to be his father, and discovers that he is horrified to be of such low birth. His greatest test comes after the defeat of Arawn. Offered a life of eternal peace in the Summer Country, Taran refuses, stating that he has promises to fulfill and tasks to complete, knowing full well that his life may be hard and unhappy. His choice has proved that he is the new High King of Prydain; having mastered himself, he may now lead others. He is, in a sense, a kind of everyman for, as Alexander says in the author's note to *The Book of Three*, we are "all assistant Pig Keepers at Heart."

TIPS FOR PARENTS AND TEACHERS: Upper elementary students with a liking for heroic fantasies will find the ideas of the Prydain books challenging but not excessively complex. They can be read after C.S. Lewis' "Chronicles of Narnia" but before the fantasies of writers like Susan Cooper, Alan Garner, or J.R.R. Tolkien.

Mishka, by Victor Ambrus, Frederick Warne & Co., New York, 1975. Ambrus uses strong shapes against a blank background to capture the humorous predicament of his young hero.

❦Ambrus, Victor *(1935 –   )*
English

Born in Budapest, Hungary, Victor Ambrus began drawing at age six with his grandfather, depicting historical events and horses. During summer vacations, the family often visited small Hungarian villages, and he used his memories of the places he saw to create the settings for many of his adaptations of folktales. During the Soviet invasion of Hungary, Ambrus fled to England where he entered the Royal College of Art, receiving a diploma in 1959. During his second year at the College he provided pictures for *White Horses and Black Bulls*, the first of over two hundred books he was to illustrate. Among the children's writers whose works he has illustrated are Hester Burton, William Mayne, Rosemary Sutcliff, K. M. Peyton, and Ian Serraillier.

In 1965, after having been twice named a runner-up, Ambrus received his first Kate Greenaway Medal for *The Three Poor Tailors*, one of several humorous Hungarian folktales he has retold and illustrated. Others include *Brave Soldier Janosh* (1967), *The Seven Skinny Goats* (1969), and *The Sultan's Bath* (1971). His other folktales include *The Little Cockerel* (1968), *A Country Wedding* (1973), and *Mishka* (1975). Ambrus has said that in adapting the stories he tries to use as few words as possible, allowing the pictures to communicate the action. The illustrations themselves make use of bright colors which, Ambrus feels, parallel the bold but simple language of the stories. For *Mishka* and *Horses in Battle* (1975), Ambrus won his second Kate Greenaway Medal.

In *Dracula* (1980) he uses comic book techniques in a humorous account of the old legends.

TIPS FOR PARENTS AND TEACHERS: In his illustrations, Ambrus delights in emphasizing the humorous elements of the stories he retells. Students in the upper elementary grades, who are developing a keen awareness of the nature of humor, can examine the illustrations to discover how the humor is created.

❧Andersen, Hans Christian *(1805 – 1875)*
❧ *Danish*

Although during his lifetime Hans Christian Andersen, the "ugly duckling of children's literature," was noted as a writer of novels, plays, and poetry for adults, he is now best known for his children's fairy stories. They have been translated into over one hundred languages and illustrated by some of the world's best known artists for children.

Andersen was a lonely, imaginative child. In his home town of Odense, Denmark, he made puppet plays and often listened to old stories told by his father or the inmates of an asylum at which his grandmother worked. As a teenager, he decided to make his fortune in the theatres of Copenhagen; but when he failed he attended school, the oldest boy in his class. After graduation in 1827, he began a writing career in earnest, publishing a collection of poems and a semi-autobiographical novel. His first children's stories appeared in 1835, and were enthusiastically received. Andersen soon became famous and, in his travels through Europe and England, was received by famous artists, authors, and musicians, and several heads of state. In 1867, Odense welcomed home its most famous son, and the city was illuminated in his honor.

Although one of Europe's most acclaimed writers, Andersen seems to have been unhappy during his adult life. He never married and in his autobiography, *The Fairy Tale of My Life*, tells of sadness in love. He was deeply enamored of the renowned singer Jenny Lind, "the Swedish Nightingale." Much of his life was spent in the homes of friends and he longed for a family of his own. When he died in 1875, after a long illness, presumably cancer, he was staying at the home of close friends.

As critics have often noted, many of the children's stories are in a sense about Andersen himself. And if Andersen saw himself in some of his stories, he also tried to view his life as a story, calling his autobiography *The Fairy Tale of My Life*. "The Ugly Duckling" is often seen as a treatment of the author's own life. Misunderstood, mistreated, and rejected, the title hero spends a lonely winter before being recognized as the magnificent swan he is. Andersen himself is reported to have told his mother, "First you go through terrible suffering, and then you become famous."

In addition to revealing aspects of Andersen's own view of his life, the tales also reflect aspects of the literary trends of the nineteenth century. At this time, folklore had become very popular, in part because of the work of Jacob and Wilhelm Grimm, whom Andersen knew. During the later part of the century, the Scottish writer George MacDonald created a series of mystical fairytales, and throughout the century English and European writers used Oriental effects in created fairy worlds. Other popular subjects of the age were the nobility of the common man, the anguished wanderings of a lonely hero, and the death of a helpless and innocent child.

While an understanding of Andersen's life and these literary trends provides a useful background to his writings, it does not fully describe his great successes. One of Andersen's major achievements is his ability to create convincing stories about inanimate objects. As French critic Paul Hazard noted, "Andersen is unique in his capacity for entering into the very soul of beings and of things."

Often inanimate objects are used to satirize human nature; by representing recognizable failings in unlikely objects, Andersen emphasizes the ridiculousness of many people. In fact, satire plays a large role in many of Andersen's stories. That children might not understand these aspects did not bother the author for, as he wrote to a friend, "Now I dip into my own bosom, find an idea for the older people and tell it to the children, but remembering the father and mother are listening." Chief of Andersen's targets are the pomposity and vanity most often found in royalty. His satire is at its best in "The Emperor's New Clothes," in which the title hero, vain over his wardrobe, would rather walk about nude than admit his limitations.

Andersen's best stories generally involve quests in which the central figures must prove that they are worthy of achieving an important goal. Gerda shows her love and bravery in her long northward trek to rescue Kay in "The Snow Queen"; Karen is willing to lose her feet and do penance to escape from the red shoes which symbolize her vanity in "The Red Shoes." In the story of the same name, the Little Mermaid gives up her tongue and accepts the possibility of annihilation to win immortality. While she does not gain the love of her prince, she does earn a second chance to gain a soul.

One of Andersen's best quest stories is "The Wild Swans," based on a traditional folktale. At the beginning and the end of the story Elise lives in royal splendor; however, only at the end has she proved that her inner goodness equals her outer station. When her brothers have been turned into swans and she has been cast out by her witch-stepmother, Elise has a chance to prove herself. After great danger and much suffering and persecution, she rescues her brothers and marries a prince.

The central figures in many of the tales are children, "my little spiritual children," as Andersen called them. Because of their age or social status — many are poor orphans — they are vulnerable as they enter into what the author referred to as "the wide world." Because of inner strengths, they achieve their own kinds of triumph. For example, although she freezes to death, the Little Match Girl is reunited in Heaven with her grandmother. None of these children is a fully developed literary character, but rather a symbol of an aspect of childhood confronting a larger world.

Perhaps the major reason for Andersen's continued popularity with younger and older readers is this ability to infuse his stories with an unobtrusive yet important symbolism which transforms them from mere entertainments into treatments of universal themes. For example, "Thumbelina" is more than a story of romantic wish fulfillment; it is a tale in which the forces of love and life emerge victorious over those of ignorance and death. Throughout the story, Thumbelina is associated with flowers, sunlight, and winged creatures: symbols of life. The frog and toad who wish to marry her live beneath the ground, creatures of darkness. The former is ignorant and ugly; the latter old and narrow-minded. Marriage to either of them would crush Thumbelina's delicate, loving spirit. By rescuing a nearly frozen swallow, she displays her selfless courage and, through his agency, arrives at a paradise where she finds the love and fulfillment she has earned. The dark forces which have tried to control her have been left behind.

Andersen has been criticized for the sentimentality found in many of his stories and for a cynical, satiric quality some critics consider beyond the reach of his young readers. However, in his best stories, he created a convincing fantasy world, portrayed well a variety of human emotions, and delineated significant quests. These aspects of his work have justly earned him acclaim as one of the finest of all writers for children.

TIPS FOR PARENTS AND TEACHERS: In the middle elementary grades, students can examine the quests undertaken by Andersen's characters, noticing how they earn the right to reach their goals. The importance of such symbols as snow in "The Snow Queen" or light and darkness in Thumbelina can be considered. Upper elementary students can appreciate the satire in works like "The Emperor's New Clothes" and "The Princess and the Pea." At all levels, children can compare different illustrated versions of the same story, making judgments on which ones they think best reflect the themes of the particular tale.

❦Animal Stories

Animal stories are of ancient date. From earliest times, cultures around the world have included tales about animals in their folklore and mythology. People who believed that animals possessed spirits and could often take human shape created stories in which animals embodied their religious and secular beliefs. Not surprisingly, when books for children became popular in the early nineteenth century, many of the traditional animal stories were adapted for young readers, capitalizing on children's imaginative abilities to endow animals with human personalities. These folktales were the forerunners of one of the most popular types of modern children's stories, the animal fantasy.

During the later part of the nineteenth century, increased scientific study of animals, along with growing interest in Darwin's theories of evolution and humanitarian efforts to ameliorate the conditions of domestic animals, contributed to the development of the realistic animal story. While each of these types of stories deals with animals, each is distinctively different, possessing unique characteristics and requiring different standards of evaluation.

1. Animal fantasies: The first point to consider in analyzing or assessing animal fantasies is that the characters are not real animals—they are literary animals. That is, while they may possess some of the characteristics of actual animals, they possess personalities that no animals have. Neither are they human beings; not only do they look different, they are usually not tied to the moral and cultural codes of human beings and they generally possess different life-styles. The skillful creator of an animal fantasy draws on characteristics of the animal world and aspects of human nature and combines these to create a unique being — a literary character which would be totally unbelievable in the real world but which functions convincingly within the confines of a story. Some of these literary characters bear closer resemblance to their natural counterparts than others; however, all of them must be judged by how convincing they are in their stories. In reading an animal fantasy the following questions should be asked: how convincing are the characters' actions and thoughts? are they presented consistently? are they appropriate for the story being told?

Three of the earliest masters of the animal fantasy, Rudyard Kipling, Beatrix Potter, and Kenneth Grahame, reveal the range of approaches to the animal story. Kipling used wild animals from India in *The Jungle Books* (1894–95). While they act physically like animals, they talk to each other and evolve a complex social hierarchy. Kipling's purpose was, among other things, to develop his theories of social organization and leadership; to do this he showed how each of the species in the book related to the other animals. Beatrix Potter wrote stories about small wild and domestic animals found in England. Her most famous character, Peter Rabbit, is like members of his species in his preference for garden vegetables and his vulnerability. However, he is also like a little boy: he wears clothes, which he regularly loses, and he is reckless and disobedient. By making Peter a rabbit, Potter emphasizes the danger of the situations in which he finds himself; by making him behave like a little boy, she makes his actions understandable to the child reader. Like Kipling, Kenneth Grahame in *The Wind in the Willows* (1908) is interested in presenting a cross-section of social types: Badger is the solitary, self-reliant individual; Mole, the young innocent learning the ways of the world; Rat, the dreamy, poetic individual; and Toad, the lover of the latest, most fashionable objects. However, like Potter, Grahame dresses his animals and gives them homes with furnishings. While Kipling's animals most closely resemble creatures in nature, Grahame's seem more like human beings. However, the characters of these three authors are neither human nor animal; they exist believably only within the books in which they appear and must be judged accordingly.

Other animal stories in which the characters possess both animal and human characteristics include Richard Adams' *Watership Down* (1972), Leo Lionni's *Frederick* (1967), Robert O'Brien's *Mrs. Frisby and the Rats of NIMH* (1971), William Steig's *Sylvester and the Magic Pebble* (1969), and Robert Lawson's *Rabbit Hill* (1944).

A favorite setting for many animal fantasies is a barnyard. Such a locale gives the author the opportunity to create a variety of animals representing a cross-section of character types. Often such fantasies satirize human nature, the implication being that if animals can resemble human beings the reverse may also be true. Stories in this tradition include *Chanticleer and the Fox* (1958), the medieval beast fable retold and illustrated by Barbara Cooney; and Roger Duvoisin's stories about Petunia and the Goose. The best-known of course, is E.B. White's classic *Charlotte's Web* (1952). Although Charlotte, the spider, is able to write human words in her web, the animals behave in much the same manner as barnyard animals do. However, the different species talk to each other, and each animal possesses a distinct personality. Wilber, at first childishly egocentric, becomes a mature, self-confident pig; Templeton, the rat, is always totally selfish and gluttonous; Charlotte is the model of friendship and self-sacrifice.

Another important type of animal fantasy has animals interacting with human beings. Such interaction is seen in sections of *Wind in the Willows* and E.B. White's *The Trumpet of the Swan* (1970). In some stories, the animals are pets who live with the family and become almost human members of the family. Paddington the Bear in the books by Michael Bond and Lyle the Crocodile in Bernard Weber's picture books are such characters. Not only are the situations very humorous because of the ludicrousness, but they also represent a dream that many pet owners have of being able to converse with their animals on a human level.

   2. Realistic animal stories: While animal fantasies have their roots in ancient myth, legend, and folktales, realistic animal stories are relatively modern. During the nineteenth century, biological sciences developed rapidly, and with them, interest in the behavioral patterns of animals. When biologist Charles Darwin advanced the theory that man had descended from animals and that only the most superior of animal species survived, interest in the lives of animals increased. Realistic animal stories began to appear during the later part of the nineteenth century.

   Several problems face the writer of this kind of story. First, the major interest in most fiction is character analysis; however, it is impossible to know if animals think and, if they do, what they think. The author is forced to two extremes: either he must be studiously objective in his reporting, making his work almost like a scientific description, or he must attribute human personalities to his characters, thus coming perilously close to fantasy. Second, lives of animals seem to be dominated by two biological urges: feeding and reproduction. The daily and yearly cycles of their lives are thus very predictable and, as such, relatively poor story material. The author is thus faced with the problem of making his story both accurate and exciting.

   These problems were faced by the first major writers of stories about wild animals, Sir Charles G.D. Roberts (1860–1943), a Canadian novelist and poet, and Ernest Thompson Seton (1860–1946), an American writer who was born in England and had lived in Canada. Both men were careful observers of nature and both were influenced by the studies of Darwin. They solved the problems by choosing to write only about superior animals, ones which they believed were possessed of more than mere instinct. In the preface to his novel *Red Fox* (1905), Roberts outlined his approach: "Once in a while such exceptional strength and such exceptional intelligence may be combined in one individual. This combination is apt to result in just such a fox as I have made the hero of my story." In such works as *Wild Animals I Have Known* (1899) and *The Biography of a Grizzly* (1900) by Seton, and *The Kindred of the Wild* (1902) and *Kings in Exile* (1909) by Roberts, the realistic animal story of the wilderness reached its high point. While later authors have produced fine books, most realistic animals stories of the twentieth century have dealt with more familiar domesticated animals.

   Beginning with Anna Sewell's *Black Beauty* (1877), horse stories have been extremely popular with young readers. Presented as an autobiography, and with thinly veiled comments about the need to treat horses humanely, the book has been criticized for its sentimentality. Perhaps the foremost twentieth-century writer of stories about horses has been Marguerite Henry, whose *King of the Wind* (1948) was named winner of the Newbery Medal. Dog stories have also been extremely popular. Among the best known of these are Jim Kjelgaard's *Big Red* (1956), and Sheila Burnford's *The Incredible Journey* (1961).

An interesting variation of the animal story is that portraying the relationships between human beings and animals usually considered wild. Marjorie Rawlings' *The Yearling* (1936) portrays sensitively the friendship between a boy and a fawn; *Julie of the Wolves* (1972) by Jean George is a powerful depiction of the encounter between an Eskimo girl and a pack of Arctic wolves. Farley Mowat's *Owls in the Family* (1961) humorously describes a young boy's discovery of baby owls and their misadventures as family pets.

TIPS FOR PARENTS AND TEACHERS: In choosing animal fantasies, it is important to examine the success with which the author creates literary animals — are they convincing and consistent? Realistic animal stories should avoid sentimentality and making animals overly human in their thoughts. Cuteness is one of the great weaknesses of both realistic animal stories and fantasies. Authors should respect their readers and their stories and should not falsify their characters in an attempt to be cute. Animal stories are enjoyed most by readers in the middle and upper elementary grades.

Anno, Mitsumasa *(1926 –)*
Japanese

Born in Tsuwano-cho, Japan, Mitsumasa Anno loved drawing when he was a small child. After attending normal school, he began a long career as a teacher. His career as a children's author-illustrator began on a trip to Paris, when a visit to the tomb of Van Gogh and a study of the works of Dutch painter Escher inspired him to create *Strange, Strange Pictures*. Published in the United States as *Topsy Turvies* (1970), it won awards in several countries. This was followed by *Upside-Downers: More Pictures to Stretch the Imagination* (1971), *Dr. Anno's Magical Midnight Circus* (1972), *Anno's Alphabet* (1975), *Anno's Counting Book* (1975), *The King's Flower* (1976), *Anno's Journey* (1977), and *Anno's Animals* (1979).

Anno's purpose in his books can best be described by the subtitle for the American edition of his first work, "Pictures to Stretch the Imagination." Through the use of optical illusion, unobtrusive but significant details, and hidden figures, he challenges the viewer to become actively involved in the interpretation of the pictures. The first two books, *Topsy Turvies* and *Upside-Downers*, create a sense of realism through bold use of color and strong sense of line, but then upset that realism through optical illusions. His best known pair of books, *Anno's Alphabet* and *Anno's Counting Book*, are not simple concept books. In the first, optical illusions are used so that in examining the effect one becomes more aware of the actual shapes of letters. In *Anno's Counting Book*, each page of landscape contains a series of interacting objects so that numbers become more than an abstract concept. *Anno's Journey* shows the author wandering across a European landscape in which are found such well-known real and imaginary figures as Little Red Riding-hood, Don Quixote, and Beethoven. The viewer with a background in art will notice echoes of masterworks by Millet, Renoir, and Seurat. *Anno's Animals* uses watercolors and pen and ink to hide dozens of animals in a naturalistically portrayed woodland setting.

TIPS FOR PARENTS AND TEACHERS: Anno's picture books are for all ages and encourage the active participation of attentive readers. Adults reading the books with preschoolers and early elementary school children should lead children into discovering some of the visual tricks and surprises and then invite them to search on their own for others.

Ardizzone, Edward *(1900 – 1979)*
English

Born in Indochina and raised in England, Edward Arizzone became a children's author almost by accident. When his wife asked him to tell a story to settle down their rather energetic children, he recalled the coastal steam-ships he loved watching as a boy and told an adventure of a little boy on one of them. The story was popular and was often retold with modifications and additions and, needing money, Ardizzone made it into a book. *Little Tim and the Brave Sea Captain* (1936 — revised and reissued with new illustrations in 1955) has been a perennial favorite. In following years, more Tim stories appeared: *Lucy and Tim Go to Sea* (1938), *Tim to the Rescue* (1949), *Tim and Charlotte* (1951), *Tim in Danger* (1953), *Tim All Alone* (1956), *Tim and Ginger*

(1965), *Tim to the Lighthouse* (1968), and *Tim's Last Voyage* (1972). *Tim All Alone* was the winner of the first Kate Greenaway Medal, awarded for excellence of illustration in a British children's book. *Little Tim and the Brave Sea Captain* received the Lewis Carroll Shelf Award as a book worthy of standing next to Carroll's classic *Alice in Wonderland*. Among his other stories are *Nicholas and the Fast-Moving Diesel* (1947), *Johnny the Clockmaker* (1960), and *Sarah and Simon and No Red Paint* (1965). He has also illustrated over one hundred books by such writers as Mark Twain, Hans Christian Andersen, James Reeves, Eleanor Farjeon, Philippa Pearce, Eleanor Estes, and Walter de la Mare.

The heroes of Arizzone's stories are generally ordinary children on exceptional adventures. In their adventures, the children make complete breaks from their normal worlds, sailing boats or handling runaway trains. When Tim is on his maritime voyages he does not think about his mother or father, but they are ready to receive the young hero at the end of each story. There is one exception: *Tim All Alone*, considered by many critics the best of the series. The story opens with the young sailor returning home to find his house empty and a "to let" sign on the porch and then describes his generally lonely, sometimes tearful, but finally successful search for his mother.

Ardizzone has written and spoken often of his theories of writing and illustrating. The text of a story, he says, should be relatively short, about two thousand words, containing the basic plot and should be written in a flowing style which the adult reader can repeat several times. The illustrations fill in the emotions and characterization. They should be suggestive, evoking the desired moods by the positioning and movement of the figures rather than by detailed facial portrayals. Background in a picture is also an important means of indicating aspects of character. His illustrations are done in either pen and ink, or pen and ink with pale watercolors added, media which help to create suggestive rather than definitive meanings.

TIPS FOR PARENTS AND TEACHERS: Although children in the early elementary grades find the adventures of Ardizzone's characters exciting, they identify most with the emotions of the characters and these can be discussed. Young readers can examine the illustrations of *Tim All Alone* to see how they reveal the hero's changing feelings.

Armstrong, William *(1914 –)*
American

Born in rural Virginia near Lexington, William Armstrong began writing as a teenager. One of his first stories, the account of a cat's attack on a nest of birds, was rejected by his teachers as plagiarism; however, when he attended college it won first prize in a literary competition. His first children's book, *Sounder* (1969), winner of the Newbery Medal, is set in an unnamed area of the South, in an unspecified time after the Civil War, and describes the life of a sharecropping black family after the father has been sent to prison for stealing a ham to feed his family. The focus is on the boy, searching for his father and growing to manhood, and the dog, Sounder, who waits patiently for the return of his master.

Sounder draws on many sources: a tale Armstrong heard as a child, the Virginia countryside he loved as a child, and his knowledge of the Bible and classical literature. The opening note to *Sounder* links the story to the *Odyssey*, particularly to Telemachus' search for his long-absent father and the patient loyalty of the dog Argus. However, whereas the *Odyssey* is the story of a triumphant homecoming, *Sounder* is one of grim fortitude and endurance. By leaving his characters nameless, Armstrong transforms *Sounder* from a local and particular legend into the portrayal of universal grief, suffering, and love. *Sounder* was made into a motion picture in 1972 starring Paul Winfield and Cicely Tyson.

Since the publication of *Sounder*, William Armstrong has written several other books for children, none of which has received critical acclaim. They include: *Animal Tales* (1970), *Barefoot in the Grass* (1970), a biography of Grandma Moses, and *The Mills of God* (1973), a Depression-era story about a boy and his dog.

TIPS FOR PARENTS AND TEACHERS: Upper elementary and junior high school students should be given an opportunity to compare *Sounder* in its book and film versions. This activity allows them to see the differences in the two art forms and to comment on which one is more successful in its treatment of the basic story.

Asimov, Isaac *(1920 –   )*
American

Born in the Soviet Union, Isaac Asimov came to New York at age three. His father forbid him to read pulp magazines on sale at the family candy store, but did allow him to read science fiction magazines, and when Asimov published his first story in 1938, it was a science fiction tale entitled "Marooned Off Vest."

Asimov has become one of the most prolific writers in North America, with over two hundred titles to his credit. He is perhaps best known for his science fiction books, in which he combines his scientific knowledge with his ability to tell a fast-moving story, and for his informational books in which he makes scientific material understandable for the layman. Under the pseudonym Paul French, he wrote five novels for younger readers about an astronaut called Lucky Starr. During the past twenty years, he has written many nonfiction books for younger readers. Their range is wide: science (including *Breakthroughs in Science*, 1960); history (including *The Kite that Won the Revolution*, 1963); the Bible (including *Asimov's Guide to the Bible*, 1968 and 1969); and a series on the origin of words (including *Words from the Myths*, 1961).

TIPS FOR PARENTS AND TEACHERS: Because Asimov's non-fiction books are clear and generally concise, they are useful for students needing basic information on a wide variety of subjects.

Babbitt, Natalie *(1932 –   )*
American

Born in Dayton, Ohio, Natalie Babbitt majored in art at Smith College. After graduation, she married Samuel Babbitt, whose *The Forty-Ninth Magician* (1966) was the first book she illustrated. In 1967, she began her own career as an author with a narrative nonsense poem, *Dick Foote and the Shark*. Since then, she has written another poetry book, *Phoebe's Revolt* (1968), and seven works of fiction: *The Search for Delicious* (1969), *Kneeknock Rise* (1970), *The Something* (1970), *Goody Hall* (1971), *The Devil's Storybook* (1974), *Tuck Everlasting* (1975), and *The Eyes of the Amaryllis* (1977).

Natalie Babbitt's stories are fantasy. But, as she has said, she is more interested in the different ways people react to events than in the events themselves. In *The Search for Delicious*, Gaylen, the twelve-year-old messenger of the king, discovers many different answers as he searches for the food which can serve as the best example of the word "delicious" in a new dictionary. In *Kneeknock Rise*, Egan, determined to find a practical explanation for the mysterious spirit Megrimum, finds that people prefer to maintain their imaginative beliefs. *Tuck Everlasting* is the work of Natalie Babbitt which seems most likely to endure. Set in the late nineteenth century, it is the story of the brief meeting between young Winnie Foster and the Tuck family which, nearly a century earlier, had accidentally drunk from a fountain of immortality.

TIPS FOR PARENTS AND TEACHERS: Although Babbitt's situations are hypothetical, the reactions to them are real. Students in the upper elementary grades can consider how they would respond in similar situations.

Barrie, Sir James Matthew *(1860 – 1937)*
Scottish

When he was growing up in Scotland, James Mathew Barrie began writing stories for his mother. "They were all sorts of adventure," he was later to report. "Happiest is he who writes of adventure; no characters were allowed within if I knew their like in the flesh, the scene lay in unknown parts, desert islands." After receiving his MA from the University of Edinburgh (1882), he moved to London to pursue a career as an author and dramatist. While there, he began telling stories to children he used to meet in Kensington Gardens. To the children of Sylvia and Arthur Davies he narrated special adventures which were the seeds of what were to become his most famous stories, the adventures of Peter Pan and his human friends.

In 1902, some of the stories Barrie had told the Davies children were included in his adult work *The Little White Bird*. The six chapters, later released as *Peter Pan in Kensington Gardens*, are about Peter, who "escaped from being human when he was seven days old; he escaped by the window and flew back to the Kensington Gardens." In 1911, the novel *Peter and Wendy* appeared.

Barrie began to work on a play about Peter Pan in 1903 and offered it to British and American producers in 1904. Rehearsals began in October of that year and, after delays and revisions, "Peter Pan: or the Boy Who Wouldn't Grow Up," opened in London on December 27. It received almost instant acclaim, and a year later it became a success in the United States. Since then, it has become one of the most popular of all children's plays. Two motion pictures have been made of "Peter Pan," a 1924 Famous Players-Lasky production, and a 1952 Walt Disney animation. In 1955, the NBC television production with Mary Martin attracted the largest single television audience to that time and, in 1976, NBC produced another version starring Mia Farrow.

The continuing popularity of "Peter Pan" among children arises from the excitement of its fast-paced action, the convincing quality of its fantasy, and its memorable characters. In rapid succession, Michael, John, and Wendy Darling meet Peter, learn to fly, and begin the long journey to Neverland where "adventures . . . were of daily occurrence." In the stories, readers can fulfill vicariously their fantasies: being able to fly and being heroes against pirates as ferocious as any they have read about. And, as Michael, John, and Wendy do, they may return to a loving home at the end of the story.

Although, with the exception of his portrayal of Peter, Barrie gives his characters little depth, he does make them memorable. Captain Hook, "the only man that the Sea-Cook feared," (presumably a reference to Robert Louis Stevenson's Long John Silver), is lonely and melancholy. A vicious man, he is nevertheless terrified of the crocodile who wishes to devour him and is concerned that everything be done according to good form. Wendy, "one of the kind that likes to grow up," thrives on her role of mother to the Lost Boys, and her greatest horror when she is captured is her discovery that "the ship had not been scrubbed for years."

Peter Pan's character is more complex. His fear is that he will grow to be a man, and so he runs away to Neverland where he can control the adventures he is in. He is willing to be pretend father to Wendy's mother, but asks the girl anxiously, "It is only make-believe, isn't it, that I am their father?" Although described as cocky and conceited, Peter is extremely upset when the Darling children decide to return home, taking the Lost Boys with them: "Of course, he cared very much, and he was so full of wrath against grown-ups, who, as usual, were spoiling everything." Self-sufficient, he nonetheless feels a longing as he sits outside the window watching the children's happy homecoming: "He had ecstasies innumerable that other children can never know; but he was looking through the window at the one joy from which he must be forever barred." For Peter, as for Mark Twain's Huck Finn and, perhaps Astrid Lindgren's Pippi Longstocking, there will never be a sense of belonging to a family.

As is the case with many books originally intended for children, there is much in *Peter and Wendy* which is most fully appreciated by adult readers. The story contains much satire. Barrie, who admired Robert Louis Stevenson and wrote approvingly of R. M. Ballantyne's nineteenth-century adventure classic, *The Coral Island*, intends a great deal of his story to be a parody of the pirate and Indian adventure novels. In fact, in the book, the narrator often remarks about the correct way of doing things in adventure stories. In the description of Hook's battle with Peter, Barrie ridicules British notions of proper schoolboy behavior: "With a magnificent gesture Peter invited his opponent to pick up his sword. Hook did so instantly, but with the tragic feeling that Peter was showing good form." As he dies, Hook has the satisfaction of making Peter act in a manner showing bad form. By having the Darling children raised by a dog, and by having Wendy mouth parental platitudes in Neverland, Barrie satirizes many conventional views of child rearing. Finally, Barrie allows the adult reader to view Peter and the adventures ambivalently. The boy hero experiences a joyous freedom, but he also shows signs of arrested development. In the end, the reader, young or old, identifies with the Darling children, not their exciting, but somewhat pathetic, night visitor.

TIPS FOR PARENTS AND TEACHERS: Early and middle elementary aged readers enjoy the fantasy and exciting adventures of Peter Pan. In the upper elementary and junior high grades, students can study the story as parody, noticing Barrie's satire of conventional adventure stories, and can consider the implications of a life where a person never grows to adulthood.

Baum, L. Frank *(1856 – 1919)*
American

When Frank Baum's *The Wonderful Wizard of Oz* was published in 1900, the author, who was born in Chittenango, New York, had worked variously as a dramatist, reporter, newspaper and magazine editor, salesman, and store owner. He had written two children's books, *Mother Goose in Prose* (1897), and *Father Goose, His Book* (1899), the latter selling over 60,000 copies. When he set out to write *The Wonderful Wizard of Oz*, which first bore the tentative titles of "The Emerald City," "From Kansas to Fairyland," and "The Fairyland of Oz," he wanted to create a uniquely American fairy tale. He stated in the "Introduction" that: "The old-time fairy tale, having served for a generation, may now be classified as 'historical' in the children's library; for the time has come for a series of newer 'wonder tales.' . . . [This book] aspires to being a modernized fairy tale in which the wonderment and joy are retained and the heartaches and nightmares are left out."

The Wonderful Wizard of Oz is not a complex book. It recounts the circular journey of Dorothy's departure from and return to home, during which she comes to appreciate the gray land of Kansas and her dour aunt and uncle. Once at Oz, the book delineates the three stage quest of Dorothy and her friends; the hopeful journey to Oz in which the girl's unlikely companions acquire, unknown to themselves, the virtues they seek; the dangerous trip to the western lands of the Winkies in which they discover their new attributes as they help free the country from the curse of the Wicked Witch; and the voyage to the Quadling country, where Dorothy's friends prove their loyalty before becoming kings themselves. None of the characters is portrayed with much depth, but each elicits the reader's sympathies with his recognizably human weaknesses and uncertainties.

As many recent critics have noted, *The Wonderful Wizard of Oz* is historically important. In his introduction to *The Annotated Wizard of Oz* (1973) Michael Patrick Hearn has noted that the book was the first truly American fantasy. Unlike the nineteenth-century American writers Nathaniel Hawthorne, who retold the Greek myths for children, and Howard Pyle, who wrote a masterful version of the Robin Hood story, Baum chose a distinctly American region for his adventure: the agricultural, midwestern United States. As David Greene has stated in *The Oz Scrapbook* (1977): "Baum achieved universality by combining the folktale element with elements familiar to every child." The central figure is a thoroughly American Dorothy Gale, simple and plain-spoken, filed with wonder but not overcome by it as she visits Oz.

The Wonderful Wizard of Oz received favorable critical attention when it was first published and thus began a long history which included over forty sequels, several plays and motion pictures, a merchandising industry, and many critical studies. Baum himself wrote thirteen sequels beginning with *The Marvelous Land of Oz* (1904) and concluding with *Glinda of Oz* (published in 1920, the year after his death). Often he seems to have written the books only because popular demand would insure sales. In fact, sales were so strong that after Baum's death the publishers, Reilly and Lee, hired Philadelphia author Ruth Plumly Thompson to continue the series. Beginning in 1921 with *The Royal Book of Oz* and concluding in 1939 with *Ozoplaning with the Wizard of Oz*, she wrote nineteen annual volumes. Her successor was John R. Neill, who had illustrated all the Oz books except the first (which had been illustrated by W.W. Denslow). Neill wrote the volumes which appeared in 1940, 1941, and 1942. Later contributors to the series were Jack Snow, Rachel R. Cosgrove, Eloise McGraw and Lauren Wagner, and Baum's son, Frank Joslyn Baum.

The first of Baum's stage plays based on *The Wonderful Wizard of Oz* was a musical extravaganza which opened in Chicago in 1902. Although it differed widely from the book, its existence testifies to the popularity of the story. Other Oz books provided the basis for three more musicals and many stage and radio plays, perhaps the most interesting being *The Wiz* (1975), a Broadway production with an all-black cast. The story's motion picture history began in 1910 with *The Wonderful Wizard of Oz*, a silent film, the first of six Oz pictures produced during Baum's life. The best known motion picture,

MGM's *The Wizard of Oz*, with Judy Garland as Dorothy, Bert Lahr as the Cowardly Lion, Ray Bolger as the Scarecrow, and Jack Haley as the Tin Woodman, has become one of the most widely viewed of all motion pictures since its initial release in 1939. Since the early 1960s, it has appeared annually on network television.

In *The Oz Scrapbook*, David Greene reports that as early as 1903 products related to Oz began to appear, and that since then toys, games, clothes, postcards, glasses, puzzles, puppets, and other articles have been merchandised.

Since the early 1900s, the Oz stories by Baum and his successors have become among the best selling of all American children's books, with over seven million copies having been bought. Although librarians have often criticized the stories as being of inferior literary quality, children do not seem to have shared that view.

TIPS FOR PARENTS AND TEACHERS: Reading or classroom discussion (in the middle and upper elementary grades) can be timed to coincide with the annual television showing of the Judy Garland film. Students can discuss differences between the film and the book and can suggest which works most successfully. The "Oz" books can precede reading of such fantasies as C.S. Lewis's *Chronicles of Narnia*.

Bawden, Nina *(1925 –   )*
English

Born in London, the daughter of Charles and Ellalaine Mabey, Nina Bawden and her brother, along with thousands of other school children, were evacuated from London when World War II broke out. She spent three years in Wales during which time, she has said, she became very aware of the moods of adults. She began her career as an adult novelist with the publication of *Who Calls the Tune* (1953) and had published several novels when her children asked her to write a story for younger readers. The result was *The Secret Passage* (1963), published in the United States as *The House of Secrets*, in which three young children, after the death of their mother, are sent by their father to live with Aunt Mabel and become involved in a dangerous adventure. Bawden has discussed the importance of adventure for children: "In real life they can't make anything happen. All they can do is stand by and watch. In adventure stories they can see themselves taking part in the action and not only that. They can also test themselves, measure themselves against the characters in the book."

In 1971, Nina Bawden published *Squib*, a work several critics see as a turning point in her writing for children. The title character is a small, strange, shy child who often plays with other children at the park. The focus of the story is on the other children and their hypotheses about this little boy of whom they know nothing: has he been kidnapped and held for ransom? Is a terrible giant fattening him for a later dinner?

In *Carrie's War* (1973), Bawden drew on her own experiences during World War II. Carrie and her brother Nick are sent to Wales and there become involved in the family struggles between Samuel Evans, their mean and puritanical guardian, and his widowed sister. Both Carrie and her brother grow in understanding during the year. The story is set in a past-present framework. Carrie, now a widow with three children, revisits the valley and tells the children of the events of the past.

In *The Peppermint Pig* (1975), four children and their mother must move from London to a small Norfolk village where they live with aunts. During their year there, each of the children matures. The peppermint pig of the title is a runt the family acquires.

Bawden has spoken about her view of writing for children and about the way they perceive the world: "Children don't always feel what adults expect them to feel, or see what adults expect them to see. They inhabit the same world but look at it so differently. . . . They are detached, attentive and sometimes quite cruel observers of what goes on in the adult world." One of Bawden's major concerns is the relationship between children and adults, as seen from the children's point of view. Often these children are displaced: orphans, of divorced or widowed parents, or living in strange surroundings. They are courageous as they adjust to their new situations and try to come to terms with the adults who control or try to control their lives.

TIPS FOR PARENTS AND TEACHERS: As children in the middle elementary grades become more independent, they often become increasingly critical of many adults. An interesting activity is to have children pretend they are living with one of the adults in a Bawden novel. They can write a letter to a friend commenting on that adult.

❦Beauty and the Beast (1756)
Literary fairy tale
by Madame Leprince de Beaumont

This story of the beautiful girl who rescues an enchanted prince from his beast form first appeared in the eighteenth century. However, its major motif, the marriage of a human being to an apparent beast, is an ancient one. In Greek mythology, the mortal Psyche marries the god Cupid and, because she is unable to see him, fears that she may be living with a monster. In the Scandinavian folktale "East of the Sun and West of the Moon," the heroine marries a prince who has been changed into a polar bear. The story first appeared in France when Madame Gabrielle Suzanne de Villeneuve, following the current fashion of writing fairy tales in the manner of Charles Perrault, composed a version of the story which was over three hundred pages long. Sixteen years later, her countrywoman Madame Leprince de Beaumont, working as a governess in England, wrote a much shorter version which served as the basis of most nineteenth-century retellings.

Iona and Peter Opie have called "Beauty and the Beast" "the most symbolic of the fairy tales after 'Cinderella,' and the most intellectually satisfying." Certainly in its presentation of character, setting, and action, it evokes many meanings and emotions. The chief symbol is the rose Beauty asks for. At first it represents her loving nature, for she, unlike her sisters, has not asked her father for lavish gifts. To the Beast, it is one of the few objects of pleasure in his lonely world. Having lost it, he requests something more beautiful in return and receives Beauty, a spiritual rose. Although the Beast lives in a magnificent palace, Beauty must change her attitude before the place becomes an earthly paradise. She must pass the test imposed to see if she understands the differences between appearance and reality. The final transformation of the Beast is not so much the release from a magic curse as it is an indication of the fact that Beauty has perceived his true goodness.

TIPS FOR PARENTS AND TEACHERS: In the upper elementary and junior high grades, students can examine the character development of Beauty as her goodness is tested and her experience increases. The symbolic settings and the significance of the rose can also be discussed. Students enjoy comparing the various pictoral representations of the beast and deciding which one is closest to their mental images, and why.

Behn, Harry *(1898 – 1973)*
American

Born in Prescott, Arizona, Harry Behn grew up in the desert and mountain country of the Southwest. As a boy, he was an avid reader, and Hans Christian Anderson, William Blake, and George MacDonald were his favorite writers. Of them, he was later to say, "Their search was for a wholeness of vision eternally renewed by children, a healthy wonder that helps to cohere an unstable society fractured by causes and clouded by reason." He spent much of his time with the Indians, playing with many of the boys, and listening to the old tales of elders. From these people, he learned "a ceremonial response to the earth, to the dancing sun and singing winds; how to live in a world as magical as a dream; to speak with a soft voice as whitewing doves do on evenings in summer." After graduation, he lived for a summer with the Blackfoot people of Montana.

In his poems, Behn "tried to capture those early years of primitive awareness." The arousing of wonder and delight based on our earliest, poetry. "All we have to do . . . to find the source of poetry," he wrote, "is to track back within ourselves, back to the beginnings of the ancient energies that have come to us in myth. . . . Poetry is such experience, fractured and reformed into shapes that the mind . . . can assimilate. Poetry is a pursuit (in words) of all beautiful mystery." He particularly hoped that his poems would be read by children in cities, for he felt that they had been most cut off from the natural rhythms and energies of life. In the Indians, who lived close to the earth, he found people who had maintained a direct contact with nature.

Behn's poems deal with rural subjects; many are set in New England, the majority in the Southwest. Often they are about the simple, ordinary aspects of a child's life. His best poems are about the mysteries of nature and of time as perceived and experienced by the child. Like the English Romantic poet William Blake, Behn believed that the child possessed visionary powers.

There are three types of time in Behn's poetry: that measured by clocks, that experienced by a child, and that by which nature ceaselessly moves. In *All Kinds of Time* (1950), a five-year-old ponders the mysteries of time. At first he personifies clocks and takes one apart to try to find answers, only to discover that "even their ticking is just talk. Tick-talk." Then he tries to compare time to the known elements of his life: "Seconds are bugs . . . seasons are wild flowers tame flowers golden flowers and snow . . . centuries are George Washington." He comes to understand that the rhythms of the seasons are a kind of time. The poem concludes with the clock the boy dismantled running crazily and then stopping. He explains that the only part he left out was a "tiny wheel with a spring/ like a butterfly's tongue . . . " which, he suggests, "may be now or perhaps, forever." The image is important: the spring looks like something from nature; time is not mechanical, it is a part of nature. The poem is simple, yet profound. The language and imagery are a child's, as is the vision. The poem is what Behn has called "a ceremony of innocence."

Many of the nature poems celebrate the continuity of time and the rhythms of the seasons. In "Waiting," dormant plants and hibernating bears await spring; "September" is a time "When summer is almost gone/ And autumn's almost begun."

The most intense experiences in the poems generally take place when the individual is alone, in the quiet, still times of dawn or dusk. In "Early," Behn writes:

> Before the sun was quite awake
> I saw the darkness like a lake
> Float away in a little stream
> As swift and misty as a dream.

"Now" describes twilight as "forever between/ Music and silence, the invisible and the seen." One of Behn's most profound poems about a solitary experience in nature is "The Errand," from the *Golden Hive* (1967), which the author has called "a book of poems about stillness." Riding alone across the desert, a boy delivers a book to the empty farmhouse of his father's friend and, as the day ends, he returns home:

> Nothing happened. The sun set,
> The moon came slowly up, and yet
> When I was home at last, I knew
> I'd been on an errand I'd never forget.

Beneath its descriptive surface lies the profound experience of a boy's growing up.

Behn has been highly praised for *Cricket Songs* (1964) and *More Cricket Songs* (1971), the translations of many of the seventeen-syllable Japanese poems known as Haiku. Each of them is, he has stated, "an experience of illumination," and each fulfills his criteria for a good poem: "Anything or any experience, to become a poem, must be presented with a careful incompleteness of information."

TIPS FOR PARENTS AND TEACHERS: Like all good poems, Behn's are for all ages. *All Kinds of Time* and *The Little Hill* (1949) can particularly be enjoyed in the early elementary grades; *Cricket Songs* and *More Cricket Songs*, in the middle elementary grades; and *The Golden Hive*, in the upper elementary grades.

Belloc, Hilaire *(1870 – 1953)*
English

Born in St. Cloud, France, Hilaire Belloc was brought up in England. An Oxford graduate, he was unable to receive a fellowship because he was

Roman Catholic, and he had to earn a living by his writing. Although he earned his major reputation as a writer of biographies and histories, he achieved a small but significant place in the history of children's literature because of four volumes of poetry: *The Bad Child's Book of Beasts* (1896), *More Beasts for Worse Children* (1897), *Cautionary Tales for Children* (1907), and *New Cautionary Tales* (1930). Taken as a group, these poems offer humorous and good-natured satire of the instructive and morally edifying children's poetry which had been written in the nineteenth century. Lewis Carroll with his parodies and Edward Lear with his nonsense limericks and songs had proved that poetry for children need not be somber; and Belloc followed in their pioneering footsteps, but in his own distinctive style.

The Bad Child's Book and *More Beasts*, both illustrated by Basil Blackwood, satirize many nineteenth-century poems which tried to serve as vehicles for teaching biology. In the *Cautionary Tales*, Belloc imitates the approach of such early nineteenth-century poets as Ann and Jane Taylor, who often described the miserable ends of children who were disobedient, dishonest, or stubborn. However, Belloc makes his poems humorous by exaggeration, making his characters improbable in both their personalities and actions. Thus the endings of his poems are not horrifying but ludicrous. Because James runs away from his nurse, as he certainly ought not to have done, he is eaten by a lion. Sara Bing, because she cannot read, is tossed into a hedge by a bull.

TIPS FOR PARENTS AND TEACHERS: Belloc's poems are particular favorites with children in the middle and upper elementary grades. They can be used to introduce the idea of parody by comparing them with heavily moralistic poems. Students can attempt to write their own humorously moralistic poems, imagining ridiculous punishments for their own misdeeds.

Bemelmans, Ludwig *(1898 – 1962)*
American

Born in Meran, in the Austrian Tyrol, Ludwig Bemelmans was a lonely and rebellious child. He was a failure in school and when, at age sixteen, he shot a hotel manager for whom he was working, he left for America rather than be sent to reform school. His idea of America had been formed by reading the adventure stories of James Fenimore Cooper, and he expected to find wild Indians living on the outskirts of New York. Shortly after his arrival in New York, Bemelmans began taking art classes and became recognized as an illustrator during the 1920s.

May Massee, children's editor of Viking, suggested that he write a children's book. The result was *Hansi* (1934), a depiction of everyday life in the Austrian mountains, based on the author's memories of his own childhood. Several of his other children's books also drew on Bemelmans' Austrian background: *The Castle Number Nine* (1937), *The High World* (1954), and *Parsley* (1955). His love and knowledge of New York are reflected in *Sunshine* (1950) and *The Happy Place* (1952), and that of Paris and London in the Madeline books.

Bemelmans' most famous story, *Madeline*, a Caldecott Honor Medal book, appeared in 1939 but had been conceived many years before. Recuperating in a French hospital after a bicycling accident, he met a little girl who proudly showed him the scar from her recent appendicitis operation. He remembered the French convent in which his mother had been raised and, putting the two together, developed the story. Bemelmans did not return to *Madeline* for fourteen years, writing in the meantime five other children's stories which are now seldom read, and twelve books for adults. The idea for *Madeline's Rescue* (1953), a Caldecott Medal book, came from several children who asked him to write a sequel with a dog in it. Sometime later, he saw a dog retrieve a wooden leg floating in the River Seine in Paris and the idea for the story emerged. Bemelmans created three more sequels — *Madeline and the Bad Hat* (1956), *Madeline and the Gypsies* (1959), and *Madeline in London* (1961) — none of them as successful as the first two books. Bemelmans' last children's story, *Marina*, appeared in 1962, the year of his death.

In most of the stories there is a great deal of chaos. However, at the end of the stories, order is restored and the central characters are safe at home. This pattern is best illustrated in the Madeline stories. The opening words and pictures depict the orderliness of the girls' lives as they eat, brush their teeth, walk, and sleep. They are watched over by Miss Clavel, whose life is constantly being unsettled by Madeline and later her friend Pepito. The books close with the various crises overcome and the girls secure and ordered in their beds.

TIPS FOR PARENTS AND TEACHERS: As much of the humor in the Madeline stories is created by the illustrations, pre-school children should be encouraged to linger over the pictures. In the early elementary grades, students can be led to discover how the neat orderly lines are disrupted when the chaos, usually initiated by Madeline, begins.

Bianco, Margery Williams (1881 – 1944)
English

Born in London, Margery Williams moved with her family to New York after the death of her father. She later remembered packing her toys and having to send a stuffed horse to the Children's Hospital because it was too big to take with her. She began writing during her teens and in 1902 *The Late Returning*, the first of her five novels for adults, was published. After she, her husband Francisco Bianco, and their children returned to England after World War I, she began writing for children. *The Velveteen Rabbit*, with illustrations by the celebrated English painter William Nicholson, was published in 1922. It was the first of several books she was to write about the toys in her own and her children's nurseries. During the 1930s, she began writing realistic children's novels: *A Street of Little Shops* (1932), *Winterbound* (1936), *Other People's Houses* (1939), and *Forward, Commandos!* (1944). Although one of these books, *Winterbound*, was awarded a Newbery Honor Medal, they are seldom read now. They are told with the author's customary charm, good humor, and sympathy; however, too many of the objects and ideas are dated.

Margery Bianco's stories of nursery toys have been favorably compared to Collodi's *Pinocchio*, Rachel Field's *Hitty, Her First Hundred Years*, and A.A. Milne's Winnie-the-Pooh stories. Pamela Bianco recalled that her mother often wrote to her as though the dolls and toys she was discussing were alive, and the author herself stated: "By thinking about toys and remembering toys, they became suddenly very much alive — Poor Cecco and Tubby and all the family toys that had been so much a part of our lives." The vividness of these stories arises from the fact that she told them from the toys' point of view.

The first of the toy series, *The Velveteen Rabbit*, has become a minor children's classic. Early in the story, the title hero learns from the wise skin horse that "when a child loves you for a long, long, time, not just to play with you, but REALLY loves you, then you become Real." At the end of the story, because of a boy's affection, it is transformed into a living rabbit. *The Little Wooden Doll* (1925) deals with a toy's greatest fear, being abandoned, and its greatest need: "Deep in every doll's heart there is a longing to be loved by a child." Like Andersen's "The Steadfast Tin Soldier," *Poor Cecco* (1925), considered by many critics to be Bianco's finest children's novel, treats the secret life of toys when human beings are absent.

Bianco tried to capture the child's own vision in her stories. It was essential, she believed, to write about what interested oneself, for children are quick to detect an author's lack of interest: "That is all there is to writing a story. It is the believing in it." She felt that stories were an important means of developing a child's imagination: "It is through imagination that a child makes his most significant contacts with the world around him, that he learns tolerance, pity, understanding, and the love for all created beings."

TIPS FOR PARENTS AND TEACHERS: Children in the early elementary grades who still treat their stuffed animals as living beings will particularly enjoy *The Velveteen Rabbit*. In the middle elementary grades children can see that what applies to the rabbit applies to people, who also need love to be completely alive.

Biography

Although of all forms of literature biography seems to be the one most founded in fact, it is also the form which is most susceptible to deviation from the truth. That is because biographies have not always been treated as life records; in fact, they have often been used as propaganda, as famous people — saints, secular leaders, and more recently major achievers in science, the arts and sports — have been used as role models. Biographies about them have been written in attempts to show young readers how to behave and live well, and as a result the lives themselves have been shaped to meet these goals. Events have been underemphasized or exaggerated, have been deleted or even invented so that the individual in question seems to be a paragon of virtue, whether he or she was or not in actual life.

The writer of biography for younger readers faces many challenges. Like all biographers, he must be accurate and objective while at the same time giving personal insights and presenting his own point of view or interpretation of the subject. But, in addition, he must write with an awareness of the fact that his audience is not adult. He must first of all be aware of the restrictions society places on him for, as critic Margery Fisher has noted, "The Establishment exercises a powerful, invisible influence on the field of junior biography." Often this has meant that certain people and certain aspects of other peoples' lives could not be discussed. More important, it meant that biographies were often expected to be cultural tracts in which the heroic subjects were embodiments of accepted social values. The success story is a typical example of this type of writing: by living according to cultural rules, the subject achieved greatness. This was particularly seen in early biographies dealing with American statesmen. Parson Weems, in *The*

Life of George Washington (1808), set a pattern which prevailed well into the twentieth century and which is still seen in biographies dealing with sports figures and major entertainers. As Marilyn Jurich has humorously remarked, "Generally, if one is to be an honest-to-goodness hero — either in this country or elsewhere — he must have known some kind of economic deprivation. Riches are not justified if the rags have not been flaunted beforehand."

A more significant problem facing the biographer is the relative lack of experience of his young readership. The lives of great men are often introspective and as such are beyond the understanding of most children; moreover, their outer lives are generally involved with historical, political, and economic forces which are also not understood by children. Also, the subjects of these biographies are adults, and it may well be that the child's understanding of the nature of adulthood differs from that of the adult.

Within these limitations, the biographer's general response has been to emphasize the story element of biography, to choose as subjects those elements of people's lives which are physically dramatic and exciting and hence comprehensible and interesting to children. Often biography is fictionalized with scenes and dialogues that operate within the range of probability rather than of verifiable fact. If this is the case, however, the author must make it clear, either in footnotes or in the text, that the scenes he presents are fabricated and are what quite likely might have been rather than what actually was. The author must also avoid the tendency to be ahistorical, that is, to make the subject so contemporary to the reader that the flavor of other times is lost.

Until the last three decades, the majority of American biographies dealt only with those figures considered to be within the mainstream of American life. Members of minority groups and controversial figures were relatively ignored. Such has not been the case since then. Most notable have been books dealing with the black American experience. Such historical figures as Frederick Douglass (*The Life and Times of Frederick Douglass*, adapted by Barbara Ritchie, 1966) and Harriet Tubman (*Harriet and the Promised Land*, by Lawrence Jacob, 1968), and modern figures like Martin Luther King (*Martin Luther King, Jr.: Man of Peace*, by Lillie Patterson, 1969) and Shirley Chisholm (*Fighting Shirley Chisholm*, by James Haskins, 1975) have received fair and sympathetic treatments that would have been impossible until recently. Native Americans have also been considered, in such works as Doris Garst's *Crazy Horse: Great Warrior of the Sioux* (1950) and Doris Martin's *Pocahontas* (1964). Biographers have not shied away from controversial figures, as is evidenced by the publication of such works as James Terzian and Kathryn Cramer's *Mighty Hard Road: The Story of Cesar Chavez* (1970), Arnold Adoff's *Malcolm X* (1970), and Edgar Wyatt's *Geronimo, the Last Apache War Chief* (1952).

Influential American women have also been the subjects of biographies. Iris Noble wrote *Susan B. Anthony* (1975); Margaret Davidson, *The Story of Eleanor Roosevelt* (1969); and Johanna Johnston, *Harriet and the Runaway Book: the Story of Harriet Beecher Stowe and Uncle Tom's Cabin* (1977).

TIPS FOR PARENTS AND TEACHERS: In choosing biographies for young readers, the adult is faced with two problems: which book gives the best treatment of the person in question, and which book will be best understood by the child at a particular reading and maturity level? In analyzing books about a particular individual the adult should, where possible, compare the book with an adult biography to be able to see the completeness of the children's biography, its accuracy, and its point-of-view. When more than one children's biography exists about the same person, several should be read. This will enable the adult to evaluate specific books. When two equally good ones are found, children can be introduced to both, thus being given an opportunity to compare differing approaches. Generally, younger children do not have the mental development necessary to understand life stories about people from different times or cultures. Thus, biography is best introduced in the middle elementary grades. At this time, children should be given biographies which give a sense of the personalities of the subjects and which emphasize important achievements. Upper elementary and junior high students can read more complex biographies, ones which reveal both the strengths and weaknesses of people and the complexities of the issues and decisions of their lives.

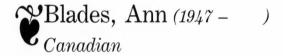

Blades, Ann *(1947 –   )*
Canadian

Born in Vancouver, Canada, Ann Blades began painting at age eleven, but did not contemplate writing a book until 1968 when, teaching in northern British Columbia, she created a story for her students and painted some watercolors for it. The story, *Mary of Mile 18*, published in 1971, was named the Canadian book of the year for children. In it the central figure discovers a lost wolf-pup, but cannot keep it until it proves its value to the family. *A Boy of Taché* (1973) is based, like *Mary of Mile 18*, on the people and settings of northern British Columbia. In 1977, Blades published *The Cottage at Crescent Beach*, reminiscences of her childhood, and illustrated *Jacques the Woodcutter*, a French Canadian folktale. Her illustrations for *A Salmon for Simon* (1978),

Betty Waterton's story about a little Indian boy who feels inadequate because, unlike his sisters, he cannot catch fish, earned Blades the Amelia Frances Howard-Gibbon Award for outstanding illustrations in a Canadian children's book. While Ann Blades is a competent writer, the success of her books results mainly from her watercolor illustrations, which are the appropriate vehicle for the dominant subject of her works: the simple lives of children who are in harmony with those around them and who learn to adapt to their environments.

TIPS FOR PARENTS AND TEACHERS: Because they deal with emotions of children in real life situations, Blades' books are enjoyed by early elementary aged children. These children can be invited to discuss how they would have reacted in similar situations and can examine how Blades makes use of different colors to suggest a variety of emotions.

Blake, William *(1757 – 1827)*
English

Born in London, William Blake began writing and painting as a young boy. He also began experiencing those visions which came to him throughout his life. He lived most of his life in London, engraving works of literature and writing and illustrating his own poetry. Although he was friendly with many of the political radicals of his day, Blake lived a quiet life, cultivating his unconventional ideas but never publicizing them. His poems were vastly different from those written by Ann and Jane Taylor, two of the most widely read children's poets of his day. Unlike their works, in which obviously contrived situations were presented to exemplify morals, Blake's lyrics presented his imaginative visions.

Taken as a whole, the *Songs of Innocence* (1789) are usually placed in rural settings. In the "Introduction," Blake speaks of "pleasant glee," "merry chear," and "happy songs." "The Lamb" presents a child's ingenuous questions to the animal and his identification of the lamb with both himself and Christ as a child. In "The Echoing Green," children play happily before reminiscing old people, and then return home as evening falls. Night is not a fearful time, for the child is protected by loving nurses, parents, and God. The strongest emotions, as described in "The Divine Image," are mercy, pity, peace, and love. Two of the poems, "Holy Thursday" and "The

Chimney Sweeper," are set in London, but in them the children are sustained by their joyous love of God.

Several of the poems in *Songs of Experience* (1794) have the same titles as poems in *Songs of Innocence*. However, their themes and emotions are almost completely opposite to those of the poems from the earlier volume. "Holy Thursday" is a bitter condemnation of the repression of children. In "The Chimney Sweeper," the little boy laments: "They clothed me in the clothes of death, / And taught me to sing the notes of woe," In "The Divine Image," the strongest emotions are cruelty, jealousy, terror, and secrecy. The city is a place blighted by "dark Satanic mills," and in "London," the poet sees "in every face I meet / Marks of weakness, marks of woe." Often born of diseased mothers, children lead tragic lives. In "Infant Sorrow," Blake writes, "Into the dangerous world I leapt, / Helpless, naked, piping loud."

One of Blake's major achievements as a poet for children is his ability to see the world as children do. There may be joy in seeing the lamb, but awe and terror in questioning the tiger. As twentieth-century poet Harry Behn, who freely acknowledged the influence of Blake on his works, wrote: "Children see a world in every least thing." Blake expressed this idea in the opening lines of his poem "Auguries of Innocence."

> To see a World in a Grain of Sand
> And a Heaven in a Wild Flower,
> Hold Infinity in the palm of your hand,
> And Eternity in an Hour.

Not widely read in his own day, Blake is now seen as the first major English poet for children.

TIPS FOR PARENTS AND TEACHERS: Because of their clear images and the sensitive, child-like emotions they contain, Blake's poems can be read to children even at the preschool age. It is not necessary to analyze the poems, although good students in the upper elementary grades may enjoy contrasting similar poems in *Songs of Innocence* and *Songs of Experience*.

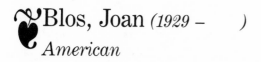Blos, Joan *(1929 –)*
American

Born in New York City, Joan Blos studied clinical psychology at City College and in 1958 became a member of the faculty at the Bank Street School of Education in New York City. In 1970, she began teaching children's literature at the University of Michigan and in 1977 became the American editor of the critical journal, *Children's Literature in Education*. Although she had written texts for children's picture books, it was not until the publication of *A Gathering of Days: A New England Girl's Journal, 1830–32* in 1979 that her work received critical attention. Winner of the Newbery Medal, it is the story of Catherine, a fourteen-year-old living in rural New Hampshire. In addition to describing the day-to-day events of her life, she details several major events which take place: giving aid to an escaped slave, her father's remarriage, the death of her closest friend, and her preparation for leaving home. As she says at the conclusion of her diary, "This year, more than others, has been a lengthy gathering of days, wherein we lived, we loved, were moved; learned how to accept." In discussing the novel, Blos noted that she attempted both to capture the flavor of rural life of the times and to present themes as important today as they were during the nineteenth century: "Sex as well as its consequences, the challenge to children when respected adults hold conflicting opinions, the making of new families out of shattered parts, the personal responsibility that lies between the socially accepted and the morally right."

TIPS FOR PARENTS AND TEACHERS: In the upper elementary and junior high grades, *A Gathering of Days* can be read along with such other novels about nineteenth-century life as *Caddie Woodlawn* (Carol Brink) and the "Little House" books (Laura Ingalls Wilder). Students should study selected passages of the diary to see what they reveal about Catherine's character and the changes it undergoes.

Blume, Judy *(1938 –)*
American

Judy Blume has called herself a child of suburbia. Born in Elizabeth, New Jersey, she grew up in a middle-class Jewish family, where she enjoyed a rich imaginative life, often making up stories with herself as heroine and movies with herself as star. She attended New York University, she has said, because it was expected that she would find a husband and learn a profession to fall back on, should that ever become necessary. In 1959, she married attorney John Blume, and in the 1960s began to raise two children, daughter Randy and son Lawrence.

Judy Blume became interested in writing when, her children having reached school age, she needed a challenge and enrolled in a creative writing course at New York University. Out of the course came two books: *The One in the Middle is the Green Kangaroo* (1969), a picture book illustrated by Lois Axeman, and *Iggie House* (1970), a novel about a black family's move into a white neighborhood. However, it was not until she wrote *Are You There God? It's Me, Margaret* (1970) that she felt she had found her own style and subject matter. Using what she has called her almost total recall of events of her life after age eight, Blume tells the story of Margaret Simon who, moving from New York to New Jersey, wrestles privately with her doubts about religion and shares with her new girlfriends her anxieties about developing breasts and beginning menstrual cycles.

Are You There God? It's Me, Margaret quickly became a success with young readers and was followed by several other books about children facing the problems of growing up. *Freckle Juice* (1971) deals with the humorous attempts of Andrew Marcus to grow freckles so that he won't have to wash his face. In *Then Again, Maybe I Won't* (1971), thirteen-year-old Tony Miglione confronts his sexual growth and worries about wet dreams, a stomach disorder, and a social-climbing family. *Tales of a Fourth Grade Nothing* (1972) is a series of short stories about the misadventures of Peter Hatcher, whose greatest troubles are caused by a baby brother who falls from a jungle gym while attempting to fly and swallows Peter's pet turtle. *It's Not the End of the World* (1972) traces Karen Newman's attempts to cope with the breakup of her parents' marriage. *Otherwise Known as Sheila the Great* (1972) follows the somewhat insecure heroine through the activities of a summer vacation. *Blubber* (1974) deals with the peer group cruelties of fifth graders.

In *Deenie* (1973), Judy Blume moved outside her own experiences to deal with a medical problem. The heroine is a seventh grader who is intent on making the cheerleader team and whose mother hopes that her daughter will become a professional model. It is discovered that she is suffering from scoliosis (a curvature of the spine) and must wear a body cast. Judy Blume did extensive research for the book, visiting hospitals and studying patients' reactions. The result is a story which is both sensitive and accurate in its portrayal of both clinical details and a young teenager's reactions to a major trauma in her life.

Three of Judy Blume's most recent novels make a departure from the earlier books. *Forever* (1975) portrays the first sexual love affair of two high school seniors who learn that their passions do not last. *Starring Sally J. Freedman as Herself* (1976) was Judy Blume's longest book to that time. She stated that all the earlier books were a rehearsal for this one, in which the events and reactions of the heroine closely parallel those of the author's younger life. *Wifey* (1978), an adult novel, deals with a woman's restlessness in her marriage, her love affairs, and her final reconciliation with her husband. It perhaps draws on Judy Blume's own feelings during the breakup of her marriage. She remarried in 1976 and now lives with her husband, Thomas Kitchen, in New Mexico. Her most recent books are *Superfudge* (1980), more tales of Peter Hatcher and his brother, and *Tiger Eyes* (1981) about a girl's coping with her father's death.

Judy Blume does not believe that she is writing books about problems, but stories about individuals and their particular interests and concerns. This aim has led her to deal with subjects generally considered taboo among writers and adult buyers of realistic children's fiction. At the beginning of the 1970s, Judy Blume was thus a pioneer in portraying the actual concerns of children and teenagers. She is sympathetic towards her characters, saying that they are very real to her and that while writing she almost becomes them. She is also respectful of her readers, noting "I think young people need to learn that others share their feelings — that no matter what your problem is, you're not alone."

The reason for the popularity of Judy Blume's books among young readers is not difficult to discover. They seek neither to sermonize nor to educate; rather they present the world as it appears to a specific young person. Generally a story is narrated by the central character so that the reader focuses on his perceptions. The hero's concerns are those that are most important to children from the ages of eight or nine to fifteen or sixteen: parents, peer group pressures, awakening sexuality, death, and religion. These are treated without condescension. No firm conclusions are reached; adaptability and greater understanding are the usual results for the characters.

Are You There God? It's Me, Margaret represents Judy Blume's writing talents at their best. The book treats one year in the life of a girl who has moved to a new school. Although she can talk to her paternal grandmother and her school friends, she prefers to confide in God, to whom she privately addresses prayers throughout the book. Blume skillfully interweaves the many threads of the story: Margaret's fears that she may be sexually abnormal, her awakening interest in boys, her growing appreciation of her first-year teacher, her unkindness to Laura Danker, the biggest girl in the class. The climax occurs as Margaret's parents and her maternal grandparents quarrel over religion. The girl sobs, "How could they talk that way in front of me! Don't they know I'm a real person with feelings of my own!" Margaret learns that she is a real person; equally important, she learns that others are real people too.

In spite of their tremendous popularity — perhaps, in part, because of it — Judy Blume's works have often been criticized by adults. It has been said that she gives young readers what they want rather than need; that she doesn't challenge them. She has also been accused of shaping her plots to meet bibliotherapeutic ends. Perhaps most significantly, her use of the first person narrator has been criticized as limiting the scope of her vision; the reader is not given other points of view. Judy Blume has admitted this limitation of her work, but has then remarked that she aims to present honestly the particular point of view of a specific central character. She has noted that, were she to write about another character in the same book, a totally different approach might be taken.

"I think," she has remarked, "my only responsibility is to be truthful to the kids." While her books are unlikely to become classics, they are, in their honest portrayal of the children who are the characters and in their honesty to the children who are readers, significant children's novels of the 1970s.

TIPS FOR PARENTS AND TEACHERS: Because of their great popularity and the honesty with which they treat their subjects, Judy Blume's books should be made available to upper elementary and junior high school readers. Because they present limited reading challenges, they should be supplemented by the works of such authors as Norma Klein.

Blyton, Enid *(1897 – 1968)*
English

Born in London, Enid Blyton as a girl expressed an interest in music. It was not until she began teaching and discovered that she enjoyed telling stories to her pupils that she began a writing career which would see her publish over 600 books that would sell millions of copies and be translated into dozens of languages. Her first book, *Real Fairies*, a collection of poems, appeared in 1923, and by the end of the decade she had published twenty-two volumes. Her production increased with each decade, and her most prolific year was 1950, when thirty-two of her titles appeared; three books appeared in 1968, the year of her death. A recent bibliography of her works occupies nearly fifteen pages of small type.

Not only the volume, but also the range of Enid Blyton's output is surprising. Most of her books were novels and collections of stories. Many of her characters appeared frequently in series; Nobby, a toy elf, was the hero of over fifty books. The Famous Five, the Adventurous Four, and the Secret Seven had many adventures. Blyton retold many traditional stories from Homer, the Bible, and Aesop, and even adapted some of the adventures of de Brunhoff's Babar. There were volumes of plays and poems, and books which reflected her interest in nature.

There are many reasons for Blyton's tremendous popularity with children. Critic Sheila Ray has noted that Blyton presents "exciting and undemanding reading material." Gillian Avery comments that in her girls' stories, Blyton "ministered to the girls' taste for comfort and security." For casual book buyers, the very presence of Blyton's well-known name prominently displayed on a book's cover was an inducement to purchase. However, her books have not generally been praised by critics or librarians, having been attacked as being bland, simplistic, and unliterary.

TIPS FOR PARENTS AND TEACHERS: Because they are relatively unchallenging, Blyton's books should not provide the basis of children's literary fare. For beginning and slower readers they are good "starter" material; however, the adult should read them stories with greater linguistic and thematic complexity.

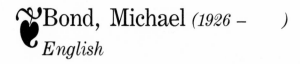

Bond, Michael *(1926 –   )*
English

Born in Newbury, Berkshire, and raised in Reading, Michael Bond decided when he was a young boy to do something creative and sent a cartoon to *Punch*. It received a kindly rejection. After serving in World War II, he worked with the BBC as a cameraman. In 1947, *London Opinion* published his first short story and after that he wrote several stories, articles, and radio plays.

Bond began writing for children as a result of an incident which happened to him at Christmas, 1957. He noticed a small bear which had been left on a shelf in a London department store, bought it, named it after the nearby Paddington Station, and gave it to his wife as a stocking stuffer. A story began to form in his mind, and within ten days he had written *A Bear Called Paddington*. Published in 1958, it is the story of a small bear from Darkest Peru who is discovered, all alone in Paddington Station, by the Brown family. The book quickly became very popular, and more volumes of his adventures were published, many of them illustrated by Peggy Fortnum, whose depictions of Paddington have done much to establish his character.

In 1966, Bond began a series of books about a new character: Thursday, an orphan mouse who lives with the Cupboardosity family, a group of mice residing in an organ loft in *Here Comes Thursday!* (1966). A third group of Bond's books deal with Olga da Polga, a guinea pig who lives with a human family she calls the Sawdusts. The series includes *The Tales of Olga da Polga* (1971) and *Olga Carries On* (1976). Bond has written several other children's books, including many about Parsley, a lion, and two books of plays about Paddington's adventures.

In creating the stories, Bond certainly has followed his theories about successful writing. He has stated that, "I don't think that you can really write a book unless you believe in the characters," and that a writer must draw on real life experiences and people. He also believes that, "If you write *for* children, you run the risk of writing down."

Paddington's adventures occur for three reasons: he is a stranger, a native of Darkest Peru adapting to the new and different life of modern London. Moreover, he is a small bear learning to live with a human family. Most important, he is Paddington, a highly individualistic character, and an adventure-prone bear. As he says, "Things are always happening to me. I'm that sort of bear." Throughout his misadventures, Paddington demonstrates that he is a bear who can land on his feet. He is good-natured and makes many friends who are all willing to help in his many times of need. He is practical in money matters. For those who displease him or try to take advantage of him, he has a withering stare, taught him by his Aunt Lucy for use in emergencies. Although young readers may occasionally laugh at the bear's ludicrous assumptions and awkward predicaments, they can sympathize with his brave attempts to assert himself in a large and sometimes unfriendly world.

TIPS FOR PARENTS AND TEACHERS: Early elementary aged children who have read several Paddington stories can make up their own adventures describing how the bear would react to people, places, and events they know about.

Bontemps, Arna *(1902 –   )*
American

Born in Alexandria, Louisiana, and raised in Los Angeles, Arna Bontemps became involved in the resurgence of black culture known as the Harlem Renaissance while living in New York in the 1930s. He formed a friendship with another noted black author, Langston Hughes, with whom he collaborated in writing his first children's book, *Popo and Fifina, Children of Haiti* (1932). In the following years, in addition to writing many adult works, Bontemps produced several books for children. His many biographies of significant black figures were important contributions in a period when there were few biographies for children about black people written by black authors. Among Bontemps' biographies are *Father of the Blues* (with W.C. Handy, 1941), *The Story of George Washington Carver* (1954), and *Famous Negro Athletes* (1964). His *The Story of the Negro* (1948) is considered one of the finest histories written for young people and received a Newbery Honor Medal. Bontemps collaborated with Jack Conroy in writing two tall tales, *The Fast Sooner Hound* (1942) and *Sam Patch, the High, Wide, and Handsome Jumper* (1951). He has also written short novels for children: *Sad Faced Boy* (1937), *Lonesome Boy* (1955), and *Mr. Kelso's Lion* (1970). *Lonesome Boy*, perhaps the best and most widely read of these, is the story of Bubber, who so loves playing his trumpet that he ignores his grandfather's warning, "You'd better mind where you blow that horn, boy," and ends up playing for the Devil's ball.

TIPS FOR PARENTS AND TEACHERS: Bontemps' nonfiction works are a must for elementary and junior high school library collections. In junior high, *Lonesome Boy* can be studied as a representative tall tale and as a cautionary tale about the dangers of carelessness.

♥Boston, Lucy Maria *(1892 –   )*
English

Born in Lancashire, England, Lucy Boston first saw the Manor, a nine-hundred-year-old house near Cambridge and the principal setting of nearly all her books, in 1915. After purchasing it in 1939, she restored it as nearly as possible to its earliest Norman form, and during World War II used it as a music club for members of the Air Force.

In 1954, at the age of sixty-one, Lucy Boston published *Yew Hall*, an adult novel, and *The Children of Green Knowe*, a children's fantasy, and began a literary career in which she was to write fourteen books in twenty-two years. *The Children of Green Knowe* is the story of nine-year-old Tolly, who is sent to live at Green Knowe after his father has remarried and moved to Burma. Lonely and wishing "he had a family like other people," he discovers warmth and security with his great-grandmother, Mrs. Oldknow. In the story Tolly develops a friendship with the ghosts of Toby, Linnet, and

Alexander, ancestors who had lived in the seventeenth century and died in the Great Plague.

Four more Green Knowe books appeared in the next ten years. In *The Chimneys of Green Knowe*(1958 — published in the United States as *Treasure of Green Knowe*), Tolly returns to Green Knowe for a school vacation and, finding that a much loved family portrait of Toby, Linnet, and Alexander may have to be sold because of financial difficulties, decides to discover the long-lost family jewels. He has matured greatly since the beginning of *The Children of Green Knowe*. Whereas in the earlier novel he had come to Green Knowe lonely, desolate, and insecure, now he feels at home and returns from school with great excitement. Moreover, in this story he actually travels to the past and takes an active part in events.

Tolly and his great-grandmother do not appear in *The River at Green Knowe* (1959), considered by critics to be the weakest in the series. The house has been rented for the summer to Dr. Maud Biggin, who brings along her eleven-year-old niece Ida, and two orphans: Oskar, whose father had been killed in Poland, and Ping, an Oriental boy who has apparently lost both parents. Left much on their own, the children spend their vacation exploring the river, discovering real and fantastic people and creatures.

A Stranger at Green Knowe (1961), Lucy Boston's best-known book, won the Carnegie Medal as the best British children's book of the year. Mrs. Boston had been impressed by a photograph of a gorilla in a London zoo, and on visiting the zoo had been moved by the strength, pride, and power of this almost human figure. The novel centers on the relationship between Ping, invited by Mrs. Oldknow to spend the summer with her, and the gorilla Hanno, who, escaping from the zoo, seeks refuge in a heavy thicket adjacent to Green Knowe. In the end, Hanno, after saving Ping from the charge of an enraged cow, is shot by the big game hunter who had originally captured him in Africa. Ping, the displaced child, is given a permanent home at Green Knowe.

Early in *An Enemy at Green Knowe* (1964), the fifth book of the series, Mrs. Oldknow tells Tolly and Ping: "It [Green Knowe] has enemies, and it needs guarding all the time." At this time, the enemy is Dr. Melanie D. Powers, in reality a witch in the service of an unseen demon. She uses a series of curses in an unsuccessful attempt to force Mrs. Oldknow to sell the house. The old lady, a bastion of strength in earlier stories, is here fearful and relatively helpless, requiring all the aid Ping and Tolly can give her in defeating the dark forces.

After *An Enemy at Green Knowe*, Lucy Boston left the series for several years, publishing an adult novel, *Persephone*, in 1969 (released in the United States as *Strongholds*), her autobiography, *Memory in a House* (1973), and six stories designed for readers younger than those of the Green Knowe books.

Of these, the best, and the author's own favorite, is *The Sea-Egg* (1967), in which two boys on a seaside vacation discover an egg which hatches into a triton who takes them on miraculous sea adventures.

Mrs. Boston's most recent story, *The Stones of Green Knowe* (1976), may well be the last of the series, gathering together as it does occupants of the house from the past and the present. The central character is Roger, a boy living in Norman times when Green Knowe was being built. Proud of the dwelling, "he passionately wanted the new house to be there forever." When he discovers two mysterious stones in a dense forest, Roger learns he can travel into the future, where he meets later inhabitants of Green Knowe: Toby, Linnet, and Alexander; Susan; and Tolly and Mrs. Oldknow. In the final scene, all these characters are gathered together, and Mrs. Oldknow, transformed into her girlhood self, gives Roger a ring, a family heirloom which he can take back nine hundred years so that it can again be passed through generations, symbolizing the continuity of Green Knowe.

The foundation of the Green Knowe books is the author's knowledge of the house and its past, both of which she describes with accuracy and love. However, each of the books required that she engage in extensive research, the results of which had to be unobtrusively included within the narrative. Green Knowe itself is a symbol of permanence and of continuity through and between changing centuries. Although it is an idyllic retreat, it is threatened by the encroachments of the modern world, as is most evident in *A Stranger at Green Knowe* and *The Stones of Green Knowe*.

Mrs. Oldknow presides over the house. While she does not play a major role in the action of the stories, being more a catalyst for the children, she is able to instill in them a sense of the history of the place and her own love for it. Moreover, she has a deep understanding of children, realizing that they must be allowed to explore and learn on their own, but with the assurance of her love and help should they need it. Although she does not intrude, she shares intuitively with them the excitement they feel in their adventures, reliving through them her own youthful joy at Green Knowe.

Each of the Green Knowe books was illustrated by the author's son, Peter.

TIPS FOR PARENTS AND TEACHERS: In the middle and upper elementary grades, students have usually developed enough of an historical consciousness to understand the time travels of the characters. *A Stranger at Green Knowe* can be examined as a study of the conflict between nature and civilization and can be compared to Jean George's *Julie of the Wolves*.

Briggs, Raymond (1934 –   )
English

Born in London, Raymond Briggs studied at the Wimbledon School of Art, and the Slade School of Fine Art in London, where he decided to become an illustrator. His work began to receive wide attention in 1962, when he published *Ring-A-Ring O' Roses*, the first of three books in which he illustrated a small group of traditional nursery rhymes. *The White Land* followed in 1963. *Fee Fi Fo Fum* was published in 1964 and was named a Greenaway Honor Book.

In 1966, *The Mother Goose Treasury* was published. Winner of Briggs' first Kate Greenaway Medal, it took two years to prepare as Briggs selected over 400 nursery rhymes and then sought the most effective means of presenting them. The book contained over 800 illustrations, some of them very small, some in full-page illustrations or two-page spreads. They reflect the diversity of tone and subject matter of the poems in the collection.

During the 1960s, Briggs illustrated the works of such writers as William Mayne and Ruth Manning-Saunders, and provided the pictures for a series of adventure books about such figures as Charles Lindbergh and von Richthofen, the Red Baron.

In 1970, Briggs drew on the traditional story of Jack and the Beanstalk for his original sequel, *Jim and the Beanstalk*. Set in the twentieth century, it tells of the title hero's discovery of a mysterious beanstalk growing outside his window. Climbing the vine, he meets the old, weak-eyed, bald, and toothless son of Jack's giant. Jim returns to earth three times to acquire the incredibly large eye glasses, false teeth, and wig the old man needs. The humor arises not only from the parallels and discrepancies between this story and the original, but also from the details of the illustrations.

In 1976, Briggs won his second Greenaway Medal for *Father Christmas*, the portrayal of an overworked, somewhat cranky old man who, awakened from a dream of warm summer sunshine, must put up with a cold outhouse, miserable weather, tight chimneys, and rooftop TV aerials as he performs his annual duties. There are compensations: a drink of VSOP cognac at one house, and a gift of the same when he returns home. The book is presented in comic book fashion, with several panels on each page and dialogue enclosed in balloons. A sequel, *Father Christmas Goes on Holiday* (1975), traces the course of the hero's long-awaited vacation, first in France, where he wears a French beret and white shorts; later in Scotland, where he dons a kilt; and finally in Las Vegas, where, attired in a tuxedo, he plays the tables and watches the shows. Briggs' most recent books are *The Snowman* (1978), a wordless picture book which describes the dream adventures of a boy who thinks that his snowman has come to life, and *Fungus the Bogeyman* (1977), about an underground creature. These books have been well received.

TIPS FOR PARENTS AND TEACHERS: Jim and the Beanstalk makes a good follow-up to "Jack and the Beanstalk" in the middle elementary grades. After noticing the similarities and differences in the two stories, children can comment on what they would have done in this situation or in another situation where they met a well-known folktale character.

Brink, Carol *(1895 – 1981)*
American

Born in the then-pioneer town of Moscow, Idaho, Carol Brink lived with her grandmother and aunt after the death of her parents. Life on the farm was happy but lonely, and the girl enjoyed listening to stories of her grandmother's life in frontier Wisconsin, making up stories of her own, reading, and riding through the Idaho countryside on her pony. Her career in children's literature began after she decided she could write better stories then those appearing in her own children's Sunday School newspapers. In 1934, she published *Anything Can Happen on a River*, which draws on the Brink family's adventures on a small boat they had bought and sailed on France's River Seine.

In 1935, she published *Caddie Woodlawn*, a novel which won the Newbery Medal, has been translated into ten languages, and adapted by the author as a play. The book was created around the stories the author had heard about her grandmother's Wisconsin childhood. In the introduction, Brink noted: "The names are partly true, partly made up, just as the facts of the book are mainly true but have sometimes been slightly changed to make them fit better into the story." The novel traces a year in the life of the young heroine. During the first autumn, she is a tomboy roaming the woods with her brothers, playing practical jokes on her uncle, and befriending the Indians. But, by the following autumn, Caddie realizes, "What a lot has happened since last year . . . . How far I've come! I'm the same girl and yet not the same."

In *Caddie Woodlawn*, Brink followed her own theories of how to write: "I like to start with something I know — a place, a person, an experience — something from which I have had an emotional reaction." In this case it was her grandmother, whom she made the heroine. In addition, Carol Brink engaged in extensive research about the life of the period, and spent many summers with her husband in a primitive cabin in Northern Wisconsin, where she became thoroughly familiar with the landscape described in the book.

The popularity of *Caddie Woodlawn* led Carol Brink to write a sequel, *Magical Melons, More Stories about Caddie Woodlawn* (1944) about the adventures of the family from 1863 to 1866, after they had moved to Red Cedar River. Among Brink's other novels for children are *Two Are Better than One* (1968) and *Louly* (1974), a depiction of the lives of two young girls living in the early years of the twentieth century, in which she draws on memories of her Idaho childhood; *Baby Island* (1937), a humorous story of two girls who are shipwrecked on an island with four babies; and *Winter Cottage* (1968), the account of a family living in a wilderness cabin during the Depression.

TIPS FOR PARENTS AND TEACHERS: Readers in the middle elementary grades can compare Caddie's adventures with those of Laura in the "Little House" series by Laura Ingalls Wilder. Readers should notice the steps by which Caddie matures during the year portrayed in the book.

Johnny Crow's Garden, by L. Leslie Brooke, Frederick Warne & Co., New York, 1903. Personification and realistic animal anatomy are combined by Brooke to achieve the comic effects of Johnny Crow's Garden.

In Johnny Crow's Garden.

❧Brooke, L. Leslie *(1862 – 1940)*
English

When Leslie Brooke was a small boy growing up in Birkenhead, his father regularly improvised rhymes for him and his brother about a character called Johnny Crow. One of the children would name an animal and the father would be required to invent some ridiculous antic, ending the verses with the phrase, "in Johnny Crow's Garden." In 1891, Leslie Brooke began his career as a professional illustrator, succeeding Walter Crane as the illustrator of the annual volumes of children's novelist Mrs. Molesworth. Before the turn of the century, he provided, among others, the illustrations for *The Nursery Rhyme Book* (1897), edited by Andrew Lang, and *The Jumblies and Other Nonsense Verses* (1900), and *The Pelican Chorus and Other Nonsense Verses* (1900), both by Edward Lear.

It was not until 1903 that Brooke published the work for which he is most famous: *Johnny Crow's Garden*. When his children were born, he continued his father's tradition of making up Johnny Crow verses. His wife suggested that, combined with his illustrations, they would make a good children's book. So popular was the first edition that a second printing was called for in 1904. By its fiftieth anniversary, it had been reprinted twenty-six times, and it remains in print yet. The second book of the series, *Johnny Crow's Party*, appeared in 1907 and the third, *Johnny Crow's New Garden*, dedicated to Brooke's eldest grandson, in 1935.

In 1904, Brooke illustrated the four retellings of traditional stories which many critics feel to be his best work. *Tom Thumb, The Golden Goose, The Story of the Three Bears*, and *The Story of the Three Little Pigs*, combined in 1905 as *The Golden Goose Book*, follow very closely the texts of earlier versions but are given added humor and dimensions of meaning by Brooke's illustrations. During the period preceding World War I, he illustrated the works of others and published illustrated versions of nursery rhymes. Of his later books, only *Ring o' Roses* (1922) and *Johnny Crow's New Garden* (1935) are widely read today.

The Johnny Crow trilogy and the four retellings of traditional tales combined in *The Golden Goose Book* are Brooke's best works. Of the former, Brooke remarked that at first he had wondered how he might unify a group of little poems. He provided unity three ways: through the development of the title character, in the presentation of a fully realized setting, and in the creation of a loose and slight but definitely sequential plot. Johnny Crow is the creator of order and the perfect host. Because he is concerned for each of his guests as individuals, he is able to create a sense of order and harmony. Johnny's garden seems to have a beneficial effect on the animals. Quiet and ordered, it has enough space to allow each animal to follow his own interests, and it also seems to be a refuge from the cares of the world outside. The illustrations for the Johnny Crow books provide meanings not found in the slender text. Against the tranquil setting, Brooke places characters who are true to their animal natures and who also reflect human foibles.

Brooke's gifts of expanding the meanings of the text and infusing humor into the story through his illustrations are also seen in *The Story of the Three*

Bears. The bears are presented with anatomical accuracy, and, should bears ever live in houses, this is the way they would look and act. The family is completely humanized. While the text merely notes that one is a "Little, Small, Wee Bear," the illustrations reveal that he is a typical only child, somewhat rambunctious and spoiled by his doting parents. The richness of the story is increased by the setting Brooke has created. The family lives in comfort and security. Surrounding the cottage are well-kept borders filled with flowers for the bees who occupy the three hives near the front door. The interior of the house is tastefully decorated, with a bear motif on the door knocker, paintings, and bedspreads. By making the house so much an extension of the bears' personalities, Brooke makes Goldilocks' entry more of an intrusion. She is out of place, and worse, she is an invader of private property.

TIPS FOR PARENTS AND TEACHERS: Preschool and early elementary aged children enjoy the humor of Brooke's illustrations. They should be encouraged to discuss the personalities of the animals depicted in that "Johnny Crow" books. In the middle elementary grades, children can discuss the appropriateness of the illustrations for the traditional stories.

❦Brown, Marcia *(1918 –)*
American

Drawing and storytelling was an important part of the early life of Marcia Brown, who was born in Rochester, New York. She and her sisters often received boxes of crayons for Christmas and spent the holidays creating pictures and stories. Her favorite authors included Howard Pyle and Hans Christian Andersen, and her favorite stories, *Tales from the Arabian Nights* and the folktales retold by the Grimm Brothers and Charles Perrault.

Her first book, *The Little Carousel* (1946), was based on observations she made from the window of her apartment in the Sicilian section of New York. It is the story of Anthony, who cannot afford a ride on a portable carousel but who finally earns one by helping the operator. In 1947, she won the first of six Caldecott Honor Medals for *Stone Soup*, the retelling of a traditional folktale.

Beginning in 1950, Marcia Brown won five consecutive Caldecott Honor Medals, for *Henry Fisherman* (1949), the story of a little Caribbean boy who earns the right to help his father; *Dick Whittington and his Cat* (1950), the

English legend of the poor boy who became the Lord Mayor of London; *Skipper John's Cook* (1951), the tall tale of a boy who gets a job on a New England fishing boat; *The Steadfast Tin Soldier* (1953), the first of three Hans Christian Andersen stories she retold and illustrated; and *Puss in Boots* (1954), another rags-to-riches folktale. This amazing record of successes was climaxed in 1954 when she published *Cinderella*, winner of the Caldecott Medal.

During the later 1950s, Marcia Brown retold and illustrated such works as *The Flying Carpet* (1956), a tale from *The Arabian Nights*, and *The Three Billy Goats Gruff* (1957); and wrote stories of her own based on her observations from her extensive travels. *Felice* (1958) was created after she had watched a Venetian cat lowered to the street in a basket; *Tamarindo!* (1960) tells of Sicilian boys who search for a runaway donkey and lose their clothes to some curious goats. Her love and interest in traditional stories led to the creation of her second Caldecott Medal book, *Once a Mouse . . .* (1961). In Italy, she was given a book of old East Indian tales, and she adapted for younger children the fable about a mouse who is rescued by an old hermit and turned into a tiger; it attacks the master, who then transforms the ungrateful animal back into a mouse.

Since the publication of *Once a Mouse . . .*, Marcia Brown has concentrated on the retelling and adapting of traditional stories. *Backbone of the King* (1966) is the Hawaiian story of a father and son who prove their loyalty to an ungrateful king. Other work included adaptations and illustrations of two more Andersen stories, *The Wild Swans* (1963) and *The Snow Queen* (1973), and two Russian tales, *The Neighbors* (1967) and *The Bun* (1972), the last a variation of *The Gingerbread Man*.

In many of her own stories and those she has adapted, a major theme recurs: the success of the child in a world in which he is considered insignificant. Lonely Anthony in *The Little Carousel* is rewarded by the owner whom he helps; Dick Whittington grows up to become Lord Mayor; Henry proves himself worthy of helping his fisherman father; Cinderella marries the prince; children rescue the lost donkey; and, as boys, the Hawaiians Paka'a and (later) his son succeed in men's worlds. Related to this success theme is that of gratitude: people are rewarded or punished as they appreciate the deeds done for them by these heroes.

While a successful writer, Marcia Brown is best known for her art work. She has often stated that the role of the storyteller in a book is to create in words and pictures a vehicle which will enable the reader or viewer to feel the essence of the story that the author, too, has felt. To achieve this, she carefully chooses the medium and style which best expresses the theme and mood of each book. She has stated: "A child is individual; a book is individual. Each should be served according to its needs." Before creating the pictures, she engages in extensive research: the medieval cottages and houses of Dick Whittington are accurately depicted, Cinderella mirrors the elegant costumes of the seventeenth-century French court. Scenery is appropriate: the rugged Scandinavian mountains form the backdrop of *The Three Billy Goats Gruff*; Sicilian hills and beaches appear in *Tamarindo!*. Marcia Brown has said the "color is not so important as the richness of the message told by the illustrations." However, when color is used, it must enhance mood and them. For *Shadow* (1982), an adaptation of African folklore, Brown was awarded an unprecedented third Caldecott Medal.

TIPS FOR PARENTS AND TEACHERS: In the early elementary grades, children can discuss the moral of *Once a Mouse . . .* and can notice how the illustrations subtly reveal the changes that take place. In the middle elementary grades Dick Whittington's perseverance can be considered. In the upper elementary and junior high grades, students can examine how, like Barbara Cooney, Brown varies her artistic style according to the culture being presented.

Brunhoff, Jean de *(1899 – 1937), and* Brunhoff, Laurent de *(1925 –   )*
French

French artist Jean de Brunhoff often listened to his wife tell stories to his two small children, Laurent and Mathieu. One of these was about a little elephant, and de Brunhoff decided to draw a series of pictures for it. He showed these to his sons, listened carefully to their reactions and then created a large picture book, *The Story of Babar, the Little Elephant*. It was published in France in 1931 and quickly became a success, selling over 50,000 copies. It appeared in the United States in 1933 and in England a year later. He then created six more Babar stories, four of which were published before his death in 1937: *The Travels of Babar* (1932; first edition in English, 1934), *Babar the King* (1932; English translation, 1935), *Babar's ABC* (1936; English translation, 1941), and *Babar's Friend Zephir* (1936; English translation, 1937). Posthumous publications were *Babar at Home* (1938; English translation, 1938), and *Babar and Father Christmas* (1941; the English edition had appeared first, in 1940).

De Brunhoff's son Laurent had studied to become an artist and, after World War II, he decided to continue his father's series. *Babar and that Rascal Arthur* appeared in 1947 and was published in the United States as *Babar's Cousin* (1948). When the book appeared, critics marvelled at how close Laurent de Brunhoff had come to duplicating his father's style. In all, Laurent de Brunhoff has written and illustrated twenty Babar books, several of them very short stories in small format. He has also initiated two series of his own, in which he has developed his own style, one much freer than that used in his Babar stories. Among the titles are *Bonhomme* (1965), the author's favorite, and *Serafina the Giraffe* (1965).

Although the books were written for young children, they have attracted a surprisingly large amount of critical attention from adults. The town created by Babar has been called both middle-class and a utopian socialistic society. Babar, riding his bicycle, exploring caves, and travelling to America, has been seen as a king who never loses the common touch and also as a perpetual infant. For one critic, the early stories are "a primer in power politics," as Babar leaves his primitive society, is educated in Europe, returns home to become ruler, and creates a modern nation with bread and circuses for all.

The continued appeal of the Babar books among children is more straightforward. As picture books, they use vivid color, clearly presented central figures, and backgrounds containing dozens of tiny, fascinating details. As stories, they have several recurring, easily recognizable characters: kindly older people and elephants, loving parents who allow their children considerable freedom, several enegetic children, and an irascible monkey. And in nearly all of the stories appears Babar, an elephant who looks somewhat ridiculous in his neatly tailored suits and royal robes, but who maintains his grace and equanimity through all his adventures and misadventures.

TIPS FOR PARENTS AND TEACHERS: The early Babar stories should be read to preschool chldren in sequence, thus giving a sense of the character's growth to adulthood and kingship. In the early elementary grades the personalities of the characters can be discussed.

Burgess, Thornton W. *(1874 – 1965)*
American

Born in Sandwich, Massachusetts, Thornton W. Burgess worked as the cashier and assistant bookkeeper of a shoe store, later as a reporter, and finally as an associate editor of *Good Housekeeping Magazine*. To supplement his income, he took a job with *Country Life in America*, a widely read periodical of the day, writing a monthly nature calendar. After his day's work he used to compose story letters for his son and later submitted them to a publisher. They appeared in 1910 as *Old Mother West Wind*. A sequel was published the following year.

He soon began to support his family entirely by his writing. Eight "Mother West Wind" books had appeared by 1918. In 1912, he began a daily newspaper feature which continued for forty-five years and which provided the basis for nearly all of his more than sixty children's story books. He also wrote a series of nature guides for children, four books especially for the Boy Scouts, and for several years in the 1920s and 1930s hosted a weekly network radio program, "Radio Nature League." By the time of his death in 1965, he had written over 11,000 individual stories, and sales of his books had reached six million copies, with many of the books having been translated into foreign languages. Some of the most widely read Burgess titles are *Mother West Wind's Children* (1911), *Mother West Wind "Why" Stories* (1915), *The Adventures of Grandfather Frog* (1915), *The Adventures of Danny Meadow Mouse* (1915), *Happy Jack* (1918), and *Lightfoot the Deer* (1921).

Burgess believed that stories were an important way of teaching children about nature and described his own works as being a mixture of accurate observation and imagination: "When I began writing animal stories for children, it was with the sole purpose of teaching the facts about the forms of animal life most familiar to American children. I endeavored to do this by stimulating the imagination, which is the birthright of every child." Often criticized for the sentimentality of his stories, Burgess was a pioneer, being one of the first writers of the twentieth century to make animal stories available to a wide, diverse, and rapidly growing reading public.

TIPS FOR PARENTS AND TEACHERS: Because the Burgess stories overly humanize their animal characters, and because they are often of inferior quality, they should be supplemented with works by such writers as Kenneth Grahame, Beatrix Potter, Charles G.D. Roberts, and Ernest Thompson Seton.

❧Burnett, Frances Hodgson *(1849 – 1924)*
❧ *English*

Born in Manchester, England, Frances Hodgson Burnett learned to read at a very early age and throughout her childhood told stories to her friends and schoolmates. After the family moved to Knoxville, Tennessee, in 1865, her interest in storytelling continued, and in 1868, *Godey's Lady's Book*, a popular publication of the day, printed her first story, "Hearts and Diamonds." Although she is now chiefly remembered as a writer for children, most of her books were intended for adults, and during the later decades of the nineteenth century she was considered one of the more significant women writers of her day and was even compared to George Eliot.

Her first children's book, *Little Lord Fauntleroy*, appeared in 1886. It is the story of the son of an outcast English nobleman, living in reduced circumstances in New York. Little Cedric Errol and his mother are given news that he is to be the heir to his grandfather's title and fortunes, and mother and son return to England. Originally serialized in *St. Nicholas Magazine*, the novel was an immediate success, selling over forty thousand copies the first year. So popular was it that an unauthorized play was announced; in retaliation, Frances produced her own version, *The Real Little Lord Fauntleroy*, staged first in London and later in New York. As a result of the success of her play, the novel, and artist Reginald Birch's illustrations, *Little Lord Fauntleroy* hair styling and clothing for boys became very popular, much as had Kate Greenaway frocks for girls.

The success of *Little Lord Fauntleroy* encouraged Burnett to write *Sara Crewe, or What Happened at Miss Minchin's*. Published in 1888, this is the story of a rich little girl who is given preferential treatment at a fashionable boarding school until her father dies penniless and the child is relegated to the role of a servant. Only at the end of the book is she returned to her fortunes; however, she retains her kind and good nature throughout her tribulations. Burnett returned to this story twice. In 1902, she wrote a play, performed in London, called *A Little Princess*, a drama about Sara Crewe to which were added several characters and incidents. In 1905, she published *A Little Priness*, a novel based on but much longer than the original *Sara Crewe*.

Although in the twenty years before her death in 1924 she continued her prolific writing career, public acceptance of her works steadily declined until publication of *The Secret Garden* in 1911. Generally considered her finest work, *The Secret Garden* is another story of wish fulfillment. Mary Lennox, a homely, sickly, and unpleasant little orphan from India and Colin Craven, a wealthy but also sickly and unpleasant Yorkshire child, discover health and happiness as they work together in the garden which gives the book its title.

In her last years, Burnett's health and vitality steadily declined. She died on October 29, 1924, shortly after having seen the motion picture premiere of *Little Lord Fauntleroy*, starring Mary Pickford in the title role.

Little Lord Fauntleroy, A Little Princess, and *The Secret Garden*, the only works of Burnett still generally read, all fit into one of the most popular story forms for children: the Cinderella story of the child who overcomes many obstacles to achieve happiness and often wealth. Adults also play significant roles in the development of the children. The parents in each of the three novels are either dead, absent, or, if present, generally ineffectual. However, people like Lawyer Havisham, who tells Cedric of his inheritance; Ram Dass, who oversees the refurnishing of Sara's attic room; and Mrs. Sowerby, who provides for Colin and Mary from her limited means but large heart, are not unlike the fairy godparents of folktales: they help the heroes actualize their inner potentials. The influence the children themselves have on the misanthropic individuals close to them is also important. Cedric's innate good nature overcomes the long-standing bitterness and loneliness of his grandfather, and Sara's kindness helps ease the deep guilt of her father's partner. As Mary and Colin grow in happiness, the pervading gloom of Misselthwaite is gradually dissipated until, at the novel's conclusion, the "magic" influences Mr. Craven, who is reunited with the son he'd virtually abandoned at the time of his wife's death.

The focus of the three novels is on the fulfillment of the Cinderella quests of the four central characters: Cedric, Sara, Mary, and Colin. In *Little Lord Fauntleroy* and *A Little Princess*, the fairytale element is only thinly disguised and within the stories there are statements which indicate that the children themselves are aware of the fairytale quality of their adventures. Speaking of Sara's fall from her privileged position, Becky remarks, "It's [Sara's situation] exactly like the ones in the stories . . . . Them pore princess ones that was drove into the world." In *Little Lord Fauntleroy*, the author makes the link to fairytales explicit: "If the castle was like the palace in a fairy story, it must be owned that little Lord Fauntleroy was himself rather like a small copy of the fairy prince, though he was not at all aware of the fact." In *The Secret Garden*, the fairytale elements are almost completely submerged beneath the realistic portrayal of character, actions, and setting, and the result is a more satisfying novel.

TIPS FOR PARENTS AND TEACHERS: The Secret Garden is still popular with children in the middle and upper elementary grades. They enjoy discussing the many ironies in the story as the children continually surprise the adults around them. By examining the changes in the garden, students can see how these reflect the changes in the characters of the children.

Burnford, Sheila *(1918 –   )*
Canadian

Born in Scotland and educated in northern England, Sheila Burnford and her family moved to Canada after World War II, settling in Port Arthur in Northern Ontario. As her children grew, Sheila Burnford began writing, producing scripts for the local puppet theatre and contributing essays to such British magazines as *Punch*. In 1961, she drew on her memories of household pets to write *The Incredible Journey*, the account of the two-hundred-and-fifty-mile journey of a cat and two dogs. Crossing the rugged northern wilderness, they confront a variety of human, animal, and geographical dangers before being reunited with their master. Although it has since been criticized for elements of anthropomorphism and sentimentality, it became an immediate success. Not intended by its author as a book for children, it received the Canadian Children's Book of the Year award, has been translated into over twenty languages, and made into a full-length motion picture.

Her second children's book, *Mr. Noah and the Second Flood* (1973), a modern version of the Biblical story, emphasizes man's lack of reverence for nature. Most recently, she has written *Bel Ria* (1977), the story of a little circus dog who wanders through France and England during World War II. The title hero, like the animals in *The Incredible Journey*, is highly intelligent and influences the lives of the people he meets on his travels.

TIPS FOR PARENTS AND TEACHERS: To help children in the middle elementary grades better understand the hardships of *The Incredible Journey*, it would be useful to display a map of the area north of Lake Superior and pictures of the rugged landscape. Ask children whether either they or their pets could survive making such a long trip in the north woods.

Burningham, John *(1936 –   )*
English

Born in Farnham, Surrey, John Burningham studied at London's Central School of Art, worked for several years painting posters, and tried unsuccessfully to get jobs as a book illustrator. He decided that the only way

way he could get such work was to write and illustrate his own stories, which he did.

His first published book, *Borka: the Adventures of a Goose with No Feathers* (1963), quickly became a success and was awarded the Kate Greenaway Medal. Several other animal stories followed: *Trubloff: The Mouse Who Wanted to Play the Balalaika* (1964), *Humbert, Mister Firkin, and the Lord Mayor of London* (1965), *Cannonball Simp* (1966), and *Harquin: The Fox Who Went Down into the Valley* (1967). While each story deals with different animals, all have a common theme: the need of the central character for security and a sense of self-worth. Each of these books, along with his *ABC* (1964), reflects Burningham's work as a poster painter. Each full or double-page spread is clearly designed with central figures simply and boldly outlined. Vivid foreground colors are used, with a variety of tones employed to depict backgrounds and convey moods. Often Burningham will use the white spaces of his pages to isolate and focus attention on his main characters.

In 1970, Burningham won his second Kate Greenaway Medal for *Mr. Gumpy's Outing*, a work which marks a departure from the style of his earlier works. The plot is simple: the title hero invites two children and several animals for an outing in his boat. After the occupants capsize the boat, they dry out and return to Mr. Gumpy's home for an afternoon tea. During most of the book, Burningham places a black and white sketch opposite a full-color, full-page painting. Each of the sketches shows the boat becoming ever more crowded; each of the paintings, the individual people or animals who ask to join the outing. Double-page, full-color spreads show the boat over-turning the tea party. A sequel, *Mr. Gumpy's Motor Car* (1973), uses similar techniques and a similar situation.

Burningham's most recent books, *Come Away from the Water, Shirley* (1977) and *Time to Get Out of the Bath, Shirley* (1978), mark a new stage in his development as an author and illustrator. In the first, Shirley and her parents go to the seashore and, while the adults read, the girl imagines herself involved in exciting pirate adventures. In the second, she takes a bath and has further adventures. The books are based on a contrast between the world as experienced by a child and by an adult. Burningham communicates the idea almost entirely by pictures. Facing each other are two pictures, a subdued one capturing the moment as the parents see it, and a vividly colored one, from Shirley's point of view.

TIPS FOR PARENTS AND TEACHERS: Early elementary aged children will be able to discuss the emotions felt by the characters in the early Burningham stories. After reading the Shirley stories, children can be invited to talk about similar experiences they have had. They can draw two pictures, one depicting the event from their own point of view, the other as they think their parents might have seen it.

Burton, Hester *(1913 –   )*
English

Born in Beccles, Suffolk, historical novelist Hester Burton enjoyed reading fast-paced adventure stories during her childhood. At Oxford University, while studying English literature under the guidance of J.R.R. Tolkien and C.S. Lewis, she first acquired an interest in history.

Burton's first children's novel was *The Great Gale* (which appeared in the United States as *The Flood at Reedsmere*). Published in 1960, it is a fictionalized account of the storm of 1953 which devastated England's east coast. The central characters are Mark and Mary Vaughan, two children who heroically rescue two old cottagers. It was followed in 1962 by *Castors Away!*, the first of Burton's historical novels and the winner of a Carnegie Honor Medal. During the autumn of 1803, at the time of the Battle of Trafalgar, Edmund, Tom, and Nell Henchman, vacationing at the seashore, become involved in efforts to rescue a sinking ship and save a drowning man. The shadow of the great battle is ominously present in the background, and young Tom joins Nelson's fleet as a gunner's boy. *Time of Trial* (1963), winner of the Carnegie Medal, is set in 1801 and is the story of Margaret Pargeter, who "wanted to know only the normal, laughing, happy things in the world." Her idealistic father holds dangerously radical notions, and when a tenement collapses, killing several occupants, he writes a pamphlet entitled "The New Jerusalem," for which he is imprisoned. Margaret must struggle in the face of the hostility toward her father, must witness the destruction of his bookstore by an angry mob, and must cope with her growing love for Robert Kerridge, whose wealthy parents do not approve of her.

Since *Time of Trial*, Hester Burton has written several other novels which use late eighteenth- or early nineteenth-century settings. *No Beat of Drum* (1966) deals with the 1830 Farm Riots, and *The Rebel* (1971) is the story of Stephen Parkin, who travels to Paris at the height of the French Revolution.

Hester Burton has dealt with two other periods of English history. The mid-seventeenth century is the setting of *Thomas* (1969), which deals with the Great Plague and the struggles of the Quakers, and *Kate Rider* (1974), in which the Roundhead heroine worries about her Royalist friends. The early years of World War II form the backdrop for *In Spite of All Terror* (1968), in which Liz Hawtin, an orphan from the London slums, is sent to the country during the blitz and plays a role in the sea rescues of the Battle of Dunkirk.

For Burton, one of the attractions of writing about the early nineteenth century is the fact that it was a time "when it was not all safe to be young." It is an appropriate era in which to develop one of her major situations: "young people thrown into some terrible predicament or danger and scrambling out of it unaided." Her heroes and heroines are usually ordinary individuals who respond heroically when they find themselves caught up in forces beyond their control: a flood, a London riot, the blitz, the French Revolution.

TIPS FOR PARENTS AND TEACHERS: By using young characters with whom junior high aged students can identify, Burton brings troubled times to life for her readers. Students should note that the characters not only become involved in exciting adventures, but also must face difficult moral problems.

The Little House, by Virginia Lee Burton, Houghton Mifflin, Boston, 1942. Rural details and circular designs are reintroduced into the illustrations to show the Little House's return to happiness.

❦Burton, Virginia Lee *(1909 –   )*
❦ *American*

Born in Newton Center, Massachusetts, the daughter of the first dean of the Massachusetts Institute of Technology, Virginia Lee Burton spent her childhood years in Massachusetts and California. Her major interest was ballet, which she studied in her teens and which influenced the rhythmic patterns of her art, drawing, and painting. While enrolled in art classes at the Boston Museum of Fine Arts, she met her future husband, George Demetrios, one of the instructors.

Her first book *Jennifer Lint*, the story of a particle of dust, was rejected by thirteen publishers; when her four-year-old son fell asleep as she read it, she admitted its failure. Between 1937 and 1943, Burton wrote and illustrated the five books on which her reputation mainly rests. Each was created for her children and each was, she has said, tested on them in manuscript form. With the exception of *Calico the Wonder Horse* (1941), written in an attempt to wean her boys from their love of comic books, each is based on life around her. *Choo Choo: The Story of a Little Engine Who Ran Away*, (1937), in which the title heroine wearies of a life of responsibility but finally discovers that the familiar is best, was based on the author's memories of a locomotive on the Gloucester Branch of the Boston and Maine Railroad. The steam shovel heroine of *Mike Mulligan and His Steam Shovel* (1939) she first saw digging the basement of the Gloucester High School. *Katy and the Big Snow* (1943) uses as its star the snow plough who was "the pride and joy of the Gloucester Highway Department." The Demetrios' own house served as the basis for *The Little House* (1942), winner of the Caldecott Medal. During this period she illustrated four books by other writers, the most notable being *Fast Sooner Hound* (1942) by Arna Bontemps and Jack Conroy, the tall tale of a dog who races railroad trains and beats them.

With the growth of her sons, Virginia Lee Burton's interest in the creation of picture books declined. However, she created two more books of her own and illustrated two others. *Maybelle, the Cable Car* (1952) was written to celebrate her childhood memories of San Francisco and to assist in the fight to prevent these historic vehicles from being taken off their routes. *Life Story* (1962), her last book, on which she did eight years research, was a survey of the development of the Earth from its creation to the present. In 1947, she designed and illustrated *Song of Robin Hood*, a collection of old ballads modernized by Ann Malcolmson and set to music by Grace Castagnetta. It won a Caldecott Honor Medal. In 1949, she illustrated Hans Christian Andersen's *The Emperor's New Clothes*, a favorite from her childhood.

Although Virginia Lee Burton is an accomplished writer, having a sensitivity for the rhythms and nuances of words, she considered herself primarily a visual artist, a teller of stories mainly through pictures. For her, a tale began with a series of pictures to which words were later added. Like many artists, she worked with a story board, setting each picture in sequence and studying its effect on the total design. In addition, the components of each page — color, line, details, and the arrangement of type — work together to become a total entity. In *Choo Choo, Calico* , and *Son of Robin Hood*, she revealed her skillful use of black and white. Silhouettes were used in *Calico* to imitate but transcend the style of comic strips, while in *Song of Robin Hood*, blacks, greys, and whites create striking designs which remind one of medieval manuscripts. Her use of full color could be as brilliant as in the rollicking *Mike Mulligan*, or as muted as in the nostalgic *Little House* and *Maybelle*.

Her use of line was very important in the creation of mood and theme. Swirls depict the frenzied actions of Choo Choo, Mary Anne, and Katy. Rolling hills and winding roads, which reflect the influences of Wanda Gág, indicate the passage through time and/or space; curved, rounded lines usually indicate happiness and contentment. The Little House sits on her rounded hill in the country, and the houses of Popperville in *Mike Mulligan* are arranged in a circle. Sharp, angular lines signal the disruptive forces associated with progress. The tiny details found on nearly every page of her works contribute to the story. Burton once wrote that "every detail, no matter how small or unimportant must possess intrinsic interest and significance and must, at the same time, fit into the big design of the book." Endpapers and introductory pages are also important: the wall-paper like endpapers of *The Little House* and *Maybelle* depict histories of transportation and thus introduce the past-present contrasts of the stories. The dedication page of *The Little House* depicts a ring of daisies and so foreshadows the circle designs and the daisy refrain found within the story.

In her books, Burton examined two closely related themes: the need of the individual to feel useful and be recognized, and the superiority of the older, simpler ways over the modern, progressive industrialized life. Her themes are most fully explored in *The Little House*. The opening third of the book emphasizes the harmony which has long existed among the house, its human tenants, and the environment. The only changes are the alternations of the seasons and the generations. However, with assembly line quickness and efficiency, a highway is built, slashing diagonally across and through the gentle curves of the rural landscape, destroying the old ways. The negative effect that the increasing urbanization has on the physical environment is equalled by the effect it has on people, who rush about frantically and apparently without purpose. They never once notice the Little House, or, by extension, the old virtues and way of life it represents. At the end, the House is moved to the country. By travelling through space, it reaches a spot where the old-fashioned, rural way of life, with its close harmony with nature, still exists.

TIPS FOR PARENTS AND TEACHERS: The Little House and *Mike Mulligan* are excellent books to introduce early elementary children to the importance to meaning of visual details, color, and design. After looking carefully at single pages, they can discuss the emotions of the characters, and after comparing earlier and later pages, they can notice visual changes and what these signify. *Maybelle the Cable Car* can be used in the middle elementary grades as the starting point for a discussion of the relative merits of old and new objects.

Byars, Betsy *(1928 –   )*
American

Born and raised in Charlotte, North Carolina, Betsy Byars began her career as a writer while raising four children in Morgantown, West Virginia. After trying unsuccessfully to write mysteries, she decided to write for a younger audience and published her first book in 1962: *Clementine*, the story of a toy dragon.

Byars' next three children's books, *The Dancing Camel* (1965), *Rama, the Gypsy Cat* (1966), and *The Groober* (1967), received scant critical acclaim, and it was not until 1968, with the publication of *The Midnight Fox*, that her work began to receive wide attention. This story, the author's favorite, illustrated her ability to portray accurately the thoughts of children in a crisp and lean prose style. Sent to spend the summer on his aunt's farm, the narrator, Tom, is unhappy until he sees a black fox and spends much of his time trying to get further glimpses of it. There is little action in the story; its impact comes from the vivid depiction of the boy's accounts of his thoughts and emotions. *Trouble River* (1969), Byars' next novel, has a pioneer setting. Twelve-year-old Dewey Martin and his grandmother escape hostile Indians by boating down a dangerous river on a raft the boy has built.

A newspaper clipping about swans who regularly left a beautiful pond on the grounds of a university provided the inspiration for Byars' best-known story, *The Summer of the Swans* (1970), winner of the Newbery Medal. The heroine, Sara Godfrey, a young teenager, has reached a difficult period of her life: "Up until this year, it seemed, her life had flowed along with rhythmic evenness. . . . Now, all that was changed. She was filled with discontent, an anger about herself, her life, her family, that made her think she would never be content again." However, when her mentally retarded brother Charlie becomes lost looking for the swans she had shown him a day earlier, she finds a focus. Searching for the boy, Sara overcomes the ugly duckling feeling she has had. The beauty of the book comes from Byars' sensitive portrayal of Charlie's response to his world.

Since publication of *The Summer of the Swans*, Betsy Byars has written several books about the development of love and understanding between individuals. In *The House of Wings* (1972) a boy and his grandfather care for a wounded crane; in *The Winged Colt of Casa Mia* (1973), a boy and his uncle raise a colt who has wings; *The Pin Balls* (1977) brings three unwanted children together in a foster home. In many of these stories, parents are absent, and the children must adapt to other grownups, maturing in the process.

Betsy Byars' other titles are *The 18th Emergency* (1973), *After the Goat Man* (1974), *The Lace Snail* (1975, illustrated by the author), *The T.V. Kid* (1976), *The Night Swimmers* (1980), and *The Cybil Ware* (1981).

TIPS FOR PARENTS AND TEACHERS: Upper elementary and junior high aged readers will find Byars' works satisfying reading, responding to her sensitive portrayal of problems they can recognize. Students should be encouraged to notice both the self-reliance the characters reveal and their interrelationships with other children.

Caldecott Medal

At its 1937 meeting, the American Library Association accepted the offer of Frederic Melcher to donate a medal to be awarded annually "to the artist of the most distinguished American picture book for children published in the United States during the preceding year." The editor of *Publishers' Weekly*, Melcher had been instrumental in the development of Children's Book Week, and had previously donated the Newbery Medal to the American Library Association in 1921. Named after Randolph Caldecott, the nineteenth-century English picture book illustrator, the Medal was to be awarded only to a citizen or resident of the United States and was to be in recognition of the pictures rather than the text, although the text was expected "to be worthy of the book." The winning book was to be chosen by the twenty-three member Caldecott-Newbery Medal Committee, composed of members of the Association's School Libraries Section and the Section for Library Work with Children. Since 1958, the members of the Committee have been drawn from the Children's Services Division, which absorbed the two earlier groups.

In 1938, the first Caldecott Medal was presented to Dorothy Lathrop for her illustrations to *Animals of the Bible*. Between then and 1982, it has been awarded to forty-four artists. Eight of them have been husband and wife artist teams: Ingri and Edgar d'Aulaire, Maud and Miska Petersham, Berta and Elmer Hader, and Leo and Diane Dillon. Six artists have received the Caldecott Medal twice: Robert McCloskey (1942 and 1956), Marcia Brown (1955 and 1962), Barbara Cooney (1959 and 1980), Nonny Hogrogian (1966 and 1972), and Leo and Diane Dillon (1976 and 1977). The Dillons are the only artists to have won the award in consecutive years. Eleven of the artists have been foreign born: Ingri and Edgar d'Aulaire, Miska Petersham, Roger

Duvoisin, Nicolas Mordvinoff, Ludwig Bemelmans, Feodor Rojankovsky, Marc Simont, Nicholas Sidjakov, Beni Montresor, Uri Shulevitz, Peter Spier, and Paul Goble. Only one person has won both the Caldecott and Newbery Medals: Robert Lawson for *They Were Strong and Good* and *Rabbit Hill*, respectively. Gail Haley, who won the Caldecott Medal for *A Story, A Story*, also won the British Greenaway Medal for *The Post Office Cat*.

Each year, in addition to the Caldecott Medal, the Committee names a number of runners-up or Honor Books. These are titles which finished strongly in the voting. The number of Honor Books varies from year to year.

At present, the Caldecott-Newbery Medal Committee is composed of twenty-three members: the executive of the Children's Services Division (president, president-elect, past-president, and treasurer), eight persons elected from general membership of the Children's Services Division, the five members of the Book Evaluation Committee, and six members appointed by the president (the latter are selected to give the Committee as broad-based a representation as possible). Each member of the Committee nominates at least three books for consideration and the Committee receives nominations from the general membership. Committee members read each book nominated and meet at the midwinter meeting of the American Library Association to vote on the titles, four points being awarded for first-place, three for second, and two for third. In order to be declared the Caldecott Medal winner, a book must have received either twelve first-place votes or a total of forty-eight points. The Committee then decides how many of the runners-up should be named Honor Books.

The winning titles are announced shortly after the meeting and the medals are presented at a special banquet at the American Library Association Conference held in the early summer. On this occasion, the winners deliver their acceptance speeches, which are later printed in *Horn Book* and *Top of the News*.

Writing in 1957 about the Caldecott Medal winners to that date, Esther Averill stated, "As a body of published work, the Caldecott Award books seem to lack a common bond." This statement is still valid, for, using artistic excellence as the criterion, the Committee has chosen books about many subjects. A large number of the books deal with realistic subjects; however, during the 1970s all but one of the award-winning books were fantasies or folktales. Reflecting the increased awareness of America's ethnic minorities, two of the medal-winning books of the 1970s were adaptations of African folktales, two of American Indian folktales, and one an alphabet book about African customs.

Inevitably, the choices of the Committee have sparked controversy. Some critics have stated that winners are not popular with children; however, the Children's Services Division has replied that popularity is not a criterion for excellence. It has also been suggested that, in recognition of past excellences artists have been awarded the Caldecott Medal for inferior books. However, for over forty years, the Caldecott Medal has been the most distinguished picture book award in the United States. The book which receives it may count on vastly increased sales and will be certain to receive great attention from librarians and teachers.

The History of the Newbery and Caldecott Medals, by Irene Smith (New York: Viking, 1957), gives a detailed account of the two awards. The acceptance speeches of Caldecott Medal winners have been collected in three volumes: *Caldecott Medal Books, 1938–1957*, edited by Bertha Mahoney Miller and Eleanor Whitney Field (Boston: Horn Book, 1957); *Newbery and Caldecott Medal Books, 1956–1965*, edited by Lee Kingman (Boston: Horn Book, 1965); and *Newbery and Caldecott Medal Books, 1966–1975*, edited by Lee Kingman (Boston: Horn Book, 1975).

TIPS FOR PARENTS AND TEACHERS: By studying all of the Caldecott Medal Books and the Honor Books, adults will become aware of changing styles and themes in picture books and will see how the different artistic media can be used to enhance or expand upon the verbal components of the books.

The Randolph Caldecott Picture Book, by Randolph Caldecott, Frederick Warne & Co., London, 1976. Caldecott indulges in his love of comic situations in this illustration from "The Diverting History of John Gilpin."

❧Caldecott, Randolph *(1846 – 1886)*
English

Born in Chester, England, Caldecott as a young boy revealed the interests and talents which were to make him the most renowned nineteenth-century children's illustrator. By age six, he was making wood carvings of animals. He studied briefly at the Manchester School of Art and then moved to London, where he contributed illustrations to such papers and magazines as *London Graphic* and *Punch*.

In August, 1872, he joined his friend and future biographer Henry Blackburn in Europe; over one hundred of his sketches of the trip appeared in Blackburn's *A Tour in the Toy Country* (1872), the first book Caldecott illustrated. He was established as a major illustrator in 1876 with the publication of *Old Christmas: Selections from the Sketch Book by Washington Irving*. In the next ten years, he illustrated many books, including three by noted children's author Juliana Horatia Ewing, and a selection of Aesop's Fables.

In 1878, *The Diverting History of John Gilpin* and *The House that Jack Built*, the first two of the famous Randolph Caldecott picture books were published by George Routledge and Sons. Caldecott had created these in collaboration with the highly respected engraver Edmund Evans, who had worked with children's book artist Walter Crane and was later to work with Kate Greenaway. The venture was a success, the 10,000 copies of each of the books selling very quickly at one shilling each. Thereafter, for the next seven years, Evans and Caldecott produced two volumes annually.

Although Caldecott has been praised for the variety and range of his artistic talents, his reputation rests on his sixteen picture books for children. At their best, for example in *Hey-Diddle-Diddle* (1882), *John Gilpin's Ride*, and *A Frog He Would a-Wooing Go* (1883), they represent a perfect blend of text, art, and engraving. In choosing texts, Caldecott seems to have selected those which best complemented his style and gently satiric bent. The rhythmic quality of the language was important, as it could be harmonized with the rhythmic, flowing quality of the art. Each of the works contained a great deal of action and, with the exception of *The Babes in the Wood* (1879), all were capable of humorous interpretation. The focal point in many of the narratives is some kind of ridiculous disaster: John Gilpin is carried off on a runaway horse; a courting frog is devoured by a duck; a dog bites a man and dies. Much of the action takes place on horseback and in the country, allowing Caldecott to indulge his love of drawing horses and rural scenes. Seldom are the actions of the main characters performed in solitude; generally there are crowds and thus the artist has opportunities to include many satiric sketches.

Caldecott's art work has made the picture books the classics they are. The simplicity of line, the accurate depiction of topography, animals, and people, the subtle use of color, and the fluidity and rhythm of the pictures are all qualities of his work that critics have constantly praised. Caldecott's pictures are far more than illustrations: they are interpretations and extensions of the actions. His sense of narrative development seems to have been a major principle in his illustrations. This can be seen in *Bye Baby Bunting* (1882), where the pictures expand the meaning of the simple four line lyric into a story of a father's long, frustrating, and unsuccessful hunting trip.

This interpretation and extension of meaning is achieved by Caldecott's inclusion of details not found in the words. In *An Elegy on the Death of a Mad Dog* (1879), the reasons for the dog's turning on his master are made clear in the illustration: the man is paying attention to a kitten while the dog sulks in the corner. In *A Frog He Would a-Wooing Go*, the suitor's actions are watched by a human family which is at first amazed, but which becomes more and more concerned as the drama progresses to its disastrous conclusion. This use of detail is best seen in the three pictures which accompany the single line "And the dish ran away with the spoon" in *Hey-Diddle-Diddle*. The first shows the elegantly dressed dish running from a party with a dainty spoon, much to the amazement of the onlookers: a wine decanter, a pitcher, and several plates. The second shows the two lovers sitting quietly, shyly, and lovingly together on a bench, while the third reveals the outcome of their precipitous actions. Father knife and mother fork sternly lead their daughter home, while the dish, surrounded by four mourning plates, lies in pieces on the floor, the victim of either his own rash acts or the father's anger.

With the exception of *The Babes in the Woods*, so untypical of Caldecott's work in many ways, and apparently a concession to Victorian pathos, the general tone of the picture books is humorous and gently satiric. Caldecott once wrote to a friend, "Please say that my line is to make to smile the lunatic who has shown no sign of mirth for many months." Although human foolishness, vanity, and hypocrisy are portrayed in the pictures, the tone is not caustic. The foolish suitor who rejects a milk maid who has no dowry is shown being unceremoniously lifted onto the back of a bucking cow; John Gilpin, so dignified as he starts on his ill-fated ride to Edmonton, clings to the horse's mane as his wig and hat fly off behind; the three jovial huntsmen stare stupidly at a pig which they mistake for a "Lunnon alderman."

TIPS FOR PARENTS AND TEACHERS: For preschool and early elementary aged children familiar with the verses illustrated by Caldecott, a look at his books can add to their literary experiences. They can be asked to provide their own words to the story after carefully studying the illustrations.

Cameron, Eleanor *(1912 –)*
American

Born in Winnipeg, Canada, Eleanor Cameron and her family moved to southern Ohio when she was three, and to California when she was six. Here she spent her childhood and her early teens, gathering memories which would later be used in her novels, sending stories to the children's page of the Berkeley *Daily Gazette,* and spending hours at the local public library. When her seven-year-old son David, who had been reading the Doctor Dolittle books, asked if she would write a space story about a small planet, with himself and his friend Chuck playing important roles, she wrote her first children's novel, *The Wonderful Flight to the Mushroom Planet* (1954).

The five Mushroom Planet books, which combine imaginative fantasy and scientific knowledge, trace the adventures of two boys, David Topman and Chuck Masterson, and their strange older friend, Mr. Tyco Bass, a descendant of people from the tiny, unknown planet of Basidium. In *The Wonderful Flight to the Mushroom Planet,* the boys are sent in their homemade rocket to Basidium, where they help the inhabitants overcome a blight affecting the food supply. In *Stowaway to the Mushroom Planet* (1956), they find a home for Theo, Mr. Bass' lonely wandering cousin, and thwart the plans of Horace Q. Peabody, who would destroy the peace of the tiny planet by opening it to human exploitation.

The third and fourth books, *Mr. Bass's Planetoid* (1958) and *A Mystery for Mr. Bass* (1960), introduce another character of Basidium descent, the eccentric inventor Prewytt Brumblydge. David and Chuck help him out of difficulties which he, in part, creates. The final volume, *Time and Mr. Bass* (1967), is set almost entirely in Wales, the ancient earthly home of all individuals descended from Basidium. The two boys help their friend in the decoding of an ancient scroll, the contents of which will enable him to destroy evil forces which have long threatened his people.

The Mushroom Planet books contain a great deal of exciting adventure. Two relatively ordinary boys become involved in and play important roles in events closed to other human beings. Taken as a group, the books also contain an increasing seriousness as the boys are required to face and understand large issues. In the first two books, they must consider the implications of their discovery of Basidium, a place with "no traffic, no factories, no hustle and bustle, no war." They realize that they cannot reveal their new knowledge without jeopardizing life on the planet. *Time and Mr. Bass* deals with the relativity of time and the conflict between the forces of good and evil.

The three best-known of Eleanor Cameron's "California" novels are *A Room Made of Windows* (1971), *The Court of the Stone Children* (1973), and *Julia and the Hand of God* (1977). The first and third are set in the 1920s and deal with the growing maturity of Julia Redfern. In *A Room Made of Windows,* she is troubled over the romance between her widowed mother and her employer and struggles to become a writer. *Julia and the Hand of God* is an unusual sequel, for it deals with the girl's life before the time of the first novel. Living unhappily with her grandmother, she learns to resolve the conflicts in her life. *The Court of the Stone Children* is considered by many critics to be Eleanor Cameron's finest novel. The heroine, Nina Harmsworth, unhappy because her family has moved to San Francisco from a small mountain town, becomes fascinated with a private museum. Here she makes contact with the spirit of Dominique, a French girl from the Napoleonic era.

In her articles, published in *The Green and Burning Tree* (1969), Eleanor Cameron speaks frequently of the essential seriousness of writing for children and writes critically of those authors who do not maintain that seriousness. All good fantasy must contain, she states, "essential truths of the human condition." One of these, she believes, is "the necessity to perceive." In her books, her characters must perceive the realities and truths of the worlds in which they find themselves and of their own inner beings.

TIPS FOR PARENTS AND TEACHERS: In addition to being read as entertaining fantasy, the Mushroom Planet books can be used in the middle elementary grades to introduce important social themes: the relationship between conquered and conquering peoples and the need to respect the environment. *Time and Mr. Bass* and *The Court of the Stone Children* can be read by older children before tackling the more complex fantasies of Alan Garner and Susan Cooper.

Carroll, Lewis: pseudonym of Charles Lutwidge Dodgson *(1832 – 1898)*
English

While he was growing up in Daresbury, Cheshire, Charles Ludwidge Dodgson, the eldest son and third of ten children of Charles Dodgson, a minister, exhibited that love of nonsense which later appeared in his literary classics, *Alice's Adventures in Wonderland* and *Through the Looking-Glass*. He was also a serious student and, in 1851, entered Christ Church, Oxford, beginning an association which lasted for the rest of his life. After graduating with first class honors in mathematics, he began teaching mathematics at Christ Church. He also began publishing poetry in various magazines, and first used his famous pseudonym in 1856. "Solitude" appeared in *The Train* under the name Lewis Carroll, which he later explained was a latinization of his first and middle names.

During the latter part of the 1850s, Dodgson formed the first of his many friendships with children and to three of them, the daughters of Christ Church Dean Henry George Liddell, he first told what was to become his most famous story. While taking the girls on a boating excursion on July 4, 1862, Dodgson related several adventures about Alice; more were told on another excursion a month later, and at the request of Alice Liddell, the author wrote them down and provided illustrations. "Alice's Adventures Underground" was presented to the girl in 1864, and in the same year, at the encouragement of many friends, including novelist George MacDonald, the author considered publishing it. Revised and expanded, and illustrated by well-known political cartoonist John Tenniel, *Alice's Adventures in Wonderland* appeared in November, 1865. A sequel, *Through the Looking-Glass and What Alice Found There*, also illustrated by Tenniel, appeared in 1871.

The Alice books quickly became very popular, and by the time of Dodgson's death in 1898, had sold over 180,000 copies. In 1869, German and French editions of *Alice's Adventures in Wonderland* appeared, and by the turn of the century it was available in Italian, Russian, Swedish, and even short-hand. It has now been translated into over forty languages. The popularity of the book prompted Dodgson to bring out a facsimile of *Alice's Adventures Underground* in 1886, and *The Nursery "Alice"* in 1889, the latter a simplifica-tion of *Alice's Adventures in Wonderland*, accompanied by colored enlarge-ments of the Tenniel drawings. As had been the case with the first edition of *Alice's Adventures in Wonderland*, *The Nursery "Alice"* experienced difficulties in its progress through the press. Dodgson rejected the first set of illustra-tions as being too gaudy; they were offered to an American publisher who also rejected them, saying that they were not sufficiently bright.

Alice in Wonderland was first performed on the stage in 1886, and since then Dodgson's stories have been the basis of many dramatizations. They have also been transformed into films, the two best-known being the 1927 Pathé version starring W.C. Fields, and the 1951 Walt Disney animated version. The books have been frequently reprinted in the twentieth century, with illustrations by such well-known artists as Salvador Dali, Arthur Rackham, Charles Robinson, and Leonard Weisgard. In 1977, *The Wasp and the Wig: The "Suppressed" Episode of Through the Looking-Glass*, which Dodgson had dropped on Tenniel's advice, was published. There have been many parodies and sequels by various writers.

Since their initial publications, the Alice books have been the subject of more critical and scholarly commentary than any other children's book. Writing of their historical significance, critic Roger Lancelyn Green noted, "The revolutionary nature of Lewis Carroll's achievement cannot be exaggerated." At a time when most children's books were heavily moralistic and didactic, Dodgson wrote stories intended solely to entertain and delight. Drawing on the knowledge of children he gained from his many friendships with young people, he was able to understand and present the child's point of view. In Wonderland and the Looking-Glass country, Alice reacts as most children would under such unusual circumstances.

Although Dodgson denied that the Alice books had serious symbolic meanings, critics have delighted in interpreting the stories in a variety of ways. In 1972, to celebrate the one-hundredth anniversary of the publication of *Through the Looking-Glass*, Robert Phillips edited *Aspects of Alice: Lewis Carroll's Dream Child as Seen Through the Critic's Looking-Glass*. In the articles in the collection, the books are interpreted as reflections of Dodgson's own life, as rebellions against Victorian children's literature, as elaborate studies of logic and mathematics, as satires of the church and the educational systems of the times, as parodies of widely read poems, and as case studies in Freudian or Jungian psychology. While some of these articles seem far-fetched, many of them reveal the rich complexity of Dodgson's stories.

During the 1860s and 1870s, Dodgson wrote several mathematics books, most notable of which was *Euclid and His Modern Rivals* (1879). In 1867, he published "Bruno's Revenge" in *Aunt Judy's Magazine*. This story became the basis of two long and somewhat moralistic fairy tales, *Sylvie and Bruno* (1889) and *Sylvie and Bruno Concluded* (1893).

In 1874, while walking across the Surrey Downs, Dodgson had the idea for his best-known nonsense poem, *The Hunting of the Snark*: "I was walking on a hillside, alone, one bright summer day, when suddenly there came into my mind one line of verse — one solitary line — 'For the Snark *was* a Boojum, you see.' I knew not what it meant, then; I know not what it means, now; but I wrote it down." The poem, published in 1876, describes the sea voyage and search for the snark by ten unusual individuals: a bell-man, boots, bonnet-maker, barrister, broker, billiard-marker, banker, beaver, baker, and butcher. The snark is neither seen nor captured, but manages to carry the baker away. Dodgson received many letters asking him what a snark was and admitted that he did not know. In fact, he refused to allow artist Henry Holiday to include an illustration of the snark in the book, preferring that readers create their own mental pictures. Dodgson remarked about the poem's meaning, "Words mean more than we mean to express when we use them; so a whole book ought to mean a great deal more than the writer meant . . . . The best that I have seen is by a lady (she published it in a letter to a newspaper) — that the whole book is an allegory on the search for happiness."

In 1881, Dodgson resigned from the mathematics lectureship at Christ Church, feeling that he no longer needed the income it provided and that he wished to devote more time to his writing. A year later he was elected curator of the Common Room at Christ Church, a position he held for nine years. On January 14, 1898, he died at Guildford, Surrey.

TIPS FOR PARENTS AND TEACHERS: The Alice books need to be carefully introduced to children, as their complexity can often be intimidating. One way of increasing interest in them is to treat them as giant puzzles. In the upper elementary and junior high grades, students can examine Alice's adventures in Wonderland for clues that reveal what kind of a child she was in the waking world. Children with a knowledge of chess can see parallels between that game and events in *Through the Looking-Glass*. Many of the poems in both Alice books are parodies of well-known and dull nineteenth-century children's poems. After comparing Carroll's versions to the originals, students in junior high can write their own parodies of the poems, using modern situations.

Ciardi, John *(1916 –   )*
American

Born in Boston's Little Italy, John Ciardi studied literature at Tufts University and the University of Michigan, where he earned an MA and won the 1939 Hopwood Poetry Award, the University's most prestigious literary award. He has taught at Kansas City University, Harvard, and Rutgers, and has published over twenty-five books of poetry.

Ciardi's first poems for children, many of them published in *The Reason for the Pelican* (1959), were written for his nieces and nephews. In his second book of children's poetry, *I Met a Man* (1961), Ciardi used a controlled list of words provided by his publishers and tested his poems on his daughter Myra. Several other volumes followed, including *The Man Who Sang the Sillies* (1961); *John J. Plenty and Fiddler Dan* (1963), a verse adaptation of the fable of the grasshopper and the ant; *The Monster Den* (1966), written for and about his daughter and two young sons; and most recently, *Fast and Slow* (1975).

Ciardi has criticized much children's poetry, saying that it seems to have been created with "a sponge dipped in warm milk and sprinkled with sugar." Not surprisingly, his own chldren's poetry is much different. Remembering his own youth, he notes that childhood is noisy, boisterous, and violent, and he tries to incorporate these qualities in his own poems, adding to them a sense of humor.

Although a few of Ciardi's poems are written from the point of view of a child, the narrator is generally an adult who seems to be lecturing children on the proper methods of behavior, but who understands his listeners' feeling that such rules and the adults who impose them are often foolish.

TIPS FOR PARENTS AND TEACHERS: Ciardi's nonsense poems make excellent reading for families who sometimes think they are the only ones to quarrel and experience chaos. A book like *Fast and Slow* is a humorous way to introduce concepts to preschoolers.

Cinderella
Folktale

This story of the mistreated heroine who eventually achieves happiness is probably the best-known of all folktales. Hundreds of versions have been discovered around the world. Many of them are older than the famous retelling of Charles Perrault and the Brothers Grimm, while others are adaptations of these French and German versions. Before Charles Perrault published "Cendrillon" in *Histoires ou Contes du temps passé, avec des Moralités* in 1697, the Cinderella story existed in many cultures. Because of the emphasis on daintily fitting shoes, it is believed to have originated in the Orient, where small feet were considered signs of beauty. In fact, the earliest surviving version cames from ninth-century (A.D.) China. Two early versions also existed in the British Isles: the Scottish story "Rashin Coatie," and the Irish "Tattercoats."

After the versions of Charles Perrault and the Brothers Grimm appeared, the Cinderella story was firmly established in the mainstream of children's literature. Dozens of adaptations and translations appeared in English. The story was brought to America where, as author-critic Jane Yolen has noted, it was modified to suit American beliefs. In 1949 it was made into a Walt Disney animated cartoon. The story was also adapted by many North American Indian tribes. In "Poor Turkey Girl," a Zuñi tale, a poor Indian maiden is rewarded for her kindness to the birds she tends with magnificent clothes to attend the great dance. However, because she fails to return to the birds by sundown, they desert her, and she resumes her wretched condition. In "Oochigeas and the Invisible Boy," a Micmac tale, a mistreated youngest sister wins the hand of a great warrior, who "had known all along

. . . that Oochigeas had courage under her gentleness — and a brave spirit makes all things possible."

The two best-known versions, those of Perrault and the Brothers Grimm, are very different in both individual details and overall tone. Living on the edges of the elegant French court of the late seventeenth century, Perrault was a sophisticated author; the Brothers Grimm, students of oral literature and linguistics, attempted to transcribe accurately the oral stories reported to them. Thus, in Perrault's retelling, the tale bears the flavor of the French court and the clothes described were those fashionable at the time. The Grimms' version lacks much of this elaborate description.

The major differences between the two versions relate to the roles of the heroine's father and natural mother, the means by which the girl is able to arrive at the ball, the fate of the stepsisters, and the character of Cinderella. In Perrault's version, the father is of no importance. After marrying, he falls under the influence of his new wife, who "ruled him with a rod of iron," and disappears from the story. The Grimms' father, by contrast, makes what is suggested to be a hasty remarriage and when the messengers arrive at the house with the shoe, denies his daughter, saying, "There is still a little stunted kitchen wench which my wife left behind her." The effect of this treatment is to make Cinderella even more victimized than she was in the Perrault account.

The Grimms' version opens with the mother's death-bed promise to her daughter: "I will look down on you from heaven and be near you." The tree Cinderella plants on her mother's grave and the birds in it are extensions of the mother's benevolent spirit. Perrault does not include the mother, but introduces a fairy godmother who provides all that Cinderella needs. In the Grimms' version, the birds help her as she helps herself. Their Cinderella takes a more active role in shaping her destiny. As psychologist Bruno Bettelheim has noted, "hard and difficult tasks must be performed before Cinderella is worthy of a happy ending."

At the end of the tale, Perrault's stepsisters repent of their wickedness, are forgiven by Cinderella, and marry lords of the court. In the Grimms' version, they mutilate their feet in their attempts to fit the slipper and are blinded by the guardian birds. The final sentence states: "And thus, for their wickedness and falsehood, they were punished with blindness all their days". The explicit emphasis on their evil natures has the implicit effect of enhancing Cinderella's virtue. Perrault emphasizes Cinderella's innate good nature: she is patient and when she prepares her sisters for the ball she resists the temptation to create tangles in their hair; she helps them find husbands. Throughout this version she is a more passive heroine than that portrayed by the Brothers Grimm. Their heroine actively seeks to go to the ball and must perform various tasks before she can do so.

TIPS FOR PARENTS AND TEACHERS: In the early elementary grades, children can be asked to judge which of several illustrated versions of the story is most successful. In the middle elementary grades, they can discuss the significance of the differences between the Perrault and Grimm versions. Upper elementary and junior high students can examine versions from several cultures, seeing how each version reflects the cultural values of the people who created it.

♥Cleaver, Elizabeth *(1939 –   )*
Canadian

Born in Montreal, Canada, Elizabeth Cleaver was educated in Montreal, except for three years during her teens when she lived with her family in Hungary. Her first illustrations for a children's book appeared in *The Wind Has Wings* (1968), a collection of Canadian poetry, which was the first winner of the Amelia Frances Howard-Gibbon Award for outstanding illustration in a Canadian children's book and is distinguished by her use of collage. Her next two books, *How Summer Came to Canada* and *The Mountain Goats of Temlaham*, companion volumes published in 1969, are retellings of Indian legends. *The Miraculous Hind* (1974), the legend of the founding of Hungary, won the Canadian Library Association's Bronze Medal as the children's book of the year. Richly illustrated in collage, it is the product not only of Cleaver's sensitive artistry, but also of her extensive research into Hungarian customs and costumes.

In 1977, her illustrations of the West Coast Indian legend, *The Loon's Necklace*, a pourquoi story in which an Indian gives up his necklace in gratitude for the bird's role in restoring his sight, received the Howard-Gibbon award. *Fire Stealer* (1980), an Ojibway legend, was also awarded a Howard-Gibbon Medal. *Petrouchka* (1980), an adaptation of the Stravinsky ballet, received the Canada Council prize for children's literature.

TIPS FOR PARENTS AND TEACHERS: In the early elementary grades, students can be shown how Cleaver uses collage, making line patterns, textures, and colors convey the emotions of her stories. In the middle elementary grades, the North American Indian legends can be used along with social studies units about native peoples. Students can be encouraged to see how closely Cleaver imitates Indian art styles.

Cleaver, Vera *(1919 –   ) and*
Cleaver, Bill *(1920 – 1981)*

American

Vera Cleaver was born in Virgil, South Dakota, and Bill in Seattle, Washington. After they met and married during World War II, they began writing short stories, publishing over two hundred of them before writing their first children's book, *Ellen Grae* (1967), the story of a garrulous tomboy who discovers that the local half-wit had secretly buried his parents in a nearby swamp. In *Lady Ellen Grae* (1968), the heroine has further adventures which help her in the difficult process of growing up. The Cleavers' later books have also dealt with this theme of characters, often from rural backgrounds, who must struggle by themselves to confront the difficult worlds in which they live. Among the better-known of their novels are *Where the Lilies Bloom* (1969), in which fourteen-year-old Mary Call tries to keep her father's death a secret so that she and her brothers and sisters will not be taken to a foster home; *The Whys and Wherefores of Littabelle Lee* (1973), about a sixteen-year-old girl living in the Ozark Mountains, trying to care for herself and two aging grandparents; and *The Kissimmee Kid* (1981), the story of twelve-year-old Evelyn, who discovers that her brother is involved in cattle rustling. Among the Cleavers' other books are *Grover* (1970), *I Would Rather be a Turnip* (1971), *Me Too* (1973), and *A Little Destiny* (1979). Although they are warm-hearted in their treatment of the characters, the Cleavers' books are also tough: living in difficult environments, and in demanding situations, the characters must courageously confront complex moral situations.

TIPS FOR PARENTS AND TEACHERS: The Cleavers' books make good reading for students in the upper elementary and junior high grades who prefer realistic fiction. In studying these novels, students should be encouraged to discuss the nature of the moral dilemmas faced by the characters.

Collodi: pseudonym of Carlo Lorenzini
(1826 – 1890)

Italian

Like his most famous character, Pinocchio, Carlo Lorenzini (Collodi, his pen name, was taken from his mother's birthplace) was often a very naughty child. Born in Florence, Italy, he often created disturbances at school, frequently receiving punishments from his teacher and scorn from his classmates. However, he reformed and after studying for the priesthood, he became a soldier, government official, newspaper writer, and author of humorous books and school texts. At the request of a friend, he began writing a story which was serialized in *The Children's Journal*, a new Italian magazine. It proved very popular and in 1883 was published in book form as *Pinocchio*. Within a few years, it had sold over one million copies in Italy alone and was being translated into many other languages. During the twentieth century, it has been adapted several times, with the most famous adaptation being the 1940 Walt Disney animated movie. As many critics have noted, these adaptations alter the character of Pinocchio drastically, making him far more innocent and less naughty than Collodi's original.

Pinocchio came into being because Geppetto wanted to have a puppet with which to make money. However, when the marionette was completed, he came to life and began making life miserable for his new father. Throughout the fast-paced, exciting, and humorous story, Pinocchio is constantly promising to be better to the adults around him. However, because of his dislike for school, his aversion to hard work, his egotism, and his gullibility, he soon breaks these promises and, as a consequence, often finds himself in very great danger. His failings lead him finally into being turned into a donkey and, in this form, being sold to a man who wishes to use his skin to cover a drum.

Although Pinocchio is thoughtless and often cruel, he is not basically evil; he has the seeds of goodness within him. His desires to do well are sincere; it is his inexperience and youthful egotism which betray him. One of Collodi's great achievements in this classic is his ability to present convincingly Pinocchio's mixed character. While he is a make-believe character and not even human until the book's closing pages, Pinocchio reflects qualities most chldren have in varying degrees. In an age in which most children's books were often blatantly didactic, *Pinocchio* was an accurate presentation of elements of children's natures.

Collodi is also an excellent humorist. He portrays his hero in such a way that, although young readers can recognize parts of themselves in him, they can feel superior to him. In similar circumstances, they would not have been so foolish and so gullible. Much of the young reader's joy comes from his being able to predict, if not specifically at least generally, the consequences of the puppet's actions. However, the child can also identify with Pinocchio's moments of remorse and his real love for his father.

Pinocchio is not, however, without moral intention. As an educator, Collodi believed in the values of school so despised by his fictional hero. As he leads his readers through a series of exciting, funny, and often moving episodes, he is also gently reminding them of the values of education and of obedience to those adults who love them.

TIPS FOR PARENTS AND TEACHERS: Many of the elements of *Pinocchio* are like those of myths and fairy tales. His being swallowed by the shark, for example, reflects the Biblical adventures of Jonah. Children in the middle elementary grades enjoy spotting similarities between this novel and folktales they know. They also enjoy predicting the traps into which Pinocchio stumbles before he actually walks into them. This story can be compared to Margery Williams Bianco's *The Velveteen Rabbit,* in which a toy also comes to life because of love.

Chanticleer and the Fox, adapted and illus. By Barbara Cooney, T.Y. Crowell, New York, 1958. A simple, medieval hut is in direct contrast to the strutting pride of Chanticleer in Barbara Cooney's satiric illustration.

Cooney, Barbara *(1917 –   )*
American

Born in Brooklyn, New York, Barbara Cooney grew up on Long Island and spent her summers in Maine. Her mother, a painter, encouraged her interest in art, and at college she majored in the history of art, a subject which was to be invaluable in her later career when she adapted the style of her illustrations to the period of the story. After graduating from Smith College in 1938, she spent a year at the Art Students League in New York. The first book she illustrated was Carl Malmberg's *Ake and His World*, published in 1940, and the first book she wrote and illustrated herself, *King of Wreck Island*, appeared in 1941.

Barbara Cooney did not create any stories between 1943, when she published *Captain Pottle's House*, and 1958, when her Caldecott Medal-winning *Chanticleer and the Fox* appeared. However, she acquired a reputation as an important illustrator, working on twenty books by such authors as Lee Kingman, Ruth Seeger, and Louisa May Alcott, for whose *Little Women* she provided illustrations for a 1955 edition.

Her most famous book, *Chanticleer and the Fox*, an adaptation of "The Nun's Priest's Tale," a fourteenth-century satirical poem by Geoffrey Chaucer, grew from her desire to draw chickens. She had been intrigued by her neighbors' hens and shortly after had read Chaucer's tale. Extensive research followed: several of the neighbors' chickens were moved to her home to be observed and sketched; the herbs in her garden were studied and those of them also found in Chaucer's England were included in the illustrations; the social history and costumes of the fourteenth century were examined thoroughly. Finally, the text, based on Robert Lumiansky's modernization, was adapted to the picture book form. Implicit references to the Canterbury pilgrims and long passages discussing medieval dream theory were omitted.

In her Caldecott acceptance speech, Barbara Cooney stated that her aim had been "to convey in my pictures what Chaucer conveys in his words: that people — in this case chickens — can be beautiful and lovable even when they are being ridiculous." Chanticleer, the vain rooster who is captured and nearly eaten by a flattering fox, is portrayed both realistically and satirically. The first illustration of him takes over three-quarters of a two-page spread. There is no background; the complete focus is on Chanticleer, as the rooster would have wished it. The incline of his head and his strutting posture reveal his vanity. Many of the illustrations are done on scratchboard. This medium Barbara Cooney had used with great success in earlier works; but she was to use it less after *Chanticleer and the Fox*, preferring to vary her medium to suit the subject matter.

During the 1960s, Barbara Cooney illustrated works of Margaret Wise Brown, Walter de la Mare, Virginia Haviland, and Edward Lear. For three of the books she illustrated, French versions of Mother Goose, "Wynken, Blynken, and Nod," and "The Owl and the Pussy Cat," she travelled to France, sketching and gathering background material. In 1961, she published an adaptation of *Cock Robin* and, in 1966, an adaptation of the Grimm Brothers' *Snow White and Rose Red*. During the 1970s, she has branched into a new area, the illustration of three Greek myths adapted by Penelope Proddow: *Dionysus and the Pirates* (1970), *Hermes, Lord of Robbers* (1971), and *Demeter and Persephone* (1972), each using the styles of Greek art. In 1977, she illustrated Jean Craig's adaptation of the Grimms' *The Donkey Prince*, using the style of fifteenth-century Renaissance painting. For her illustrations for *Ox-Cart Man* (1979), a poem by Donald Hall, she received her second Caldecott Medal. In them she copied the style of American primitive painting.

TIPS FOR PARENTS AND TEACHERS: In the early elementary grades, *Chanticleer and the Fox* can be related to such satirical barnyard stories as *Petunia* by Roger Duvoisin and to stories of narrow escapes like Potter's *The Tale of Peter Rabbit*. The *Ox-Cart Man* can be related to early American history lessons in the upper elementary grades. In junior high, students examining artistic styles from various eras will enjoy noticing how Cooney adapts her work to suit the period of the tale.

Walter Crane as a Book Illustrator, by Rodney K. Engen, St. Martin's Press, New York, 1976. Crane's illustration for "Beauty and the Beast" is noted for the accurate and elegant reproduction of clothing and architecture.

🍂 Crane, Walter *(1845 – 1915)*
English

Born in Liverpool, Crane moved with his family at age two months to Torquay, where for the next twelve years he enjoyed the rural scenery and seashore. An avid sketcher, he often helped his portrait painter father, from whom he received much of his early art instruction. In 1863, he illustrated J.R. Wise's *The New Forest: Its History and Scenery* and, as a result, was introduced to Edmund Evans, the top color engraver of the time and later publisher of the children's books of Kate Greenaway and Randolph Caldecott. In 1865, Crane began a collaboration with Evans which was to influence profoundly the publication of children's books. In that year, George Routledge published two of Crane's books, *The Railroad Alphabet* and *The Farm Yard Alphabet*. In future years, Crane produced many of these small-sized, children's books, the last, *The Sleeping Beauty in the Wood*, in 1876. The toy books, as they were called, were so popular that the publishers twice issued collected volumes, each containing eight titles earlier published singly.

In 1877, Crane collaborated with Evans on *The Baby's Opera*, the first of three books on which much of the former's enduring reputation rests. A collection of traditional rhymes with piano arrangements by his sister Lucy Crane, the book is a masterpiece of design. The second book, *The Baby's Bouquet* (1878), contained several foreign songs and was less successful than its predecessor. *The Baby's Own Aesop* was published in 1887, and the three were combined and published in 1899 as *Triplets*.

Crane continued to illustrate children's books during the 1880s, although he had become more interested in education and the socialistic theories of William Morris. He provided pictures for several of the novels of Mary Molesworth and, in 1882, with Lucy published *Household Stories from the Collection of the Brothers Grimm.*. Among other books, he illustrated Hawthorne's *A Wonder Book* and Oscar Wilde's *The Happy Prince.*

Although Crane's children's books are not so popular as those of his contemporaries Kate Greenaway and Randolph Caldecott, he was more influential than they were in the development of children's literature in the nineteenth century. Given the lack of quality in most of the children's books of his time and the infancy of color printing, Crane's insistence on quality in the total design of the book and Evans' skill as a color engraver were instrumental in advancing the art. Crane's philosophy of the picture book is summarized in this statement from *Of the Decorative Illustration of Books Old and New* (1896): "Every child, one might say every human being, takes in more through his eyes than his ears, and I think much more advantage might be taken of this fact." Thus, in designing a book, Crane considered all visual aspects: color, line, border, calligraphy, page size, paper texture, end pages, and cover, as well as subject matter.

Crane believed that inclusion of exquisite details in pictures was one of the means by which the taste of the child is educated and his imagination liberated: "The best of designing for children is that the imagination and fancy may be let loose and roam freely, and there is always room for humor and even pathos, sure of being followed by that ever-living sense of wonder and romance in the child heart." The intricacy and solidity of the details make the realm of the stories more convincing to young readers, thus strengthening their imaginations, which Crane felt were being deadened by the utilitarian approaches of his day. Moreover, the richness of the backgrounds serves as a means of weaning children from the tasteless products to which they were generally exposed.

To achieve his effects in book illustration and design, Crane made use of many periods and types of art : medieval illumination with its integration of text and decoration, Greek pottery with its firmness of line, and Japanese print art with its flat quality and sense of color. Although he used many bright colors in his toy books, Crane made color subservient to his bold, firm lines.

Crane's work as an illustrator and designer of children's books was probably most successful in *The Baby's Opera*. The lyrics and scores of each of the thirty-six traditional rhymes are surrounded by a decorative border containing title and figures appropriate to the particular song. The use of two or three colors for each border gives a subdued effect and aids in the creation of a balanced page. The volume contains eleven full-color, full-page illustrations which depict specific actions of individual poems. These are relatively free of the ornamentation found in his other works. The title page, cover, and endpapers, as well as the small quarto size, all combine to complete the design of this superior children's book.

TIPS FOR PARENTS AND TEACHERS: A century after they were published, Crane's illustrations provide preschoolers with a good introduction to quality art. Children should be encouraged to linger over individual pictures noticing how they relate to aspects of the story they depict.

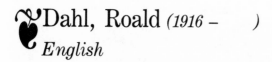

Dahl, Roald *(1916 –   )*
English

Born in Wales, Roald Dahl attended school in England and, rather than enroll at Oxford, accepted a job with the Shell Oil Company, working in Tanzania. In 1942, he was assigned to Washington as assistant air attaché and while there began publishing stories in magazines. After his marriage to actress Patricia Neal, he began telling stories to his children, later publishing them. His first children's book, *James and the Giant Peach* (1961), is a story of a young orphan who enters into a giant peach, meets a group of talking insects, and travels in the peach across the ocean to New York. A theme running through the story is James' progressive growth to maturity. His clear thinking prevents disaster from striking during the strange adventures.

Charlie and the Chocolate Factor, Dahl's best-known and most controversial children's book, appeared in 1964. In it, Charlie Bucket, living in poverty with his parents and grandparents, wins a ticket which admits him to the wonderful chololate factory of Willie Wonka. There he watches as four other ticket-winning children are carried off as a result of their bad habits and manners. On one level, the story is a parody of the Victorian cautionary tale, in which bad children were severely punished. The story has been attacked for its racist portrayal of the Oompa-Loompas, African pygmies who labor in the factory. A later edition of the book has removed the racial references.

Among Dahl's other books for children are *The Magic Finger* (1966), about a girl who uses her powers to cure a neighboring family of its enthusiasm for hunting; *Fantastic Mr. Fox* (1970), an account of unsuccessful attempts of three farmers to destroy a sly animal; and *Charlie and the Great Glass Elevator* (1972), in which the boy, and his parents, grandparents, and Willie Wonka have a series of astounding adventures.

TIPS FOR PARENTS AND TEACHERS: Although Dahl's books have created controversy, particularly among those who do not share his moral views, they are very popular in the middle elementary grades, where students enjoy the humor and admire the courage of his characters.

Daugherty, James *(1889 – 1974)*
American

Born in Ashville, North Carolina, James Daugherty listened to his grandfather tell stories about Daniel Boone and often sketched while his father read to him from the classics. He studied art at the Corcoran Art School in Washington and at the Philadelphia Art Academy. The first book he illustrated was Stewart White's *Daniel Boone, Wilderness Scout*, which was published in 1926. In following years, he illustrated several classics, including Harriet Beecher Stowe's *Uncle Tom's Cabin* (1929), Washington Irving's *Knickerbocker's History of New York* (1928), Francis Parkman's *Oregon Trail* (1931), and Mark Twain's *Adventures of Tom Sawyer* (1932). He also illustrated several stories written by his wife, Sonia Medvedeva: *Mashinka's Secret* (1932), *Vanka's Donkey* (1940), *Wings of Glory* (1940), and *Way of an Eagle* (1941).

Andy and the Lion, the first book Daugherty both wrote and illustrated, was published in 1938 and named a Caldecott Honor Book. Based on George Bernard Shaw's *Androcles and the Lion*, it tells of how the title hero, who is very interested in lions, discovers one on the way to school and manages, with the aid of a pair of pliers he always carries in his pocket, to remove a large thorn from the beast's paw. Some months later, while Andy is at the circus, the same lion escapes from his cage. The two recognize each other and are later treated as heroes. Through the medium of Daugherty's illustrations, sweeping sketches colored a tawny lion-yellow, the story is transformed into a humorous American tall tale.

Daugherty's second book, *Daniel Boone* (1939), was awarded the Newbery Medal. It was written at a time in which, as Daugherty wrote in his acceptance speech, "suble propaganda more deadly than bombs is trying to undermine the walls of our faith." At times Daugherty presents the frontiersman's westward movement as being like a Biblical quest: "Daniel stepped from his boyhood into the kingdom of a man in a world almost as new as Genesis." At other times, he sees Boone as a man betrayed by his idealism: "You were a romantic. You neglected your opportunities to get in on the ground floor." His illustrations, in black, green, and brown, capture the ruggedness of the terrain and the violence of frontier life.

Daugherty wrote several other books about the American past: *Poor Richard* (1941), *Abraham Lincoln* (1943), *The Landing of the Pilgrims* (1950), *Of Courage Undaunted: Across the Continent with Lewis and Clark* (1951), and *Marcus and Narcissa Whitman, Pioneers of Oregon* (1953). He also edited selections of the works of Walt Whitman, Henry David Thoreau, and Ralph Waldo Emerson. His interest in the causes of freedom led to his writing *The Magna Carta* (1956), in which he noted the "unquenchable love of liberty and justice" of the English.

During the 1950s and early 1960s, Daugherty continued illustrating books. Two of these are stories by his wife: *Ten Brave Men* (1951) and *Two Brave Women* (1953). For his illustrations for Benjamin Elkin's *Gillespie and the Guards* (1956), he received a Caldecott Honor Medal. In this story about three brothers with incredibly keen eyesight, Daugherty's drawings reveal the sense of humor which had characterized many of his earlier works.

TIPS FOR PARENTS AND TEACHERS: In the middle elementary grades, students can notice how the illustrations of *Andy and the Lion* illustrate the many ironies of the story. Junior high students can compare the historical biographies to those by such writers as the Petershams, the d'Aulaires, and Robert Lawson.

d'Aulaire, Edgar Parin *(1898 –)*, *and* d'Aulaire, Ingri (Mortenson) Parin *(1904 –)*

American

The d'Aulaires, who met each other while art students in Paris, came from vastly differing backgrounds. Edgar, born in Munich, Germany, was the only child of a well-known Italian society painter and his American wife. Ingri grew up in Norway, and at age fifteen showed her art work to Harriet Backer, the foremost woman painter in Norway, who encouraged her to study art, which she did in Oslo, Munich, and Paris. The couple were married in 1925 and resumed their careers. They travelled extensively in Europe and visited Northern Africa; at one time, to support themselves, they fished and sold their catches in Norway. In 1929, Edgar went to American and Ingri joined him shortly after.

The Magic Rug (1931), the d'Aulaires' first children's book, was based on sketches of Tunisia which they had sent to Ingri's niece in Norway. It set a pattern which was to mark the d'Aulaires' work to come, being based on their first-hand knowledge of the area they were describing and drawing. Their second book, *Ola* (1932), brought them into prominence as writers and illustrators for children. It is the story of a small boy who awakens one long northern winter night and begins a journey in which he views and participates in activities and customs in a variety of Norwegian settings.

In 1936, the d'Aulaires published *George Washington*, the first of seven books celebrating the lives of the discoverers, explorers, and builders of America. In addition to doing background research, they camped extensively in Virginia, trying to experience the land as it would have been experienced by their subject a century and a half earlier. For the second of the series, *Abraham Lincoln* (1939), the d'Aulaires were awarded the Caldecott Medal. Much of the book deals with Lincoln's early life on the prairies, and the d'Aulaires made their customary camping trip, braving lightning storms and floods in Illinois. The Lincoln who emerges is not a distant figure: his cleverness, honesty, leadership, and sense of humor are presented through specific incidents. Strangely, the story does not include Lincoln's assassination, but concludes with his triumphs as president. Later books in the series dealt with Leif Ericson, Pocahontas, Benjamin Franklin, William Cody, and Christopher Columbus.

During the 1960s, the d'Aulaires produced two books which marked a significant new direction in their work: *d'Aulaires' Book of Greek Myths* (1962) and *Norse Gods and Giants* (1964). In nearly 200 oversized pages, *d'Aulaires' Book of Greek Myths* traces the creation and deals with Zeus and his family, minor gods, nymphs, satyrs, centaurs, and mortal descendants of Zeus. Maps, family trees, border illustrations, and full-page illustrations in two and four colors depict major characters and incidents. *Norse Gods and Giants* follows a similar format. It is the more successful of the two books, as it is based on the northern cultures with which the d'Aulaires were more familiar. Moreover, the method of stone lithography, which produces a somewhat coarse and rough textured picture, was a more appropriate medium for the illustrations of the Norse book than for those of the Greek one.

TIPS FOR PARENTS AND TEACHERS: The biographies of American heroes should be complemented with biographies by other authors, giving students in the upper elementary grades an awareness of the fact that biographies are interpretations as well as factual records. The two mythology books are excellent for upper elementary students.

❦ de la Mare, Walter *(1873 – 1956)*
❦ *English*

Like many people who became children's writers, Walter de la Mare was a dreamy, lonely, and often unhappy child. His literary career began while he was a student at the famous St. Paul's Cathedral Choir School in London. He founded and did much of the writing for the school magazine, *The Chorister's Journal*. At age eighteen he began work for the Anglo-American Oil Company, where he stayed until a Civil List pension gave him the financial independence necessary to devote his full time to writing. Although in his lifetime he produced over eighty books for adults — novels, plays, poetry, and essays — he is chiefly remembered for his books for children. In fact, for his *Collected Stories for Children* (1947) he received England's coveted Carnegie Medal, awarded for distinguished contributions to children's literature. De la Mare's best works for children can be divided into three categories: retellings of traditional stories, original stories, and poems.

Told Again (1927) and *Stories from the Bible* (1929) reflect de la Mare's great love of the traditional stories he heard as a child. In the former, he adapts nineteen folktales, including such favorites as "Cinderella," "The Sleeping Beauty," "Little Red Riding Hood," and "Jack and the Beanstalk." His versions are considerably longer than the originals, containing more dialogue, character development, and description. In this way, he is better able to give young readers a sense of the settings and the life-styles of times gone by. Of the Bible, de la Mare wrote, "All that man is or feels or (in what concerns him closely) thinks; all that he loves or fears or delights in, grieves for, desires and aspires to is to be found in it, either expressed or implied." While expanding on the Old Testament stories he included in the collection, de la Mare captured the rhythm of the originals as well as the spirit of the great events described.

De la Mare's own stories for children reflect his love of the old folktales; in fact, many of them are "literary folktales" incorporating into them character types and situations reminiscent of traditional tales. In "Dick and the Beanstalk," a young boy who loved the stories he read discovers Jack's beanstalk, now dry and withered. However, when he climbs it, he discovers a descendant of Jack's giant and doesn't quite know what to do when the giant visits earth, causing many problems. Several stories make use of such traditional themes as the patient daughter ("A Penny a Day") and the cruel master ("The Three Sleeping Boys of Warwicksire"). In the shorter pieces, the good, kind, and virtuous defeat the evil and selfish. The best of his stories were gathered in *Collected Stories* (1947).

The best known of de la Mare's longer works is *The Three Mulla-Mulgars* (1920, later published as *The Three Royal Monkeys*). In it, three small monkeys travel across a wintery and dangerous landscape in search of the Valleys of Tishnar, their ancestral home and the place to which their father had departed several years earlier. The story focuses on Nod, the smallest, youngest, but cleverest of the three brothers. It is, in fact, the story of his growth to maturity, and the adventures he experiences and the settings he passes through symbolize the stages of his growth. Although the story starts somewhat slowly, the pace soon picks up and readers find themselves both thrilled and deeply involved with the adventures and the small hero.

Because it is often specifically English in its descriptions and because it often deals with ideas and customs now considered somewhat old-fashioned, much of de la Mare's poetry for children appears difficult on first reading. However, even the outdated poems contain such beautiful word and sound patterns that the music itself is pleasing to the ear. The best of de la Mare's poems are those dealing with universal qualities of nature and haunting supernatural occurrences. In the former group, "Seeds," "Snowflake," "Snow," and "Silver" are perhaps the best-known and loved. Such works as "The Listeners" and "Nobody," with their delicate hints of the strange, unknown, and unseen elements of life, speak to imaginative, sensitive minds as forcefully today as they did when they were first written. Often the ability to feel the moods of the poems is as important as the ability to understand the meanings clearly. As de la Mare wrote, "We can, . . .

particularly when we are young, delight in the sound of the words of a poem
. . . without realizing its *full* meaning."

TIPS FOR PARENTS AND TEACHERS: For young children, the reading
of nearly all of de la Mare's poems will be a rich introduction to the beauties of
the sounds and rhythms of language. The poems dealing with English
landscape can serve as a complement to a reading of Frances Hodgson
Burnett's *The Secret Garden.* Upper elementary aged school children who
have enjoyed reading adventure stories about soldiers, sailors, and pirates
will enjoy reading the poems on the same subject. "Dick and the Beanstalk"
is an interesting follow-up to a reading of "Jack and the Beanstalk." Good
readers who have responded to J.R.R. Tolkien's *The Hobbit* may find it
interesting to compare Bilbo's journey to that of the young hero of *The Three
Mulla-Mulgars.*

dePaola, Thomas (Tomie) Anthony
(1934 –   )
American

Born in Meriden, Connecticut, Tomie de Paola studied art at the Pratt
Institute and California College of Arts and Crafts. He is one of the most
prolific contemporary illustrators, with over sixty books to his credit in
fifteen years. His own stories can be divided into three categories: old tales
retold, stories of childhood experiences, and information books. *Strega Nona*
(1975), for which de Paola won a Caldecott Honor Medal, is an Italian folktale
in which Big Anthony, like the Sorcerer's Apprentice, gets into trouble with
magic. Two of de Paola's stories about children deal with nighttime experiences. An early work, *Fight the Night* (1968), deals with a little boy who, not
wanting to go to sleep, decides to fight the night. In *When Everyone was Fast
Asleep* (1976), two young children are taken on a marvelous dream journey.
Nana Upstairs, Nana Downstairs (1973) is the sensitive portrayal of a little boy's
relationship with his ninety-four-year-old great-grandmother and his ad-
justment to her death.

In his information books, de Paola combines a humorous story line with
a clear, simple, and accurate presentation of facts. *Charlie Needs a Cloak* (1973)
describes the processes of shearing, carding, spinning, dying, and weaving
wool. The pictures show Charlie's sheep protesting and interfering at every

step. In *The Quicksand Book* (1977), Jungle Girl falls into a quicksand pool where she receives an erudite lecture on appropriate actions from Jungle Boy, who then forgets his own advice when he, too, falls in the pool.

TIPS FOR PARENTS AND TEACHERS: In the middle elementary grades, children are best able to enjoy the visual humor of de Paola's books. After examining the format of the information books, upper elementary aged students can create one of their own, based on their science studies.

Why Mosquitoes Buzz in People's Ears, by Verna Aardema, illus. by Lee and Diane Dillon, Dial Press, New York, 1975. The Dillons illustrate the exaggerated reports of various animals in *Why Mosquitoes Buzz in People's Ears.*

Dillon, Leo *(1933 –   ), and*
Dillon, Diane *(1933 –   )*
American

Born only eleven days apart, Leo and Diane Dillon came from very different backgrounds. Leo grew up in Brooklyn, the son of a Trinidad couple. As a child, he enjoyed drawing and studied at Parsons School of Art, where he met Diane Sorber, whom he married in 1957. She had been born in Glendale, California, and, like Leo, had drawn and painted in childhood. She has remarked that art was a constant for her in a life marked by frequent family moves.

After their marriage, the Dillons worked in advertising and later freelanced, creating album covers, magazine illustrations, movie posters, and paperback book covers. They achieved international prominence in 1975 for their illustrations for Verna Aardema's *Why Mosquitoes Buzz in People's Ears,* winner of the Caldecott Medal. A West African pourquoi story, it relates in cumulative fashion the results of an iguana's failure to say hello to his friend the python. In their Caldecott acceptance speech, the Dillons remarked: "We believe that the role of the illustrator is not simply to duplicate the text, but to enlarge on it, to restate the words in our own graphic terms." Using watercolors applied by air brush, pastels, and India ink, they captured the cumulative effect by placing several animals on each two page spread, and the animals' sense of confusion by having them sitting in jumbled fashion.

In 1977, the Dillons became the first persons to win consecutive Caldecott Medals, when *Ashanti to Zulu: African Traditions*, by Margaret Musgrove, was named the top American picture book of 1976. An alphabet book treating the customs of twenty-six cultural groups, it required extensive research. The Dillons remarked that, "We wanted to combine realism with the elegance of a fairy tale," and that, in doing research, "we began to appreciate the grandeur in ordinary living."

After *Ashanti to Zulu*, the Dillons illustrated another African folktale, Verna Aardema's adaptation of the Masai tale, *Who's in Rabbit's House?* (1977). Returning one evening to her home, Rabbit finds the door locked and hears a voice announce, "I am the Long One. I eat trees and trample on elephants." After much confusion, the mystery is solved: the Long One is a caterpillar playing a trick. As in *Why Mosquitoes Buzz in People's Ears*, the illustrations include elements not found in the text. The Dillons present the story in the form of a play in which African villagers don masks and play the various animal roles. The book's preface notes that "as the story unfolds, the masks change expression, showing merriment, horror, astonishment." Background details are also important: for example, a group of lions watching from a distance are puzzled by the antics of the actors.

The Dillons' most recently illustrated book is *Children of the Sun* (1980), by Jan Carew. It tells of the twin children of the sun, who are sent away to discover their destinies.

TIPS FOR PARENTS AND TEACHERS: In the middle elementary grades, students should be encouraged to notice the cause-effect relationships between actions in *Why Mosquitoes*. Middle elementary students who have read African trickster stories involving rabbits can appreciate the irony of the trickster being tricked in *Who's in Rabbit's House?*

Dodge, Mary Mapes *(1831 – 1905)*
American

Although born in New York City, Mary Mapes Dodge grew up in the country, helping her father, who was a well-known agricultural scientist.

After the death of her husband, whom she married in 1850, she began writing to support her two small children, putting down on paper the stories she had told them. Her first book, *Irvington Sketches* (1864), was so well received that her publishers asked her to write a children's novel dealing with the Civil War. Not interested, she instead wrote a novel set in Holland, *Hans Brinker, or the Silver Skates*. Published in 1865, it was an immediate success and within thirty years it had gone through one hundred editions and been translated into six languages. For the work Dodge was awarded the Montyon Prize of the French Academy. The novel tells of a poor but honest brother and sister and their invalid family, who recover wealth the father had hidden long ago and lead happy and prosperous lives. A standard story which makes use of the theme of hard work, honesty, and goodness being rewarded, it is notable for its vivid depictions of scenes and customs which the author was not to see herself until several years after the book was written. Dodge also wrote other children's books, none of them read today.

However, she played an important role in the most important nineteenth-century children's magazine, *St. Nicholas Magazine*. She had been a magazine editor during the 1860s and in 1873 was asked to be the founding editor of *St. Nicholas*. She served in that position until her death in 1905. Regarded by most critics as the finest children's magazine of all times, it was designed to delight young readers while at the same time subtly inculcating middle-class American values. Under Dodge's leadership, the magazine published works by such well-known authors as Mark Twain, Frank Stockton, Howard Pyle, Frances Hodgson Burnett, and Rudyard Kipling. Although the magazine was published until 1940, it enjoyed its greatest popularity during the years of her editorship.

TIPS FOR PARENTS AND TEACHERS: While it is somewhat old-fashioned and slow-moving in places, *Hans Brinker* is still enjoyed by upper elementary aged children who like reading about different customs and different times. Children who live near a library which has copies of *St. Nicholas* should be given the opportunity to peruse it. Not only will they enjoy looking at a magazine which their great-grandparents may have loved, but also they will find many stories of lasting interest.

du Bois, William Pène *(1916 –   )*
American

Born in Nutley, New Jersey, William Pène du Bois lived with his family in France for six years. His arithmetic teacher had a passion for neatness and from him du Bois learned the order and discipline which marked his work habits and are evident in his art. He also became interested in the writings of Jules Verne and because of them also became interested in unusual mechanical devices. Returning from France, du Bois decided to become an author and illustrator of children's books. Between 1936 and 1941, when he entered the United States Army, he published six books, *Elizabeth, the Cow Ghost* (1936), *Giant Otto* (1936), *Otto at Sea* (1936), *The Three Policemen* (1938), *The Great Geppy* (1940), and *The Flying Locomotive* (1941). Du Bois in these humorous stories gently satirizes human nature and reveals his interest in circuses and machines.

The Twenty-One Balloons (1947), the first book du Bois published after the war, was awarded the Newbery Medal. Set in the 1880s, it is the story of Professor William Waterman Sherman who, after forty years as a school teacher in San Francisco, decides to fly around the world in a giant balloon of his own making. However, he is forced down on the volcanic island of Krakatoa, where he finds a Utopian community of elegant dressers and gourmet cooks. The volcano erupts and the Professor, with the inhabitants, escapes on a giant raft borne aloft by twenty-one balloons. When Sherman finally ditches the raft in mid-Atlantic and is rescued and returned to San Francisco, it is discovered that he has circumnavigated the globe in forty days, half the time taken by the hero of Jules Verne's famous novel, *Around the World in Eighty Days*. In addition to allowing du Bois to indulge in his love of gadgets and balloons, *The Twenty-One Balloons* provided him with an opportunity to satirize mankind.

During the 1950s and 1960s, du Bois published several more picture books, each of them humorously developing an absurd situation. Among the books are *Bear Party* (1951), a Caldecott Honor Book which describes how a wise old Koala devises a means of ending the incessant quarrelling of his fellows. *Lion* (1956), also a Caldecott Honor Book, about a place in Heaven where artists draw pictures of the animals who are to be placed on various planets; and *The Alligator Case* (1965), in which a boy detective solves a circus mystery. Du Bois has also written several books to illustrate moral lessons: *Lazy Tommy Pumpkinhead* (1966) and *Porko Von Popbutton* (1969) are two of them. *Bear Circus* (1971) is a companion piece to *Bear Party* and describes how the bears, discovering a wrecked circus plane, use the costumes and equipment themselves.

Du Bois is a painstaking artist and will create only one picture a day. Often he will paint the pictures of a story first, using the completed illustrations as the basis for his narrative. He has written of his work that, "In making my own books, I always try to put more in the pictures than in my stories. I try to make them jump from chapter to chapter like a program of vaudeville acts, full of rather unusual action from the far reaches of our globe."

TIPS FOR PARENTS AND TEACHERS: In the middle and upper elementary grades, children can discuss the elements of satire found in du Bois' stories. *The Twenty-One Balloons* makes a humorous complement to science classes about volcanoes.

Duvoisin, Roger *(1904 – 1980)*
American

Born in Geneva, Switzerland, Duvoisin enjoyed drawing as a child and studied art and music. Before moving to the United States in 1925, he worked as a stage designer, potter, and textile designer, and had painted posters and murals in France and Switzerland.

His first book, *A Little Boy Was Drawing*, was created in 1932 for his son, who had been drawing a story in which the characters on the page came to life. *Donkey-Donkey* (1940) was the first of Duvoisin's many books to present a fable-like moral in a barnyard setting. The title hero had to learn to accept his long ears. During the 1930s and 1940s, Duvoisin illustrated many books, including *The Pied Piper of Hamelin* (1936), *Mother Goose* (1936), and the first of many nature books written by Alvin Tresselt, *Bright Snow, White Snow* (1947), for which he won the Caldecott Medal.

Duvoisin continued his prolific output into the 1950s, 1960s, and 1970s. He illustrated sixteen more books for Alvin Tresselt, the best-known of which is *Hide and Seek Fog* (1965), a Caldecott Honor book, and works of many other writers including Charlotte Zolotow. In the 1950s, he created two of his best-known characters: Petunia, a silly goose who learns important lessons about false pride, wisdom, and cooperation, and Veronica, a hippopotamus who first feels inconspicuous in her jungle river habitat and later becomes an accepted member of another barnyard community. Seven Petunia stories have been published, beginning with *Petunia* in 1950, and five Veronica stories, the first, *Veronica*, appearing in 1961. In 1954, Duvoisin provided the illustrations for his wife's story *The Happy Lion*, the tale of a lion who discovers that the people of a tiny French town are not so friendly when he leaves his cage. Eight further adventures in the series have appeared. Another major work of the period is *A for the Ark* (1952), a humorous alphabet book in which Noah has trouble keeping the animals in alphabetical order: two bears wish to enter under *u* for their Latin name *Ursus*.

In the 1970s, he continued illustrating books by his wife Louise Fatio and wrote and illustrated six books of his own, one Petunia and one Veronica story, three other barnyard fables, *Jasmine* (1973), *Periwinkle* (1976), and *Crocus* (1977), and *See What I Am* (1974), a concept book about color. His last book, posthumously published, was *The Importance of Crocus* (1980).

In his work as an author and illustrator, Duvoisin develops two major themes: the need to maintain a common sense view of oneself and one's place in the world, and the need to be more sensitive to the world of nature which is being constantly threatened in a machine-oriented age. Duvoisin has freely admitted his didactic concerns, stating that the picture book allows him to exercise "that little sneaking desire to teach and to moralize, to pass on to children what we think of our world." In his animal stories, he has utilized the common device of making the barnyard a symbolic world in miniature, with the animals placed in learning situations. At the end of each of the stories, the conflict that has existed between the central figure and the other barnyard animals has been resolved and a sense of cooperation, interdependence, and friendliness prevails. Duvoisin prevents his moral lessons from becoming obtrusive because of the humor with which the situations are described and the obvious affection he feels for his fallible characters.

For Duvoisin, the meanings of a picture book are created through the interaction of illustrations and text. He has worked with great care on two major aspects of illustration, color and design, both of which he considers the artist's greatest vehicles for experimentation. Color is used to convey mood and atmosphere. The use of the white of the page in relation to a few carefully chosen and placed colors is important to Duvoisin, who described its function in *Bright Snow, White Snow*: "What looks more like snow than the white pages of a book? All the artist has to do is let the white speak for itself. A red spot on the page and you have the feeling of a red brick house whose roof is confused with the snowy hills behind. In the snow landscape everything is guessed rather than clearly seen." Design, the layout of objects and colors on a page, is as important to Duvoisin as the actual content of the pictures. For him, a well-designed page helps to "tell the story with more simplicity, more verve, clarity, and impact; to give importance to what is important; to eliminate what destroys the freshness . . . . A well-designed page will . . . educate the child's taste and his visual sense."

TIPS FOR PARENTS AND TEACHERS: Duvoisin's picture books are best enjoyed by preschool and early elementary aged children. They can discuss the morals of the animal stories and relate them to their own lives.

The nature books can be used to complement science lessons in the early elementary grades.

Emberley, Ed *(1931 –   ), and* Emberley, Barbara *(1932 –   )*
American

Born in Malden, Massachusetts, Ed Emberley began drawing as a child and, after completing high school, studied at the Massachusetts School of Art, where he met and married Barbara Collins, a student of fashion design. Since publishing *The Wing on a Flea* (1961), a book about shapes, he has produced over two dozen books, several of them in collaboration with his wife.

Ed Emberly is best known for his illustrated versions of traditional songs, including *Yankee Doodle* (1965); *One Wide River to Cross* (1966), a Caldecott Honor book; *London Bridge is Falling Down* (1967); and *Drummer Hoff* (1967), winner of the Caldecott Medal. He has also produced a number of concept books which invite reader-viewer involvement. *Green Says Go* (1968) describes primary and secondary colors, explains how colors communicate certain meanings, and suggests that the younger reader think of other meanings associated with color. In *The Wizard of Op* (1975), a series of pictures of optical illusions, he informs the viewer that the eye, not the picture, does the work.

Although Emberley has employed a variety of media, his best books use either woodcuts or pen sketches combined with washes. *The Story of Paul Bunyan* (1963), written by his wife, uses blue and brown woodcuts to suggest the skies and forests of the rugged frontier. *Drummer Hoff*, adapted by Barbara Emberley from a traditional rhyme, is also executed in woodcuts; however, several bright colors and thick pen outlinings are used to create stylized pictures. In addition to illustrating the simple cumulative poem, the pictures satirize military life.

In his work of the 1970s, Emberley generally used pen sketches and washes. Two of the best in this style are *A Birthday Wish* (1977) and *Ed Emberley's ABC* (1978). In the first, a little mouse blows out a candle on his cake and starts a chain of events which leads to his wish coming true. In the latter, each letter is given a two-page spread containing four small pictures, each one marking a stage in the formation of the letter. For example, an ant in the skywriting airplane forms the letter A.

TIPS FOR PARENTS AND TEACHERS: The Emberleys' illustrated song books make excellent supplements for music lessons. Preschool and early elementary aged children should look carefully at the sequencing of the pictures in books like *Drummer Hoff* and *A Birthday Wish*, noticing the changes that take place from page to page.

Estes, Eleanor *(1906 –   )*
American

Although Eleanor Estes had always wanted to be a writer, it wasn't until 1941 that her first book was published. *The Moffats*, the first of sixteen books for children, is the story of Rufus, Janey, Joe, and Sylvie, who live with their widowed mother in the town of Cranbury, a fictionalized version of West Haven, Connecticut, where the author grew up. Although worried that the landlord will sell their house, as he does in the final chapter, the children lead exciting and happy lives. Two more books about the family were published. *The Middle Moffat* (1942) tells of the children's life in their new house, and *Rufus M.* (1943) highlights the youngest's adventures, told against the background of World War I. Both books were awarded Newbery Honor Medals.

After an excursion into fantasy in *The Sun and the Wind and Mr. Todd* (1943), Eleanor Estes returned to realistic fiction in *The Hundred Dresses* (1944), her third Newbery Honor book. This is the story of an outsider, Wanda Petronski, who, to compensate for her poverty, tells her classmates that she has one hundred dresses at home. Unlike the Moffat stories, which presented a generally carefree life, this story, sensitively illustrated by Louis Slobodkin, deals with more unpleasant aspects of children's natures.

Only four of the books Estes has written since 1944 remain widely read. Two of these deal with the Pye family, also residents of Cranbury. *Ginger Pye* (1951), winner of the Newbery Medal, tells of how a brother and sister lose their puppy on Thanksgiving Day and recover him six months later. *Pinky Pye* (1958) describes the adventures of the Pye family on a summer vacation on Fire Island, where they adopt an abandoned kitten and help in the search for a rare pygmy owl.

In *The Witch Family* (1960), Estes returned to fantasy. Two friends, Amy and Clarissa, create, through their imaginative drawings, witches whom they then banish to an "awful, high, lonely, bare, bleak, and barren glass hill!" Although the children have made the witches, they become involved in the adventures and the story becomes an interesting study of the relation between the creators and their creatures.

The Alley (1964) draws on the writer's memories of her Brooklyn residence. Living in a faculty housing complex, Connie discovers that the apparently inviolable area is a target for robbers and, with her friend Billy Maldon and other neighborhood children, finds the robbers.

Eleanor Estes' reputation rests on her Newbery Medal and Honor books. In them, the events of the stories are such as children normally experience: getting a first library card, buying a pet, playing games, visiting the beach, and reacting to the other children and adults they meet.

The center of the Estes' children's world is the home. Neither the Moffats nor the Pyes have much money and the children are aware of the fact but not oppressed by it. Mrs. Moffat and Mr. Pye are loving and supportive; like the adults in E. Nesbit's stories, they generally allow the children freedom of movement, remaining background figures. Brothers and sisters are cooperative but independent and not above being mildly disapproving of each other at times. Beyond the home are the school and the community at large. Friendship is important for the children in Estes' books and the idea of the best friend constantly recurs. Learning to deal with different types of people is also important, as Peggy and Maddie learn in *The Hundred Dresses*, and Mariana in *The Coat-Hanger Christmas Tree* (1973). In this larger world there is also evil. Ginger Pye is stolen and Connie Ives' home is robbed. "If only," Connie muses in *The Alley*, "outside-the-Alley people abided by outside-the-Alley laws as well as inside-the-Alley people did by inside-the-Alley Katy laws."

TIPS FOR PARENTS AND TEACHERS: Dealing as they do with children's early encounters with the world beyond the home, Estes' books appeal to readers in the elementary grades. Individual episodes in "The Moffats" books can be read as short stories and introduced at the times of the year which parallel the seasons in the stories.

Just Me, by Marie Hall Ets, Viking, New York, 1965. The quiet, isolated world of the small child is captured by Marie Hall Ets in this illustration from *Just Me*.

Down near the woods I met an old turtle. He wasn't doing anything at all. "Turtle," I said, "I want to walk like you. Let me see how you walk."

❧Ets, Marie Hall *(1893 –   )*
American

Born near Milwaukee, Marie Hall Ets, as a child, enjoyed art lessons and wandering alone in the woods watching wild animals. After studying interior design at the New York School of Fine and Applied Art, she worked as an interior decorator in San Francisco and as a social worker in Chicago and Czechoslovakia. Marie Hall Ets first combined her artistic ability and knowledge of children in the early 1930s when she created a cloth book for her nephew (published in 1948 as *Little Old Automobile*). *Mr. Penny* (1935), her first published book, is the story of a kindly but poor old man whose sole concern is the happiness of his "family": a horse, a cow, a goat, a pig, a lamb, a hen, and a rooster. Two sequels followed: *Mr. Penny's Race Horse* (1956), a Caldecott Honor Book, and *Mr. Penny's Circus* (1961). A fourth book with similar characters, *Mr. T.W. Anthony Woo: The Story of a Cat and a Dog and a Mouse* (1951), was a Caldecott Honor Book. In 1939, Ets published *The Story of a Baby*, her favorite book, capturing in a series of sensitive drawings the growth of the fetus and the early months of a child's life.

During the 1940s, Marie Ets began writing and illustrating stories examining the world as perceived by a small child. *In the Forest* (1944) and *Another Day* (1953) describe a small boy's encounter with his forest friends. Among other books depicting the small child's experiences are *Play With Me* (1955), and *Just Me* (1965), both Caldecott Honor Books. In the former, the first story Ets illustrated in full color, a little child noisily approaches a number of small animals, asking them to play, and is sad when they run away. In *Just Me*, a boy enjoys imitating animal sounds, but is happiest being himself and accompanying his father on a boat ride.

During the 1950s, Ets spent time in Mexico and among Mexican-Americans in southern California, and the result was *Nine Days to Christmas: A Story of Mexico* (1959), winner of the Caldecott Medal, about a small child who waits anxiously for her first Posada, or Christmas party. *Gilberto and the Wind* (1963) and *Bad Boy, Good Boy* (1967) are sensitive and sympathetic portrayals of Mexican-American children.

While she was a student of social work, Ets became interested in how children interpreted drawings, and when she began illustrating she "tried to keep my eye and mind on the child — not the art critics." Her language is simple yet sensitive, expressing observations as a child would. Generally her pictures are presented with soft-edged oval borders suggestive of the perceiving eye of a child. Although Ets seldom uses four colors, when she does they are muted. Her pastels delicately suggest the living world of which her characters are gradually becoming aware.

TIPS FOR PARENTS AND TEACHERS: Ets' picture books make excellent quiet-time reading for preschool children. Early elementary aged children not familiar with Mexican culture will learn much from reading *Nine Days to Christmas.*

Fables

Fables are short narratives in which the characters, usually animals, are involved in actions the consequences of which are designed to illustrate specific morals. The best-known fables are of ancient date, having originated in Greece and the Far East. Aesop, who is reported to have been a Greek slave living in the sixth century B.C., told hundreds of the stories, including "The Fox and the Crow," "The Town Mouse and the Country Mouse," "The Fox and the Grapes," and "The Hare and the Tortoise." It is said that Aesop placed his morals and satiric messages in the mouths of animals so that he could avoid punishments that would have followed if the ruling class had realized he was criticizing his contemporaries. Aesop's "Fables" were translated into Latin and, during the Middle Ages, spread through Europe where they were again translated into many languages.

Two other widely known fable collections originated in ancient India. The "Panchatantra" was a group of stories designed to show people how to lead good lives, and the "Jataka Fables" were tales about the life of the Buddha in his various incarnations. Living with different types of animals, he acquired the wisdom which made him a great teacher. Both of these collections travelled to Europe and, like Aesop's fables, were very popular in the Middle Ages.

With the invention of printing in the late fifteenth century, volumes of these stories soon appeared. One of the first books published by English printer William Caxton was *Aesop's Fables* (1484). In the seventeenth century, Frenchman Jean de la Fontaine drew from Aesop and the "Oriental fables" to create a number of verse stories which maintain their popularity today.

The fables have proved very popular with modern children's authors and illustrators. In 1962 James Reeves published *Fables From Aesop*, with illustrations by Maurice Wilson. Alice and Martin Provensen's illustrations to Louis Untermeyer's *Aesop's Fables* (1965) remain popular. Marianne Moore translated *The Fables of LaFontaine* in 1954, and Joseph Gaer published *The Fables of India* in 1955. "The Hare and the Tortoise" has been illustrated by Paul Galdone (1962) and Brian Wildsmith (1967). Other illustrated versions of individual tales include *The Frogs Who Wanted a King* (Margot Zemach, 1977), *Once A Mouse* (Marcia Brown, 1961), and *The Monkey and the Crocodile* (Paul Galdone, 1969).

While the fable has been associated with the authors and cultures noted above, many modern writers have written in the fable form. Of these the most noteworthy are Leo Lionni and Arnold Lobel. In such picture books as *Swimmy* (1963), *A Color of His Own* (1976), and *Frederick* (1967), Lionni told simple stories which illustrated the importance of the individual, particularly the unusual individual with special talents, and emphasized the value of recognizing and respecting this individuality. In his Caldecott Medal winning *Fables* (1980), Lobel created twenty original fables to illustrate such morals as "The highest hopes may lead to the greatest disappointments," and "It is always difficult to pose as something that one is not."

TIPS FOR PARENTS AND TEACHERS: Although the fables are short and contain few characters and actions, their simplicity is deceptive. Their morals are generally abstract, and the reader must have developed fairly sophisticated conceptualizing processes to be able to understand them. Therefore, fables are best introduced to children in the middle elementary grades. After students have read a number of fables and have discussed the basic characteristics of the form, they can write their own fables. The teacher can introduce a moral and discuss it; then the class can consider appropriate characters and actions and each student can write a fable.

❦Fantasy

Fantasy is both one of the oldest forms of literature and one of the most popular with readers. Nevertheless, because it includes so many elements, so many types of stories, it is extremely difficult to define. Fantasies take place in the past, the present, and the future; they are set on and under the Earth, in imaginary lands, and in outer space; they contain ordinary human beings, but also tiny people and giants, aliens, and supernatural beings; and the actions that take place in them are not those we would see or experience in our everyday lives. No matter what the nature of the particular work, fantasy stories all have one thing in common: the events that take place in them are not governed by the normal laws of physics, the conditions of time and space as we know them. Even when they closely approach reality, the characters engage in actions which are, at best, highly improbable in the world as we know it.

From earliest times, folktales, myths, and hero tales of all cultures have been fantasy. While the stories they created may have contained elements of their religious beliefs, they also reflected a world controlled by supernatural powers and/or operating according to nonnatural as well as natural laws. During the seventeenth and eighteenth centuries, many of the conventions of folktales were used by such French writers as Charles Perrault, Madame Villeneuve, and Madame Leprince de Beaumont to create what are called literary folktales— that is, stories using patterns found in the traditional, anonymous works, but consciously created by known authors. Perrault's "Cinderella," "Puss in Boots," and "Donkey-Skin," and Beaumont's "Beauty and the Beast" are among the best-known. The literary folktale has remained popular since then, with two of its best practitioners being Hans Christian Andersen (in works like "Thumbelina" and "The Snow Queen") and Jane Yolen (in works like "The Girl Who Cried Flowers" and "The Hundredth Dove.").

During the middle and later nineteenth century, fantasy for children flowered. Many of the great English writers wrote fantasies for children, among them Charles Dickens (*The Magic Fishbone*, 1974), and John Ruskin (*King of the Golden River*, 1851). However, the two most important fantasists for children, and those whose works are still widely read today, were Lewis Carroll and George MacDonald. Carroll's *Alice's Adventures in Wonderland* (1865) and *Through the Looking-Glass* (1871) are both dream journeys which present convincingly the reactions of a relatively ordinary child as she enters confusing and frustrating dream worlds. George MacDonald in *At the Back of the North Wind* (1870), *The Princess and the Goblin* (1871), and *The Princess and Curdie* (1882) created fantasy worlds in which young heroes and heroines were engaged in quests which tested their moral worth. It is not an overstatement to say that the works of these two men profoundly influenced children's fantasy in the twentieth century. Maurice Sendak, the modern author-illustrator, reflects the impact of these two men in nearly everything he has written.

As the publishing of books for children flourished and the establishment of library services for young readers developed in the twentieth century, the range and volume of fantasy has expanded greatly. The following paragraphs are intended to give a brief overview of types of modern fantasy and a sampling of some of the books in each category.

One of the most popular types of children's fantasy has always been the animal story. Early folktales and fables made frequent uses of animals and these have frequently been retold in the twentieth century. At the turn of the century, Beatrix Potter and Kenneth Grahame created what have remained among the most favorite of animal fantasies. In her little books about such characters as Peter Rabbit, Squirrel Nutkin, and Jemima Puddleduck, Potter combined both the vulnerability of animals and the character failings of children into stories in which adventure and mild moral lessons are pleasingly linked. In *Wind in the Willows* (1908), an entire animal society is presented, as a group of creatures interact with each other and the forces of civilization. Modern animal fantasies of note include E.B. White's *Charlotte's Web* (1952) and Robert O'Brien's *Mrs. Frisby and the Rats of NIMH* (1971). In the former, several barnyard animals learn the values of friendship and cooperation; in the latter, a group of rats given super mental abilities as a result of laboratory experiments search for a perfect community. Several important picture book artists have created animal stories, among them Leo Lionni (*Frederick*, 1967), Wanda Gág (*Millions of Cats*, 1928), and William Steig (*Sylvester and the Magic Pebble*, 1969).

Travels into new, unusual lands have been a staple of fantasy for several centuries. The eighteenth-century writer Jonathan Swift, satirizing contemporary interest in travel literature, sent the hero of *Gulliver's Travels* (1726) into unusual countries where he met tiny people and giants, among others. Sections of Swift's book became popular with children very quickly and have been frequently republished since then. Nineteenth-century French writer Jules Verne sent his hero on an undersea journey in *Twenty Thousand Leagues Under the Sea* (1870). While such voyages are commonplace today, they were unheard-of at that time.

Modern fantasy journeys can be categorized according to the destinations of the travels: trips to alternate universes, to distant countries and planets, and through time into different eras. Frank Baum's "Oz," J.M. Barrie's "Neverland," and C.S. Lewis's "Narnia," are examples of alternate universes. In the stories of these authors, basically ordinary children like Dorothy (*The Wonderful Wizard of Oz*, 1900), the Darling children (*Peter and Wendy*, 1911), and the Pevensies (*The Lion, the Witch, and the Wardrobe*, 1950), find themselves transported into lands where the normal laws of reality are suspended and unusual characters and settings are the rule. Each of their stories is completed with a return to the normal world, but not before they have undergone experiences which aid them in developing as individuals.

Unknown lands, on Earth or beyond it, have always fascinated writers of fantasy; the very unknown quality makes it possible for the authors to introduce strange powers and creatures. Early in the twentieth century, Edgar Rice Burroughs used Africa as the setting for his Tarzan stories because, being largely unexplored, it provided a locale for a variety of odd civilizations with which Tarzan made contact. Canadian fantasist Catherine Anthony Clark has used the wildernesses of British Columbia as the settings for many of her fantasies (*The Golden Pine Cone*, 1950; *The Sun Horse*, 1951). Space travel has held greater appeal for fantasists. Eleanor Cameron, in a series of books about the Mushroom Planet, and Madeleine L'Engle, in *A Wrinkle in Time* (1962), have used interplanetary and interstellar journeys as means of portraying the growth to maturity of their characters.

Time travel provides both a convenient means of moving characters into settings which are non-normal and a way of examining the theme of the nature of time. An example of a group of works which does both is Lucy Boston's "Green Knowe" series, in which children of the twentieth century living in an ancient stone manor make contact with and visit children from earlier historical periods. In addition to providing interesting portrayals of the other times, Boston considers the relationship of past and present, of how people from the past can influence the present and the reverse. Other stories in which children from the present journey into the past include Philippa Pearce's *Tom's Midnight Garden* (1958), William Mayne's *A Game of Dark* (1971), and E. Nesbit's *The House of Arden* (1909).

Self-contained universes figure prominently in many stories. From the beginning of such stories, the reader is expected to recognize that he is experiencing a completely independent realm. Perhaps the most famous independent world is J.R.R. Tolkien's Middle Earth, as seen in *The Hobbit* (1937) and *The Lord of the Rings* (1954–56). Such worlds operate entirely according to their own laws and principles. Lloyd Alexander in his "Chronicles of Prydain" creates another such world. In a setting which resembles the wilder areas of Wales, his heroes and heroines fight mighty battles against the forces of evil. Ursula K. LeGuin's "Earthsea Trilogy" takes place entirely within an oceanic archipelago in which laws of magic rather than those of science control nature and people.

The normal world is the locale of many fantasies. In these stories unusual events or characters are found in familiar settings. In fact, most of the impact of these kinds of works arises from the discovery that such marvelous occurrences or beings can be part of what is usually so routine a place. Talking animals and animated toys and machines are often found in fantasies for young children, who often give human personalities to objects and animals in their play. In E.B. White's *Charlotte's Web* (1952) and in Roger Duvoisin's stories about Petunia the Goose, barnyard animals interact in ways similar to those of the child readers. Rumer Godden, Margery Williams

Bianco, and Collodi have all written tales in which dolls come to life, experiencing human emotions and conflicts. Perhaps the best-known writer about animated machines is Hardie Gramatky who, in *Little Toot* (1939) and other tales, has made machines undergo great emotional conflicts.

Often stories deal with characters one would not normally expect to find in real life. Mary Norton, in a series of books about the Borrowers, portrays the lives of tiny people who live hidden in the houses of normal-sized "human beans." In Alan Garner's *The Weirdstone of Brisingamen* (1961) and *The Moon of Gomrath* (1963), magical creatures from the past suddenly appear in rural England, while in William Mayne's *Earthfasts* (1966) an eighteenth-century drummer emerges from the ground into the modern world. In all of these stories, much of the impact arises from the fact that ordinary humans confront these beings and must come to terms with them or conquer them.

No matter what kind of fantasy one is reading, it must be convincing for it to succeed. As Diana Waggoner has written in *The Hills of Faraway: a Guide to Fantasy* (1978), "The author of an honest fantasy must convince the reader of two things: first, that his world is plausible; second, that the story he sets in that world is plausible." Initially, the writer must get his reader to accept the "reality" of the world being created; if the reader does not accept it early in the story, the work will be a failure. The author must be able to concretely present described settings, making the world of the work tangible to the reader. Characters must be plausible so that, whatever types of creature they may be, they have recognizable personalities which develop consistently during the story. "Ordinary" human beings must experience surprise and wonder at the extraordinary characters and settings they come in contact with. Finally, the stories, no matter how unusual the material they deal with, must be internally consistent; even though the laws of the world of the story may differ from the laws of our world, they must operate in a consistent manner throughout.

TIPS FOR PARENTS AND TEACHERS: Because fantasy is such a popular form of story for children, the adult should try to introduce young readers to the best fantasies available. After reading a number of fantasies of each type noted above, the adult can evaluate each one according to the criteria discussed, noticing which ones are more successful than others. Because children will have been exposed to so many inferior fantasies on television, it is important that they be given only good works, thus helping them to become better readers. Animal and toy stories work well with pre-school and early elementary readers; the heroic and mythical fantasies, such as C.S. Lewis' "Narnia Chronicles" and Lloyd Alexander's "Chronicles of Prydain" can be introduced in the middle elementary grades. Ursula K. LeGuin's "Earthsea Trilogy" and Tolkien's *Lord of the Rings* are very popular with good readers of junior high school age.

♥Feelings, Tom *(1933–   ), and*
♥Feelings, Muriel *(1938–   )*
American

Born in Brooklyn, Tom Feelings became interested in black history as a child and, after completing his art training at the School of Visual Arts in New York, began a comic strip, "Tommy Traveler in the World of Negro History," which ran in the *New York Age* for 1957 to 1959. He then worked as a free-lance artist before moving, in 1964, to Ghana in West Africa where he illustrated for *The African Review*, a monthly magazine. He referred to his two years there as "one of the most meaningful and rewarding experiences of my life." Returning to America, he married Muriel Gray in 1968. Educated at California State University at Los Angeles as a teacher of art and Spanish, she had taught for two years in Kampala, Uganda.

Together, Tom and Muriel Feelings set out to create books about African life for black children. The first of these, *Zamani Goes to Market* (1970), describes the pride of a small child leaving his village for the first time. The Feelings' best known books, *Moja Means One: Swahili Counting Book* (1971) and *Jambo Means Hello: Swahili Alphabet Book* (1974), both Caldecott Honor Books, have been highly praised for their portrayal of daily African life. Tom Feelings has also illustrated several other books about black history and culture. Among these are Letta Schatz' *Bola and the Olea's Drummers* (1967), Julius Lester's *To Be a Slave* (1968), and Lucille Warner's *From Slave to Abolitionist: The Life of William Wells Brown* (1976).

TIPS FOR PARENTS AND TEACHERS: Preschool and early elementary children can use the alphabet and counting books not only to develop basic concepts, but also as an introduction to an unfamiliar culture. The illustrations should be carefully examined, with the adult helping the young reader to understand the way of life being depicted.

♥Folktales

In *The Folktale*, Stith Thompson noted that the oral tale "is the most universal of all narrative forms." Folktales have been found all over the world and have presumably existed since the earliest periods of human history. They are easily recognized: short, highly stylized stories, they contain stock characters, events, and settings. In fact, similar motifs and tale types have been found in different cultures in widely separated parts of the world. Folktales are also embodiments of beliefs of specific cultures. For example, over three hundred versions of the Cinderella story have been discovered from China to the southwestern United States. The human emotions portrayed are similar in nearly all of the versions; however, the individual manifestations of these emotions reflect the customs and beliefs of the group telling the story.

Folktales possess recognizable stylistic patterns. Retold over generations, they acquired, particularly in the hands of skillful narrators, several verbal formulas. This is most evident in European tales, which often begin with such a phrase as "once upon a time" and, when there is a marriage at the conclusion, end with the words "they lived happily ever after." Within stories, certain phrases are often repeated at key points, as is seen in such stories as "The Story of the Three Little Pigs" and "East o' the Sun and West o' the Moon." Many of the stories of the Plains Indians begin with the words "Coyote was going along." Not only do these stylistic devices help to give shape or pattern to the stories, but also, as we shall see, they may have implicit significance as well.

Psychologists and critics have noted that although the folktales generally contain imaginary characters and situations, they symbolize basic human concerns. They are, as European scholar Max Lüthi suggested in *Once Upon a Time: On the Nature of Fairy Tales,* "a poetic vision of man and his relationship to the world." Each story presents the central character with the opportunity to achieve fulfillment, both within himself and in relation to his social and natural environment. The characters are presented as types rather than as individuals. They embody basic aspects of human nature and experience essential human dilemmas. In the tales most often read to children today, the main actors are frequently children, vulnerable beings in a world of adults and threatening natural and supernatural forces. Orphans and youngest children are important characters as they are the most vulnerable, and, if they emerge victorious at a tale's conclusion, their achievements seem even greater. In order to survive and to triumph, they must face severe tests, engage in great struggles, and make wise choices. Often they take on royal roles, for as Lüthi has noted, "to be a king [or queen] is an image for complete self-realization." Thus, while readers or listeners cannot all become kings or queens, they can, like the characters in the story, work to achieve as complete a self-realization as possible.

In the search for self-fulfillment, the central character is generally alone; responsibility for achieving one's destiny rests with the individual himself. Usually the character makes a dangerous physical journey, leaving a home which for various reasons is no longer secure. The geography is austere; dark, threatening forests and violent weather abound in folktales, symbolizing the unknown and perilous aspects of the quest. The negative characters encountered — witches, giants, dragons, and malicious, hypocritical human beings are most common in European stories — symbolize the evils that must be overcome. The hero does have helpers such as fairy godmothers or talking animals, or possesses magic objects; but these are only effective when he realizes his inner potential. The hero must develop and/or exhibit such positive virtues as courage, cleverness, and kindness if the external aid he receives is to be beneficial and if he is to pass successfully his progressively more difficult tasks. Not all folktale characters develop these qualities, and they receive appropriate punishments. In many African and North American trickster tales, the central hero, because of his mischievousness, does not receive the rewards he expects. His cleverness backfires because it is selfishly motivated.

The implicit significance of the content of folktales is often reinforced by the stylistic devices. The stock "once upon a time" opening of European tales not only helps a fantastic tale achieve credibility by removing it from familiar times and places, it also emphasizes the universality of the themes present: the conflicts are not local but of all times and for all places. If the central characters live "happily ever after," it is because they have developed as human beings to such a degree that they deserve the happiness they receive. Repetition is also significant; it helps to show that because events become increasingly difficult, a continuing personal development is necessary for ongoing success and achievement.

While they embody universal processes of individual growth, folktales also reflect elements of the specific cultures in which they are told. The supernatural characters in them are those found in the beliefs of the various cultures: malicious dragons in Northern Europe, Baba Yaga in Russia, trolls in Norway, the Little People in England, shape-shifting animals in North America, Jizo in Japan. These beings had very definite characteristics which would have been well-known to original listeners and are thus part of the implicit meanings of the stories. Modern readers who are aware of their specific connotations will be able to appreciate individual stories more fully.

Over the last two centuries, several theories have been advanced to explain the origins of folktales. The German scholars Jacob and Wilhelm Grimm, two of the earliest collectors of folktales, believed that such stories were the fragmentary pieces of earlier myths which had broken up over the centuries and lost their specifically religious content. "Little Red-Cap" they traced back to a solar myth; her being devoured by the wolf and later rescued represented the setting and rising of the sun. During the nineteenth century, several scholars, influenced by the prevailing theories of the origins of language, argued that all folktales originated in India, the "cradle of civilization," and gradually spread throughout the world. This single place of origin explained for them the existence of similar motifs and tale types in different locations. In contrast to this theory, referred to as "monogenesis," Andrew Lang and other folklorists in the late nineteenth and early twentieth centuries argued that the similarities arose because there were a limited number of basic situations and emotional responses and that these were common to all people. Lang advanced the theory of polygenesis: similar stories found in widely separated areas had developed independent of each other. Twentieth-century psychologist Carl Jung suggested that the tales originated in archetypes or fundamental images found within the unconscious minds of everyone. Since all people were similar psychologically, they produced similar stories.

No matter what the nature of their origins, it is known that many stories have travelled from one culture to another. For example, it is believed that the Grimm Brothers' version of "Little Red-Cap" is derived from Perrault's "Little Red Riding Hood," which slowly travelled across Europe, gradually altering its shape. Many well-known European stories were brought across the Atlantic with the explorers, traders, and colonizers, and were adapted to specific local conditions. North American tales also travelled widely. The trickster Coyote appears in some Indian nations as the Old Man (Nape). The tale of "The Blind Boy and the Loon" is found across the Canadian and Alaskan Arctic and is found amongst the Indians of the Northern Pacific coast.

Over the centuries, writers have been adapting these oral stories to their own purposes. In Homer's *Odyssey*, for example, the hero's exploits among such beings as the cyclops are believed to have been derived from earlier folktales. In the fourteenth century, English poet Geoffrey Chaucer used many well-known fables and folktales in his *Canterbury Tales*. However, it was not until 1697, when Frenchman Charles Perrault published *Histoires ou Contes du temps passé, avec des Moralités*, a collection of eleven fairy tales, that folktales came to the attention of a large, international reading public. Containing such now well-known stories as "Sleeping Beauty," "Cinderella," "Puss in Boots," "Little Red Riding Hood," and "Bluebeard," the work was published in English in 1729, and fostered a vogue for fairy tales which lasted throughout the eighteenth century. Perrault's stories, which contained much implicit wit and satire, were highly polished literary works, reflecting in both style and content the grace and elegance of the seventeenth-century French court.

In the late eighteenth century, a scientific interest in traditional literature developed, and in 1812 Jacob and Wilhelm Grimm published *Kinder-und Hausmärchen (Nursery and Household Tales)*, a book of folktales they had collected from friends, relations, neighbors, and nearby peasants. Although the brothers, particularly Wilhelm, often edited the materials, they were not attempting to adapt the stories for children, but hoped to preserve a record of one aspect of a disappearing culture. However, the stories were quickly seized upon by publishers interested in selling books for the rapidly increasing juvenile market.

Because the writing, publishing, and purchasing of children's stories have always been in the hands of adults, it was inevitable that many people objected to certain elements of traditional tales. Not having originally been created specifically for children, they often contained violence and sexual incidents considered inappropriate for young readers, and, since the early nineteenth century, they have frequently been adapted to fit adult ideals of what constituted suitable reading for youngsters. The famous English illustrator, George Cruikshank, an advocate of the temperance movement, retold the tale of "Jack and the Beanstalk" in such a way as to show that the giant's problems were caused by excessive drinking. In his version, the giant is not killed at the end; rather he becomes a teetotaller and leads a socially useful life. Some versions of "The Story of the Three Little Pigs" have been changed so that the first two pigs do not die but rush to safety in their brother's brick home. The wolf is not boiled alive and eaten, but flees from the area in terror, never to be seen again. In the case of children's versions of Eskimo and Indian stories, adaptation has often been even more drastic. The cultural and religious beliefs of these peoples, because they are so different from those of the dominant Anglo-European culture, have at times been viewed as foolish superstition, the products of unenlightened, primitive minds; and characters have been presented according to European standards, with only their physical appearances and geographical surroundings relating them to their true cultures.

These remarks are not intended to suggest that all children's adaptations are debased, simplistic versions of the original materials. In fact some of the finest children's authors and illustrators have created excellent versions of folktales. Among them are Walter Crane, Leslie Brooke, Walter de la Mare, and Wanda Gág in earlier years, and more recently, Paul Galdone, Marcia Brown, Gerald McDermott, Tomie de Paola, Christie Harris, and Alison Lurie. However, in choosing a children's version of a folktale, the selector should ascertain how close it is to the original version and, particularly in the case of stories dealing with ethnic minorities, how accurate it is in its reflection of the culture in question.

TIPS FOR PARENTS AND TEACHERS: Because of their basic simplicity, many folktales make an excellent introduction to literature for preschoolers. Stories with easy-to-follow plots and a great deal of repetition, like "The Three Little Pigs" and "The Three Billygoats Gruff," are easily grasped by young children. In the early elementary grades, children should be encouraged to discuss the appropriateness of the pictures in illustrated versions of the better-known tales, and should be exposed to simpler folktales from a variety of cultures. In the middle elementary grades, more complex tales such as "Hansel and Gretel" or "The Sleeping Beauty" can be considered, and students can begin to discuss the stories as reflections of the culture from which they came. Upper elementary students can survey the entire range of folktales, noticing the cultural variations in the treatment of common themes and the psychological implications of some of the tales.

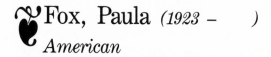

Fox, Paula *(1923 –)*
American

The characters in Paula Fox's stories travel: across the street, into new parts of town, to different cities, across the country, and even across the Atlantic ocean. They are like the author herself who, during her childhood, lived in New York City, Cuba, and New Hampshire, attending nine schools before she was twelve years old. During her adult life, she has called New York City, London, Paris, and Warsaw home and has worked as a machinist, teacher, reporter, and author. She did not begin to publish stories until her two sons were grown up; *Maurice's Room*, her first children's book, appeared in 1966, and since then she has written twelve more children's books and four novels for adults. In 1974, she was awarded the Newbery Medal for *The Slave Dancer*. In 1978, she received the Hans Christian Andersen Medal, in recognition of her career as a children's writer.

Paula Fox's early children's books deal with the problems contemporary children face as they mature in a confusing world. *How Many Miles to Babylon* (1967), her first novel to achieve wide critical recognition, tells of a small black boy being cared for by three old aunts while his mother recuperates from a mental breakdown. Wandering out of school one day, he is caught by three older boys who force him to assist them in their dog-stealing operations. After a terrifying night, he returns to the security of his home and finds that his mother has returned from the hospital. In *Stone-Faced Boy* (1968), Gus, the middle child in a family of five, cannot express the emotions inside him, until, one winter night, he searches the woods to find his sister's lost dog. *Blowfish Live in the Sea* (1970) is the story of twelve-year-old Carrie and her nineteen-year-old half-brother Ben, who has become moody and withdrawn. Accompanying him to Boston, where he is to rejoin his semi-derelict father, she comes to understand his problems more fully and learns to appreciate her own parents. The characters in these stories, like the one in the nursery rhyme "How Many Miles to Babylon?," must make a circular journey through a nighttime world which is both literal and symbolic. Their return to the daylight world of their own lives signals their increased sensitivity towards others and understanding of themselves.

Fox's most significant children's work to date has been *The Slave Dancer* (1973), her only historical novel. Set in pre-Civil War times, it recounts the adventures of Jessie Bollier, a young teenager who is kidnapped near his home in New Orleans and taken on board a slaver bound for Africa. It is his duty to play his fife for the human cargo to dance by, thus giving them enough exercise to maintain them in saleable condition. On the return journey, the boat is shipwrecked and Jessie finds himself on the Mississippi shore with one of the slave boys he'd tacitly befriended. Returning to New Orleans, he slips back into the accustomed patterns of his life, but discovers that he has been deeply affected inwardly. In addition to its exciting, fast-paced adventures, the book succeeds because of its striking depictions of the boy's reactions to the brutality and horror of conditions on the ship.

Since *Slave Dancer*, Paula Fox has written only two children's books, *The Little Swineherd and Other Tales* (1978), a collection of folk-like stories, and *A Place Apart* (1980), the account of a teenage girl who must adjust to her father's death, life in a new town, and her mother's upcoming remarriage.

In her Newbery acceptance speech for *The Slave Dancer*, Paula Fox wrote, "Each novel deepens the question. It does not answer it." The question, the central one in each of her books, is how the individual is to find a meaningful place in the world, one in which he can maintain his integrity while responding to others. The journey must be taken alone. If there are parents around, as is not often the case in Fox's novels, they are generally not of much help. However, there are other adults — a long-lost aunt, an old man met in the park, a portrait painter — who do help the young heroes help themselves in their processes of maturing. Although in *Maurice's Room*, *A Place Apart*, and *The King's Falcon* (1969), the central characters move to new homes, the final destination is usually the home from which they have departed. However, they return changed, more confident individuals, more able to cope with the world which had earlier so confused them.

One of Fox's most significant qualities as a novelist is her ability to focus each novel on a major symbol which, while profound in its implications, is accessible to younger readers. In *Maurice's Room*, the junk the boy collects represents his individual creativity; for Ben, the blowfish parallels the inflated falseness he sees not only in his father but in the society around him; Jessie Bollier's fife, which had once been a means of earning money, now is the instrument by which the suffering slaves are kept alive so that they can bring more profit to the slavers; the geode given to Gus by Great Aunt Hattie is an emblem of the inner qualities which are hidden behind his expressionless face.

TIPS FOR PARENTS AND TEACHERS: Middle elementary aged students who are familiar with fairy godmothers and their roles will enjoy discussing how the older people help the heroes in *A Likely Place* (1967) and *Stone-Faced Boy*. Older students can discuss why the ring is so important to James Douglas in *How Many Miles to Babylon* and the sketch of his mother to the hero of *Portrait of Ivan* (1969). For students in junior high school, *The Slave Dancer* is an excellent case study of how the horrors of slavery affected not only the slaves themselves but also those who caught, shipped, and sold them.

Freeman, Don *(1908 – 1978)*
American

Born in San Diego, Don Freeman grew up there and in St. Louis. After high school graduation, he hitchhiked to New York where he took classes at the Art Students League and earned a living playing the trumpet. In 1943, he illustrated William Saroyan's novel *The Human Comedy,* and since then he has illustrated books by James Thurber (*White Deer*, 1945), Ann Nolan Clark (*Third Monkey,* 1956), Astrid Lindgren (*Bill Bergson and the White Rose Rescue*, 1965), Julia Cunningham (*Burnish Me Bright*, 1970), Richard Peck (*Monster Night at Grandma's House*, 1977), and many other authors.

At the encouragement of a friend, Don Freeman submitted to an editor a story he and his wife had created for their son. It was published as *Chuggy and the Blue Caboose* in 1951 and was the first of over two dozen picture books Freeman was to write and illustrate before his death in 1978. His second book, *Pet of the Met* (1953), received wide critical acclaim. The story of a mouse, Maestro Petrini, who lives with his family in the Metropolitan Opera House and earns his living turning the pages of the prompt book, it reflects Freeman's love of music and the theatre, and reveals his ability to develop, in words and pictures, convincing characters and fast-paced plots. Freeman received a Caldecott Honor Medal for *Fly High, Fly Low* (1957), the story of two pigeons who build their nest in the curves of a letter in a giant sign atop a San Francisco building. Of Freeman's other children's books, the best known are *Beady Bear* (1954), about a teddy's feelings of insecurity; *Norman the Doorman* (1959), in which a mouse wins a sculpture contest at the Majestic Museum of Art; *Dandelion* (1964), about a lion who decides not to put on airs; and *The Guard Mouse* (1967), set at London's Buckingham Palace.

TIPS FOR PARENTS AND TEACHERS: After discussing the emotions of Freeman's characters, early elementary aged children can relate these to their own emotions and experiences.

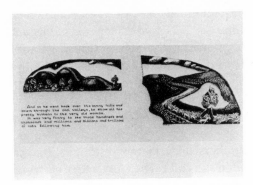

Millions of Cats, by Wanda Gág, Coward, McCann, & Geoghegan, New York, 1928. Gág integrates text and illustrations in this two-page spread so that visual and verbal rhythms interact.

Gág, Wanda *(1893 – 1946)*
American

Born in New Ulm, Minnesota, the eldest of seven children, Wanda Gág grew up in a family where art and literature formed a major part of life. Her father died when she was fifteen, leaving the family with little money, and after a long illness her mother died. She was torn between keeping the family together and becoming an artist, but with energy and dedication was able to do both. She taught in a country school for a year after her own graduation from high school and then received scholarships for study at the St. Paul Institute of Arts and the Minneapolis School of Art. In 1917, Wanda Gág moved to New York to study at the Art Students League.

Her first children's book, *Millions of Cats*, was published in 1928 and was named a Newbery Honor book. Highly praised then, it is now recognized as being of considerable historical significance. Along with William Nicholson's *Clever Bill* (1927), it is one of the first major picture storybooks to be published in the United States. Two more books followed: *The Funny Thing* (1929) and *Snippy and Snappy* (1931). Her fourth picture book, *ABC Bunny* (1933), in which a wandering and inquisitive rabbit provides continuity, was also named a Newbery Honor book.

During the 1930s, Gág focused on her writing, returning to the Grimm Brothers' stories she had heard as a child. In 1936, she published *Tales from Grimm*, which included such favorites as "Hansel and Gretel," "Rapunzel," and "The Frog Prince." For the work she did extensive research, studying tales in the original German and reading many variants and versions by other collectors. In addition, in her illustrations she strove for accuracy in the details of clothing and architecture. The second volume of the series, *Snow White and the Seven Dwarfs* (1938), was written at the request of critic Anne Carroll Moore, who had been upset with the recently released Walt Disney cartoon movie. For the book, Gág was awarded a Caldecott Honor Medal. *Three Gay Tales from Grimm* was published in 1943, and *More Tales from Grimm* appeared posthumously (1947). Wanda Gág received a second Caldecott Honor Medal for *Nothing at All* (1941), the story of an invisible dog, the only one of her children's books with illustrations in color.

Wanda Gág's achievement as a children's writer is two-fold: as a creator of stories in which pictures and text work together to communicate meanings, and as one of the major twentieth-century adaptors of the Grimm Brothers' tales. Her own stories show the influence of folktales she heard so often as a child. The language of each story is carefully controlled to provide a maximum amount of rhythmic repetition in the folktale manner. In *Millions of Cats*, the refrain "there were hundreds of cats, thousands of cats, millions and billions and trillions of cats" is repeated six times to emphasize the ludicrous and unexpected complications the old man encounters in his initially simple quest. In *Nothing at All*, the dog repeats the phrase "I'm busy/Getting dizzy" for nine days as he whirls himself into visibility.

The illustrations, all in black and white with the exception of those in *Nothing at All*, enhance the moods of the words. Though using only black and white, Wanda Gág is able to achieve a great variety of effects. In *Millions of Cats*, the kitten left after the other millions have destroyed each other is first seen as a tiny black object in the corner of the page, almost covered by bushes. A two-page spread indicates the stages of its growth and the final illustration shows the cat still small, but in the center of the page, balanced between its loving owners.

Wanda Gág called her adaptations from the Grimms "free translations," remarking that it was virtually impossible at times to capture in English the nuances of some of the words. In her "Introduction" to *Tales from Grimm*, she outlined her approach. Basically, she considered the stories from a child's point of view, the way she had responded to them when she was a girl and the way she felt the modern child reader or listener could best understand them. Portions of the stories intended for adults were either simplified or omitted. Dialogue was used more than in the originals, and repetition was employed more freely.

At times, Gág's descriptions achieve symbolic levels, as in this passage from "Hansel and Gretel": "They felt small and strange in the large, silent forest. The trees were so tall and the shade was so dense. Flowers could not grow in that dim, gloomy place — not even ferns. Only pale waxy mushrooms glowed faintly among the shadows, and weird lichens clung to the tree-trunks." Here the gloom of the forest parallels the feelings of the lost children.

Much of the charm of the four books of retellings of Grimm Brothers' stories comes from the illustrations Wanda Gág supplied. She was careful to see that they enhanced overall mood while still being faithful to the text. In *Snow White*, visual repetition is used to advance theme. Each time the disguised queen visits Snow White, an illustration covering the top one-third of two pages shows the heroine in the house at the right and the dwarfs at work, far away on the left. Separating them is the queen and over her head are clouds which, in successive illustrations, become darker and lower as the queen becomes more dangerous.

TIPS FOR PARENTS AND TEACHERS: Preschoolers enjoy discussing the circumstances of the main characters in Gág's books. In the middle elementary grades, students can carefully examine specific passages from the folktales, noticing how they help create mood, and can compare Gág's versions of the well-known tales with other modern adaptations.

Galdone, Paul *(1914 –   )*
American

Born in Budapest, Hungary, Paul Galdone moved with his family to New Jersey when he was fourteen. The family located shortly after in New York, where Galdone worked at a variety of jobs during the day so that he could attend art school at night. After serving in the United States Army during World War II and working for four years in the art department of Doubleday & Co. publishers, he decided that he wanted to illustrate children's books. The first book he illustrated was Ellen MacGregor's *Miss*

Pickerell Goes to Mars (1951). Since then he has illustrated close to two hundred books.

Galdone is best known for his adaptations of traditional folktales and for his illustrations for Eve Titus' "Anatole" series, two books of which, *Anatole* (1956) and *Anatole and the Cat* (1957), were named Caldecott Honor Books. Using only three colors, black, blue, and red, in depicting the adventures of the French mouse, his sketches capture the flavor of the French background and the courage of the mouse's encounters with the human world. In adapting folktales, Galdone makes his illustrations parallel the stylized quality of the language, while at the same time conveying the humor of many of the situations. In *The Three Bears* (1972), *The Little Red Hen* (1973), and *The History of Mother Twaddle and the Marvelous Achievements of Her Son Jack* (1974), his abilities are seen at their best.

TIPS FOR PARENTS AND TEACHERS: In the early elementary grades, students can study the facial expressions of Galdon's characters as clues to their emotions.

Garfield, Leon *(1921 –   )*
English

Born in Brighton, Sussex, Leon Garfield decided as a boy to be a writer, but after World War II he worked for many years as a biochemist in hospitals. Reading Robert Louis Stevenson's *The Master of Ballantrae* inspired him to write a novel set in the eighteenth century. *Jack Holborn* (1964) is the story of a London orphan who stows away aboard a ship which is taken over by pirates. Garfield's second novel, *Devil-in-the Fog* (1966), received critical praise. It is the story of how poor George Treet finds himself the heir of John Dexter, a nobleman. Three of the books Garfield wrote before 1970 were named runners-up for the Carnegie Medal. *Smith* (1967) is about a London pick-pocket whose life is endangered when he witnesses a murder. In *Black Jack* (1968), a young man and woman find true love. *The Drummer Boy* (1969) details the horrors of war. Garfield has written several other novels about eighteenth- and early nineteenth-century life, among them *The Apprentices* (1978), originally published as twelve short books. Garfield's historical novels have been praised for their accurate and vivid details, fast-paced narratives, clear delineation of character, and vibrant prose style. In 1971, he collaborated with author-critic Edward Blishen to retell several Greek myths.

The God Beneath the Sea, which won the Carnegie Medal, grew from Garfield's long-standing interest in the myths and from his desire to "impose a narrative order on the Greek myths, linking apparently disparate events." The individual stories are combined and told so that the book reads like a novel. The two writers retold the story of Heracles, whom Garfield has described as "a rather Dostoevskian figure," in *The Golden Shadow* (1973).

TIPS FOR PARENTS AND TEACHERS: In the upper elementary grades, the historical novels make an excellent introduction to the more violent aspects of eighteenth-century life. The retellings of the Greek myths have been successfully used to introduce junior high school students to the richness of mythology.

Garner, Alan *(1935 –   )*
English

Born in Congleton, Cheshire, near Alderley Edge, the major setting for his first two novels, Alan Garner decided to become a writer after reading *Lord of the Flies*. He studied at Oxford and then returned to Cheshire possessing, he has said, a far greater concern for his roots than he would have had if he had never left. He bought and restored a fourteenth-century house near the Edge, where he lives with his wife and children

Garner's first book, *The Weirdstone of Brisingamen* (1960), which he says took him two years to write and one-and-a-half to find a publisher, is in the author's eyes his worst. It is the story of Colin and Susan, two young children who are sent to live in the country while their parents are abroad. Exploring along Alderley Edge, the children are attacked by goblins and rescued by Cadellin, a wizard who tells them of dark forces which can only be defeated by recovering a missing gem, the Weirdstone.

In a sequel, *The Moon of Gomrath* (1963), Susan's spirit is captured by a Brollachan, a force of darkness and evil, and only Colin, by gathering a legendary flower found only at full moon, can save her. In many ways, this pair of novels is wildly undisciplined. The books' greatest success lies in their presentation of the intensity of the emotions and the courage, which a dwarf calls "fear mastered," displayed by Susan and Colin.

Elidor (1965), Garner's third novel, marks a departure in this treatment of the supernatural and is a more mature and controlled book. Exploring a demolished Manchester slum, four brothers and sisters are suddenly transported into the parallel universe of Elidor, a land laid waste by forces of evil which also threaten the children's world. The salvation of Elidor depends on the safety of four treasures, a spear, a sword, a cauldron, and a stone, which are entrusted to the children to take back to Manchester.

Owl Service (1967), Garner's fourth novel and winner of the Carnegie Medal, moves away from the Manchester and Alderley settings to an isolated Welsh valley. The central characters are three teenagers: Alison and Roger, an English half-brother and sister on vacation with their parents, and Gwyn, a Welsh boy native to the area. When Gwyn, investigating strange noises in the attic, brings down a set of china and Alison traces the owl patterns on them, powerful forces are released in the valley. Gwyn, deeply troubled and seeking his place in the valley; Roger, bitter over his mother's desertion of him and his father; and Alison, now on the verge of womanhood, are possessed by this power and by their own maturing emotions.

Garner's position as one of Britain's foremost fantasists was established by these four books. His next novel, *Red Shift* (1973), interrelates the lives of young people living in second-, seventeenth-, and twentieth-century England. *The Breadhorse* (1975), *The Stone Book* 1976), *Tom Fobble's Day* (1977), *Granny Reardum* (1977), and *The Aimer Gate* (1978) are stories about working people and are intended for young readers. *Fairytales of Gold* (1979) is a collection of four stories using traditional motifs, while *The Lad of the Gad* (1980) retells five Gaelic tales.

The focus in Garner's fantasies is a child or young teenager who, though generally very average, feels obligated to embark on a very important quest which will pit him against great forces. Roland, the central figure in *Elidor*, is perhaps the most interesting of these children. His name is linked by the book's motto to Childe Roland, subject of a traditional ballad and a nineteenth-century poem by Robert Browning. He was an untested knight who had to confront physical and spiritual wastelands. Roland, who has been continually teased by his family for living too much in an imaginary world, must, on entering Elidor, rescue his brothers and sisters who have failed to possess special treasures. Later, when the others try to deny their Elidor experiences, he remains loyal to his vision, fearful though it is. He confronts the dangers because "he knew that it was up to him to do something." That something is to aid in the restoration of light to Elidor and, in so doing, to prevent the spread of evil on Earth.

The quests are enacted in settings which alternate between real and fantastic worlds. In *The Weirdstone* and *The Moon*, Alderley Edge has superimposed on it a world which possesses figures of the High Magic and the Old Magic. By having the setting so concretely presented, Garner makes the intrusion of the fantasy world more convincing. Elidor is a parallel world: the facts that its lack of color and vegetation is similar to the demolished

Manchester slum and that the ruined church the children enter is in both worlds emphasize that the light of Elidor which the children must save is one which influences Earth also. The valley setting of *The Owl Service*, isolated from the outside world, is not so much a contrast between the physical and the nontangible worlds as a proof that time is not a continuum, that powerful emotions exist in a kind of eternal present. As Alison muses, "'Yesterday,' 'today,' 'tomorrow' — they don't mean anything. I feel they're here at the same time: waiting."

TIPS FOR PARENTS AND TEACHERS: Garner's fantasies make challenging reading in the upper elementary and junior high grades. Students who have enjoyed the fantasies of C.S. Lewis and Lloyd Alexander will not find excessive difficulty in tackling his works.

George, Jean Craighead *(1919 –   )*
American

Born in Washington, D.C., Jean George grew up in a family of naturalists and spent most of her summers in the outdoors, studying wildlife. She wrote and painted as a child and, after her university studies, worked as a reporter and author-artist for newspapers in Washington. In 1944, she married John George, and in 1948 co-authored with him *Vulpes, The Red Fox*, the first of six animal biographies they were to write together. She has also written over thirty books of her own, the best known being *My Side of the Mountain* (1959), a Newbery Honor Book, and *Julie of the Wolves* (1972), winner of the Newbery Medal.

The plots of many of George's books deal with her young heroes and heroines learning about the ways of wild creatures. In *The Summer of the Falcon* (1962), June Pritchard comes to understand the sparrowhawk her brothers have given her. Luke Rivers, in *Gull Number 737* (1964), studies the habits of birds living near Boston's Logan Airport. Lost in the Arctic tundra, Julie, in *Julie and the Wolves*, realizes that she can survive only by carefully observing the habits of a wolf pack and discovering a means of communicating with them.

In several of her stories, George portrays the delicacy of the ecological balance and the threat to this balance of man's often unthinking actions. In *Who Really Killed Cockrobin: An Ecological Mystery* (1971), a brother and sister, noticing a dead bird on their lawn, undertake an investigation to discover the reason for its death and find a chain of causes leading back to an industrial plant. In *Julie of the Wolves*, the Arctic tundra represents an ideal state of nature; however, the encroachments of civilization signal its inevitable destruction. Oil drums litter the frozen ground and bounty hunters shoot wolves from planes, needlessly breaking the cycles of nature. In *Going to the Sun* (1976), Marcus, who has followed in his father's footsteps as a big game hunter, comes to realize that shooting even a few mountain goats may lead to their extinction.

As Jean George's characters grow in their understanding of nature, they also begin to understand themselves better. *My Side of the Mountain* and *Julie of the Wolves* describe the growth to maturity of young people who spend a winter in the wilderness. Both Sam Gribley and Julie-Miyax Edwards see the wilderness as a kind of paradise but learn that they must return to the modern, civilized world. Sam lives in a hollow tree on family land in the Catskill Mountains, but is discovered in the spring and visited by many curiosity-seekers. He is told by his adult friend, Professor Bando, "Let's face it Thoreau, you can't live in America today and be quietly different. If you are going to be different you are going to stand out, and people are going to hear about you; and in your case, if they hear about you, they will move you to the city or move to you and you won't be different any more."

Fleeing from the Alaskan town of Barrow in order to avoid consummation of her prearranged marriage with her retarded cousin, thirteen-year-old-Eskimo girl Julie becomes lost in the tundra. Her goal is San Francisco, to her the epitome of civilization and the antithesis of the old Eskimo ways she has come to dislike. However, living with a pack of wolves, she learns the value of the old ways lived in harmony with nature. After the head wolf is shot from an airplane, Julie wanders into an Eskimo village where she learns that her father has capitulated to the ways of civilization. Stoically, she elects to remain in the village, realizing that the old ways are doomed. Her process of maturing has led to a bitter and ironic outcome.

TIPS FOR PARENTS AND TEACHERS: In the upper elementary and junior high grades, students can examine the moral dilemmas experienced by George's characters as they are caught between the forces of civilization and the rhythms of the natural world. In considering *Julie and the Wolves*, readers should notice how the wolves symbolize the old ways and how and why Julie's attitudes to these old ways change. *Julie* can be compared to such other survival stories as Armstrong Sherry's *Call It Courage* and Scott O'Dell's *Island of the Blue Dolphins*.

Goble, Paul (1933 –)
American

Born in Surrey, England, Paul Goble became interested in American Indians when he was a child. His mother read him the books of Grey Owl and Ernest Thompson Seton, and he later read the works of Black Elk. In 1959, after finishing his studies at the Central School of Art and Design in London, he made his first trip to the United States, visiting the Indians of the northern plains. He returned several times and, in 1977, settled in the Black Hills of South Dakota. He illustrated several books written by his son Richard, and in 1976 he received national attention for his illustrations for Richard Erodes' collection, *The Sound of Flutes and Other Indian Legends*. *The Girl Who Loved Wild Horses* (1978), which he wrote and illustrated, was awarded the Caldecott Medal. A synthesis of many legends, it was written, Goble stated, as an attempt "to express and paint what I believe to be the Native American rapport with nature." *The Gift of the Sacred Dog* (1980) is a plains Indian legend about the coming of the first horses. Goble's vividly colored, stylized paintings reflect the Indian background of the story and capture its emotional intensity.

TIPS FOR PARENTS AND TEACHERS: Goble's art provides an excellent introduction to the physical and spiritual lives of the northern plains Indians and is a good supplement for social studies lessons in the upper elementary and junior high grades.

Godden, Rumer *(1907 –   )*
English

Born in Sussex, England, Rumer Godden spent most of her childhood in India. When she was thirteen, she returned to England with her sister to attend school. In 1936 she published *Chinese Puzzle*, the first of her seventeen adult novels, and in 1947 *The Doll House*, the first of her eighteen stories for children. It was written, she said, because "I wanted to see if I could write a real novel in the tiny compass of a doll's house, and make it acceptable for children."

Considered by many critics to be Godden's best children's book, *The Doll House* is the story of five dolls who make up the Plantagenet family and their human owners, Emily and Charlotte Dane. The story, which has an emotional intensity and depth of characterization not often found in doll stories, introduces the reader to Godden's psychology of dolls: "It is an anxious, sometimes dangerous thing to be a doll. Dolls cannot choose; they can only be chosen; they cannot 'do,' they can only be done by; children who do not understand this often do wrong things."

Godden wrote several more stories about dolls: *Impunity Jane* (1954), *The Fairy Doll* (1956), *The Story of Holly and Ivy* (1958), and *Candy Floss* (1960), each of them similar to *The Doll's House*. However, in *Miss Happiness and Miss Flower* (1961), she wrote a doll story of a different nature. Drawing on her own memories of attending school in England,she tells the story of Nona, who receives two Japanese dolls, and, as she sets about designing a true Japanese house for them, gains confidence and acquires a sense of being part of a family herself.

Rumer Godden has written two short books about mice, *The Mousewife* (1951) and *Mouse House* (1957), and several realistic novels, the best of which is *The Kitchen Madonna* (1967), about a lonely and possessive nine-year-old boy who builds a kitchen icon for the family's Ukrainian cook. Godden has also retold an old folktale, *The Old Woman Who Lived in a Vinegar Bottle* (1972), and has written a verse narrative, *St. Jerome and the Lion* (1961).

TIPS FOR PARENTS AND TEACHERS: Readers in the middle elementary grades are best able to appreciate the moral and psychological themes of Godden's doll stories. They can compare them to *The Velveteen Rabbit* by Margery Williams Bianco and can write stories about their own toys.

Grahame, Kenneth *(1859 – 1932)*
English

Kenneth Grahame, author of *The Wind in the Willows*, once wrote that he remembered clearly everything that occurred to him between the ages of four and seven, and certainly the habits and attitudes he developed then were to influence his adult writing. Born in Edinburgh, Scotland, he was sent to live with his grandmother in Berkshire after the death of his mother. Only five years old, he became a lover of solitude and spent hours wandering across the countryside and along the riverbank, two areas which were to influence his classic animal fantasy. Grahame wanted to study at Oxford University; however, his relations chose for him a career in the Bank of England. Bitterly disappointed, he began work as a gentleman clerk in 1878.

While working at this conventional job, Grahame developed literary interests and established his reputation with *The Golden Age* (1895) and *Dream Days* (1898), two books which, although written for adults, describe life from a child's point of view. The best-known story in the two books is "The Reluctant Dragon," the tale of the friendship between a boy and a poetry-writing dragon and the complications that arise when St. George arrives in the area to slay the beast.

Grahame wrote little in the decade following the publication of *Dream Days*. In 1898, he accepted the Secretaryship of the Bank and, in 1899, married Elspeth Thomson. In 1900, his only son, Alistair, was born. In 1906, the Grahames moved from London back to the Cookham Dene area in the Berkshires, the place he had so loved as a child. He retired from the Bank in 1907.

Grahame's most famous book, *The Wind in the Willows*, began as a series of bedtime stories told to Alistair from the time the boy was four years old. Some time later, he wrote several of them as letters to his son, who was vacationing at the seaside. At the encouragement of a friend, he turned them into a book which, after having been rejected by several publishers, appeared in 1908. Not widely acclaimed at first, *The Wind in the Willows* soon became a favorite, and over one hundred different editions have now appeared. The stories have been illustrated by such well-known artists as Ernest Shepard, Arthur Rackham, and Tasha Tudor, and have been made into a play by A.A. Milne (*Toad of Toad Hall*, 1929) and a Walt Disney movie.

After the publication of *The Wind in the Willows*, Grahame wrote little. He travelled abroad often and when at home was somewhat of a recluse. Alistair died beneath a railroad train in 1920, an apparent suicide. Grahame himself died of a cerebral hemorrhage in 1932.

There are many reasons for the continued popularity of *The Wind in the Willows*. Grahame told a simple yet well-paced story. The major episodes center on the eccentric Toad and the misfortunes created by his violent enthusiasms. Those stories involving the other two main characters, Rat and Mole, are less frenetic, offering a change in pace and tone. The settings are both accurately described and made symbolically important. The River Bank is a stable area in which animals live peacefully and close to nature and is presided over by the mythical god Pan, the helper and healer of the creatures. The Wild Wood and the Wide World represent areas in which the residents are dominated by extreme lawlessness and extreme civilization, respectively; the River Bank is the ideal happy medium.

Grahame's central characters are all animals and his work has been compared to Beatrix Potter's animal stories and Rudyard Kipling's *The Jungle Books*. Like these writers, his contemporaries, Grahame presents characters which are a mixture of human and animal qualities, but which take on distinct, unique identities of their own. Many critics have noticed that *The Wind in the Willows* contains no major women characters and that, while the animals perform various daily chores, they are free of the responsibilities of adult life. These absences may well account for the great appeal of the book for children, for the life depicted is one children often see as ideal. The major characters, while not as irresponsible as J.M. Barrie's Peter Pan, do lead relatively carefree existences.

Several major themes run through *The Wind in the Willows*. The first examines the importance of one's home, what as Grahame calls "the special value of some such anchorage in one's existence." Friendship plays a major role in the stories. While respecting each other's individuality and peculiar needs, each character is ready to help others in need. Implicit throughout the book is a sense of nostalgia, a pastoral longing for a simpler, rural world. When Grahame wrote *The Wind in the Willows*, the English countryside was being rapidly transformed by modern technology. Even the River Bank is threatened: steam launches and motor cars disrupt the peace. Toad is particularly vulnerable to the modern world, as is seen in his frenzied response to automobiles. Biographer Peter Green has written, "The social picture which *The Wind in the Willows* presents is not life as Grahame thought it was, or had once been: it is his ideal version of what it *should* be, his dream of the true Golden Age."

TIPS FOR PARENTS AND TEACHERS: Children in the middle and upper elementary grades can notice the importance of the settings to the various animals and what happens to them when they move out of their appropriate locales. Students can be asked to consider whether or not Toad has really reformed at the end of *The Wind in the Willows*.

The Kate Greenaway Treasury, William Collins, New York, 1967. This illustration reflects both the static quality of Greenaway's figures and the dress styles she made famous across Western Europe.

Greenaway, Kate *(1846 – 1901)*
English

Born in London, Kate Greenaway, daughter of well-known engraver John Greenaway, was sent at age two to a farm near Rolleston, Nottinghamshire. Although she lived there for only two years, the sight and sounds of this rural area made a vivid impression on her and influenced the illustrations of her mature years. Most of her childhood was spent in London, playing with and making clothes for her large family of dolls, watching her engraver father at work, sketching, and attending school. At age eleven, she began her formal art training and a year later won her first prize. Later schooling included classes at Heatherley's and the Slade School of Art. In 1868, her watercolor drawings were exhibited at the Dudley Gallery in London, and during the early 1870's she worked as a free-lance artist. Her first children's book, *Under the Window* (1878), was a great success, over 70,000 copies selling in England and over 30,000 in French and German editions.

In 1880, *Kate Greenaway's Birthday Book for Children* appeared, followed in 1881 by *A Day in a Child's Life*, with music by Miles Foster, and in 1882 by *Little Ann and Other Poems*, an illustrated selection of poems by Ann and Jane Taylor that had been childhood favorites of Kate Greenaway. In 1883, she created the first of the very popular almanacs which were to be published yearly, with the exception of 1896, until 1897. Success followed on success: *The Language of Flowers* (1884), *Marigold Garden* (1885), a second collection of her own poetry, *Kate Greenaway's Alphabet* (1885), *A Apple Pie* (1886), a new illustrated version of an old and popular alphabet book, and illustrated versions of Bret Harte's *The Queen of the Pirate Isle* (1886), and Robert Browning's *The Pied Piper of Hamelin* (1888).

Kate Greenaway was the most popular children's author of the 1880s. The quaint, rural, late eighteenth-century clothing seen in her books became the rage in France, and from there spread through Europe, into England, and across the Atlantic to the United States. It has been said that "she dressed the children on two continents." Many illustrators copied her style, but as the *Dictionary of National Biography* observed, "although she had many imitators, she had no formidable rivals." Her popularity waned during the last ten years of the nineteenth century, a fact which seems to have disturbed her considerably. Her only major publication then was *The April Baby's Book of Tunes* (1900), a group of songs and music for which she supplied the illustrations.

Kate Greenaway is remembered today as a member, with Walter Crane and Randolph Caldecott, of the great triumvirate of illustrators whose works proved that quality picture books for children could be financially successful. Her achievement is much different from theirs. Both Crane and Caldecott chose largely traditional material to illustrate and did not generally include children in their books. However, as her biographers M.H. Spielmann and C.S. Layard suggest, Kate Greenaway was "the interpreter-in-chief of childhood," being concerned with making children and their approach to life around them the focus of her work.

Kate Greenaway chose rural areas as her chief settings. However, even though one occasionally sees the rolling hills and villages of England, more often the setting is a garden, carefully cultivated and delicately arranged. Generally the time of year is spring or summer, as the harshness of late fall and winter would not have produced the effects she desired. The gardens seem almost visionary, for although the details are based on her careful observations, they have an almost perfect quality about them, never seeming to have been touched by the ravages of nature. Greenaway herself was aware of this visionary quality, writing once to a friend, "You can go into a beautiful new country if you stand under a large apple-tree and look up to the blue sky through the white flowers — to go to this scented land is an experience. I suppose I went to it very young before I could really remember and that is why I have such a wild delight in cowslips and apple-blossoms — they always give me the same feeling of trying *to remember*, as if I had known them in a former world."

Her characters are generally young children in action. Occasionally adults appear, usually chiding or comforting mothers, slender and graceful, a contrast to the artist, who was short and plump. Like the settings they appear in, the children, with few exceptions, are neat and graceful. Although they dance, row boats, skip, or play at shuttlecock, their clothes are never ripped or spoiled. Greenaway's children live in an idyllic world, one without pain or sorrow, where life is a round of school, tea parties, and games.

TIPS FOR PARENTS AND TEACHERS: Although slightly "old-fashioned," Greenaway's picturebooks are still enjoyed by preschoolers. *A Apple Pie* is a good beginning alphabet for two- and three-year-olds. Her version of *The Pied Piper* can be used in the early elementary grades, as can *Under the Window* and *Marigold Garden*, and her collections of poems.

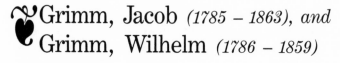 Grimm, Jacob *(1785 – 1863), and* Grimm, Wilhelm *(1786 – 1859)*

German

Born in Hanau, Hesse, two of nine children, Jacob and Wilhelm Grimm spent their childhood in Hanau, Steinau, and Cassel. Jacob entered Marburg University in 1802, and Wilhelm entered a year later. Here the elder brother fell under the influence of Friedrich Savigny, a professor of Roman law who encouraged the student's interest in history and fostered in him a scientific attitude toward studies of the past. After graduation Jacob became private librarian of King Jérôme Bonaparte of Westphalia, a position which allowed him much time to pursue his own research. At this time, the brothers began collecting folktales and in 1812 published the first volume of their most famous book, *Kinder- und Hausmärchen (Nursery and Household Tales)*. Although the book was criticized in Vienna as a work of superstition, it became very popular, and Jacob and Wilhelm began work on a second edition, which appeared in 1815. A third volume consisting mainly of detailed notes and commentary was published in 1822. Later editions, mainly the work of Wilhelm, were issued in 1833, 1836, 1839, 1841, 1843, 1847, 1850, 1853, and 1858. The work was very popular in other countries, and the first English edition, *German Popular Tales*, translated by Edgar Taylor, was published in 1823. *Household Tales* has been translated into over sixty languages.

Although very close, the brothers had very different personalities. Jacob was a quiet, reserved scholar, working diligently until his death on his various projects. Wilhelm, who suffered ill health during his adult life, had a more poetic nature, and enjoyed social life more than his brother. Jacob lived with Wilhelm most of his life, enjoying the position of favorite uncle in the family circle.

The *Household Tales* emerged as a result of the literary trends of the times and the brothers' personal interests. During the eighteenth century, literary versions of traditional tales had enjoyed a great vogue, with the tales of Frenchman Charles Perrault having the most popularity. With the emergence of the Romantic movement in Western Europe towards the end of the century, writers and scholars became interested in the traditional literatures of their various countries, finding in them stories which, it was felt, could bolster national pride. However, until the Brothers Grimm began their work, little scientific study of traditional literature had been made. With their interest in the examination of the past, the two began to collect oral stories from their Hessian neighbors. Their object was not to provide a group of entertaining tales, but rather to record accurately the materials they gathered. They gathered the tales from many sources: family members, neighbors, friends, and nearby peasants. After the success of the first volume, their task became easier as many people sent them stories collected in other areas.

The Grimms were interested in discovering the ultimate origin of the stories they collected, and advanced several hypotheses. Their most important theories were that the stories may have developed from Indo-European originals and that they were fragments of myths which had broken down into simpler stories. In the "Preface" to the second volume, Wilhelm wrote,

"[The household tale] has preserved most purely the nature of early epic poetry and has transmitted a whole element of it down to our present times. It is a poetry which belongs to the childhood of the race — and therefore children take to it so readily." This view is not generally held today.

Since their time, the study of folklore, of which they were the major pioneers, has advanced greatly, and modern researchers, who have much more information available, have made extensive categorizations of the tales they collected. In his "Folkloristic Commentary" in *The Complete Grimm's Fairy Tales* (1944), scholar Joseph Campbell has divided the tales in the following manner: animal tales, including "The Wolf and the Seven Little Kids" and "The Bremen Town Musicians"; tales of magic, including "Rapunzel," "Hansel and Gretel," "Little Red-Cap," "Little Briar-Rose," "Cinderella," and "Snow White"; religious tales, including "The King of the Golden Mountain"; romantic tales including "King Thrushbeard"; tales of the stupid ogre, including "The Peasant and the Devil"; and jokes and anecdotes, including "Clever Elsie," "Hans in Luck," and "Clever Hans."

Although not collected originally for children, the tales soon entered the area of children's literature. In 1869, English author John Ruskin noted, "[Children] will find in the apparently vain and fitful courses of any tradition of old time, honestly delivered to them, a teaching for which no other can be substituted, and of which the power cannot be measured; animating for them the material world with inextinguishable fire, fortifying them against the glacial cold of selfish science, and preparing them submissively, and with no bitterness of astonishment, to behold, in later years the mystery of the fates that happen alike to the evil and the good."

Within the first hundred years of their publication, the stories were illustrated by some of the foremost artists in the field. In England, these included George Cruikshank, Walter Crane, and Arthur Rackham. During the twentieth century, many distinguished illustrated editions of single stories have appeared. Among them are Wanda Gág's *Snow White and the Seven Dwarfs* (1938), Nancy Eckholm Burkert's *Snow White and the Seven Dwarfs* (1974), Adrienne Adams' *Hansel and Gretel* (1975), and Bernadette Watt's *Rapunzel* (1974).

There are many reasons for the popularity of many of the stories with children. As with most folktales, these are short, with sharply patterned plots, clearly defined characters, and quickly moving narratives. While they contain many unusual characters and strange occurrences, they present situations with which children can identify. "Hansel and Gretel" reflects a child's fear of desertion, and, in their bravery, the brother and sister reflect a heroism admired by young readers. In stories like "Cinderella," repressed individuals survive and then triumph against great odds. In stories about simpletons, children can feel superior to the ridiculous characters. In the stories there is little moral complexity: the good are rewarded and the evil, punished. In those tales containing magic, there is a sense of wonder to which children are particularly responsive.

Although they are favorites with children, the *Household Tales* have often been criticized by adults responsible for selecting books for young readers. The violence and terror contained in many of the stories have been seen as unsuitable for young children. Accordingly, many of them have been adapted, with the more unsettling aspects either omitted or toned down. Even Wanda Gág, a highly respected adaptor of the tales, lessened the horror, noting, "a certain amount of goriness if presented with a playful and not too realistic touch, is accepted calmly by the average child."

TIPS FOR PARENTS AND TEACHERS: The Grimm's stories are not all suitable for children, and adults should read all of the tales to select those which will most interest young readers. In addition to hearing the old favorites, children should be introduced to lesser-known tales. Where possible, a number of illustrated versions of the same tale should be available for perusal. The Grimm's stories can be discussed most fully in the middle and upper elementary grades.

The Post Office Cat, by Gail E. Haley, Scribner's, New York, 1976. The lonely, terrifying life of a young cat in London is captured by Haley in *The Post Office Cat*.

♥Haley, Gail *(1939 –   )*
American

Born in Charlotte, North Carolina, Gail Haley spent her childhood in the rural North Carolina village of Shuffletown and took her formal art training at the Richmond Professional Institute. She privately printed her first book, *My Kingdom for a Dragon* (1962), selling 1000 copies. It is the story in woodcuts of a knight who refuses to betray a dragon he befriends. A second book, *The Wonderful World of Marguerite* (1964), was illustrated in pen and ink.

During the 1960s, she mainly illustrated books by others, and she refers to this period as her apprenticeship.

While living in the Caribbean on a government-sponsored educational project, Gail Haley became interested in Caribbean folklore and began the research which was to lead to the publication of *A Story, A Story* (1970). A West African tale about an old man, Ananse, who undergoes a series of trials so that he may bring the Sky God's stories to his people, the book won the 1971 Caldecott Medal. Since then, Gail Haley has created six picture books: *Noah's Ark* (1971), the story of a modern day Noah who rescues the world's animals from pollution; *Jack Jouett's Ride* (1973), in which an enterprising boy living in Revolutionary times outwits the British; *The Abominable Swamp Man* (1975), a presentation of the need for a fantasy life; *The Post Office Cat* (1976), a recreation of a nineteenth-century British legend and winner of the Kate Greenaway Medal as the top British picture book of the year; and *Go Away, Stay Away* (1977), an account of the Swiss rituals dealing with the coming of spring. *The Green Man* (1979) tells of the adventures of a young man who refuses to believe in a legendary forest spirit.

Gail Haley's main interest is in the presentation of traditional myths, legends, and folktales. When she won the Caldecott Medal, she spoke of the importance of the old stories to African children. Her statement that the stories educated children into the culture and history of their people, while at the same time encouraging their own imaginative creativity, can be applied to her own work. She tells and illustrates each story in such a way that the young child hearing and seeing each book will respond to the cultural and human elements expressed in it.

Haley chooses an appropriate medium for each book: for *A Story, A Story*, woodblocks in vivid colors suggest both the stylized quality of folktales and the brightness of the African setting. In *The Post Office Cat*, the use of subdued greys and blues is appropriate for the cold, foggy city, and bold lines capture the feeling of the large, unfriendly areas into which the lonely cat wanders. *The Green Man* approximates the style of medieval tapestries.

TIPS FOR PARENTS AND TEACHERS: Haley's books provide introductions for students in the early and middle elemtnary grades to a wide variety of cultures. *A Story, A Story* can be read with other African trickster stories; *The Post Office Cat*, with the English folktale "Dick Whittington"; and *The Green Man*, with many of the Robin Hood stories. Upper elementary students can notice how Haley varies her artistic style to reflect the cultures of the stories.

Hamilton, Virginia *(1936 –   )*
American

Born in Yellow Springs, Ohio, the descendant of an escaped slave, Virginia Hamilton grew up surrounded by her Perry relatives. She later wrote, "The relationship of my relatives to past and present is something I learned as a child . . . . I know what an exceptional spiritual experience is the extended family." As a child, she often heard her family tell stories, many of them based on their past; she read, enjoying Nancy Drew books; and she wrote stories herself. She studied at Antioch College and Ohio University before going to New York, where she worked at various jobs while learning the craft of writing. In 1960, she married the poet Arnold Adoff and several years later, the couple, with their two children, returned to Yellow Springs to live. "Having lived ten and more years in New York," she wrote, "I discovered that my mind had never left Ohio."

Hamilton's first novel, *Zeely* (1967), tells of Elizabeth Perry, a young girl spending the summer on her uncle's farm who becomes infatuated with Zeely Taber, a statuesque swineherder whom the girl imagines to be a Watutsi princess. Elizabeth fabricates stories about her heroine, only to be confronted by Zeely speaking of her lonely life and emphasizing that one should see reality as it is. The girl then rejects her fantasy world, remarking meekly, "Things are what they are, I guess."

In *Zeely*, the central character attempts to create a romantic past; in Hamilton's second novel, *The House of Dies Drear* (1968), the young hero, Thomas Small, learns about a real element of Afro-American history, the Underground Railroad. Moving with his family to an Ohio college town, Thomas discovers that the mysterious house the family lives in was once a station on the Underground Railroad and that two escaped slaves and an abolitionist had been murdered in it.

Time-Ago Tales of Jahdu (1969) is the first of three books of literary folktales about a mischievous and magical trickster who resembles figures from African folklore. In his adventures, he outwits the giant Trouble, annoys many of his friends, and gives the grass and ocean their present characteristics. The stories are set within a contemporary framework. Sitting with his babysitter in Harlem, Lee Edward asks the old lady to tell him Jahdu stories. In the final story of the second book, *Time-Ago Lost: More Tales of Jahdu* (1973), Lee Edward dreams that he meets Jahdu and learns that he himself is beginning to grow up. *Jahdu* (1981) is an easy-to-read account of the trickster's further adventures.

Hamilton's third novel has a New York setting. *The Plant of Junior Brown* (1971), a Newbery Honor Book, is the story of two boys, Junior Brown, overweight, neurotic, and musically gifted, and Buddy Clark, a boy of the streets who knows how to fend for himself. Because of his own problems and the pressures placed on him by his equally neurotic mother, Brown retreats steadily from reality. The book was the first of Hamilton's novels in which plot was subordinated to intensive character analysis.

In the early 1970s, Hamilton wrote two biographies about major figures in black history: *W.E.B. DuBois: A Biography* (1972), and *Paul Robeson: The Life and Times of a Free Black Man* (1974). Of these books, she has said, "I had hoped, by writing the personal history of a real individual through the disciplined presentation of facts, to create an illusion of total reality: to give readers the feeling that they walked along with the subject in his life."

Virginia Hamilton's most highly acclaimed novel, *M.C. Higgins, the Great* (1974), winner of the Newbery Medal, is set in rural Ohio and deals with a young person's coming to terms with his past. The title hero wishes to escape from the family's mountainside home, which is threatened by a slag heap above it. He is also in conflict with his father, Jones, who is equally as proud and headstrong as he. By confronting his emotions, he learns his deep love and loyalty to his father, the land, and his past.

Arilla Sun Down (1976), the story of a girl of Black and Indian background, arose, the author stated, from two sources: "My interest in a reputed part-Indian ancestry — my grandmother was said to be part Cherokee — and my firsthand experience as a parent in an interracial family." After the publication of *Arilla Sun Down*, Hamilton wrote, "I've become less preoccupied with my own roots. Only so much can be said about one's heritage, and five or so books on the subject seem quite enough." Accordingly, she has most recently turned to fantasy. *Justice and Her Brothers* (1978) is a story of a girl who possesses strange powers which are necessary for her survival. Two sequels, *Dustland* (1980) and *The Gathering* (1981), trace her adventures in the future worlds.

In discussing her philosophy, Hamilton has written, "Life is continuous, going in a circle." This statement can be applied to her Ohio stories. The first, *Zeely*, relates the adventures of Elizabeth Perry; the last, *Arilla Sun Down*, is about a girl whose mother's maiden name is Perry. Both Elizabeth and Arilla, who are struggling to define themselves, may be seen as personae of the author, who has said that she weaves tales "out of the mystery of my past and present," and that "my characters are for the most part based on me." The individual must not attempt to create a false past as Elizabeth does, but must explore the past, as Thomas does in *The House of Dies Drear*, must listen to the voices of the cultural past as M.C. Higgins does, or to those of one's personal past as *Arilla Sun Down* does.

Virginia Hamilton's characters are black, as Hamilton is herself, and their specific concerns relate to black culture and history. Hamilton wrote, "I attempt in each book to take hold of one single theme of the black epxerience and present it as clearly as I can." However, writing from within a specific area of the American experience, Hamilton achieves a universality: "More than anything, I write about emotions, which are part of all people." Her heroes and heroines are not ordinary. They are generally loners, sensitive and often deeply troubled as they search for patterns to give order to their lives. They have a will to survive in the confusion of the modern world.

TIPS FOR PARENTS AND TEACHERS: While Hamilton's novels can be read as illustrations of how contemporary black children relate to their heritage, they can also be read as major statements of the nature of the human condition. In the upper elementary grades, students can notice how Zeely moves away from and then back to reality. Junior high readers of *M.C. Higgins, the Great* should consider the symbolic implications of the setting and of the characters M.C. meets.

❦Hansel and Gretel
Folktale

Although this story was first collected by the Brothers Grimm in 1812, the theme of abandoned children has a long history in traditional literature, extending at least as far back as the Biblical episode of Moses' abandonment in the bulrushes. As Iona and Peter Opie have noted in *The Classic Fairy Tales*, Perrault's "Hop o' My Thumb" ("Le petit poucet") deals with a similar motif. However, the Grimm Brothers' version has become the most popular treatment of the theme and is, along with "Cinderella," one of the best known European folktales.

Reasons for the great popularity of this story are easy to perceive. Faced with threats to their lives, the children act heroically to survive. The three adults in the story offer no security: both the stepmother and the witch want to destroy them; the father is completely helpless. The settings of the story clearly and graphically emphasize the insecurity. The vast, dark, tangled forest is a perfect embodiment of the terror and bewilderment the children feel during much of the story.

At first, the children cherish false hopes that they will be able to return home and find security; later, they think that the witch's house will offer nourishment and sanctuary. Indeed, it represents false security, as they soon discover. However, when they clearly perceive the reality of their situation, they shape their own destinies. On their return to their father, their house has become a home.

TIPS FOR PARENTS AND TEACHERS: This story deals with the very great courage of children who face extreme danger. Versions of the story which understate the danger or the evil of the witch diminish this courage. Children in the middle elementary grades can discuss the characters of the children, the terror of the forest, and the deceptive quality of the gingerbread cottage.

Harris, Christie *(1907 –   )*
Canadian

Born in Newark, New Jersey, Christie Harris as a baby moved with her Irish parents to Canada's west coast province of British Columbia, the setting of most of her books. Her first book, *Cariboo Trail* (1957), published when she was fifty years old, reflected her interest in the history of western Canada, an interest which led to her later books, *West with the White Chiefs* (1965) and *Forbidden Frontier* (1968). The activities of her family provided her with the materials of several other books she wrote in the 1960s: *You Have to Draw the Line Somewhere* (1964), *Confessions of a Toe-Hanger* (1967), and *Let X Be Excitement* (1969).

Christie Harris has achieved her greatest success as a reteller of the history and legends of Canada's west coast Indians. In 1963, she published *Once Upon a Totem*, a collection of five legends based on the figures carved on totem poles, and in 1966, *Raven's Cry*, the winner of the first of her two Canadian Library Association Children's Book of the Year awards. The book is an historically accurate, but fictionally rendered account of the Haida nation from the early contact times to the disintegration of its culture in the first half of the twentieth century. Several other books about Indian life and culture followed. *Once More Upon a Totem* (1973) is a second, and generally more successful collection of legends. *Sky Man on the Totem Pole?* (1975) combines traditional legends with the modern notions of astral travelling and visitors from space. In 1976, she published *Mouse Woman and the Vanished Princesses*, her second book to win the Canadian Library Association Children's Book of the Year award, another collection of Indian tales. The legends are unified around the title heroine, a narnauk, or spirit, who takes the shape of either a tiny mouse or an old grandmother in her efforts to help erring mortals. Later collections of Mouse Woman stories are *Mouse Woman and the Mischief Makers* (1977), *Mouse Woman and the Muddle Heads* (1979), and *The Trouble With Princesses* (1980). The basic Indian belief contained in the stories is the necessity for a harmonious interrelationship between and a respect for all creatures. The retellings of the legends are much longer than the originals and they lack the anecdotal and episodic quality characteristic of Indian tales. Using the devices of the European storyteller and writing for a non-native audience, Christie Harris gives deeper portrayals of character and fuller depictions of setting; she also employs the devices of choric repetition common to many Old World folktales.

TIPS FOR PARENTS AND TEACHERS: In the middle and upper elementary grades Harris's retellings can be used to introduce the Indian culture of the Pacific Northwest. As short stories, they are also careful studies of character development and, as such, can be related to non-Indian stories dealing with similar human qualities.

❧Hero Tales

Throughout the ages, in cultures from around the world, legends, sagas, and epics have been created celebrating the deeds of great heroes; these stories continue to hold readers and listeners, young and old, spellbound. Why do these stories about people who may never have existed, and who, if they did, probably were not nearly so great as the stories suggest, hold such interest for us? In *The Hero with a Thousand Faces*, Joseph Campbell writes,

> Whether we listen with aloof amusement to the dream-like mumbo jumbo of some red-eyed witch doctor of the Congo, or read with cultivated rapture thin translations from the sonnets of the mystic Lao-tse; now and again crack the hard nutshell of an argument of Aquinas, or catch suddenly the shining meaning of a bizarre Eskimo fairy tale: it will always be the one, shape-shifting yet marvellously constant story that we find.

In his study, Campbell examines hundreds of folktales, hero tales, and myths from around the world to discover the structural similarity underlying them all: what has been called the monomyth. Although there are biographies of many heroes from many cultures, there is, he argues, only one basic life story: the quest of the individual to discover his own identity and his role in society.

Many twentieth-century psychologists, most notably Carl Jung, have argued that this quest is one taken by all people and that this is the reason that hero tales have been so important in all cultures. We can identify with the aspirations and struggles of an heroic figure, for they are ours as well. However, unlike the average reader or listener to a hero story, the hero enacts his drama on a larger stage. He is more powerful and influential than we are, and the events of his life, including the conflicts he experiences, affect not only himself, but also the people he leads. He is superior to us; he represents a higher level of human potential and achievement. We can sympathize with what he is going through; but we can look up to him because we could never fulfill our quests in so grand or heroic a manner as he does.

In *The Hero with a Thousand Faces*, Campbell discusses the specific stages of the hero's quest. It is a life-story, a complete biography beginning with birth and ending with death. The first stage, the birth and youth of the hero, indicates that he has a special status, that there is something unique about him setting him apart from other people. His birth is mysterious. Often he is the product of a union between a god and a mortal, a sky-father and an earth-mother. Perseus, the Greek hero, was the son of Zeus, king of the gods, and Danae, daughter of the king of Argos. The hero is, or may appear to be, an orphan: Moses, hidden in the bulrushes, is raised by the Pharoah's daughter; Arthur, the British hero, is raised as a ward of Sir Ector. The birth of the hero may be marked by marvelous occurrences. In some versions of the black American legend of John Henry, the moon stops and then moves backwards on the night he is born.

The importance of all of these aspects is that the young hero is markedly different from other children. This often places great difficulties on him as he must work harder to prove himself. Almost from birth he is faced with the task of defining who he is. He must usually go through an arduous process of education, guided by an old, wise tutor, as Arthur is by Merlin, before he is recognized for the leader he is.

Having assumed his role of leader, the hero must display both courage and wisdom and must lead through example. His physical tasks appear to be overwhelming, even impossible. David must destroy Goliath, a giant before whom all the soldiers of Israel tremble; in Norse stories, Sigurd must kill the dragon Fafnir. The hero must help his people in times of great need: Robin Hood steals from the hypocritical, rich authority figures to help England's downtrodden women and peasants; Nanabozho, the Ojibway Indian hero, must rescue his people who are threatened by a flood caused by the evil Windegos. However, courage or strength, such as that exhibited by John

Henry or Beowulf, the Anglo-Saxon hero, is not always in itself enough. Both Robin Hood and Ulysses, the Grecian hero, succeed through trickery and guile; David perceptively realizes that he must employ small but superior weapons in confronting the heavily armored Philistine giant.

Although superior, the hero is not generally perfect. The love of adventure and trickery displayed by Ulysses and Robin Hood often create dangers for themselves and their followers. The idealistic King Arthur fails to realize that the greatest threat to his kingdom is man's fallen nature. In fact, the hero's failing can bring about his final defeat and death. Though they are superior to other people, the great heroes are all mortal. The death of the leader is a major element of the great hero tales: Beowulf dies killing a fire-drake while all but one of his men hide in terror; John Henry dies of exhaustion after having driven more steel than the steam drill; Robin Hood is betrayed by an hypocritical, evil prioress. Nanabozho and Arthur do not die, but leave the world, supposedly to return in times of great need.

Although in general outline the stories of the heroes are much the same throughout the world, each hero tale is unique, an embodiment of the culture which produced it. In depicting the characters and actions of their great leaders, people have celebrated those ideals they have most admired. Ulysses is a great humanist, affirming the Greek beliefs in the value and dignity of human beings in an often hostile natural and supernatural universe. Beowulf and Sigurd embody the physical and mental courage so admired by the fierce warriors of northern Europe. Robin Hood possesses the qualities of the ideal English yeoman; King Arthur, those of the chivalrous medieval knight. John Henry, a member of a then-downtrodden race, is a symbol both of his people's dignity and of modern man's struggle against the encroachments of technology. The modern reader should be aware of both the basic structure of hero tales and the specific cultural forms they take.

The hero tales most commonly adapted as children's stories have their origins in epics, sagas, romances, and ballad cycles. Although all of these are long narrative poems focusing usually on the great deeds of a central character, there are differences between them. The term *epic* usually refers to those poems which follow the style and structure of Homer's *Iliad* and *Odyssey*. Sagas are those stories of Icelandic or Scandinavian origin. Romances, generally products of the later Middle Ages, deal with the chivalrous adventures of knights. The ballad cycles are collections of shorter, rhymed narrative poems all dealing with the same subject.

The stories contained in these traditional narratives may originally have developed around historical events and actual people. In retellings over the years, these have been magnified in importance until the heroes have become larger than life. Stories totally unrelated to the original material attached themselves to it and motifs from folklore and mythology were added. At a specific point in time, all of the materials were unified into one coherent narrative. The resulting product, be it the *Odyssey*, *Beowulf*, or the *Volsunga Saga*, has remained basically constant since its creation and represents the form in which the specific story is best-known today.

The hero tales most widely known in the English-speaking world are the *Iliad* and the *Odyssey* (Greek), the stories of the Trojan War and the wanderings of Ulysses (Odysseus); *Beowulf* (Anglo-Saxon), the exploits of the killer of monsters and dragons; *Le Morte d'Arthur* (English), the adventures of the Knights of the Round Table; *Robin Hood* (English), legends of the honest savior of the poor; and several Norse (Icelandic and Scandinavian) sagas, the best known of which is probably the *Volsunga Saga*, the account of the deeds of the great warriors and their descendants. Perhaps because it is such a relatively new area, North America has fewer clearly developed hero tales. However, such characters as Daniel Boone, John Henry, and Nanabozho are among the best-known pioneer, black American, and Indian heroes.

Many popular television programs and motion pictures avidly consumed by young people make use, consciously or unconsciously, of elements from the hero tales. For example, the mysterious origin, the silver bullets, and the recognizable costume of the Lone Ranger find parallels in elements from the Robin Hood stories. The recent motion pictures about Superman deal with a mysterious birth, the boyhood and education of the young hero, and his ultimate, self-sacrificing leadership. George Lucas, in preparing for his "Star Wars" films, studied the traditional hero tales thoroughly. The orphan Luke Skywalker must go through a long, arduous training, guided by Yoda and the spirit of Obi-wan Kenobi, before becoming a Jedi Knight. The student who is aware of the traditional patterns and symbols will be able to consider these modern works in a new light, and with a basis for comparison will be better able to make evaluative judgments about them.

TIPS FOR PARENTS AND TEACHERS: Hero tales can best be introduced in the middle elementary grades, when students can discuss universal traits of such characters as the young King Arthur, Robin Hood, Nanabozho, and John Henry. In the upper elementary grades, a variety of heroes can be examined. Children can notice similarities among them and can also notice how specific heroes reflect the beliefs of the cultures creating them. Homer's *Iliad* and the *Odyssey* are suitable for the junior high grades. Robert Graves' *The Seige and Fall of Troy* (1962), Barbara Picard's *The Odyssey of Homer Retold* (1952), and Padraic Colum's *The Children's Home* (1962) are very good versions of these ancient classics.

Hogrogian, Nonny *(1932 –   )*
American

Born in the Bronx, New York City, Nonny Hogrogian studied art at Hunter College and the Pratt Institute before working as a book designer and illustrator. Her first illustrations were for Nicolette Meredith's *King of the Kerry Fair* (1960), and since then she has illustrated over two dozen books, including several for her husband, poet David Kherdian.

Nonny Hogrogian is one of only five artists to have won the Caldecott Medal twice (the others being Robert McCloskey, Leo and Diane Dillon, and Barbara Cooney). She received her first award for the illustrations of Sorche Nic Leodhas' adaptation of the traditional Scottish ballad *Always Room for One More* (1965), and her second for the illustrations for her own adaptation of the Armenian folktale, *One Fine Day* (1971). For the former, Hogrogian sketched the figures and the Scotsman's cottage in pen and ink and used gray washes and purple pastels to suggest the fog and heather of the Highlands. For the latter, she used bright oils in depicting the quest of the fox to recover his tail, cut off by an old woman whose pail of milk he had stolen. In 1976, Hogrogian won a Caldecott Honor Medal for her adaptation of *The Contest*, an Armenian folktale.

TIPS FOR PARENTS AND TEACHERS: One Fine Day can be used in the early elementary grades to emphasize the relationships in the food chain and the idea of the interdependence of living beings. It can also be compared to such cumulative stories and poems as "The House That Jack Built."

Houston, James *(1921 –   )*
Canadian

Born in Toronto, Canada, James Houston first visited the Canadian Arctic, his home for fourteen years and the setting for nearly all his books, in 1948. There he steeped himself in Eskimo culture and was influential in having the now-famous stone carvings brought to the attention of the rest of the world.

It was not until 1965, after he had moved to the United States, that Houston began writing stories of the Canadian North. His first book, *Tikta'*

Liktak (1965), the story of an Eskimo boy who is stranded on an ice floe during spring breakup and survives great physical and spiritual hardship before being reunited with his family, won the Canadian Library Association Children's Book of the Year award in 1966. His second book, *Eagle Mask* (1966), is about the coming of age of an Indian of the northwest coast.

Houston won his second Canadian Library Association Children's Book of the Year award for *The White Archer* (1967), in which Kungo, an Eskimo boy, learns the arts of hunting from an old man, all the while meditating revenge against the Indians who had killed his mother and father and carried off his sister. In *Akavak* (1968), a boy makes a perilous journey so that his dying grandfather can see a brother. *Wolf Run* (1971) deals with the Caribou Eskimo and their struggle against starvation, while *Ghost Paddle* (1972) returns to the Indians of the northwest coast, describing a young prince's attempts to restore peace with a neighboring tribe. *Kiviok's Magic Journey* (1973) deals with the supernatural as an Eskimo woman and her children are stolen by the wicked trickster Raven. *Frozen Fire* (1977), much longer than his retelling of traditional stories, uses a present-day setting, treating the confrontation of the old and new ways, as an Eskimo boy and his American companion search the frozen wastes for the latter's missing prospector father. A sequel, *Black Diamonds*, appeared in 1982. *River Runners* (1979), the story of the relationship between an Indian and a white boy, was named the Canadian Children's Book of the Year. The struggle to survive plays a large part in each story which is enacted in a harsh, unyielding landscape where cold, fierce animals and starvation are ever-present dangers.

Unlike traditional Eskimo stories, which are generally extremely short and contain little characterization, Houston's are longer, with an unfolding plot and greater character portrayal. Much of their beauty emerges from Houston's prose style: concrete in its portrayal of setting, its simple vocabulary and sentence structure give it a measured dignity. Houston's own accompanying illustrations, often in wax pencil on acetate, are accurate, but more important, they reflect the harshness of the environment and the dignity and courage of the characters who confront it.

TIPS FOR PARENTS AND TEACHERS: For middle and upper elementary aged readers Houston's Indian and Eskimo tales are exciting adventures and perceptive studies of character growth. Students should notice how each event gives the hero a chance to grow as an individual. The culture conflict stories will help upper elementary and junior high children to understand better the social upheavals which have occurred in the Far North.

Hughes, Shirley *(1929 –   )*
English

When she was growing up in Liverpool, award-winning author-illustrator Shirley Hughes was an avid reader, and, with the other children in her family, often wrote, illustrated, and dramatized stories. After studying at the Liverpool Art School and the Ruskin School of Art in London, she began illustrating books and since then has created pictures for over one hundred stories. Discussing her role as an illustrator, she has said, "Illustrating . . . is largely concerned with trying to use your imaginative powers to get inside another person's skin, to identify with the story and work out from there, using your technique . . . to illuminate the drama of the narrative, [and] give a visual form and style to the characters and their background."

She began writing stories for her own children because she wished to have complete visual and verbal control of the stories she treated. Her first book, *Lucy and Tom's Day* (1960), describes the everyday adventures of young children. There are two sequels: *Lucy and Tom Go to School* (1973) and *Lucy and Tom at the Seaside* (1976). In the mid 1970s, she began attracting international attention with a series of full-color books describing the domestic experiences of ordinary London children. *Helpers* (1975, published in the United States as *George, the Babysitter*) describes the work and play of three small children and their sitter. *Dogger* (1977, published in the United States as *David and Dog*) relates the trauma of a small boy who loses a favorite stuffed animal. It was awarded the Kate Greenaway Medal. *Moving Molly* (1978) is the account of a child's departure to a new residence.

TIPS FOR PARENTS AND TEACHERS: Hughes' works are particularly relevant for contemporary, urban preschoolers and can be related to their own everyday experiences which are often traumatic to them.

Hunt, Irene *(1907 –   )*
American

Born in Newton, Illinois, Irene Hunt grew up on her grandparents' midwestern farm. Although she did not publish her first novel, *Across Five*

Aprils, until 1964, she had been writing and collecting rejection slips for several years before. *Across Five Aprils*, written to bring history alive to her junior high school students, is the story of Jethro Creighton, who lives on a southern Illinois farm during the Civil War. In her "Author's Note," Irene Hunt stated that, "there is hardly a page in this book on which a situation has not been suggested by family letters and records and by the stories told by my grandfather." The book was awarded a Newbery Honor Medal.

Irene Hunt's second book, *Up a Road Slowly* (1966), won the Newbery Medal. In it she drew on her memories of her father's death and her subsequent life with her grandparents. Julie Trelling's mother dies when the girl is only seven years old. Sent to live with a proper but loving maiden aunt and an alcoholic uncle, Julie becomes a secure and poised young woman, but not before she undergoes struggles in adjusting to her new home and learns to cope with the normal problems of maturing.

Irene Hunt's next two books, *Trail of Apple Blossoms* (1968) and *No Promises in the Wind* (1970), are historical. The former is a fictionalized biography of the now-legendary Johnny Appleseed. In the latter, fifteen-year-old Josh Grondowski and his ten-year-old brother take to the road during the Depression years of the early 1930s.

Since moving to Florida after her retirement from teaching, Irene Hunt has used a southern setting for her books. *Lottery Rose* (1976) deals with a subject which has received considerable notice recently: the battered child. After having been savagely beaten by his alcoholic mother and her boy-friend, Georgie Burgess is sent to live in a home and takes with him a rosebush he had won in a grocery store lottery. It represents security to him, and he gives it all his love. *William* (1977) describes the life of five children who live together to create a family. After their mother's death, the title hero and his two sisters join forces with an unwed teenaged mother and her baby.

Irene Hunt's novels could be called chronicles, as they deal with the daily lives of the characters over long periods. These children all move up roads slowly, overcoming their tragedies and handicaps. Using either the first-person narrative or a limited third-person point of view, Hunt sensitively and realistically portrays their hopes, sorrows, and uncertainties. She has said that the writer for children must have "a close affinity with his own childhood, and if he has this, it follows that he will have that same affinity for childhood in general. He must remember!"

In *William*, Sarah quotes from the Greek philosopher Heraclitus: "As all things flow, nothing abides. Into the same river, one cannot step twice." The inescapability of change is perhaps the major theme of all Irene Hunt's novels and the central characters must learn to accept and adapt to change as they slowly travel their roads to maturity.

TIPS FOR PARENTS AND TEACHERS: Hunt's historical novels make excellent reading to supplement history lessons in the upper elementary and junior high school grades. Children experiencing emotional difficulties similar to those described in the novels will find encouragement in reading such books as *William, Up a Road Slowly,* and *Lottery Rose.*

Rosie's Walk, by Pat Hutchins, Macmillan, New York, 1968. The illustrations for *Rosie's Walk* reveal actions not stated in the simple text.

across the yard

❦Hutchins, Pat *(1942 –)*
English

Born in Yorkshire, England, Pat Hutchins grew up in the country, where she often sketched animals and scenery. She studied at the Darlington School of Art and the Leeds College of Art and then worked for an advertising agency in London. She married Laurence Hutchins in 1965 and moved with him to New York where she published her first two children's books: *Rosie's Walk* and *Tom and Sam* (both 1968). She has since written and illustrated a dozen books including *Clocks and More Clocks* (1970), *Changes, Changes* (1971), *Goodnight Owl* (1972), *The House that Sailed Away* (1975), and *Happy Birthday, Sam* (1978). *The Wind Blew* (1974) was awarded the Kate Greenaway Medal. Her first novel, *The Mona Lisa Mystery,* was published in 1981.

Discussing her books, Hutchins has stated, "I try to keep my stories logical, even if a story is pure fantasy . . . . I like to build my stories up, so the reader can understand what is happening and, in some cases, anticipate what is likely to happen on the next page." Each story has a steadily progressing narrative which leads to a satisfying conclusion. In *Rosie's Walk,* a chicken takes a stroll, unaware of a fox who several times tries unsuccessfully to pounce on her. In *The Wind Blew,* a cumulative story, an increasing number of people chase after objects the wind has blown from them.

Pat Hutchins' earlier illustrations were somewhat stylized; those for more recent stories are more realistic. However, in all her books, she uses page design to indicate continuity of action from illustration to illustration and thus to create narrative movement. In *Rosie's Walk*, one two-page spread reveals the fox in midair, his eyes intent on the chicken, oblivious to the rake toward which his momentum carries him. The following two-page spread shows him landing and the rake hitting him. Rosie appears on the right-hand edge of each spread, walking toward the scene to be depicted in the following spread, unaware of the peril behind her.

The Wind Blew uses more realistic drawings to tell its simple story. By the end of the book, twelve people, including four children, a bridegroom, a palace guardsman, and a postman, are chasing objects. The right-hand side of each two-page spread becomes progressively more cluttered as the people follow the wind. Near the edge of the left-hand side of each page is seen the individual who, although he does not yet realize it, is the wind's next victim. The pages contain much humor as the chaos increases.

TIPS FOR PARENTS AND TEACHERS: Hutchins' books provide an excellent introduction to sequencing for preschoolers and early elementary aged children. Have children carefully notice the relationship between details on two or three successive pages and then notice the changes in placement of the details and, if possible, reasons for the changes.

Jack and the Beanstalk
Folktale

References to "Jack and the Beanstalk," one of the most popular of the English folktales, appeared early in the eighteenth century. The three versions which have formed the basis of most modern retellings were published in the nineteenth century and are very different from each other. Iona and Peter Opie, in *The Classic Fairy Tales*, reprint "The History of Jack and the Beanstalk," first published in 1807. In the same year, *The History of Mother Twaddle and her Amazing Son Jack* appeared. Fifty years later, folklorist Joseph Jacobs collected another version. The Opies maintain that the two 1807 versions descended from different sources and that what Jacobs collected was a literary version of *The History of Jack*. Katherine Briggs, on the other hand, argues in *A Dictionary of British Folk-Tales* that Jacobs' variant is closer to the original tale.

The History of Mother Twaddle is the least known of the three. In verse, it tells how Mother Twaddle, having found a sixpence while sweeping, sends Jack to the fair to buy a goose. Jack, of course, buys a bean, is scolded by his mother, and plants the bean. Climbing the stalk the next morning, he arrives at a giant's castle where he is met by a damsel who hides him. The damsel gives the giant wine and, when he falls into a drunken stupor, Jack beheads him and soon after marries the damsel.

This version included in the Opie's collection begins with a description of Jack's character. He has been constantly overindulged by his mother, who is now reduced to selling their cow to buy their food. Jack, however, trades the cow to a butcher for the magic beans and, the next day, climbs the beanstalk to a desolate land where he meets an old woman. A fairy in disguise, she tells Jack that the ogre had killed the boy's wealthy father and dispossessed mother and child. Accordingly, Jack must avenge the death of his father, and can "seize upon [the treasure] all with impunity," because it is really his.

The Opies' version, in addition to providing complete moral sanction for Jack's acts of thievery, also places him within the long-standing tradition of heroes, who, unknown to themselves, are of noble birth, are reduced to humble circumstances, and are required to pass dangerous tests to regain their birthright.

Jacobs' version includes neither the fairy nor an earlier happier life for Jack and his mother. The boy makes three trips and succeeds because of his daring and cunning. He is a marked contrast to his mother, who seems virtually unable to cope with the stresses they encounter and wrings her hands while Jack calls her to chop the Beanstalk. In the end, the happiness of mother and son is augmented by the fact that the new wealth makes it possible for Jack to marry a great princess.

The story was very popular in nineteenth-century America. In one version from the Appalachian Mountains, Jack successively gathers a rifle, a skinning knife, and a bedspread with golden bells. Many sequels to this story have appeared, one of the best being *Jim and the Beanstalk*, by Raymond Briggs, in which a boy meets the giant's son and makes a "new ogre" of him by supplying the giant with glasses, false teeth, and toupee.

"Jack and the Beanstalk" belongs to a large group of tales in which the title hero, named Jack, survives by his wits. The story of "Jack the Giant Killer" is a gathering together of tales about ogre slayers. In the United States, a number of "Jack Tales" have been collected in which the lazy hero prospers by virtue of his abilities as a trickster. Jack is a "literary relation" of David, the Biblical slayer of Goliath.

TIPS FOR PARENTS AND TEACHERS: In the early elementary grades, children enjoy comparing Paul Galdone's *The History of Mother Twaddle* with more familiar versions.

Peter's Chair, by Ezra Jack Keats, Harper & Row, New York, 1967. Keats uses the placement of characters on the page to reflect the boy's sense of being left out in *Peter's Chair*.

🌸 Keats, Ezra Jack *(1916 – 1983)*
American

Born in Brooklyn, New York, Ezra Jack Keats began telliing stories and drawing at an early age. His artistic ability earned him special status in his tough Brooklyn neighborhood. Some older boys, chasing him one day, discovered one of his paintings under his arm and thereafter treated him with great respect. Keats had no formal art training. When he graduated from high school, he was awarded a scholarship to the Art Students League but was unable to accept it because of financial difficulties. After World War II, he pursued a career as a professional artist, art instructor, and book illustrator.

Published in 1962, *The Snowy Day*, Keats' first book, had long been growing in the author's mind. Several years before, he had clipped from a magazine candid photos of a child whose facial expressions and clothing he had found particularly appealing. The child became the basis for Peter, the little boy who goes outdoors to explore his first snowfall, responding to it with wonder and curiosity. There is little text—Keats believing that words should be kept at a minimum, being suggestive rather than explicit. The illustrations are done in collage, a medium that Keats had not used before but which he was to use as well as any in the field of children's illustration. The book was awarded the Caldecott Medal. Later books describe Peter's adventures as he grows and investigates his inner city world. In *Whistle for Willie* (1964), he feels inferior to other children because he is unable to whistle for his dog; in *Peter's Chair* (1967), he has to cope with the arrival of a new baby in the family; and, in *A Letter to Amy* (1968), he has a series of misadventures while mailing a birthday party invitation to his special friend.

Keats remarked that it was only while he was working on *Peter's Chair* that he realized that his hero was growing up. Later books expand Peter's horizon and introduce new characters. *Goggles*, winner of a 1969 Caldecott Honor Medal, introduces Archie who, with Peter, finds an old, broken pair of motorcycle goggles, only to have older boys try to steal them. In *Hi, Cat!* (1970) and *The Pet Show* (1972), Archie finds a pet who has a tendency to upset the boys' plans. Another new character is called Louie. In *Louie* (1975), he feels shy and sensitive in front of the others; in *The Trip* (1978), he moves to a new neighborhood; and, in *Louie's Search* (1980), he hunts for a father.

Other books by Keats include a retelling of the black American legend *John Henry* (1965); illustrations for three books of poetry; and three books of humorous animal advantures: *Psst! Doggie—* (1973), *Skates* (1973), and *Kitten for a Day* (1974).

The publication of *The Snowy Day* in 1962 was a significant event, for its presentation of a black child as the central figure was unusual in picture books up to this time. The child's race is not mentioned in the text and is evident only in the pictures; thus, race is not an issue in the conflict. In later stories, Keats makes the socio-cultural milieu more explicit in the illustrations. In *Goggles*, Archie sports an Afro haircut and wears Afro clothes. Puerto Rican and white children become part of Peter's neighborhood and the physical condition of the buildings deteriorates.

Although dealing specifically with inner-city children, Keats places them in situations which have universal relevance and presents these situations as children themselves would experience them, showing how events which might be insignificant to adults are very important to youngsters. Exploring snow for the first time, being unable to whistle, and losing one's cat just before a neighborhood pet show are major concerns. Progressing from *The Snowy Day* through to *The Trip*, the children confront larger worlds, moving from the security of the house onto the street, to the store, through the alleys, and finally into new neighborhoods.

In his books, text is minimal, merely establishing essentials of the story; the pictures, in collage or acrylic, impart the deeper meanings. In *Whistle for Willie*, for example, the placing of Peter and his dog on separate blocks of paper on opposite sides of a two-page spread indicates the boy's feeling of isolation from his pet. As he becomes increasingly despondent, he is often pictured very small on the page and a hat that he puts on has the effect of making him almost blend into the wallpaper. With the success of his first whistle, Peter's smiling profile takes half of the two-page spread, and background wallpaper filled with sunbursts reflects the joy he now feels.

From the time of *Goggles* on, Keats has employed collage much less, often using only bits of torn newspaper to represent back alley debris. The strong colors of the acrylics suggest the intense emotions of the later stories: the potential violence of older boys' attempts to steal goggles, the loneliness of Louie, and the joy of discovering beauty in a blind man's apartment (in *Apt. 3*, 1971).

TIPS FOR PARENTS AND TEACHERS: The stories dealing with Peter can be read to preschoolers who are experiencing similar emotions. In the early elementary grades, children can notice how color and facial expressions convey characters' emotions. The objects found in the "Louie" books can be made easily in art classes.

Charley, Charlotte and the Golden Canary, Oxford University Press, London, 1967. The lonely life of the solitary London child is captured by Keeping in *Charley, Charlotte and the Golden Canary.*

Down in Paradise Street, Charley also felt lonely and miserable. He was not even sure where Charlotte now lived. All the new buildings looked alike.

Keeping, Charles *(1924 –   )*
English

Born in Lambeth, a poor district of London, Charles Keeping grew up in a family that encouraged creativity: his grandfather told tales of his seafaring life, and others drew, sang, or told stories. Keeping would often write and illustrate stories based on the animals he had seen. After completing his art training at Regent Street Polytechnical in London, Keeping began a career as an illustrator.

In 1966, after over a decade of illustrating others' works, Keeping published *Shaun and the Cart-Horse*, the first of over a dozen books he was to illustrate and write himself, stories drawing on his own childhood memories and the London he knows so well. Shaun is a little boy who befriends a cart horse, Queen, and her owner Uncle Charlie Peel. When Uncle Charlie becomes ill and must give up the horse, who will be slaughtered, Shaun leaves his tiny yard and goes on a long search for Queen. *Black Dolly* (1966), published in the United States as *Molly o' the Moors*, treats a similar theme, the life and aging of a cart horse who is finally returned to the happy fields of his youth. In real life these horses would have been slaughtered; however, because his publishers felt such facts would not have been acceptable in children's books, Keeping gave the stories happy endings.

Keeping's next work, *Charlie, Charlotte and the Golden Canary* (1967), was awarded the Kate Greenaway Medal as the most distinguished British picture book of the year. The origin of the story was an idea that had long preoccupied Keeping during his walks around London. "I was walking through the market when I noticed these high-rise flats. I saw these kids stuck up on the balconies and thought: they would never come down; there they are, stuck up in the modern flats, in their tiny caged balconies. Then I looked at all the kids running wild about the streets. And I thought to myself, what is best? A canary or a sparrow?" On one level, the story is of a child who is separated from and later reunited with a best friend. However, in the final illustration, Keeping has shown the children apparently caged by the grillwork of the balcony. In her move from Paradise Street, Charlotte has left freedom; the implication is that Charlie, too, will lose his paradise should his tenement be demolished.

Keeping's later works continued to explore the world of the small child. In *Alfie and the Ferry Boat* (1968), the title hero crosses the Thames River in search of Bunty, an old man who has told him stories of his supposed seafaring adventures. *Joseph's Yard* (1969) is a powerful presentation of the life of a lonely child who plants a small flower in his enclosed yard. *Through the Window* (1970) chronicles the reactions of a small boy to the people and events he sees in the street below, while *The Garden Shed* (1971) portrays the fascination with which a child watches a fire in which the statue of a woman burns. In recent books, Keeping has extended his geographical range: *The Nanny Goat and the Fierce Dog* (1973) takes place in a nearly deserted weed patch. *Inter-City* (1976), a wordless picture book, depicts a train journey through the countryside.

In his best works, Keeping shows the world as seen by a child living in the slums of London. It is an expanding world. The limit of Jacob's view in *Through the Window* is symbolized by the small area he can see from the window. In *Joseph's Yard*, the child has entered a larger but still confining world and the emotions of love, jealousy, and overprotectiveness he feels for his plant reflect his narrow view, one which he overcomes in the end. In *Alfie and the Ferry Boat*; *Charlie, Charlotte and the Golden Canary*; and *Shaun and the Cart-Horse*, the heroes enter into a larger world. Although Alfie discovers that the "Other Side of the World" is only a dance hall outside of which his old friend plays his scratchy records, he refuses to believe that Bunty is not an adventurous sailor. Shaun shows love, courage, and resolution as he ventures alone and at night out of his own neighborhood to rescue the aging horse. Charlie's travels from the old world of tenements to the new one of high-rise apartments may foreshadow his entry into a more modern life.

In the illustrations for his stories, Keeping does not use naturalistic representation, choosing instead to recreate the moods of the children through stylized drawings and impressionistic use of color. Vivid, contrasting colors are used in startling juxtaposition to suggest, Keeping has said, the violent, often discordant sounds of London life. Recently Keeping has used more subdued colors, reflective of the streets and buildings of the urban scene. A distinctive feature of his art is the use of a series of narrow lines which flow across or down each page and are shaped in such a way as to create rhythmic patterns which harmonize with the mood of the particular illustration.

TIPS FOR PARENTS AND TEACHERS: Early and middle elementary aged students can discuss the emotional growth of the characters in Keeping's stories and can examine how color and line are used to express emotions.

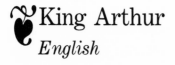King Arthur
English

Along with Robin Hood, King Arthur is the best-known of England's legendary heroes. In fact, he has often been called a counterpart of Robin Hood; for, as the former embodied the ideals of the commoners, Arthur and his Knights of the Round Table embodied those of the nobility. Surrounded by such companions as Gawain, Lancelot, and Galahad, tutored by the wizard Merlin, and armed with his famed sword Excalibur, Arthur represented the ideal ruler, defending the country and creating an internal peace and prosperity.

Whether King Arthur is based on an historical person is not known. If he is, it is probably on some now-unknown warrior chief who fought against invading Saxons in the sixth century A.D. In succeeding centuries, legends developed around him so that he became an almost bigger-than-life hero. Britons fleeing in the face of the Saxon invasions took the stories with them to France, where they were further expanded before being returned to England after the Norman invasions of the late eleventh century. During the twelfth century, Geoffrey of Monmouth wrote *History of the Kings of Britain*, in which he glorified existing stories and invented others. At the same time in France, the poet Chrétien de Troyes wrote several very popular works about Arthur and his knights. Many other writers retold old stories and invented new ones, the best-known of these being *Sir Gawain and the Green Knight*, an anonymous poem of the late fourteenth century.

The most important version of the early retellings of Arthurian legends was the fifteenth century *Le Morte d'Arthur*, by Sir Thomas Malory. William Caxton, England's first printer, published the book in 1485, noting in his preface that Arthur was a man "which ought most to be remembered among us Englishmen before all other Christian Kings." Caxton also stated that his purpose in printing the legends was moral: "[I] have done set it in print, to the extent that noble men may see and learn the noble deeds of chivalry, the gentle and virtuous deeds that some knights used in those days, by which they came to honor; and how that they that were vicious were punished and oft put to shame and rebuke."

Undoubtedly, children have heard stories about the deeds of King Arthur and his knights since the legends were first told. However, it was not until early in this century that they were specifically written for children. Howard Pyle, one of the foremost American children's authors and illustrators, published four volumes of King Arthur tales: *The Story of King Arthur and His Knights* (1903), *The Story of the Champions of the Round Table* (1905), *The Story of Sir Lancelot and His Champions* (1907), and *The Story of the Grail and the Passing of Arthur* (1910). Seen by many critics as Pyle's finest writing, the books were based on extensive historical research and reflected the author's profound admiration of the English king. In his forward, Pyle noted, "I believe that King Arthur was the most gentle knight who ever lived in all the world."

Since Pyle's time, many distinguished authors have retold the Arthurian legends. Among them are Sidney Lanier (*The Boy's King Arthur*, 1917), Rosemary Sutcliff *The Light Beyond the Forest*, 1979, and *The Road to Camlann*, 1981), and Roger Lancelyn Green (*King Arthur and His Knights of the Round Table*, 1956). One of the best-known modern adaptations for children is T.H. White's *The Sword in the Stone* (1938), which was made into a Walt Disney animated film in 1963.

Although after the publication of Malory's *Le Morte d'Arthur* there were many retellings, the basic elements of the story had been established by 1500. The central figure, of course, was Arthur. Generally, he was said to have been the illegitimate son of King Uther Pendragon. After his birth, he was taken away by the wizard Merlin to be raised by Sir Ector and did not discover his identity until, sent to fetch a weapon for his foster brother, Kay, he withdrew a sword from a churchyard stone and thus established himself as king of all Britain. The early years of his reign were spent quelling dissident factions in his realm and gathering together a group of knights who were to become the Champions of the Round Table. The greatest quest of the knights was for the Holy Grail, the sacred bowl used at the Last Supper. Many were killed and only two, Galahad and Percival, saw the Grail. The later years of Arthur's reign were marked by war and dissension. Lancelot carried on his adulterous relationship with Queen Guenevere, Gawain fought against Lancelot, and Mordred, Arthur's bastard son, betrayed his father. Arthur was transported to the enchanted Isle of Avalon from which, it was believed, he will return in England's time of greatest need.

The nature of the basic material has made adapting it for younger readers difficult. For example, the many sexual exploits and the complex religious motives (based on pagan as well as Christian beliefs) are beyond the range of younger readers. Moreover, the feudal system is much different to the governmental processes of the twentieth century. What the children's versions emphasize are the selfless dedication to spiritual quests, the steadfast loyalty to the royal leader, and the heroism and courage displayed during dangerous adventures. Riding through strange and threatening landscapes, the knights face dragons, giants, superior numbers, and supernatural adversaries. Often outmatched, they never shirk confrontations and generally emerge victorious.

TIPS FOR PARENTS AND TEACHERS: For upper elementary aged readers, R. L. Green's *King Arthur and His Knights of the Round Table* makes an excellent introduction to the Arthurian legends. With the basic outline of the story in their minds, they are ready for the more detailed treatments of authors like Pyle and Sutcliff. Junior high students can analyze the moral nature of the various knights and can compare the stages of Arthur's life with those of such heroes as Robin Hood, Beowulf, and Odysseus.

Kipling, Rudyard *(1865 – 1936)*
English

Although Kipling was born in India and although his most famous collections of stories, *The Jungle Books,* are set largely there, he lived less than a quarter of his seventy years in Asia. Of his eight children's books, one is set in the North Atlantic (*Captains Courageous*), three in England (*Stalky & Co.,*

Puck of Pook's Hill, and *Rewards and Fairies*), and one in a purely fantasy realm (*Just So Stories*). Only *The Jungle Books* and *Kim* are set in India.

When he was six, Kipling was sent to live in England under the guardianship of a Mrs. Halloway, an overly strict, religious zealot who allowed her son to bully the young boarder. The unhappy times of this period, which provided the basis for his short story "Baa Baa, Black Sheep," may well explain the unsentimental pictures of childhood Kipling was to present in the Mowgli stories and *Stalky & Co.* This latter book drew much of its material from the events of Kipling's next four years, when he was a student at the United Services College at Westward Ho in Devon. At age seventeen, Kipling returned to India as a reporter, and in 1892 he married Caroline Balestier. *The Jungle Books* appeared in 1894 and 1895 and *Captains Courageous,* published in 1897 on Kipling's return to England, was begun while he was living in Vermont.

With the exception of "Rikki-Tikki-Tavi," the tale of a young mongoose who kills two attacking cobras in gratitude to the human family who had rescued him from a flood, *The Jungle Books* are now read chiefly for the eight stories of Mowgli, the boy who was raised by wolves. Although these stories make use of Indian terrain and animals, they are almost purely literary creations, being in the tradition of legends of feral children, infants who have been reared by wild animals. Mowgli is Kipling's symbol of the good leader, the individual who, while walking alone, uses his wisdom and sense of discipline for the good of his people. His leadership is contrasted to that of the demagogue tiger, Shere Khan. However, he is a divided individual, torn between his love of and loyalty to the wild animals and his increasing attraction to human kind. In the end, his awareness that he is a man wins, and he returns to the hut of his mother and little brother.

In 1899, Kipling published his fourth children's book, *Stalky & Co.*, the work which, next to *The Jungle Books* and *Just So Stories,* is probably most read today. The nine stories of the book describe the school adventures of the poetic Beetle (who is not unlike the young Kipling), the patrician McTurk, and the ring-leading Stalky. The boys are vigorous opponents of bullies and sychophants and especially of the masters King, Prout, and Macrea, symbols of dictatorial and unjust authority. However, although characters and incidents are based on life, they are given a comic but unsentimental exaggeration which transforms them from life to literature. In 1901, Kipling published *Kim*, a book many Indian critics feel establishes him as the finest Anglo-Indian writer. Little read by children today, it is the story of an Irish boy who moves disguised among Indians on dangerous spy missions. *Kim* presents a rich and varied picture of India and a significant study of a character who, like Mowgli, is caught between two ways of life.

In 1902 Kipling published what has become his most enduring children's book, *Just So Stories*. The twelve tales in the collection are noted not only for their humor of incident and their gentle moral tone, but also for the style in which they are told and for Kipling's accompanying India ink drawings. Each story is a combination of two literary types: the moral fable and the pourquoi, or why, story explaining origins of animal and geographical characteristics. For example, the fact that the whale has a throat so constructed that he can't swallow large objects is attributed to his greed in early days. Throughout, one is aware of the kindly adult storyteller speaking quietly to a beloved audience but using such traditional formal devices of the storyteller as rhetorical questions and cumulative repetition. The illustrations, two to each story, give added dimensions for, with the accompanying glosses, they explain and expand upon ideas only lightly touched on in the story.

Although Kipling's literary fame declined during the decade, he was awarded the Nobel Prize for Literature in 1907, and in 1906 and 1910 wrote his last two children's books, the companion volumes *Puck of Pook's Hill* and *Rewards and Fairies*. The tales were originally told to his younger children, who appear in the stories as Daniel and Una and who, with the aid of Hobden, an old woodsman, come to discover Puck, the creature from folklore; they are introduced to such memorial figures from the Sussex past as a Norman knight and Roman legionnaire.

TIPS FOR PARENTS AND TEACHERS: In the early elementary grades, children who have read the *Just So Stories* can try to write their own pourquoi stories, based on unusual animals they know. They should be encouraged to recognize the ridiculousness of Kipling's explanations. In junior high school, the Mowgli stories can be contrasted to Jean George's *Julie of the Wolves*.

Klein, Norma *(1938 –)*
American

Born and raised in New York City, where she still resides with her husband and children, Norma Klein began her writing career publishing adult fiction. Dissatisfied with the books she read to her children, she felt challenged to produce a better one herself, and since then has written over a dozen, the majority of them novels for upper elementary and junior high readers. In her novels she portrays modern city children confronting contemporary problems. She has tried to avoid clichéd situations and has recognized that sexual awareness is part of the process of maturing. Her first children's novel, *Mom, the Wolf Man, and Me* (1972), is the story of Brett, child of an unwed mother. During a peace march on Washington, mother and daughter meet a man whom the mother eventually marries. The novel is an honest, unsentimental portrayal of the thoughts and experiences of the eleven-year-old heroine. Klein's other novels for children include *It's Not What You Expect* (1973), in which fourteen-year-old twins Oliver and Carla cope with the fact that their father has opted for bachelor life; *Taking Sides* (1974), about a girl who goes to live with her divorced father; and *It's OK If You Don't Love Me* (1977), the account of a first love between an outgoing New York girl and a shy midwestern boy.

TIPS FOR PARENTS AND TEACHERS: Klein's novels are most appropriate for upper elementary and junior high readers. Students experiencing problems similar to those of her characters may find reading these stories reassuring.

❤Konigsburg, Elaine *(1930 –)*
American

Born in New York City, and raised in small mill towns in Pennsylvania, Elaine Konigsburg studied to become a chemist and taught science in high school. After her children started school, she began her career as a writer. Never having read any stories which reflected the kind of world in which she grew up, she decided that she would write novels for her children that took place in the suburban, late 1960s environment with which they were familiar. Her first two books, which she also illustrated, *Jennifer, Hecate, Macbeth, William McKinley, and Me, Elizabeth* (1967) and *From the Mixed-Up Files of Mrs. Basil E. Frankweiler* (1967), received the Newbery Honor Medal and the Newbery Medal, respectively. This was the first time that an author had won the two awards in the same year.

Jennifer, Hecate, Macbeth grew out of the experiences of the author and her daughter Laurie, both of whom had been newcomers at various schools. It is the story of Elizabeth and her friend Jennifer, a black girl who proclaims herself a witch and who agrees to take Elizabeth as her apprentice. *From the Mixed-Up Files* is about Claudia Kincaid, who knew that "she could never pull off the old-fashioned kind of running away . . . . She didn't like discomfort." With her brother Jamie, she lives for a week in New York's Metropolitan Museum of Art. There she and her brother set out to prove that the museum's newly acquired statue, Angel, is by Michelangelo. Along the way, Claudia learns a great deal about herself.

The central figures of Elaine Konigsburg's next two novels, *About the B'nai Bagels* (1969) and *(George)* (1970), are boys. In the former, Mark Setzer learns that his mother and his brother will be manager and coach respectively of his Little League team. Ben Carr, hero of *(George)*, is a gifted child who has a sharp-tongued old man called George living inside of him. When Ben's father's new wife hears Ben talking to George in his sleep, she decides that the boy is schizophrenic and engages the services of a psychiatrist.

After publishing *Altogether, One at a Time* (1971), a collection of short stories, Elaine Konigsburg wrote *A Proud Taste for Scarlet and Miniver* (1973). It is the story of the twelfth-century queen Eleanor of Aquitaine, as retold by herself and three of her associates as they sit in Heaven eight hundred years after her death. Konigsburg's other historical novel, *The Second Mrs. Giaconda* (1975), is a study of Renaissance artist Leonardo da Vinci, as seen through the eyes of his irascible apprentice Salai.

Two of Mrs. Konigsburg's most recent stories deal with children who grow up in protected environments. In *The Dragon in the Ghetto Caper* (1974), Andrew Chronister moves out of his own world into a black ghetto. In *Father's Arcane Daughter* (1976), Winston and his apparently retarded sister Heidi are virtual prisoners in the home of their wealthy parents.

The majority of Konigsburg's characters are on journeys of discovery in which they must come to terms with their inner selves and with the people around them. It is a long process for, as Mark Setzer remarks after his Bar Mitzvah, "You don't become a man overnight. Because it is a becoming; becoming more than yourself." For some, the journey may never be completed, as is seen in the case of Leonardo da Vinci, torn between loyalty to his vision and the need for public approval. One must, as Ben Carr learns, be true to oneself, to the George within. This may involve being different, not in the showy way Elizabeth strives for during her early acquaintance with Jennifer, but in a deep inner way such as Claudia Kincaid discovers after meeting Mrs. Basil E. Frankweiler. Friendship is important for, according to Mark Setzer, "You need a friend who is a little different to rub against. That way you file down each other's rough edges." Elizabeth and Jennifer, Claudia and Jamie, Salai and Leonardo are such friends. However, as George tells Ben, it is not easy to achieve such relationships, for "friendship is the most unreasonable thing in the world." In growing up, it is also necessary to have parents who respect one's individuality. Mrs. Setzer realizes Mark's need for privacy, but the mother of Heidi and Winston imprisons them for her own selfish reasons.

Konigsburg's plots, like many of her titles, are audacious: a suburban grade school girl takes lessons to be a witch; a brother and sister hide out in a large museum; a boy's best friend lives inside his body; a sister returns home after having been missing for many years. Yet these unusual plots turn out to be structural metaphors for examining very real concerns: the problems of modern suburban children as they grow up.

TIPS FOR PARENTS AND TEACHERS: Students in the upper elementary and junior high grades will be most receptive to the themes of maturing presented in the Konigsburg novels. After reading a specific novel, students can consider the appropriateness of its unusual title. In discussing *From the Mixed Up Files*, readers can analyze not only the character of Claudia, but also of Mrs. Frankweiler, as it is revealed in her letter.

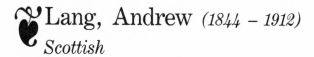

Lang, Andrew *(1844 – 1912)*
Scottish

Author of the famous "Colored Fairy Books," Andrew Lang grew up in Scotland, learning about the imaginative creatures of Scottish folklore and reading such noted writers as Charles Dickens and Sir Walter Scott. His childhood interests, combined with his studies at Oxford University in the new field of anthropology, led him into the field of children's literature. In 1884, he published *Princess Nobody: A Tale of Fairyland*, and, in 1888, *The Gold of Fairnilee*, a fantasy about hidden treasure in the Scottish Highlands. His most famous work for children, *The Blue Fairy Book*, a collection of well-known fairy tales, appeared in 1889. Over the next twenty-five years, he was to produce an annual volume for children, including eleven more "colored" fairy books, and collections of nursery rhymes, animal stories, and tales of heroes and saints, princes and princesses. He also wrote two more original fairy stories, *Prince Prigio* (1889) and *Prince Ricardo* (1893). During the 1880s, when most children's fiction was either realistic or didactic, Lang's colored fairy books helped reintroduce fantasy. Each of the twelve volumes contained over thirty stories from cultures around the world. *The Blue Fairy Book* included some of the best-known stories, while later books made many stories available to children for the first time. Much of the work for the books was done by his wife. While he selected most of the pieces, she often adapted them for younger readers.

The prefaces of several of the fairy books contain many important statements about the nature of fairytales and their relation to children. Lang notes that folktales are of ancient origin: "Men were much as children in their minds long ago, long, long ago, and so before they took to writing newspapers and sermons, and long poems, they told each other stories, such as you read in the fairy books. They believed . . . . Then, as the world became grownup, the fairy tales which were not written down would have been quite forgotten but that the old grannies remembered them, and told them to the little grandchildren." He states that the stories are similar in many different lands, that "a certain number of incidents are shaken into many varying combinations, like the fragments of colored glass in the kaleidoscope." In preparing the stories for younger readers, certain changes were made: "When the tales are found they are adapted to the needs of British children by various hands, the Editor doing little beyond guarding the interests of propriety, and taming down to mild reproofs the tortures inflicted on wicked stepmothers, and other naughty characters".

This is exactly what he did in his own stories, *Prince Prigio* and *Prince Ricardo*. In them are found such magic objects as seven-league boots and the cap of darkness, and such motifs as sibling rivalry and trapped maidens. In the first story, a disbelieving wife refuses to invite one of the fairies to the christening of the couple's long-awaited son, and as a result he is cursed with being too clever; moreover, he grows up being skeptical about the validity of magic and the existence of fairies. However, he falls in love, becomes a believer, and is instrumental in the destruction of a terrible firedrake. In the latter, Prigio's young son grows up believing in and making excessive use of magic. The king laments that the boy has things too easy, and he wishes that Ricardo had more intellect.

TIPS FOR PARENTS AND TEACHERS: The "Colored Fairy Books" provide a basic folktale collection for a school library. Reading in them, teachers can find many stories to complement those well-known to their classes. The stories from relatively unknown cultures can supplement social studies lessons.

The Story of Ferdinand, by Munro Leaf, illus. by Robert Lawson, Viking, New York, 1936. The layout of Lawson's page reveals that the people are too far away to see what is really making Ferdinand rage.

Lawson, Robert *(1892 – 1957)*
American

Born in New York City, Robert Lawson, the only person to win both the Caldecott and Newbery Medals, decided to become an artist after he won a poster contest at his Montclair, New Jersey, high school. He enrolled in the New York School of Fine and Applied Art where he studied for three years, and after World War I worked as a magazine illustrator and commercial artist. In 1930, he illustrated the first of over fifty books, Arthur Mason's *The Wee Men of Bally-Wooden*.

His illustrations for two books by Munro Leaf brought his work to national attention. Leaf wrote *The Story of Ferdinand* (1936), about a bull who preferred smelling flowers to fighting, specifically for Lawson to illustrate. The second book, *Wee Gillis* (1938), about a boy torn between living in the lowlands or highlands of Scotland, won Lawson a Caldecott Honor Medal.

In 1939, Lawson published *Ben and Me,* the first book he wrote and illustrated himself and the first of four stories recounting the lives of famous historical personages as seen from the points of view of their close animal friends. Amos (the name means a mouse, A-mos), the eldest of twenty-six children, sets out to make his way in the world, wanders into Benjamin Franklin's study, makes his home in the statesman's old fur hat, and, by his own account, influences Franklin's many achievements. Other books in the series are *I Discover Columbus* (1941), a parrot's version of the great voyage of discovery; *Mr. Revere and I* (1953), a proud old war-horse's view of the Revolution; and *Captain Kidd's Cat* (1956), a defense of the legendary pirate by his feline friend McDermot.

In 1940, Lawson won the Caldecott Medal for *They Were Strong and Good.* Criticized now for its portrayal of racial minorities, it was intended as a tribute not only to the author's parents and grandparents, but also to all the unknown Americans who "helped to make the United States the great nation it now is." A work limited by its text and often lifeless illustrations, it is historically important as one of a group of books which appeared shortly before and during World War II, extolling the history and culture of the United States. Like Maud and Miska Petersham, Ingri and Edgar d'Aulaire, James Daugherty, and Esther Forbes, Lawson sought, through children's books, to reaffirm values threatened by world war.

In 1945, *Rabbit Hill* (1944) was awarded a Newbery Medal. Set in the rural Connecticut countryside to which the Lawsons had moved in 1936, the story describes the reactions of the wild creatures to the arrival of New Folks at a nearby rundown house. To their joy, they discover that their human neighbors are sensitive and kind toward animals and, in addition to caring for sick or injured creatures, are willing to share the harvest of their garden with the animals. In *The Tough Winter* (1954), the New Folks move south for the winter, and the wild creatures must cope with a harsh caretaker, a vicious dog, and an unusually hard winter.

After 1945, Lawson devoted himself almost exclusively to writing and illustrating his own books. In addition to the stories noted above, he also wrote a series of humorous books about people with highly unlikely abilities or attributes. In *Mr. Wilmer* (1945), a downtrodden office worker discovers on his twenty-ninth birthday that he can talk to animals. In *The Fabulous Flight* (1949), young Peter Peabody Pepperell II begins to grow smaller and, when he shrinks to four inches in height, learns to fly on the back of Gus the Gull. The title hero of *Smeller Martin* (1950) finds that he can smell better than anyone else on earth. In the last book published before his death in 1957, *The Great Wheel* (1957), winner of a Newbery Honor Medal, Lawson described the invention of the ferris wheel and its success at the 1893 Chicago World's Fair.

Although his animal stories have been compared to the works of Beatrix Potter and to Kenneth Grahame's *The Wind in the Willows*, and have been placed by some critics in the centuries-old genre of the beast-fable, the animal creatures of Lawson's books are indigenous to the Connecticut countryside, use American speech rhythms, and display recognizably American character traits. They show the influence of Joel Chandler Harris' Uncle Remus stories, which Lawson heard often as a child.

Like his contemporary Robert McCloskey, Lawson often wrote stories resembling traditional American tall tales. The author asks the reader to accept an improbable premise: that a mouse, parrot, horse, or cat can exert a major influence on the actions of important figures of history; that a boy can grow down instead of up; or that a child can smell things miles away. When the reader accepts these premises, he is carried along by the author's ability to create convincing, humorous characters and often ludicrous events.

As an illustrator Lawson is noted not so much for inventiveness or historical influence as for the excellence of most of his work. In his best-known picture books, *The Story of Ferdinand* and *They Were Strong and Good*, he did not attempt to integrate pictures and text in the manner of his contemporaries Wanda Gág and Virginia Lee Burton. Rather, he placed words and illustrations on facing pages. Lawson worked in one color only, using contrasting spaces of light and dark and varying half-tones in the creation of carefully balanced pages which reflected the content of the narrative while adding elements of humor and emotion. In *Ferdinand* and *Rabbit Hill*, he revealed most fully his ability to create animal characters which, while depicted with anatomical accuracy, reflected a wide range of human traits.

TIPS FOR PARENTS AND TEACHERS: Children in the middle elementary grades should carefully study the illustrations in *Ferdinand*, noticing how they convey meanings not found in the words alone. In the upper grades, the "historical" novels make a humorous supplement to the study of great American heroes. *Wind in the Willows* by Kenneth Grahame can be contrasted to *Rabbit Hill* in the upper elementary grades.

Lear, Edward *(1812 – 1888)*
English

Although he is remembered for his humorous poetry for children, Edward Lear, who was born in London, was a generally lonely and unhappy person. One of twelve children, he suffered from epileptic seizures and was raised by his older sister. He became a famous painter and writer of travel books, but he spent much of his adult life travelling restlessly. However, he knew that he had a talent for making people laugh, and this he did in his poetry and the sketches that accompanied them.

His "career" as a poet began in 1832, when he was invited by the Earl of Derby to draw and paint the animals in the Earl's menagerie. He wrote to a friend, "The uniform apathetic tone assumed by lofty society irks me *dread-*

fully, nothing I long for half so much as to giggle heartily and to hop on one leg down the quiet gallery — but I dare not." However, he spent much time in the company of the Earl's grandchildren, reciting humorous poems to them, many of them limericks, and sketching amusing pictures which accompanied the poems. The year 1846 marked the highlight of his professional life. *Gleanings from the Menagerie and Aviary at Knowsley Hall* and *A Book of Nonsense* (which appeared under the pseudonym Derry Down Derry) were published, and he was invited to give drawing lessons to Queen Victoria.

In 1861 he published a revised and enlarged edition of *A Book of Nonsense* at his own expense, but this time under his own name. When it had achieved a moderate success, the publishing firm of Routledge purchased the copyright from him for 125 pounds. The book's popularity grew and nineteen editions appeared during the poet's lifetime. Lear published three more books of nonsense poetry during his life, including in them many of the story-poems he had written for young children he had met and befriended during his travels. *Nonsense Songs, Stories, Botany, and Alphabets* (1871) included such now well-known favorites as "The Owl and the Pussy-Cat" and "The Duck and the Kangaroo." *More Nonsense* (1872), published to capitalize on the popularity of the 1871 book, and *Laughable Lyrics* (1877) did not achieve the success of the earlier books.

Although art critics are now giving his paintings closer attention than they received during his lifetime, Lear is chiefly remembered for his children's poems and their accompanying illustrations. In writing them, Lear remarked that "Nonsense, pure and absolute, [was] my aim throughout." Children's poetry of the first half of the nineteenth century was somberly and often sternly religious or moral. Lear's poems were highly original. Along with Lewis Caroll and Laura Richards, he was responsible for introducing the notion that children's poetry could be humorous. The range of Lear's nonsense is wide: limericks, alphabets, cookery, botany, prose tales, and verse-stories; but only the limericks and story poems are still widely read.

Lear did not invent the four-lined stanza known as the limerick, but he was one of the first people to make it widely popular. In his limericks, Lear combines rigidity of form with wildness of character and situation. The first line opens with an introduction of an individual and the second line states his or her oddity: a physical deformity, a peculiarity of dress, an obsessive and eccentric habit or activity. The third line, which usually begins with "but," "so," "when," or "till," describes the consequences of the character's peculiarity for himself or others. The fourth line either presents the final outcome for the character, or restates his identity with an added qualifying adjective. Some of the adjectives applied to the characters suggest admiration: "amiable," "ingenious," and "funny." More often they are derogatory: "obnoxious," "mendacious," "vexatious," or "obsequious." The people in the limericks are absurd and eccentric, but the speaker is not; he is a normal person, detached, observing, commenting, and often judging.

Lear's story-songs, written later than the majority of the limericks, lack the gay hilarity of the earlier poems. Many critics have attributed this lack to the loneliness and unhappiness Lear felt as he grew older. The central characters are usually a group of incongruous and unlikely companions: an owl and a pussycat, a duck and a kangaroo, the nutcrackers and the sugartongs, a yonghy-bonghy-bo and Lady Jingly Jones. The main action is often a journey. The owl and the pussycat sail away forever, happy in their matrimonial devotion; the nutcrackers and sugartongs flaunt convention by leaving the table to ride away on a horse; and the daddy long-legs and the fly, ill-adapted to the world they live in, sail away to a land where they can forever play battlecock and shuttledore. Some of the one-way journeys are not happy: rejected in love, the yonghy-bonghy-bo sails sadly off; the dog with the luminous nose becomes a lonely wanderer searching for the jumblie who left him. If these diverse characters share anything in common, it is their unconventionality: they do not accept normal modes of behavior and often they react against the boredom of conventional life.

Although the characters and situations Lear depicts in his story-poems are interesting and humorous, they have been rendered memorable through his poetic craftsmanship. He carefully developed his rhyme schemes, rhythmic patterns, and stanza forms so that each story became important because of the manner of expression. He also used nonsense words of his own creation. Lear's poems were also distinguished by the spontaneous and humorous pen and ink sketches which accompanied them. It is surprising that many modern editions of Lear's works do not use these drawings, preferring instead to use the artwork of other illustrators. While their work is often very clever, it lacks the close unity with text found in Lear's own sketches.

TIPS FOR PARENTS AND TEACHERS: Limericks are best introduced in the middle elementary grades when the linguistic abilities of children are developing rapidly. If they hear dozens of limericks over several months, they become familiar with the form and can try writing their own, using literary characters or even the adults in their lives as their subjects. The characters in Lear's limericks provide excellent subjects for sketches in art classes.

Lee, Dennis *(1939 –   )*
Canadian

Born in Toronto, Canada, Dennis Lee had his first poem published in the magazine *Wee Wisdom* when he was four years old. After receiving a

Master of Arts from the University of Toronto, Lee taught at York University and the University of Toronto. In 1972, his *Civil Elegies and Other Poems* won the Canadian Governor-General's Award for Poetry.

Lee's interest in poetry for children began in the 1960s when he read Mother Goose rhymes for his two young daughters. He says that he began to "look for living nursery rhymes in the hockey sticks and high-rises that my children knew first hand." Drawing on the urban geography of Canada and using pronounced rhymes and rhythms, he created a series of poems which were published in 1970 as *Wiggle to the Laundromat*. New poems were written, older ones revised and issued together in 1974 as *Alligator Pie*, winner of the Canadian Library Association Children's Book of the Year award and one of the largest selling titles, children's or adult, in Canadian publishing history. In 1974, *Nicholas Knock*, a companion volume containing poems for older children was also published. A third collection, *Garbage Delight*, appeared in 1977 and also won the Canadian Children's Book of the Year award.

The poems in *Alligator Pie* are a mixture of chants and nonsense. The main themes of *Nicholas Knock and Other Poems* are the joy of life and the need for true liberty. The title poem is about a boy who discovers a silver honkabeast, symbol of imaginative freedom. He persists in affirming his vision against all adult opposition: parents, psychologists, police, a judge of the Supreme Court. In *Garbage Delight*, there are several of what Lee has called his "raunchy poems," pieces of nonsense and silliness. However, the dominant tone of the book is a new one, as many poems explore the quiet inner life of a small child. They celebrate what Lee refers to as "the homing instinct" in children. In 1983 Lee published *Jelly Belly*, more children's poems.

TIPS FOR PARENTS AND TEACHERS: Although written within a Canadian context, Lee's nonsense poems contain typical modern situations. *Alligator Pie* and *Garbage Delight* appeal to lower and middle elementary aged children: *Nicholas Knock* appeals to those in upper elementary or junior high school.

LeGuin, Ursula K. *(1929 –)*
American

Born in Berkeley, California, the daughter of an anthropologist and a writer, Ursula K. LeGuin began writing at an early age. After graduating from Radcliffe College in 1951 and from Columbia University in 1952, she married Charles LeGuin, an historian. Ursula K. LeGuin began submitting science fiction stories to magazines in the 1960s and, in 1966, published *Rocannon's World*, the first of her six science fiction novels for adults. The best-known of these is *The Left Hand of Darkness* (1969), winner of the Nebula and Hugo Awards, the two foremost science fiction citations.

In the 1960s, LeGuin was invited by Herman Schien, publisher of Parnassus Press, to write a fantasy for children. She was given complete freedom and, drawing on earlier stories of hers in which wizards lived and worked in a self-contained archipelago, created *A Wizard of Earthsea* (1968). It is the story of Ged, a boy who is trained to become a wizard. Filled with jealousy of a fellow student and pride in his own ability, he calls forth a dark power from the underworld. He is forced to track it down on a long journey across the seas and islands of Earthsea, and, in so doing, matures and faces the fact that the shadow is really his own darker self.

The second book of "The Earthsea Trilogy," *The Tombs of Atuan* (1971), winner of a Newbery Honor Medal, is set on an island where priestesses worship the nameless shadow of death. The current high priestess, Arha, a young woman who has been raised at Atuan since she was five years old, is filled with self-doubts and inner conflicts. In *The Farthest Shore* (1972), it is discovered that the powers of magic are disappearing from Earthsea. With the youthful Prince Arren, Ged travels through the archipelago searching for the causes. In 1976, LeGuin published a realistic novel for adolescents. *Very Far Away from Anywhere Else* is the story of Owen Griffiths, who wishes to become a great scientist.

Although "The Earthsea Trilogy" has often been compared to J.R.R. Tolkien's *Lord of the Rings* and C.S. Lewis's *Chronicles of Narnia*, it presents a unique vision. Earthsea, a world which LeGuin says she discovered rather than invented, is a land in which magic is the dominant force. Wizards, or mages, not scientists, are the wisest people. However, an individual who possesses magical powers must also accept moral responsibility for his use of them. The basis of the magic of Earthsea resides in the power of naming. Each object and individual has a true name which represents its essential nature. In knowing true names, one can control a person or thing. Thus, one must guard his own true name carefully, revealing it only to those he trusts.

Each of the Earthsea books deals with the growth to maturity of a central figure: Ged, in *A Wizard of Earthsea*; Arha, in *The Tombs of Atuan*; and Arren, in *The Farthest Shore*. At the end of *A Wizard of Earthsea*, it is reported that "Ged had neither lost nor won but, naming the shadow of his death with his own name, had made himself whole: a man: who, knowing his whole true self cannot be used or possessed by any power other than himself, and whose life therefore is lived for life's sake and never in the service of ruin, or pain, or hatred, or the dark." At the conclusion of *The Tombs of Atuan*, Arha discovers her true name, Tenar, rejects Atuan, is reborn, and returns to the world of light "like a child coming home." In *The Farthest Shore*, Ged tells Arren that he must accept the fact of his mortality: "You enter your manhood at the gate of death."

TIPS FOR PARENTS AND TEACHERS: Readers in the junior high grades can examine the character development of the main figures in the Earthsea books and can debate the moral issues found in them.

L'Engle, Madeleine *(1918 –)*
American

Madeleine L'Engle lived in New York City until she was twelve, when she moved with her parents to Europe, where she reluctantly attended boarding school. After graduating from Smith College in 1941, she met and married Hugh Franklin, an actor. In 1949, she published her first children's novel, *And Both Were Young*, the story of a girl unhappy at being sent to a boarding school. Her second novel, intended for a teenage audience, *Camilla Dickinson*, appeared two years later and portrays the title heroine's coming to terms with the imperfections of her unhappily married parents.

The life of the Franklin family provided the basis for three of L'Engle's books. *Meet the Austins* (1960) describes the impact on the family when it adopts a spoiled and bad-mannered child. *The Moon by Night* (1963) draws on a cross-country camping trip the Franklins made and is an account of twelve-year-old Vicki Austin's growth of self-awareness. In *The Young Unicorns* (1968), the Austins have moved to New York where they meet Emily Gregory, a twelve-year-old blind musician, and her friend Josiah Davidson, once a member of a street gang. In this story, the Austin children confront threatening forces of evil.

In 1962, L'Engle published her best-known novel, *A Wrinkle in Time*, winner of the Newbery Medal. Meg Murry and her young brother Charles Wallace, helped by three supernatural beings who take the form of funny old ladies, travel through the universe in search of Meg's missing scientist father. They arrive at a planet which has been reduced to a place of mindless conformity, where Charles Wallace falls under the control of the evil brain which rules the place. Aided only by her courage and her love for her brother, Meg rescues the boy.

The Murry family appears in what L'Engle has called companion stories rather than sequels. In *A Wind in the Door* (1973), dark forces threaten civilization in the form of mitochondria, small organisms living within the blood, and Meg must again save Charles Wallace. In *A Swiftly Tilting Planet* (1978), Meg has married her high school sweetheart, Calvin O'Keefe, and Charles Wallace must journey through time, existing within others' bodies, in his attempts to defeat the evil Madog.

Calvin O'Keefe plays roles in two other L'Engle stories. In *The Arm of the Starfish* (1965), Adam Eddington, a young biology student who travels to Portugal to be an assistant to Dr. O'Keefe, becomes caught up in an international plot to steal O'Keefe's secrets. *Dragons in the Waters* (1976) includes two of the O'Keefe children, Charles and Poly, who, travelling with their father aboard a ship bound for Venezuela, become involved in murder and intrigue.

Among L'Engle's other children's novels are *The Twenty-Four Days before Christmas* (1964), about seven-year-old Vicki Austin, and *The Journey with Jonah* (1968), and *Dance in the Desert* (1969), which are based on Biblical themes. She has also written adult novels and books of essays.

Critics have often noted that L'Engle's plots are extravagant, even audacious. *The Arm of the Starfish* is an international spy thriller, with incident heaped on incident; *Dragons in the Waters* is a murder mystery. In *A Wrinkle in Time*, Meg and her brother travel across space through a process known as tessering. In *A Wind in the Door*, the travel is into the human body, and, in *A Swiftly Tilting Planet*, non-corporeally, through time. However, L'Engle's plots are used as vehicles to express her major themes: the importance of the family and of love, the need for individual growth, and the ever-present danger of evil forces.

The family is the focal point of nearly all of L'Engle's stories, and during them the central figures grow in self-confidence and self-awareness. At the end of *The Moon by Night*, Vicki makes a statement that could be made by many of L'Engle's young characters: "The last time I'd sat on the rock, all the pieces of the puzzle that made up my picture had been scattered, and now they had come together I knew who I was. I was myself." The process of growth is difficult, for, as Adam Eddington discovers, it involves making choices between conflicting loyalties and deciding what, if anything, really is truth.

L'Engle explores the process of the individual's growth most successfully in *A Wrinkle in Time*. Meg Murry is insecure in herself and in her relations with her family and the larger social world. "I hate being an oddball," she laments. However, she learns that she must develop on her own and at her own pace, and during her adventures she discovers her inner strengths: "If anyone had told her only the day before that she, Meg, the snaggle-tooth, the myopic, the clumsy, would be taking a boy's hand to offer him comfort and strength . . . the idea would have been beyond her comprehension. But now it seemed . . . natural." Recognizing her responsibility for her own actions, she performs an heroic rescue.

L'Engle's treatment of her third major theme, the confrontation between good and evil, has been criticized by many reviewers, who feel she allows philosophizing to overwhelm narrative. While her characters do sometimes engage in what could be called theological dialogues, most often the themes are embodied within the plot. Mr. Cutter is intent on seizing Dr. O'Keefe's secrets not to produce human good, but to augment his power and wealth. In *A Wrinkle in Time* the dark cloud which has overwhelmed many planets now threatens Earth.

TIPS FOR PARENTS AND TEACHERS: L'Engle's books are best read in junior high when students are able to consider the moral issues they embody. In examining *A Wrinkle in Time*, readers should notice how the geography of the story provides a map of Meg's character development. Her visits to each planet and her actions and reactions on Camazotz provide her with opportunities to grow as an individual.

Lent, Blair *(1930 –)*
American

Born in Boston, Blair Lent studied at the Boston Museum of Fine Arts School and in Switzerland and Italy. His first two children's books appeared in 1964. *Pistachio*, based on his memory of a small circus he saw in France, was written by himself. *The Wave* was a Japanese folktale adapted by Margaret Hodges and was named a Caldecott Honor Book. In 1966, Lent published *John Tabor's Ride*, his own adaptation of a New England legend and a book he calls his favorite. That year, he also illustrated *Baba Yaga*, the story of an old Russian witch. Lent's early books were executed in cardboard-cuts, a medium he liked because "my ideas [were] realized much sooner," and often used only three colors, chosen to suggest both the mood of the story and its setting.

Lent has continued to illustrate retellings of old stories. In 1968, he illustrated Hans Christian Andersen's *The Little Match Girl*, trying to avoid in the pictures much of the sentimentality of the text. The same year he illustrated Elphinstone Dayrell's adaptation of the African pourquoi tale *Why*

The Sun and Moon Live in the Sky, a Caldecott Honor Book. In his pictures, Lent depicted the story as a pageant in which members of an African tribe played the various roles. For Arlene Mosel's retelling of the Chinese tale *Tikki Tikki Tembo* (1968), the story of a little boy who nearly drowns because of his exceptionally long, tongue-twisting name, Lent approximated the style of Chinese art. He received a third Caldecott Honor Medal for *The Angry Moon* (1970), William Sleator's version of a West Coast Indian tale.

Blair Lent was awarded the Caldecott Medal for his illustrations of Arlene Mosel's adaptation of the Japanese folktale *The Funny Little Woman* (1972). In this story, a woman chases a rolling rice ball into a hole in the ground and is captured by the Oni, wicked subterranean monsters.

Although Lent has changed his medium from the early cardboard-cuts to washes and has moved from the use of muted colors to vivid ones, all of his work displays a common quality: its ability to portray a sense of movement within individual pictures and between pictures. He has acknowledged the influence of motion picture techniques: "I think of the visual movement from page to page, as well as about 'long shots' and 'closeups'." In *The Funny Little Woman,* full-color illustrations of the heroine show her progress into and out of the ground. In many of the illustrations are black and white sketches which reveal what occurs above ground while the woman is a captive of the Oni: the seasons pass as the house is deserted; but as spring arrives an old man enters the house and helps the woman in her return.

TIPS FOR PARENTS AND TEACHERS: In examining *The Wave,* middle elementary aged children can notice how the illustrations create the sense of the tidal wave. In studying *The Funny Little Woman,* they can comment on the significance of the black and white illustrations to the meaning of the story.

Lewis, Clive Staples *(1898 – 1963)*
English

Born in Belfast, Ireland, C.S. Lewis as a child wrote a series of stories on animal land in which the major characters were chivalrous mice, and read widely, being particularly fond of the tales of Beatrix Potter and Norse myths. After his mother's death and his brother's departure for school, Lewis's life was "increasingly one of solitude." To prepare for his entrance exams to the university, he was sent to live with his tutor, P.L. Kirkpatrick, in

Surrey, where he read the English novelists and discovered the nineteenth-century Scottish fantasist, George MacDonald. In 1917, he entered Oxford University, but shortly after enlisted in the armed services. He was injured in France and returned to England, graduating in 1922. As a teenager, Lewis was beset with religious doubts and only during his twenties did he gradually regain the Christian faith which was to influence virtually all his writings.

After graduation, Lewis began teaching at Magdalen College, Oxford, where he formed a friendship with J.R.R. Tolkien, author of *The Lord of the Rings*. In 1954, he became Professor of Medieval and Renaissance Literature at Cambridge, where he taught for the rest of his life. Lewis was a prolific writer of essays, literary criticism, and theology, and in 1938, he wrote an adult science fiction novel which embodied many of his religious and philosophical beliefs. *Out of the Silent Planet* was followed by two sequels: *Perelandra* (1943) and *That Hideous Strength* (1945).

In 1950, Lewis published his first children's novel, *The Lion, the Witch, and the Wardrobe*. Although he was later to say that "when I wrote The Lion, I had no notion of writing the others," the idea of the Kingdom of Narnia held the author's interest and a new volume appeared annually for six years: *Prince Caspian* (1951), *The Voyage of the Dawn Treader* (1952), *The Silver Chair* (1953), *The Horse and His Boy* (1954), *The Magician's Nephew* (1955), and *The Last Battle* (1956). *The Last Battle* was awarded the Carnegie Medal, not only for its own excellence, but also in recognition of Lewis's achievements in the entire series.

The Lion, the Witch, and the Wardrobe is the story of four brothers and sisters, Peter, Susan, Lucy, and Edmund Pevensie, who have been sent to live in the country house of Professor Kirk during the air raids of World War II. Exploring the house, they enter an old wardrobe and find themselves in Narnia, where they meet the great lion Aslan and help him to overthrow the evil White Witch. Peter is established as High King and, with the other children, rules Narnia for many years. One day, the four find their way back to the wardrobe where they discover that, although years have passed in Narnia, only moments have gone by in their own world.

At the beginning of *Prince Caspian* (1951), the children, while sitting in a railway station, are again transported to Narnia where, although it is only a year later in their own lives, hundreds of years have passed in the other world. With Aslan's aid, the children defeat the usurpers of the Narnian throne, establish Caspian as king, and return to England.

In *The Voyage of the Dawn Treader*, Edmund and Lucy, with their thoroughly unpleasant cousin Eustace Clarence Scrubb, find themselves aboard a dragon-shaped ship with Caspian. It is three Narnian years later, and the king, his lands in order, searches for seven loyal lords who had disappeared during the reign of the evil usurper, Miraz. In *The Silver Chair,* Eustace and his schoolmate Jill return to Narnia, seventy years later in Caspian's reign. Jill and Eustace are charged by Aslan to find Caspian's missing son, Rilian; with the aid of Puddleglum, a Marsh-Wiggle who is pessimistic but loyal and brave, they free the boy from the spells of the Green Witch. In *The Horse and His Boy,* which takes place during Peter's reign, a young boy turns out to be Col, missing heir to the throne of Archenland.

With the sixth and seventh volumes, the series assumes an overall shape. *The Magician's Nephew* tells of the creation of Narnia and the initial entry of human beings into that land. At the beginning of the twentieth century, Digory Kirk and Polly Plummer are sent into the dead world of Charn, where the curious Digory rings a bell which releases the evil Queen Jadis from her centuries-long state of suspended animation. Inadvertently, they bring her back to London and then, with Uncle Andrew and a cab driver, into Narnia just as the mighty lion Aslan is singing it into creation. Aslan, who is aware of the evil queen's presence, announces to the talking animals that "although the world is not five hours old, evil has already entered," and proclaims that as Adam's race has done the harm (Digory's ringing of the bell), "Adam's race shall help to heal it."

The Last Battle is set entirely within Narnia. Shift, an ape, joins forces with the evil Calormene people to discredit Aslan and take over Narnia. King Tirian, a descendant of Caspian, fights the last battle of Narnia, aided by his remaining loyal subjects and Eustace and Jill. However, "Narnia is no more," and he enters through a stable door into a new world from which, along with the human children, the good creatures of Narnia enter into Aslan's country. There, Lewis writes, "we can most truly say that they all lived happily ever after."

Each of the seven books is founded on a basic premise: the introduction of ordinary boys and girls into a strange and often perilous universe. Here they experience the exciting and dangerous adventures which form the plots of the stories. As Lewis once wrote, "Dangers, of course, there must be: how else can you keep a story going?" During the stories the children are tested. Edmund, seduced by the Turkish Delight offered by the White Witch, and the disgruntled Eustace, turned into a dragon, require the grace of Aslan to be saved. Lucy, looking through a magical book, and Digory, presented with the opportunity to eat the forbidden fruit from Aslan's garden, find inner strengths to resist selfish temptations. All of the human children, familiar only with life in their schools and homes, develop the courage necessary to fight fearsome opponents and bring peace to the good subjects of Narnia.

The inhabitants of Narnia can be divided into three groups: human beings and other aliens, talking and dumb animals, and mythological creatures. Only the descendants of the cabby and his wife can be kings and queens of Narnia. Many human beings, including the Calormenes and the pirates who support Miraz, are evil. Queen Jadis and the White and Green Witches are evil forces from beyond the Narnian universe. The talking beasts seem to be the chosen creatures of Aslan, existing during better times in a golden age with the other Narnians, including the various satyrs, nymphs, dryads, fauns, and giants.

The central figure of Narnia is the great lion Aslan, creator, destroyer, protector, and judge. He is above all a being who inspires awe and, in *The Lion, the Witch, and the Wardrobe,* he is described as "good and terrible at the same time." Even to those he loves, he is demanding. The human children are given severe tests by him, and, although they greet him with joy, they treat him with reverence, respect, and a touch of fear.

In creating the *Chronicles of Narnia,* Lewis drew on his memories of his own childhood and his walks in the Irish and English countryside, his wide reading in Greek and classical mythology and English literature, and his hard-earned Christianity. Probably the greatest influence on the *Chronicles* was the Bible, as can be seen in the accounts of the sacrificial death of Aslan and the creation and final destruction of Narnia. However, in his use of his sources, Lewis does not merely transplant material, he tranforms it, making it an integral part of the imaginative world of the books.

As a result of the success of the *Chronicles of Narnia,* Lewis was often asked to present his views of children's literature. While admitting that a writer of children's stories faced limitations of vocabulary and subject matter, and could not include "reflective and analytical passages," he did not believe that juvenile stories were inferior forms of writing. In his best known essay on the subject, "On Three Ways of Writing for Children," he stated that "a children's story which is enjoyed only by children is a bad children's story," and that one wrote "a children's story because a children's story [was] the best art form for something you [had] to say." He respected his young readers: "We must treat children as equals in that area where we are their equals. Our superiority consists partly . . . in the fact that we are better at telling stories than they are."

TIPS FOR PARENTS AND TEACHERS: In the middle and upper elementary grades, students are able to examine the Narnia books as studies of the moral growth of the characters. In each of the stories, the children are placed in situations where they are tested and must make difficult ethical choices. Students can hypothesize on what might have happened if characters made other choices than those they did.

Frederick, by Leo Lionni, Pantheon, New York, 1967. Lionni uses Frederick's position on the page to indicate his relationship to his fellow mice.

Lionni, Leo *(1910 –   )*
American

Born in Amsterdam, Leo Lionni and his family moved to the United States in 1939. He worked as an art director for a Philadelphia advertising firm and for *Fortune* magazine, as chairman of the graphic design department of Parsons School of Design, and as president of the American Institute of Graphic Design. Lionni's career in children's literature began in 1959 with the publication of *Little Blue and Little Yellow*, a story about two patches of different color who learn about friendship. Since that time, he has published fifteen more picture books. *Inch by Inch* (1961), *Swimmy* (1963), *Frederick* (1967), and *Alexander and the Wind-up Mouse* (1969) were named Caldecott Honor books.

Lionni approaches each book individually, searching for the appropriate medium or style for each story. His greatest success has come in the use of collage, using different shapes, colors, and textures of paper to express the emotional tones of the various stories. With each of his books he has varied the style and/or medium to achieve suitable effects. In *Swimmy* he uses washes to create the underwater settings; in *Tico and the Golden Wings* (1964) pure gold color is employed with dazzling results; actual letters of type make up part of the illustrations in *The Alphabet Tree* (1968); and different colored comic strip balloons enclose the dialogue of the vastly different fleas of *I Want to Stay Here! I Want to Go There! A Flea Story* (1977). In all his artwork, Lionni's background as a graphic designer and advertiser is evident: shapes, space, and color are used to convey his themes.

Lionni has freely acknowledged that his stories are moral in intent, calling them fables. His major subject is the individual's coming to understand and accept himself and his place in the world. "The protagonist of my books is often an individual who is, because of special circumstances, an outcast, a rebel, a victim, or a hero." The first step is for the hero to accept himself as a unique entity. In *A Color of His Own* (1975), a chameleon must realize that he cannot be like other animals; Alexander discovers that it is better to be a real than a wind-up mouse; and Frederick is true to his own poetic being. However, friendship is vital, as is seen in *Little Blue and Little Yellow* and *A Color of His Own*. Each individual must also contribute in his own way to the general well-being.

TIPS FOR PARENTS AND TEACHERS: In the early elementary grades, Lionni's books can be used to show how pictures contribute to a story's meaning. In *Frederick*, changing colors reveal the varying emotions of the mouse family; in *Swimmy*, the hero's place on the page indicates how successful he is in his quest.

Little Red Riding Hood
Folktale

The first written version of this widely known story of the little girl attacked by a deceitful wolf appeared in Charles Perrault's *Histoires ou Contes du temps passé, avec des Moralités* (1697). Perrault may have drawn the story from an earlier work, possibly "The Old Grandmother," an old French tale in which a little girl escapes from a wolf by going outside to relieve herself. It is highly probable that his version provided the basis for the other well-known retelling, the Grimm Brothers' "Little Red-Cap." Between them, these two retellings have provided the basis for all subsequent adaptations. Interestingly, many modern adaptors have objected to the explicit violence found in both Perrault's and the Grimms' stories, particularly in the former, and have modified or removed it.

The Brothers Grimm and Perrault, while using the same characters and the same conflict, have told substantially different stories. In Perrault's, the wolf devours the grandmother and then the girl and the story ends. The Grimms extend the story: girl and grandmother are rescued from the wolf's stomach by a passing hunter, they place stones in the beast's stomach, and he dies from the great weight. When the little girl meets another wolf, she is much wiser, running to her grandmother's and helping to destroy the animal. In the former, the girl's fate is presented as an example for the reader to learn from; in the latter, the girl herself learns.

Both versions of the story have attracted a great deal of critical attention. Perrault's has been interpreted as an explanation of the fate of an innocent child in the world of experience. As Perrault states in his moral, "Children, especially pretty, nicely brought-up young ladies, ought never to talk to strangers; if they are foolish enough to do so, they should not be surprised if some greedy wolf consumes them . . . . Smooth-tongued, smooth-pelted wolves are the most dangerous beasts of all."

The Grimms' tale has been interpreted in several ways. First, it may be taken as a parable about obedience; the heroine's troubles begin when she ignores her mother's orders to stay on the path. Second, it has been related to old myths in which the sun was believed to have been swallowed every night by a monster. Third, it has been called a study of growth to maturity. Psychologist Bruno Betttelheim has noted that in the earlier stages of the story, Red-Cap, gathering flowers, has allowed self-indulgence to take precedence over duty and, in so doing, has paved the way to her "death." However, she is reborn a wiser individual: "Little Red Riding Hood lost her childish innocence as she encountered the dangers residing in herself and the world, and exchanged it for a wisdom that only the 'twice born' can possess."

TIPS FOR PARENTS AND TEACHERS: Younger readers may find the Perrault version more distressing than that of the Grimms. In the middle elementary grades, children can discuss the implications of the differences between the two versions.

Livingston, Myra Cohn *(1926 –   )*
American

Born in Omaha, Nebraska, Myra Cohn Livingston began writing poetry while she was a student at Sarah Lawrence College. Her first book, *Whispers and Other Poems* (1958), is a collection of little poems which reflect the world as perceived by a small child. In the title poem, whispers are said to "tickle" and to be "as soft as skin / letting the words curl in." In subsequent years, Myra Livingston published several more volumes of poetry: *Wide Awake* (1959), *The Moon and a Star* (1965), *Old Mrs. Twindlytart* (1967), *A Crazy Flight* (1969), *The Malibu* (1974), *The Way Things Are* (1974), and *4-Way Stop* (1976). In addition, she has written several stories which are noted for their rhythmic prose and has edited six poetry anthologies.

In her poetry, Myra Cohn Livingston seldom uses rigid, conventional stanza patterns, believing that the theme or emotion of a poem should suggest its form. Livingston deals with a variety of subjects: the passage of the seasons, holidays, the world of nature, the weather, city life, imaginary beings, pollution, strange adults. However, all are written from the point of view of the child of between ages four and ten, whose way of seeing the world is as important as that world itself. Often the focus is on the speaker's sense of self. As the idea is expressed in "One for Novella Nelson," "Me, I'm not alone./I've got myself."

TIPS FOR PARENTS AND TEACHERS: Individual poems by Livingston can be related to subjects in the curriculum and to special events of the school year. Older students can imitate specific poems, trying to use the same devices to create their own messages.

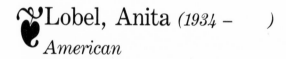

Lobel, Anita *(1934 –)*
American

Born in Krakow, Poland, Anita Lobel spent time in a German concentration camp during World War II. She studied art in Sweden and at the Pratt Institue, where she met and later married Arnold Lobel. Upon graduation, she worked as a textile designer and, in 1965, published her first children's book, *Sven's Bridge,* which she has called "a deliberately nostalgic and affectionate tribute to the folk designs of Sweden." Her second book, *The Troll Music* (1966), is a humorous folk-like story about a band of strolling musicians whose instruments are bewitched by an angry troll. *Potatoes, Potatoes* (1967) has an anti-war theme, while *The Seamstress of Salzburg* (1970) uses a traditional fairy-tale pattern. Anita Lobel's recent books include *Under a Mushroom* (1970), *A Birthday for the Princess* (1973), and *King Rooster, Queen Hen* (1975), the last written in an easy-to-read format. She has illustrated many books, including Meindert de Jong's *Puppy Summer* (1966), F.N. Monjo's *Indian Summer* (1968), Doris Orgel's *Little John* (1972), and Arnold Lobel's *How the Rooster Saved the Day* (1976). *On Market Street* (1981), also written by her husband, is an ABC book.

Anita Lobel's illustrations parallel her stylized narratives. She has said that she imagines her stories as plays or pageants and also that she has been influenced by medieval tapestries. *The Troll Music,* she wrote, "was mainly inspired by the bottom parts of medieval tapestries with the vegetation and little animals running around."

TIPS FOR PARENTS AND TEACHERS: A study of Lobel's illustrations, particularly the decorative elements, provides a lead into art classes in the upper elementary grades. Like Lobel, students can illustrate an event from the folktale of a specific culture, trying to approximate that culture's artistic styles.

❧Lobel, Arnold *(1933 –   )*
American

Born in Los Angeles, Arnold Lobel grew up in Schenectady, New York, and attended Pratt Institute in New York, where he met Anita Kempler, whom he married in 1955. He began illustrating in the late 1950s, and has worked on such books as Charlotte Zolotow's *The Quarreling Book* (1963), Edward Lear's *The New Vestments* (1970), and the Grimm Brothers' *Hansel and Gretel* (1971). For his illustrations to Cheli Ryan's *Hildilid's Night* (1971), he received a Caldecott Honor Medal. Lobel wrote his first book, *A Zoo for Mister Muster* in 1962. A year later, he published *A Holiday for Mister Muster.* Since then he has written and illustrated twelve books. *How the Rooster Saved the Day* (1977) was illustrated by his wife.

Writing about the characters in his stories, Lobel has stated, "I find that the majority of my books have as their central characters 'child substitutes' rather than real children." Mr. Muster has a child-like wonder; the hero of *The Man Who Took Indoors Out* (1974) has a child's ability to solve problems in a non-logical manner; Toad, of the "Frog and Toad" series, is childish and depends more than he realizes on his sensible friend Frog.

Lobel has established himself as a master of the easy-reader book form. The best known of his several titles are *Frog and Toad Are Friends* (1970), a Caldecott Honor Book; *Frog and Toad Together* (1972), a Newbery Honor Book; *Mouse Tales* (1972); *Frog and Toad All Year* (1976); and *Mouse Soup* (1977). Using simple words and sentence structure, he is able to give his language a poetic rhythm and make it a vehicle for his delicate characterization. His illustrations, using pale washes and few details, enhance the moods and themes of the stories without overwhelming the words. Lobel was awarded the Caldecott Medal for *Fables* (1980), a series of twenty short tales, each one illustrated with a full-page, full-color picture. Like his "Frog and Toad" series, they present simple, but profound morals.

TIPS FOR PARENTS AND TEACHERS: In addition to providing beginning reading material, Lobel's easy-readers also contain important concepts which early elementary aged children should be encouraged to discuss. Those children who enjoy writing stories can make up their own Frog and Toad or Mouse tales; others can consider how they would have reacted in situations like those of the characters.

Mathis, Sharon Bell *(1937 –)*
American

Born in Atlantic City, New Jersey, black American author Sharon Bell Mathis grew up in Brooklyn. Later she was to recall, "There's very little that can happen that hasn't happened in Brooklyn. So I grew up seeing some very shocking things but some very marvelous things. And I didn't forget any of it." An important discovery of her high school years was Richard Wright's powerful autobiography *Black Boy.* It served as her introduction to the tradition of black American literature which had been ignored in her high school curriculum. She began writing as a teenager, studied literature at Morgan State College, and contributed confession-type stories to a magazine brought out by the publishers of *Ebony.*

Mathis has published four novels. *Sidewalk Story* (1971) tells of a little girl's efforts on behalf of a family which has been evicted from its tenement. In *Teacup Full of Roses* (1972), she portrays powerfully the violent and troubled life of a black family. *Listen for the Fig Tree* (1974), considered by many critics her best novel, is the story of Muffin Johnson. Blind, Muffin must fend for herself and must help her mother, still distraught over the murder of her husband a year earlier. In *The Hundred Penny Box* (1975), winner of a Newbery Honor Medal, she sensitively explores the relationship between a boy and his one-hundred-year-old great-great-aunt. Mathis has also written *Ray Charles* (1973), a biography of the blind black musician.

Sharon Bell Mathis has written that her books are tributes to black children: "I wrote for them, with them in mind, with an idea of some of the problems that they have, which are awesome at times, but still with some of the joy of being black. Because I think there's more joy in being black than there is pain." The children in her books live in a violent world, where there is much pain, and often death, and yet they respond heroically: "You'll notice that most of the children in my books, if not all of them, are very independent, because I think that's a very special thing with black children in America. Most of them can manage, because they have to. Sometimes the parents are unable to do what they ought to do."

TIPS FOR PARENTS AND TEACHERS: Upper elementary and junior high school readers should notice how and why the characters in Mathis's novels develop courage and how they relate to the adults in their lives.

Mayne, William *(1928 –)*
English

Born in Kingston-upon-Hull, in Yorkshire, William Mayne decided to become a writer when he was eight years old. In 1953, at age twenty-five, he published his first book, *Follow the Footprints*, and he first received critical attention in 1955 with *A Swarm in May*, the first of four books based on his boyhood experiences at the Choir School in Canterbury. The others are *Chorister's Cake* (1956), *Cathedral Wednesday* (1960), and *Words and Music* (1963). Mayne's output has been prolific, over fifty books in twenty years, one of them *A Grass Rope* (1957), a winner of the Carnegie Medal. His best work can be divided into three categories: realistic experiences of children growing up; attempts to solve mysteries from the past; and time travel.

The Blue Boat (1957) and *Sand* (1964) are representative of the first type of story. In *The Blue Boat*, two boys are able to transfer their routine vacation hikes and exploration trips into great imaginary adventures, often terrifying themselves but escaping the repressive and boring life at the home of their hosts. *Sand* is set along the coast of England in a tiny village constantly battered by wind and sand. Ainsley and his friends discover a long-abandoned railroad which they work at unearthing. But more important, they discover ways of taunting Alice and her friends, in whom they are interested but before whom they are awkward.

Two of Mayne's best stories, *A Grass Rope* and *Ravensgill* (1970), set in the Yorkshire moors, focus on young people of the present trying to find solutions to mysteries from the past. In the former, Nan Owland and her younger sister Mary, with a neighbor boy, Adam Forrest, are puzzled about the old legend of hounds and a unicorn who mysteriously disappeared on the night that an innkeeper eloped with the daughter of Lord Owland. *Ravensgill* deals with a mystery of the more recent past. Bob White discovers that his grandfather had been accused of murdering his father-in-law and, in the course of the story, uncovers facts which prove the innocence of the now long-dead man.

The best-known of his books, *Earthfasts* (1966) and *A Game of Dark* (1971), are time fantasies. In the former, David Wix and Keith Heseltine are astonished when an eighteenth-century drummer boy appears out of a mound (or earthfast) in the ground. The drummer carries with him a candle he had picked up in his own time and, when it is left in the twentieth century, it unleashes strange and powerful forces which lead to the apparent death of David and to Keith's taking the candle into the depths of the cave from which it had come.

The central character of *A Game of Dark* exists in two times, moving back and forth between them in the course of the novel. In the twentieth century he is Donald, living with a religious mother and a dying father for whom he feels no love. In the Middle Ages he is Jackson, who becomes successively a page, a squire, and a field knight whose duty is to slay a dragon, or worm, which is preying on the village. In each case, the boy must make major decisions, confronting great, though physically different challenges.

No matter what his subject matter, Mayne in his best books succeeds for three reasons. First he places his characters in fully realized settings, especially in his Yorkshire novels. Second, he presents clearly the difficult and often conflict-ridden interrelationships between young people growing up. Finally, he sees the world as his characters see it, varying his viewpoint according to their ages, circumstances, and temperaments.

TIPS FOR PARENTS AND TEACHERS: Earthfasts and *A Game of Dark* can be examined in the junior high grades as studies of the main characters maturing. In *A Grass Rope* and *Ravensgill*, upper elementary students can notice how, in uncovering the mysteries, the young people are also engaged in self-discovery.

Macaulay, David *(1948 –   )*
American

Born in Burton-on-Trent, England, David Macaulay attended the Rhode Island School of Design. In 1973, he published his first book, *Cathedral: The Story of Its Construction,* for which he was awarded a Caldecott Honor Medal. Three more books which combined his interests in history and architecture followed: *City: A Story of Roman Planning and Construction* (1975), *Pyramid*

(1975), and *Castle* (1977). The last book received a Caldecott Honor Medal. *Underground* (1976) deals with a modern city, and *Unbuilding* (1980), set in the future, satirically portrays the demolition of the Empire State Building. Each book follows a standard format: the reason for the building's existence is explained and, in the following pages, plans, diagrams, and pictures of the stages of construction are presented in detailed pen and ink drawings. The text discusses the aspects of the building process. At important places in each book, panoramic two-page spreads are included, giving aerial views which show the stages of completion.

By making each of his edifices and the people responsible for building them fictitious, Macaulay is able to present more representative portraits, free from specific historical details. However, social history is included. The magnificent buildings from the past are outgrowths and expressions of the cultures of their creators. There is a note of irony in *Castle*. Of all the ancient buildings Macaulay has described, the castle took the least amount of time to finish building and it was the only one which was built to meet the needs of a warring society rather than to serve as a symbol of spiritual ideals. In *Unbuilding* Macaulay looks disapprovingly at the ease with which people decide to destroy modern landmarks.

TIPS FOR PARENTS AND TEACHERS: Macaulay's books provide excellent complements to history lessons in the upper elementary and junior high grades. Students should be encouraged to discover how Macaulay satirizes human nature in many of his illustrations.

Blueberries for Sal, by Robert McCloskey, Viking, New York, 1948. McCloskey uses exaggeration to depict the humorous confrontation of animal and human being in *Blueberries for Sal*.

❦McCloskey, Robert *(1914 –)*
American

Born and raised in Hamilton, Ohio, Robert McCloskey while a boy revealed his ability as an artist and studied at the Vesper George Art School

---

in Boston and the National Academy. His career as a children's writer-illustrator began in the late 1930s when May Massee, children's book editor of Viking Press, told him that he should draw realistically. The result, published in 1940, was *Lentil,* the humorous story of a harmonica-playing boy who helps his midwestern town in a time of crisis. *Make Way for Ducklings,* published in 1941, and based on ducks McCloskey had noticed while working in Boston, received the 1942 Caldecott Medal.

His next book, *Homer Price* (1943), is a collection of humorous stories about a boy growing up in the midwest. *Blueberries for Sal* (1948) and *One Morning in Maine* (1952), based on the adventures of his eldest daughter Sal, were named Caldecott Honor Books. *Centerburg Tales* (1952) is a continuation of the Homer Price stories. *A Time of Wonder* (1957), McCloskey's first book in full color, a depiction of children's summer activities on a Maine island, was awarded the Caldecott Medal, making McCloskey the first artist to have won the award twice. *Burt Dow: Deep-Water Man* (1963), his second full-color work, is a maritime tall tale about an old salt who takes refuge from a storm by sailing into the belly of a whale. During the 1950s and 1960s, McCloskey illustrated works of several other children's writers, including Ruth Sawyer's *Journey Cake, Ho!* (1953) and Keith Robertson's Henry Reed stories, including *Henry Reed, Inc.* (1955).

McCloskey's stories contain many autobiographical elements. His hometown of Hamilton serves as the basis for Alto in *Lentil* and Centerburg in the Homer Price stories, while Homer and Lentil are said to bear amazing physical and character resemblances to the artist as a boy. His island home, along with McCloskey, his wife Margaret, and his daughters Sal and Jane, appears in the Maine stories.

McCloskey, through the artistry of his words and pictures, is able to universalize these autobiographical elements. The design and rhythm of the illustrations capture the humor of the situations of his characters. Sal is depicted mistaking a bear for her mother; Homer, seeking a way to control mountains of doughnuts; Mrs. Mallard, bringing the Boston traffic to a halt; and Lentil, lounging in a bathtub playing the harmonica. Against realistic backgrounds, these characters are presented with sweeping, cartoon-like strokes. Color is used effectively in *A Time of Wonder* to capture the summer rhythms which influence the children's lives, and in *Burt Dow: Deep-Water Man* to emphasize the ridiculousness of the story.

Although McCloskey has maintained that he is an artist rather than a storyteller, he is, in fact, a consummate storyteller. His use of colloquial dialogue effectively creates character while his repetition of verbal patterns builds plots to exciting climaxes. The Homer Price stories, particularly those featuring Grampa Herc, reproduce the flavor of the traditional American tall tale. *A Time of Wonder*, with its unusual use of second person point of view, captures both the sounds of nature and the children's reaction to the world around them.

Like all great writers, McCloskey gives his stories universal themes. The child's need for security is seen in *Make Way for Ducklings, Blueberries for Sal,* and *One Morning in Maine;* the importance of living in harmony with the environment underlies several of the Homer Price stories and *A Time of Wonder;* and the advance of modern life is satirized in "Wheels of Progress" from *Homer Price.*

Many of McCloskey's stories echo great tales of the past. In "Homer Price and the Doughnuts," the boy hero is a modern sorcerer's apprentice, unable to turn off his Uncle Ulysses' new-fangled doughnut machine; Burt Dow, escaping a storm by docking his boat in a whale's belly, is a twentieth-century Jonah; and Gramp Herc, Homer's yarn-spinning relative, is a typical western boaster.

The continued popularity of McCloskey's stories is the result of the ability of words and pictures to communicate lively plots and convincing characters. With the exception of *A Time of Wonder* and *One Morning in Maine*, each of the stories is like the yarns spun by Grampa Herc: a combination of probable characters and improbable events. Usually, the central characters are children. Homer and Lentil can be counted upon to succeed when adults fail and Sal gains a surer sense of herself as she grows up and explores her environment. While many of the adults appear foolish, the children still have the security of knowing that they live with families and communities that are essentially protective and stable. The aging heroes, Grampa Herc and Burt Dow are, in a way, like the children; they, too, are superior to the adults who run day-to-day affairs.

TIPS FOR PARENTS AND TEACHERS: In the early elementary grades, the sense of security in *Blueberries for Sal, One Morning in Maine,* and *Make Way for Ducklings* appeals to readers. In the middle grades, students enjoy discussing the improbabilities of the Homer Price stories. Upper elementary students can compare "Homer Price and the Doughnuts" and *Burt Dow* to "The Sorcerer's Apprentice" and the Biblical story of Jonah, respectively.

Arrow to the Sun, by Gerald McDermott, Viking, New York, 1974. On the final page of the story, McDermott gathers the major figures and designs found in the book to indicate the resolution of the conflict.

McDermott, Gerald *(1941 –)*
American

Born in Detroit, Gerald McDermott began his formal art training at the age of four when his parents, impressed by his drawing ability, enrolled him in Detroit's Institute of Art. His high school years were spent at Detroit's Cass Technical, a small school which taught only artistically talented children. He then attended the Pratt Institute in New York, from which he graduated in 1964. While in high school, McDermott began creating short animated films for the enjoyment of his friends. There were no filmmaking courses at Pratt Institute, but as a summer project McDermott produced "The Stonecutter," based on a Japanese folktale he had enjoyed as a child.

After graduation from Pratt, McDermott travelled extensively in Europe, visiting many filmakers. Later he produced five animated films: "The Stonecutter" (a Japanese tale), "Sun Flight" (the story of Icarus), "The Magic Tree" and "Anansi the Spider" (both based on African folktales), and "Arrow to the Sun" (a Pueblo tale). At the encouragement of George Nicholson, then children's editor at Holt, Rinehart and Winston, he turned the films into picture books. *Anansi the Spider* (1972), the first of these to appear in book form, was named a Caldecott Honor Book. Since then, McDermott has published several other books, one of which, *Arrow to the Sun* (1974), received the Caldecott Medal.

McDermott's films and books reflect his childhood love of traditional stories, his interest in Jungian psychology, his training in graphic arts, and his study of folk art from around the world. While working on "The Stonecutter," he met Joseph Campbell, a scholar of anthropology and folklore, who clarified the artist's thinking on one of his major themes: the quest of the individual for self-knowledge and fulfillment.

Each of McDermott's stories describes a journey on which the hero is tested. In *Anansi*, the trickster-hero and his six sons survive because of their courage and quick wits. *The Magic Tree* (1973) describes the tragic growth to maturity of Mavungu, who leaves his home to rescue and marry a magic princess. However, because he reveals the secret of his new life, he loses his bride and spends the rest of his life lonely and unhappy. *The Stonecutter* (1975) is the story of Tasaku, who leaves a happy life to search for something greater and better. He is also a failed hero, being turned into a mountain because of his envious questing. In *The Voyage of Osiris* (1977), McDermott tells the story of the Egyptian god who dies but saves his people. *The Knight of the Lion* (1979) is an adaptation of the twelfth-century romance of Yvain who finds, loses, and after a long journey in which he is tested, rediscovers a beautiful lady.

McDermott's best-known book is *Arrow to the Sun*, his finest treatment of the quest for identity. Child of the Lord of the Sun and a Pueblo maiden, the unnamed hero searches for his father. Transformed into an arrow, he is shot to the sun, where his father orders the boy to undergo four tests to prove his identity. Transformed, the hero returns to earth where he leads his people in the Dance of Life.

In his works McDermott fuses the universal quest for self-fulfillment with the particular beliefs of the culture he is depicting. He also incorporates the styles of the cultures from which the stories are taken. In creating the collages for *The Stonecutter*, he was influenced by traditional Japanese art. In *Anansi* and *The Magic Tree*, he sought to approximate the vivid colors and geometric patterns of Ashanti fabrics. *Arrow to the Sun* incorporates the kiva-step design and the rainbow border pattern of the Pueblo art and uses blacks and oranges appropriate to the southwest desert country. In *The Knight of the Lion*, the only book McDermott has illlustrated solely in black and white, he avoided the ornate quality of late medieval treatment of the Arthurian cycles and sought to suggest the "force and power of the dark Celtic mythology that really underlies the legends."

TIPS FOR PARENTS AND TEACHERS: Like the myths and folktales on which they are based, McDermott's picture books appeal to a variety of ages. Early elementary students can discuss the emotions of the characters and how the illustrations reflect these. In the middle grades, the reasons for the success or failure of the quests can be analyzed. In upper elementary or junior high, the stories can be related to the cultures from which they are taken.

🦋MacDonald, George *(1824 – 1905)*
🦋 *Scottish*

Considered by many critics to be the best of the nineteenth-century fantasists, George MacDonald was a prolific writer, producing dozens of books in his lifetime: realistic novels, adult and children's fantasies, poems, plays, and essays. However, he is remembered today chiefly for two adult fantasies, *Phantastes* (1858) and *Lilith* (1895); three children's novels, *At the Back of the North Wind* (1870), *The Princess and the Goblin* (1871), and *The Princess and Curdie* (1882); and a collection of short fairy tales for children. Born into a poor Scottish family in Aberdeenshire, he studied for the ministry at the University of Aberdeen, but after three years in the ministry, resigned in 1853 to devote his full time to writing. His first book, published in 1855, *Within and Without*, was a collection of poetry and was highly praised by the critics. Although weak health often forced him to travel to Europe, he lived most of the last forty years of his life in England, supporting his wife and eleven children mainly through his writings.

MacDonald was a leader in the movement which saw the reintroduction of fantasy into children's literature during the last half of the nineteenth century. Before his time, leading writers and critics had rejected fantasy, feeling that it was foolish and not conducive to the moral education of children and stressing that children should read stories which were realistic and specifically moralistic. MacDonald, however, who had heard marvelous Celtic and Scottish legends as a child, and who had read the works of the great English and German romantics, set about writing fantasies which, while entertaining, were also morally edifying, although not blatantly so.

Many of his shorter pieces, most notably "The Light Princess" and "Little Daylight," make extensive use of the conventions of traditional folktales for both serious and satiric purposes. Each of these stories begins with the long-awaited child of a king and queen being cursed, during her christening, by an evil fairy. The Light Princess is made weightless and can only be redeemed by someone who willingly agrees to sacrifice his life for her; Little Daylight must sleep all day and becomes healthy or ill according to the phases of the moon; only by being kissed by someone who does not realize that she is a princess will she become normal. In addition to burlesquing such stories as "The Sleeping Beauty," the tales treat two serious MacDonald themes: the need for the individual to grow to maturity and the importance of people to care selflessly for others.

Two of MacDonald's best-known stories deal with children who move beyond earthly life. The emphasis is not on death, which was a favorite

Victorian subject, but on growing into greater, fuller, eternal life. In "The Golden Key," two small children, Tangle and Mossy, wander through the forests of Fairy Land in search of the door which can be opened by the golden key discovered by Mossy, the little boy. During the process of their travels, they become very old, a symbol of their growing wisdom, and at the conclusion, open a door which leads them upward into Paradise. *At the Back of the North Wind* is the story of Little Diamond, a poor but kind London child who, with the help of a beautiful lady, the North Wind, is able finally to visit the country behind the North Wind, the land of life after death. In both stories, the children reach their destinations in part because they show great kindness to other people and animals.

The two MacDonald novels most widely read today are *The Princess and the Goblins* and its sequel, *The Princess and Curdie*. The central characters are a young princess and one of her subjects, a boy who works in the king's mines. In the first book, the princess, wandering into the attic of the great house in which she lives, discovers an old lady who claims to be her great-great-grandmother and who helps her against the goblins who seek to kidnap her and make her the bride of their crown-prince. She is rescued by Curdie who, exploring the underground caverns, discovers the goblins' plans. In the second book, the focus is on Curdie, who is told by the mysterious old lady that he must help the princess and her father, both threatened by evil palace councilors who wish to overthrow the royal family. In both books, the old woman acts as a fairy godmother, helping the children not so much by direct intervention but by acting as a catalyst in the development of their inner strengths. While on one level the books are fairy tale romances filled with exciting adventures, they are on a deeper level studies of the growth to maturity of two young people.

Running through MacDonald's fantasies for children is a dominant theme: the spiritual and moral growth of the young heroes and heroines. They are surrounded by adults; parents are generally supportive, but the most helpful person is the wise, ageless, beautiful lady who sets them on their journeys and provides them with guidance. Evil beings also are found: wicked fairies, hypocritical and selfish adults, goblins. However, the ultimate fate of the children rests within themselves; they must earn their final rewards by developing the potential strengths they possess. In their quests, they move through landscapes which are both vividly portrayed and symbolically important. Two of MacDonald's favorite settings are the staircase leading upward and the underground cavern. The former may represent the progress to moral maturity and purification; the latter, the unknown recesses of the individual heart which must be explored and understood before the ascent may be undertaken.

MacDonald's legacy to children's literature is found not only in the fairytales and fantasy novels still read today, but also in the influence he has had on two of the foremost writers of modern children's fantasy: C.S. Lewis and Maurice Sendak. Lewis has called his reading of *Phantastes* one of the most important literary events of his life, and his "Chronicles of Narnia" show the influence of MacDonald's works in nearly every chapter. Sendak, who has illustrated versions of *The Light Princess* and *The Golden Key,* has often mentioned the influence of MacDonald on his picture books, particularly *Higglety, Pigglety Pop* and *Outside Over There.*

TIPS FOR PARENTS AND TEACHERS: MacDonald's shorter pieces can be best enjoyed by upper elementary school children with a knowledge of such traditional folktales as "The Sleeping Beauty." They enjoy spotting similarities to traditional tales and then noticing how MacDonald parodies them. The "Princess" books contain many passages in which the children must make difficult moral decisions; junior high aged readers may be asked to discuss these passages and their importance in illustrating character development.

Milne, A(lan) A(lexander) *(1882 – 1956)*
English

When he was a boy, A.A. Milne must have felt somewhat like his most famous creation, Winnie-the-Pooh: "of little brain." He wasn't particularly good at school and was an undistiguished university student at Cambridge, from which he graduated in 1903. However, he did enjoy writing humorous poems and decided to become a free-lance writer. He was sufficiently successful to be named the assistant editor of the humor magazine *Punch* and worked there from 1906 until the outbreak of World War I. During the war, with the help of his wife, Daphne (whom he had married in 1913), he wrote some one-act children's plays and a fantasy, *Once Upon a Time* (1917), about a war between the kingdoms of Euralia and Baroda. After the war, he enjoyed a career as a successful playwright, and also wrote poetry, novels, and short stories.

However, it is for a group of books written for, and loosely about, his son Christopher Robin that he is most remembered. *When We Were Very Young* (1924) and *Now We Are Six* (1927), two books of poems, and *Winnie-the-Pooh* (1926) and *The House at Pooh Corner* (1928), two collections of stories, were great successes in England and the United States. They have been translated into several languages including Latin and adapted as plays and animated cartoons. Milne wrote several other children's books including two plays, *Toad of Toad Hall* (1929), based on Kenneth Grahame's *Wind in the Willows,* and *The Ugly Duckling* (1941); and a collection of short stories, *A Gallery of Children* (1925). With the exception of *Toad of Toad Hall,* these other works are seldom read today.

The impetus to write the Christopher Robin books came during a rainy summer vacation in 1923. Trying to escape from the friends who often visited, Milne went to a summer house in the yard to write. At about this time, children's poet Rose Fyleman asked if he would contribute some verses to a new magazine she was editing. Liking the sound of the name Christopher Robin, he began to write verses around it. However, as Milne later stressed, the character Christopher Robin, who had the same name as his son, was not his son, who always referred to himself as Billy Moon. Stating that "no one can write a book which children will like, unless he writes it for himself first," he tried to create works which achieved technical excellence. He was later to remark, *"When We Were Very Young* is not the work of a poet becoming playful, nor of a lover of children expressing his love, nor of a prosewriter knocking together a few jingles for the little ones, it is the work of a light-verse writer taking his job seriously even though he is taking it into the nursery. It seems that the nursery, more than any other room in the house, likes to be approached seriously."

The resulting poems center on the perceptions of a young child thinking about himself, about nature, and about the wonderful characters of stories. Again stressing that the child was not his own son, Milne noted the sources for the character: "My memories of my own childhood . . . , my imaginings of childhood in general, my observations of the particular childhood with which I was now in contact."

While Milne's children's poetry is still widely read, it is not as popular as the collections of stories about Christopher Robin and his animal friends. The latter are based on the stuffed toys Milne's son had acquired over the years (Pooh had been a present to him on his first birthday). In a sense, the author considered himself their biographer rather than creator: "I described them rather than invented them. Only Rabbit and Owl were my own unaided work." The boy and his friends lived in the woods which closely resembled the area around Cotchford Farm, Surrey, to which the Milnes had moved in 1925.

The central character of the stories is Winnie-the-Pooh, a bear of little brain, who has a great love of honey and a penchant for creating verses about himself and his friends. While Pooh has what might now be called a poor self-concept early in the stories, he grows during them, becoming more competent, and he is always secure in the love of his friend Christopher Robin. In many ways Pooh and his friends are like small children, most concerned about their own affairs, but anxious to be liked by others. Pooh is always ready for a snack; Piglet wishes to make up for his diminutive size; Eeyore thinks no one likes him; and Rabbit always wants to be the leader. Christopher Robin plays an adult role in the stories, usually arriving just in time to extricate his friends from the difficulties which they have created for themselves.

After *The House at Pooh Corner,* Milne wrote no further stories about Pooh and his friends. The popularity of the four books had been so great that they were causing the real Christopher Robin to lose his privacy. Moreover, as he noted, they had succeeded so well that the reading public would expect sequels to be even better. It was best that he quit while he was ahead. Also, the character Christopher Robin was growing up. Late in *The House at Pooh Corner,* he had started going to school in the mornings. He was ready to leave the Hundred Acre Wood and his friends there. The enchanted world of early childhood was behind him.

TIPS FOR PARENTS AND TEACHERS: One of the outstanding characteristics of the Christopher Robin books is the fact that they can be read aloud so well. Preschoolers enjoy the swinging rhythms of the poems, particularly those composed by Pooh. Even though the content of some of the poems may not be understood by children, they can be used as an excellent introduction to the music of poetry. Children in the early elementary grades usually feel vastly superior to the animals in the stories. They can be invited to take the role of Christopher Robin and to explain to the animals the mistakes they have made. In doing this, they should be encouraged to be sensitive to the very tender egos of the animals.

Montgomery, Lucy Maud
(1874 – 1942)
Canadian

Like the heroine of her most famous novel, *Anne of Green Gables,* Lucy Maud Montgomery was an imaginative child. Born in Clifton, Prince Edward Island, Canada, she lived with her grandparents after the death of her mother. She later recalled, "I had no companionship except that of books and solitary rambles in wood and fields. This drove me in on myself and early forced me to construct a world of fantasy and imagination very different from the world in which I lived." After teaching for three years, working for a newspaper, studying English literature at Dalhousie University, writing stories and poems, and caring for her aging grandmother, she began work on a novel based on one of her notebook jottings: "Elderly couple apply to orphan asylum for a boy. By mistake a girl is sent them."

Anne of Green Gables, after having been rejected several times, was published in 1908 by the Boston firm of L.C. Page. It was well-received and was into a fourth printing within a few months. The author received a congratulatory note from the celebrated Samuel Clemens (Mark Twain), author of *The Adventures of Huckleberry Finn*, who called the title heroine "the dearest, and most lovable child in fiction since the immortal Alice." Since then it has been published in a dozen languages, sold millions of copies, and been made into two motion pictures and a musical. However, its early success created problems for the author; the publishers requested a sequel, and Montgomery lamented, "I feel like the magician in the Eastern story who became the slave of the 'jinn' he had conjured out of a bottle. If I'm to be dragged at Anne's chariot wheels the rest of my life, I'll bitterly repent having 'created' her." The humor of the incidents, the portrayal of Anne, and the evocation of the scenery of Prince Edward Island have made the novel Canada's greatest children's classic. However, it has not escaped criticism. Many readers have regretted the author's occasional lapses into the sentimental tone so popular in the late nineteenth-century children's fiction. She herself admitted that at least one episode, the death of Matthew Cuthbert, was included in the novel as a concession to popular taste. In order to insure better sales, she was not above giving readers what they wanted.

Several sequels appeared, including *Anne of Avonlea* (1909), *Chronicles of Avonlea* (1912), *Anne of the Island* (1915), *Anne's House of Dreams* (1917), *Anne of Windy Poplars* (1936), and *Anne of Ingleside* (1939). These books lack the spontaneity of the first novel, and Montgomery came to be tired of her heroine. As early as 1919 she wrote, "I have gone completely 'stale' on Anne and *must* get a new heroine. Six books are enough to write about any girl."

In 1911, Montgomery married Ewen Macdonald, a young minister, and moved with him to a small Ontario village. She lived in Ontario for the rest of her life, writing several other novels for girls. However, none of them ever achieved the popularity of *Anne of Green Gables*. In 1935, seven years before her death, she was named a member of the Order of the British Empire.

TIPS FOR PARENTS AND TEACHERS: Upper elementary and junior high students can study the process of Anne's socialization. After comparing her character at the beginning and end of *Anne of Green Gables*, they can see how the major events indicate her growing maturity. The students can be asked whether or not Anne gained or lost more in growing up.

Moore, Clement Clarke *(1779 – 1863)*
American

The man who wrote "A Visit from St. Nicholas" ("The Night Before Christmas") was known during his life as a distinguished scholar of theology and classics. Clement Moore served as a professor of Biblical learning and interpretation of Scripture and of Oriental and Greek literature and was a member of the Board of Trustees of Columbia College. In 1813, he married Catharine Elizabeth Taylor, who bore him nine children, six of whom had been born by 1822, when he wrote his most famous poem, "A Visit from St. Nicholas." Using as his model a rotund worker in the neighborhood, Moore told for his children the story of the night-time visit of the figure who, in the early decades of nineteenth-century America, was rapidly becoming the dominant secular figure of Christmas. The poem was anonymously published the next year when a relative sent a copy to *The Sentinel*, a Troy, New York, newspaper. The editor noted, "There is, to our apprehension, a spirit of cordial goodness in it, a playfulness of fancy and a benevolent alacrity to enter into the feelings and promote the simple pleasures of children." The poem was reprinted in many periodicals in the following years, and in 1837 Moore allowed his name to be associated with it. Since then it has been illustrated by such well-known artists as Paul Galdone, Arthur Rackham, Roger Duvoisin, Tasha Tudor, and Grandma Moses.

TIPS FOR PARENTS AND TEACHERS: There is such an interesting variety of illustrated versions that teachers and parents can invite children to look at several of them, commenting on the success of the different pictoral interpretations of the poem.

Myths

The word "myth" is commonly misused. When we hear something which we find hard to believe about a person, we often say, "Oh, that's a myth," meaning that we don't think it is true. Correctly used, the word "myth" means a story which forms part of the religious beliefs of the culture which tells it. Thus, for the people that tell them, myths are not false, they are true. In this sense, each of the stories from the Bible is a myth forming part of the religious system that makes up Christianity. Mythologies are the collections of religious stories that cultures create. It should be noted that these are not haphazard collections; they are carefully arranged or ordered to form meaningful patterns.

Generally, myths are stories about deities interacting with themselves or acting upon the natural and human worlds. While it is not known for certain how myths developed, it is generally believed they emerged as people tried to explain the natural phenomena that surrounded them and the facts of their lives: weather, the seasons, the unique features of geography, the physical characteristics of animals, the origin of the world, life, death, sin, and disease. Being unable to give "scientific" explanations, they attributed the presence of these things to the actions of supernatural forces. Gradually these forces were envisioned as gods with vastly superior powers. However, to explain the motivations of these beings, primitive people used what could loosely be described as psychology. They gave the gods human personalities to go along with their superhuman powers.

Although many societies have lived in fear of the gods who they believed controlled the world and their lives, the presence of these gods provided a measure of security. Even though the gods might be terrible in their actions, the actions had motivation. At least there were explanations for forces people could not control. A life with meaning, however dangerous, was less terrifying than a life filled with meaningless occurrences.

Scholars of mythology have found that myths from around the world treat many of the same occurrences and phenomena noted above. That is because all people must face fundamentally the same issues in their lives. However, because of the physical and social differences of cultures, myths also represented the beliefs of the specific groups creating them. For example, because the Inuit (Eskimo) people depended on sea creatures for most of their food and clothing, Sedna, the goddess of the sea, was a central figure in their myths. Not surprisingly, the Greeks, who developed intellectual discussion to a high level, often portrayed their gods as sitting in council debating issues which concerned them and the human beings whose lives they controlled.

In the Western world, the most widely known mythologies are those developed by the Greeks (and borrowed by the Romans), the Scandinavian peoples, and the Judeo-Christian nations. Not surprisingly, myths from these cultures have been the ones most frequently retold or adapted for children. In recent years, with the increased awareness of minority cultures in North America, other mythologies have been presented to children. Chief of these are the mythologies of the American Indians, the African nations, and the Polynesians.

Greek Mythology: In the beginning, Gaea (the Earth) and Uranus (the Sky) loved, producing three different groups of children: six titans (immortal giants) and their sister-wives; three one-eyed monsters, the cyclopi; and three fifty-headed giants. Uranus, fearing these last two groups, imprisoned them in Tartarus. Meanwhile, the titan Cronus turned upon his father, who fled. Assuming leadership, Cronus fathered several children, the gods, all of whom he ate except the sixth-born, Zeus, who was hidden by his mother. Grown to maturity, Zeus forced Cronus to vomit up the five other children, and, with the aid of two titans, Prometheus and Epimetheus, overthrew Cronus and established his own kingdom on Mount Olympus. He divided rule of the universe between himself, as lord of the heavens and earth, his brother Poseidon, to whom he gave the sea, and Hades, who ruled the underworld. Their interrelationships and their dealings with lesser gods and mortals form the bases of the Greek myths.

From these stories emerges a picture of a people much concerned with the dignity of mankind. If, as has been said, men create gods from their own image, the Greeks must indeed have considered men noble in potential at least; for the gods, although not perfect, did lead magnificent lives on their beautiful Mount Olympus. With one or two notable exceptions, especially the lame Haephastus, they were beautiful beings. That the gods in Greek mythology are so often faced with difficult moral choices and responsibilities reflects the high value the Greeks must have placed on making correct ethical decisions. It is true that the choices they made were not always the best and that the results were not always happy for mortals; nonetheless, the dilemmas faced by the principal mythological characters reflect a highly developed, most sophisticated sense of human existence.

Among the best-known of the Greek myths are "Prometheus," the story of the titan who brought fire to mortals and was punished by Zeus for his actions; "Cupid and Psyche," the account of how the son of Aphrodite fell in love with a mortal who, after much suffering and many tests, was made one of the gods; "Demeter and Persephone," a seasonal myth in which a young girl is abducted by the Lord of the Underworld, and Demeter, the grieving mother, brings a drought to the world until her daughter returns; "Midas," a moral allegory in which a king wishes everything he touched would turn to gold; and "Baucis and Philemon," an account of an old man and woman who are kind to the gods who visit them disguised as travellers.

Norse Mythology: Out of the darkness emerged Nifflheim, the North, a land of ice and cold, and Muspelheim, the South, a land of fire and heat.

Then the giant Ymir was born, and shortly after appeared a giant cow which provided him with food. Over a long period of time, three generations of giants were created, with Odin, a member of the third generation, becoming the most powerful. He killed Ymir, whose body provided the materials for the heavens, the earth, and the oceans, and caused Asgard, the great home of the gods, to be built. In another region was Jotenheim, the land of the giants, one of whose number, Loki, ingratiated himself with the gods, living with them much of the time. However, Loki, mischievous by nature, became malicious. His frequent tricks, once played for fun, became destructive, and he was responsible for the death of Baldur, the most loved of the Norse gods and Odin's favorite son.

Baldur's death marked the beginning of Ragnarok, the Twilight of the Gods. Seeking vengeance, the gods captured Loki whom they chained to rocks beneath a serpent, the venom from whose fangs dripped on his face. The final great battle occurred when Loki was released and with his forces warred against Odin and the gods. All were destroyed and the fires of Muspelheim swept over the world of the gods and giants. Out of the devastation emerged a new heaven in which Baldur returned to life and peace reigned.

Of all the stories of the Norse gods and giants, the best-known and most popular are those dealing with Loki and Odin's son Thor. Red-haired and possessed of the mighty hammer Molner, Thor is short-tempered and proud of his masculinity; however, often misled by the wily Loki, he has many misadventures, and at one time he has to dress as a woman. Loki, like many trickster figures, is selfish, enjoying the discomfort he causes for others. The story of Odin's quest for wisdom is also very popular. Realizing that he cannot achieve his goal without sacrifice, he gives up his eye so that he can drink from Mimir's well, the source of wisdom.

Unlike the Greek myths, which present very sophisticated psychological portraits, the Norse myths are relatively simple. The world portrayed is violent and harsh; disputes are generally settled with combat rather than debate. It is appropriate that the enemies of the gods are the Frost Giants, for they symbolize the severe weather conditions the northern poeple had to confront much of the year.

Retelling the Myths for Children: While children of various cultures grew up becoming aware of the religious stories of their people, it was not until the nineteenth century that myths were specifically adapted for children. The processes of adaptation involved adults considering what was suitable to children's powers of understanding and what was appropriate to their moral education. Often this meant that myths retold for children left out what the adaptors considered unsuitable elements, thus weakening the power and meanings of the stories. Adult choosing myths from any culture should see how close the children's versions are to the originals. While materials beyond the range of young readers' understanding should be either modified or omitted, it is a mistake either to falsify or to criticize cultural values different from those of modern readers. These should be explained to child readers as outgrowths of the beliefs of the people who created the stories.

The first major retellings of the Greek myths were those of English writer Charles Kingsley and American novelist Nathaniel Hawthorne. In *The Heroes* (1856), Kingsley retold major myths in a style which maintains its vitality today. Hawthorne's *A Wonder-Book* (1852) and *Tanglewood Tales* (1853), however, are very dated; his ornate style and his tendency to talk down to young readers limits the value of his stories for modern readers.

Among the most significant twentieth-century retellings of Greek myths are *Hermes, Lord of Robbers* (Penelope Proddow, 1971), *The Serpent's Teeth: The Story of Cadmus* (Penelope Farmer, 1971), *Lord of the Sky: Zeus* (Doris Gates, 1972), *Persephone: Bringer of the Spring* (Sarah F. Tomaino, 1971), and *Sun Flight* (Gerald McDermott, 1980). Major collections of Greek myths adapted for children include *The Book of Greek Myths* (Ingri and Edgar d'Aulaire, 1962), *Greek Gods and Heroes* (Robert Graves, 1960), and *The God Beneath the Sea* (Leon Garfield and Edward Blishen, 1971). The latter book is one of the most interesting adaptations to appear in many years. Retelling many well-known myths in novelistic style, the authors give the stories a psychological depth not usually found in versions for children.

Perhaps because they are less known, the Norse myths have not been as frequently adapted. However, several excellent collections have appeared, among them *Norse Gods and Giants* (Ingri and Edgar d'Aulaire, 1964), *The Children of Odin* (Padraic Colum, 1920), and *Thunder of the Gods* (Dorothy Hosford, 1952).

The following volumes provide good introductions to the world-wide family of myths: *A Book of Myths* (Roger Lancelyn Green, 1965), *The Beginning: Creation Myths around the World* (Maria Leach, 1956), and *The Golden Treasury of Myths and Legends* (Anne Terry White, 1959).

TIPS FOR PARENTS AND TEACHERS: Because myths are more complex than folktales, they should probably not be introduced to children until the middle or upper elementary grades. Individual myths should be read for their interest as stories and should be related to other stories children know. Simple Greek myths such as "Midas" or "Baucis and Philemon," the humorous Norse myths presenting Thor's misadventures, and the pourquoi myths of the American Indians can be introduced at first. After a period of three or four years, when children have become aware of a number of myths from a specific culture, the teacher can gather them together into a mythology, showing how the familiar stories are interrelated. In the junior high grades, the nature of mythology, the cultural basis of mythology, and the relationships between myths from different cultures can be studied.

Nesbit, Edith *(1858 – 1924)*
English

Born in London, the youngest of six children, Edith Nesbit led an unsettled life as the family moved from house to house in England, France, and Germany after the death of her father. During her teens, Nesbit, always a reader and writer, submitted pieces to magazines, and in 1876 her first work, a poem, was published in *The Sunday Magazine.* Shortly after her marriage in 1880, her writing career began in earnest. To earn money to support the family, she energetically produced essays, poems, short stories, and novels. In 1897 she published "The Treasure Seekers," a story of six young children who decide to recover the lost fortunes of their family. It appeared in *The London Illustrated News.* Further adventures appeared in other magazines and were gathered together in 1899 as *The Story of the Treasure Seekers.* The adventures of the Bastable children were enthusiastically received and later stories were collected in *The Wouldbegoods* (1901) and *The New Treasure Seekers* (1904).

Edith Nesbit's reputation as a children's writer grew as she continued to gather into book form groups of related stories originally appearing in magazines. *The Book of Dragons* (1900), her first fantasy, was followed in 1902 by *Five Children and It,* in which Cyril, Robert, Anthea, Jane, and their baby brother meet a Psammead, a sand-fairy who grants them a wish a day, but not the wisdom to use the wish wisely. In *The Phoenix and the Carpet* (1904), the same children travel around the world on a magic carpet, and in *The Story of the Amulet* (1906), believed by many critics to be Nesbit's finest fantasy, they are transported into the past with the aid of an Egyptian amulet. Her other important works of this period were *The Railway Children* (1906), the adventure of a poor family whose father has been sent to prison; and *The House of Arden* (1908) and *Harding's Luck* (1909), two related novels about children who are heirs to a titled estate but who must travel through time to overcome the difficulties which obstruct their coming into their fortunes.

In all of her best stories, Edith Nesbit followed a basic premise: a family of normal children find themselves in, or create, a situation in which they plan for themselves a course of action. However, because of their own characters and because of their misunderstanding of the natures of the situations in which they find themselves, the actions do not proceed as planned and the adventures become misadventures. Alice Bastable, talking of their affairs in *The Wouldbegoods*, perhaps best summarizes the plot of a Nesbit story, "You begin to do a noble act, and then it gets so exciting, and before you know what, you are doing something wrong as hard as you can lick." The humor of the stories arises from the unexpected events the children encounter in their adventures.

The Story of the Treasure Seekers and *The Story of the Amulet* are probably the best of Nesbit's volumes. In the former, the Bastable children feel keenly the death of their mother and the collapse of their father's business, and each suggests a way that might help increase the happiness and wealth of the family. The stories present their misguided attempts to work out each suggestion. In *The Story of the Amulet*, a group of children miss their mother, who is in Spain recovering from a serious illness, and their father, a foreign correspondent covering a war in Manchuria. Through the aid of the magic half-amulet they have purchased, they travel into the past to find the missing half, as only the complete object can grant their heart's desire: the safe return of their parents. This story possesses much more danger than was found in their earlier adventures and emphasizes the seriousness of their attempts to see the family reunited.

The incredible variety of adventures experienced in Nesbit's books arises because the children are generally left alone and not bothered by adults. They experience a "benevolent neglect" which suits them admirably for, as Oswald remarks in *The Story of the Treasure Seekers*, "having to consult about a thing with grown up people, even the bravest and the best, seems to make the thing not worth doing afterwards." However, adults are not completely absent in the stories; they are in the background providing an implicit love and security which the children feel and which allows them to pursue their adventures without worry.

TIPS FOR PARENTS AND TEACHERS: Although Nesbit's family stories are slightly "old fashioned," they do make interesting reading for middle elementary students who enjoy the mixture of "good" intentions and "bad" results. Upper elementary aged readers interested in time fantasy will find *The House of Arden* and *Harding's Luck* compelling reading.

Ness, Evaline *(1911 –   )*
American

Born in Union City, Ohio, Evaline Ness grew up in Pontiac, Michigan, and studied at the Chicago Art Institute and the Academia Della Belles Artes in Rome. In 1957, Ness illustrated her first children's book, *The Bridge*, by Charlton Ogsburn, and since then has illustrated over two dozen books by such writers as Lloyd Alexander (*Coll and his White Pig*, 1965), Elizabeth Coatsworth (*Lonely Maria*, 1960), Lucille Clifton (*Some of the Days of Everett Anderson*, 1970), and Walter de la Mare (*The Warmint*, 1976). Three of the books Evaline Ness has illustrated for others have won Caldecott Honor Medals: *All in the Morning Early* (1963) by Sorche Nic Leodhas; *A Pocket Full of Cricket* (1964), by Rebecca Caudill; and *Tom Tit Tot* (1965), an old English folktale adapted by Virginia Haviland.

Ness has also written and illustrated several books of her own, including *Josefina February* (1963), *A Gift for Sula Sula* (1963), *Exactly Alike* (1964), and *Pavo and the Princess* (1964). She has also adapted two folktales, *Mr. Miacca* (1968) and *Long, Broad, and Quickeye* (1969). Her best-known story is *Sam, Bangs, and Moonshine* (1966), winner of the Caldecott Medal. It is the tale of Samantha, who lives with her fisherman father and her cat, Bangs, and "whose reckless habit of lying" causes great trouble for her friend Tommy. As in many of her stories, the focus is on a lonely young child placed in a situation which allows for moral growth.

As an illustrator, Ness varies her media and style to suit the specific subject. For *Tom, Tit, Tot*, she used wood blocks which enhanced the simple quality of the folktale. In *Sam, Bangs, and Moonshine*, line drawings and pale gray-blue washes suggest both the fantasy world the child creates and the foggy seaside setting. The full-color paintings in *Mr. Miacca* capture the vitality of the nineteenth-century London in which the action takes place.

TIPS FOR PARENTS AND TEACHERS: After reading *Sam, Bangs, and Moonshine*, children in the early and middle grades can discuss the difference between good and bad "moonshine"—both in the story and their own lives.

Newbery Medal

At the 1921 meeting of the American Library Association, Frederic G. Melcher, editor of *Publishers' Weekly* and founder of Children's Book Week, suggested that an annual award be given to the book judged the year's "most distinguished contribution to American literature for children." The idea was accepted and, in 1922, Hendrik Willem Van Loon's *The Story of Mankind* was named winner of the Newbery Medal, named after John Newbery, the eighteenth-century Englishman who was the first major publisher of books for children. It has been awarded annually since then, and among the list of winners are books which have become classics in the field of children's literature.

During the early years of the award, votes were cast by the general membership of Children's Librarians in the ALA. In 1922, 212 votes were received, with van Loon's book receiving 163 votes. Since then, methods of selection have changed constantly; the present method of selection emerged in the late 1950s and early 1960s. Today, the Caldecott-Newbery Medal Committee is composed of twenty-three members: the executive of the Children's Services Division, members of the Book Evaluation Committee, eight elected members-at-large, and six appointed by the president of the Children's Services Division and the Young Adult Division. Each member of the Committee nominates three books and nominations are received from the membership-at-large. Each Committee member votes for three choices, with four votes being awarded for a first place, three for a second, and two for a third. Winning books must have received either twelve first-place votes or a total of forty-eight points. Winners are announced at the midwinter meeting of the ALA, and the Newbery Medal is presented at the annual conference held in early summer. Each year a varying number of runners-up are named Newbery Honor Books.

Although a book being considered for the Medal need not have been written specifically for children, it must be one which is accessible to them in language, thought, and content. The authors must be either American citizens or residents of the United States. Susan Cooper, winner of the 1976 Medal for *The Grey King*, for example, is English, but wrote the book while living in Massachusetts. Literary excellence is the sole criterion for awarding the Medal. Popularity with children is not considered, it being the belief of the evaluators over the years that awarding an excellent book the Medal would increase its popularity.

The majority of the books that have won the award have been fiction, although three biographies — Cornelia Meig's *Invincible Louisa* (1933), James Daugherty's *Daniel Boone* (1939), and Elizabeth Yates' *Amous Fortune, Free Man* (1950); one history — Van Loon's *Story of Mankind* (1921); and one book of poetry — Nancy Willard's *A Visit to William Blake's Inn* (1981), have been winners. Only three authors have won the Newbery Medal twice: Joseph Krumgold for . . . *And Now Miguel* (1953) and *Onion John* (1959), Elizabeth Speare for *The Witch of Blackbird Pond* (1958) and *The Bronze Bow* (1962), and

Katherine Paterson for *Bridge to Terabithia* (1977) and *Jacob Have I Loved* (1980). However, several medal winners, including Cornelia Meigs, Eleanor Estes, and Meindert de Jong, have had at least two of their books named Honor Books. The 1982 winner, Nancy Willard's *A Visit to William Blake's Inn*, was also named a Caldecott Honor Book in recognition of the illustrations of Alice and Martin Provensen.

Although the Newbery Medal-winning books have dealt with cultures from around the world, it is not surprising that American subjects dominate. A goodly number of these are about the past—although, particularly in recent years, with the development of novels about contemporary realism, modern subjects have dominated. As awareness of America's ethnic minorities has increased, works about black Americans have been named winners. During the 1970s, for example, four of the Newbery Medal books dealt with black Americans: William Armstrong's *Sounder* (1969), Paula Fox's *The Slave Dancer* (1973), Virginia Hamilton's *M.C. Higgins, The Great* (1974), and Mildred Taylor's *Roll of Thunder, Hear My Cry* (1976). Only fourteen of the Newbery Medal books have been fantasy, with several of these dealing with animals.

Inevitably, there has been controversy over the selections. Many of the early works have not become classics and, indeed, are seldom read today. One of the most popular children's books of all times and one which has received great critical acclaim, E.B. White's *Charlotte's Web* (1952), was only awarded an Honor Medal. None of Laura Ingalls Wilder's "Little House" books won the Caldecott Medal. Noting the large number of recent books which have dealt with contemporary problems, some critics have stated that the selections committee has been too influenced by current trends.

Generally, however, the awarding of the Newbery Medal has achieved the goals for which it was established: to publicize worthy books, to provide standards of excellence to increase the quality of children's books, and, by making the reading public more aware of the good books being written for children, to foster a climate in which good literature can be produced.

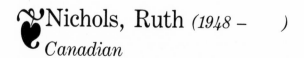

Nichols, Ruth *(1948 –   )*
Canadian

Born in Toronto, Ruth Nichols spent much of her childhood in Vancouver and many of her summers in Ontario's Georgian Bay region. These two areas are the basis for the settings of her two children's fantasies: *A Walk Out of the World* (1969) and *The Marrow of the World* (1972), winner of the Canadian Children's Book of the Year award. She began telling stories at an early age, making up a cycle of adventures about a favorite doll, and at age fourteen she won first prize in a literary competition sponsored by the government of India. She has since published two novels intended for older readers: *Song of the Pearl* (1976) and *Left-Handed Spirit* (1978).

Ruth Nichols' two children's books reflect her early interest in the works of C.S. Lewis and J.R.R. Tolkien. In *A Walk Out of the World*, a young brother and sister, Judith and Tobit, are transported into an alternate universe in which they help in the restoration of a rightful king to his throne. In *The Marrow of the World*, teenage cousins Linda and Philip are similarly transported. However, the focus is on Linda, originally from another world, and her attempts to exorcise evil from within herself and choose between conflicting loyalties. Not only do these books reveal Ruth Nichols' ability to present fully realized fictional worlds, but also they indicate her major theme: the growth of the central character's self-knowledge and sense of responsibility to others.

TIPS FOR PARENTS AND TEACHERS: Nichols' fantasies are a good follow-up to the fantasies of C.S. Lewis and lead into more complex fantasies of Lloyd Alexander and J.R.R. Tolkien. In looking at *Marrow*, upper elementary students should focus on Linda's conflicting loyalties and growth to maturity.

Norton, Mary *(1903 –   )*
English

Born in London, Mary Norton grew up in the country, where she used to imagine that tiny people crept about in her old house and beneath the flowers and shrubs of her garden. After a brief career as an actress, she married, and lived with her family in Portugal, the United States, and London. She wrote her first children's book during World War II. *The Magic Bed-Nob* (1943) is about a kindly village witch who provides a group of children with a flying bed. In a sequel, *Bonfires and Broomsticks* (1947), the children and the witch travel to the seventeenth century where they rescue a magician about to be burned at the stake. Norton's best-known children's book, *The Borrowers* (1952), winner of the Carnegie Medal, is the story of the

Clock family, the last of a race of tiny people living hidden in an old country home. When Arriety, the daughter, is discovered by a boy living in the house, a series of exciting adventures transpire, and the Clocks are forced to flee the house. The book is notable not only for the realism with which Norton portrays the Borrower's lives, but also for its depth of characterization. Both the little people and the "human beans," as they are called, are depicted in great depth. The major theme of the book is the necessity of individuals to understand each other. Three sequels have followed, none of them as good as the first book, each one recounting a phase in the lives of the Borrowers after they fled their original home: *The Borrowers Afield* (1955), *The Borrowers Afloat* (1959), and *The Borrowers Aloft* (1961). In these books Arriety becomes progressively more mature and, at the end, marries. Norton's other two books for children are *Poor Stainless* (1971), a short story about one of the Borrowers who becomes lost, and *Are All the Giants Dead?* (1975), in which a boy dreams himself into a land where fairytale characters live after their stories are finished.

TIPS FOR PARENTS AND TEACHERS: In the middle and upper elementary grades, *The Borrowers* can be studied along with such stories about tiny people as T.H. White's *Mistress Masham's Repose* and Hans Christian Andersen's "Thumbelina." Students should be invited to consider the courageous nature of the children in the story in contrast to most of the adults. *Are All the Giants Dead?* will be enjoyed by middle elementary students who are thoroughly familiar with the standard fairytales.

The Mother Goose Book, illus. by Alice and Martin Provensen, Random House, New York, 1976. The Provensens use graphic design to reinforce the thematic unity of the poems on this two-page spread.

❧Nursery Rhymes

Nursery rhymes, often referred to as Mother Goose rhymes, were not originally created for children. Short anonymous poems derived from ballads, riddles, chants, and other popular forms of poetry, they were a kind of folk poetry designed to be recited by people of all ages. Indeed, many of the poems which have been included in such scholarly books as Iona and Peter Opie's *The Oxford Dictionary of Nursery Rhymes* (1951) and William and Ceil Baring-Gould's *The Annotated Mother Goose* (1962) contain language and subjects beyond the range of children's understanding and certainly considered inappropriate for them by most adults. However, over the centuries, nurses, parents, and other adults have told countless children those rhymes which are suitable for them, and children have responded avidly, generally remembering their favorites all their lives.

It was not until the eighteenth century, when expansion of commercial printing and an increased interest in children made publishing books for young readers profitable, that the nursery rhymes were widely printed. Before that, they had been passed on by word of mouth from generation to generation. In 1744, *Tom Thumb's Pretty Song Book* appeared, containing such well-known rhymes as "Sing-a-Song of Sixpence," "Little Tom Tucker," "Hickory Dickory Dock," "Ba Ba Black Sheep," and "The House that Jack Built." The best-known of the early nursery rhyme books, *Mother Goose's Melody*, was published in the early 1760s by John Newbery, England's first major publisher of books for children. Of the fifty-one rhymes it contained, several had also appeared in *Tom Thumb's Pretty Song Book*; however, new rhymes included "Three Wise Men of Gotham," "Ding Dong Bell," "Hi Diddle Diddle," and "Jack and Jill" (spelled Gill). Newbery's book was widely reprinted and influenced collections of the poems that later appeared in England and the United States. There were large numbers of editions of nursery rhymes published over the next two hundred years, and it may safely be said that these poems are the best-known in the English language.

With the development of color illustrations for children's books in the last half of the nineteenth century, many major artists illustrated versions of the rhymes, often adding in their pictures elements of meaning not found in the words alone. Randolph Caldecott (*The House that Jack Built*, 1878; *A Frog He Would A-Wooing Go*, 1883; and many others), Walter Crane (*The Baby's Opera*, 1877), and Kate Greenaway (*Mother Goose, or the Old Nursery Rhymes*, 1882) created pictures that are as alive today as they were one hundred years ago. In the early twentieth century, Arthur Rackham (*The Old Nursery Rhymes*, 1913) and Leslie Brooke (*Ring o' Roses, A Nursery Rhyme Picture Book*, 1922) created classic illustrated versions. The books by these five authors are still in print.

Every year, new editions of nursery rhymes appear on the market; they vary in approach and in quality. Three of these have achieved classic status: Blanche Fisher Wright's *The Real Mother Goose* (1916), Marguerite de Angeli's *Marguerite de Angeli's Book of Nursery and Mother Goose Rhymes* (1954), and

Tasha Tudor's *Mother Goose* (1944). Each of these is fairly traditional in approach. Recent noteworthy editions are Raymond Briggs' *The Mother Goose Treasury* (1966), Alice and Martin Provensen's *The Mother Goose Book* (1976), and Brian Wildsmith's *Mother Goose* (1965). Feodor Rojankovsky's *The Tall Book of Mother Goose* (1942) and *The Chas. Addams Mother Goose* (1967) have humorous, off-beat pictures.

Since the time of Randolph Caldecott, single nursery rhymes have formed the basis of illustrated books. Caldecott's own books have provided the standard against which later books have been judged, for in them he made his illustrations complement and expand the texts. Among the better recent versions of single rhymes are Ed Emberley's *London Bridge is Falling Down* (1967), Peter Spier's *To Market to Market* (1967), Maurice Sendak's *Hector Protector and As I Went Over the Water* (1965), Evaline Ness's *Old Mother Hubbard and Her Dog* (1972), and Paul Galdone's *The House that Jack Built* (1961).

Although the best-known nursery rhymes are those originally collected in England, many American nursery rhymes have been collected. Two of the most highly regarded collections are Ray Wood's *The American Mother Goose* (1940) and Maud and Miska Petersham's *The Rooster Crows: A Book of American Rhymes and Jingles* (1945).

While many scholarly books have been written about the origins of the nursery rhymes, no conclusive answers have been arrived at. It is generally agreed that those most popular emerged during the sixteenth, seventeenth, and eighteenth centuries, although some have been dated earlier and new ones continue to be created. However, answers to the question why the rhymes have proved so popular with children from such diverse cultures and from many generations are easier to find. The poems are short, and they have pronounced rhythmic patterns and rhyme schemes; thus, they can be enjoyed by very young children who, while they do not understand the words, respond to the sound patterns. As listeners grow a little older, they enjoy hearing about the characters, who often have exaggerated physical features and personalities and who engage in very physical actions. The humor of many of the situations and characters appeals to young children's often highly developed sense of the ridiculous. Finally, as they become familiar with the rhymes, children enjoy repeating single lines and entire poems.

While almost universally popular with children, nursery rhymes have frequently been criticized by adults, who find in the grotesqueness of some of the characters and the violence and cruelty of many of the incidents elements which they feel will be harmful to young children. Their claims are easily refuted when we realize that they, themselves, do not seem to have suffered when they were children the disastrous effects they worry about.

TIPS FOR PARENTS AND TEACHERS: With so many collections of nursery rhymes to choose from, the adult looking for one book to present to a child should stress quality: the book must be physically durable; its illustrations should enhance the rhymes; and there should be a good selection of familiar and new rhymes. When possible, nursery schools, day care centers, and kindergartens should have three or four editions of nursery rhymes so that children can notice how different illustrators portray the same poem. In the upper elementary grades it is interesting to have students examine the poems as historical artifacts, noticing how the rhymes reflect elements of earlier eras. For example, the poem about Doctor Foster tells a lot about road conditions, and "Hark, Hark, the Dogs to Bark!" is an embodiment of fears of wandering bands of beggars. In looking at illustrated versions of single nursery rhymes, students in the early elementary grades can notice how the pictures expand on the meanings of the verses.

O'Brien, Robert: pseudonym of Robert Conly (1918 – 1973)

American

Born in Brooklyn, Robert Conly grew up on Long Island, developing his interests in music and writing. He studied at the Julliard School of Music and graduated from Rochester University with a degree in English literature. In the 1940s, he began a long career in journalism, working for such periodicals as *Newsweek* and *National Geographic*, and at the time of his death, he was senior assistant editor at *National Geographic*. When he began to write novels, he used the pseudonym of Robert O'Brien because *National Geographic* did not wish its writers to work outside the magazine. His first novel, *The Silver Crown* (1968), describes the struggle of the modern world against great forces of evil. *Mrs. Frisby and the Rats of NIMH* (1971), winner of the Newbery Medal, recounts the relationships between a widowed mouse and a group of super-rats who have developed a highly mechanized civilization. It has since been made into a full-length animated film, *The Secret of NIMH*. *A Report from Group 17* (1972) is an adult novel about biological warfare and a Russian community located close to Washington D.C. *Z for Zachariah*, posthumously published in 1975, is for young adults. The diary of a girl who has survived a nuclear war, it reflects the terror she feels when a stranger mysteriously arrives on the scene.

In his Newbery acceptance speech, O'Brien spoke of his concern about "the seeming tendency of the human race to exterminate itself." Not surprisingly, his works are concerned with survival. This is particularly true of his two best known books, *Mrs. Frisby and the Rats of NIMH* and *Z for Zachariah*. In both, the focus is on a central character who must develop courage and ingenuity in order to overcome devastating circumstances. These characters are the vehicles for O'Brien's searching studies of moral issues and of problem solving. As Mrs. Frisby notes, "All doors are hard to unlock until you have the key. All right. She must try to find the key. But where? Whom to ask?"

Mrs. Frisby and the Rats of NIMH has been the most popular of O'Brien's works and seems the most likely to become a classic. Although it is not perfect — for example, the author introduces a number of characters, including Timothy the frail mouse and Jeremy the Crow, whom he fails to develop as fully as he ought — the book is moving in its narrative and thought-provoking in its presentation of themes. With the advent of spring, Mrs. Frisby, the widowed mother of four small mice, faces a dilemma: because the farm where she lives is about to be ploughed, she must move her family to a new home; however, her son Timothy is very ill and such a move might prove fatal to him. In desperation, she turns to a group of rats living nearby and discovers that they have developed a highly sophisticated civilization. Escapees from a laboratory where they were injected with chemicals which have increased their intelligence incredibly, they are able to read and write and to operate machines. However, they are upset with their lives and wish to migrate to a locale where they do not have to steal everything they need. During the course of the novel, Mrs. Frisby and the rats are able to help others.

TIPS FOR PARENTS AND TEACHERS: Mrs. Frisby and the Rats of NIMH can be studied by upper elementary and junior high school students, who can examine the theme of interdependence, noticing how each of the characters must help others in order to survive. In examining the chapters in which the rats discuss their evolution, the students can evaluate the moral dilemmas experienced by the rats and can consider what they would do in similar circumstances.

O'Dell, Scott *(1903 –)*
American

Born in Los Angeles, Scott O'Dell spent his childhood in the many small California towns to which his father, an official with the Union Pacific

Railroad, moved. During his summers, he and his friends often paddled log boats around the coast, exploring small islands and imagining themselves great explorers. O'Dell published his first book, *Representative Photoplays Analyzed*, in 1924, and his first novel, *Woman of Spain*, in 1934. He worked as a movie cameraman, a newspaper book reviewer and editor, and during World War II served in the Air Force. Since 1950, he has devoted himself full-time to writing. While engaged in research for *Country of the Sun: Southern California — An Informal History and Guide* (1957), he found the legend of an Indian girl who had lived alone for eighteen years on one of the offshore islands. It became the basis of his first children's novel, *Island of the Blue Dolphins* (1960). Since then O'Dell has written fifteen books for children. In 1972, he became the first American to win the Hans Christian Andersen Medal, an international award given in recognition of the entire body of an author's work. Until his recent move to Westchester County in New York, O'Dell lived in southern California.

Winner of the Newbery Medal, *Island of the Blue Dolphins* is the story of Karana, a young girl who is marooned when her tribe abandons their island to escape marauding Aleuts. O'Dell describes in vivid detail the means by which the girl gathers food and defends herself against the wild animals. More important is his portrayal of the girl's psychological survival. In his Newbery acceptance speech, O'Dell spoke of Karana's character growth: "In her brief lifetime, Karana made a change from that world where everything lived only to be exploited to a new and more meaningful world. She learned that we must be an island secure unto ourselves. Then, that we must 'transgress our limits,' in reverence for all life."

O'Dell's second children's novel, *The King's Fifth* (1966), winner of a Newbery Honor Medal, is set in Mexico during the sixteenth century. It takes the form of a journal written by seventeen-year-old Esteban de Sandoval, on trial for attempting to deprive King Charles of Spain of one-fifth of the treasure found by the young man and his companions. O'Dell wrote four other children's novels dealing with the history of California and Mexico. *The Black Pearl* (1967), awarded a Newbery Honor Medal, is the story of Rámon Salazar, sixteen-year-old son of a Mexican pearl merchant who wishes to learn to be a pearl diver so that he may best his rival, Gaspar Ruiz. *The Treasure of Topo-el—Bampo* (1972), a story for younger readers, tells of the role two burros play in the new prosperity of a poor Mexican mining village. In *Zia* (1976), a sequel to *Island of the Blue Dophins*, O'Dell portrays the unhappy and lonely life led by Karana after her rescue. *Carlota* (1977), set during the time of the Mexican-American War, describes the young heroine's struggle to run the family ranch after her father's death.

O'Dell's other historical novels deal with a variety of places and times. *The Dark Canoe* (1968), which shows the influence of Herman Melville's *Moby*

Dick on O'Dell's work, is a story of three brothers on a Nantucket whaler. *Journey to Jericho* (1969) recounts a boy's cross-country journey from West Virginia to California. *Sing Down the Moon* (1970), the third of O'Dell's books to win a Newbery Honor Medal, tells of the experiences of Bright Morning during the time, immediately after the Civil War, when the federal government removed hundreds of thousands Indians from their ancestral lands. Two books are set in England. *The Hawk That Dare Not Hunt by Day* (1975) is the adventure of a boy who helps William Tyndale, first English translator of the Bible. In *The 290* (1976), a Liverpool youth signs aboard a ship bound for action in the American Civil War. O'Dell's most recent novel, *Sara Bishop* (1980), is about an orphan girl who survives in a cave during the American Revolution. Two of O'Dell's novels, *Child of Fire* (1974) and *Kathleen, Please Come Home* (1978), deal with the troubled lives of contemporary California teenagers.

O'Dell's best-known books are those written about former times, particularly the past of the western United States and Mexico. In them, he not only presents historical facts accurately and portrays his settings vividly and concretely, he also analyzes a major theme in American history: the conflicts between cultures. O'Dell has made reference to the contemporary relevance of his historical novels: "I have the feeling that the present is the past and the past is the present. The fundamental human is about the same as he was a couple of thousand years ago . . . . Human needs for love, affection, understanding, a chance to succeed at something, are about the same." However, he has stated that modern youths do not have the sense of roots or tradition possessed by many of his fictional characters.

In addition to noting the accuracy with which O'Dell handles his historical backgrounds and the vividness of his narratives, critics have praised the author's prose style and his handling of point-of-view. He mixes a simple, rhythmic style, which gives his narratives the quality of legend, with lively, realistic dialogue, which gives credibility to the characters. Most of the novels are written in the first person which, O'Dell has said, increases the credibility. More important, it enables the author to present more fully the development of his characters.

TIPS FOR PARENTS AND TEACHERS: Over twenty years after its publication, *Island of the Blue Dolphins* remains a favorite with upper elementary and junior high readers. In studying the novel, they should notice the stages of Karana's character growth. Following the reading of this book, they should be encouraged to consider the sequel, *Zia,* as an examination of the disastrous results of culture conflicts.

Oxenbury, Helen *(1938 –)*
English

Helen Oxenbury, who was born in Ipswich, Suffolk, was not originally interested in writing and illustrating children's books. She had studied theatre design before she met and married artist-illustrator John Burningham. She later remarked, "Watching my husband through every stage of his books was as good if not better than a two-year course in book illustration, and I was 'studying' under one of the best authors' illustrators in the country."

Her first book, *Numbers of Things* (1967), a counting book, revealed her sense of page design, her vivid use of color, and her strong use of line. A year later, she indicated her sense of humor in the illustrations to Leo Tolstoy's *The Great Big Enormous Turnip*. In 1969, she was awarded the Kate Greenaway Medal for two books, Margaret Mahy's *The Dragon of an Ordinary Family* and Edward Lear's *The Quangle-Wangle's Hat*. In both books, her illustrations reflected the humorous absurdity of the stories. In the latter, her double spreads of the hat reveal its enormity and its soft texture, and through her use of line and color she portrays the ridiculousness of the animals who come to live in the hat.

Oxenbury's *ABC of Things* (1971) shows her employment of incongruous groupings. For the letter "D," a dog and a duck sit at a desk; for "O," an otter clings to the neck of a surprised and annoyed ostrich; for "T," tigers and a turkey perch on a rushing locomotive. In *Pig Tale* (1973), she uses humorous verse and pictures to recount the discovery made by two pigs that their new-found wealth does not bring them happiness. During the 1970s, Helen Oxenbury has ilustrated several works by others, including Lewis Carroll's *The Hunting of the Snark* and Ivor Cutler's *Elephant Girl* (1976). One of the most popular of the books she has illustrated has been *Cakes and Custard* (1974), a collection of traditional children's rhymes chosen by Brian Alderson.

TIPS FOR PARENTS AND TEACHERS: Preschool and early elementary aged children enjoy finding and discussing the absurdities in Oxenbury's illustrations. In the middle elementary grades, *The Dragon of an Ordinary Family* can serve as an introduction to both dragon-lore and parody.

Parnall, Peter *(1936 –)*
American

Born in Syracuse, New York, Peter Parnall spent much of his childhood in the outdoors, observing animals. He briefly studied veterinary medicine at Cornell University and art at the Pratt Institute before working as art director for a small magazine and for an advertising agency. In 1964, he illustrated his first children's book, Wayne Short's *The Cheechakoes*, and since then has illustrated over fifty other books. He has also written four books of his own: *The Mountain* (1971), *The Great Fish* (1973), *Alfalfa Hill* (1975), and *A Dog's Book of Birds* (1977). For his illustrations for three books by Byrd Baylor, *The Desert Is Theirs* (1975), *Hawk, I Am Your Brother* (1976), and *The Way to Start a Day* (1977), Parnall was awarded Caldecott Honor Medals. His line drawings, to which are added limited colors, reflect the rhythm of Baylor's prose and sensitively and accurately depict the life of the southwest desert.

TIPS FOR PARENTS AND TEACHERS: In examining the illustrations for the Baylor books, upper elementary students should notice how Parnall visually embodies the main theme: the harmonious interrelationships of all elements of life.

Paterson, Katherine *(1932 –   )*
American

Born in Tsing-Tsiang Pu, China, where her parents were missionaries, Katherine Paterson, like many of her characters, moved around frequently as a child, and, particularly when living in the United States, she often felt herself an outsider. During the 1950s, she worked as a missionary in Japan, before returning to the United States, where she married John Paterson, a minister. She began writing during the 1970s, when she created *The Sign of the Chrysanthemum* for an adult education class in which she was enrolled. Since then she has written five novels and a collection of short stories. Three of her novels, *The Sign of the Chrysanthemum* (1973), *Of Nightingales that Weep* (1974), and *The Master Puppeteer* (1976), are set in Japan. Three are set in the upper southern states: *Bridge to Terabithia* (1977), winner of the Newbery Medal, *The Great Gilly Hopkins* (1978), and *Jacob Have I Loved* (1980), also a Newbery Medal winner. *Of Angels and Other Strangers* (1979) is a collection of Christmas stories originally told to her family. While set in different locales and different time periods, each of the novels is based on emotional experiences of herself and her children. Her two daughters, both adopted, provided the inspiration for *The Sign of the Chrysanthemum* and *The Great Gilly Hopkins*; her eldest son is not unlike one of the characters in *The Master Puppeteer*; her son's grief over the death of a close friend served as the starting point for *Bridge to Terabithia*. She, herself, experienced as a child the sense of loneliness and uncertainty felt by many of her young heroes and heroines.

The Sign of the Chrysanthemum and *Of Nightingales That Weep* are both set in feudal Japan. Muna, the central character of the former, is the illegitimate son of a samurai warrior. After his mother's death, he sets out to find his father so that he will have a true name. Although his quest is unsuccessful, he develops a sense of self-worth and an awareness of his responsibility to others. In the latter, Takiko, the talented daughter of a samurai, cannot accept her father's death and her mother's remarriage to a humble potter. As a member of the royal court, she witnesses the civil wars of the times and falls in love with a spy from the rival faction. Only at the conclusion of the novel does she discover her true home and role in life. In *The Master Puppeteer*, set during the eighteenth century in a time of great civil unrest, thirteen-year-old Jiro becomes an apprentice to a puppeteer, only to discover that his master works for Saburo, an unknown bandit who robs the corrupt merchants to aid the poor.

Paterson's three most recent novels are set in America. *Bridge to Terabithia*, which takes place in rural Virginia, portrays the relationship between ten-year-old Jess Aarons and Leslie Burke. The only boy and the middle child of five, Jess is very insecure. When Leslie, the daughter of two writers who have moved to the country to reassess their values, arrives, he feels threatened. However, with the girl he creates Terabithia, a kingdom in the woods, where he discovers the values of friendship. Leslie is drowned in a spring flood and Jess must learn to continue life while at the same time revering the memory of his friend. The title heroine of *The Great Gilly Hopkins* has spent her life moving from foster home to foster home. Clever and tough, she does not wish to relate emotionally to anyone except her mother, a flower child who had given her up for adoption when the girl was only three. At the end of the novel, she moves to live with her grandmother in Washington and accepts the fact that her mother does not care for her. *Jacob Have I Loved* is set on an island in Chesapeake Bay during World War II. Louise Bradshaw feels inferior to her sister Caroline, a beautiful and musically talented girl to whom her family and friends seem to pay more attention. Only when she grows up and moves to a West Virginia mountain town as a nurse does Louise understand that she, too, has an important role to play.

Although set in two different cultures and in many different time periods, Katherine Paterson's novels deal with a common theme: the troubled, often lonely, children's growth to maturity. They must discover who they are and where they belong. The quests are difficult, for they must recognize both their strengths and weaknesses and their responsibilities to others as well as to themselves. Like the animals that Jess Aarons sketches, they often find themselves in "impossible fixes"; caught between conflicting loyalties, they must maintain their integrity without violating that of others. Friendship is important, although they do not realize that at first. Often friends die, and their deaths provide the central characters with the ability to mature. Life does not always seem fair, and the children experience many disillusionments; however, in the end, they come to a fuller appreciation of the world in which they live and their places in it.

TIPS FOR PARENTS AND TEACHERS: Paterson's books are best used in the upper elementary and junior high grades. Although the titles of the novels at first appear unusual, their significance becomes apparent after the books have been finished. Students enjoy discussing the appropriateness of these titles as well as tracing the steps by which the characters grow inwardly and reach the ends of their quests, even if the ends were not what they originally expected.

Perrault, Charles *(1628 – 1703)*
French

Born in Paris, Charles Perrault practiced law before serving as a government official. After his retirement from public life in 1683, he devoted much time to writing. In 1697, he published his most famous work, *Histoires ou Contes du temps passé, avec des Moralités,* a collection of eleven fairy tales. The volume, an outgrowth of the seventeenth-century interest in old folktales, contained eight prose pieces: "La Belle au bois dormant" ("Sleeping Beauty"), "Le petit chaperon rouge" ("Little Red Riding Hood"), "La barbe bleue" ("Bluebeard"), "La chat botte" ("Puss in Boots"), "Les fées" ("The Fairies"), "Cendrillon" ("Cinderella"), "Riquet à la houppe" ("Ricky with the Tuft"), and "Le petit poucet" ("Hop o' My Thumb"). Three verse stories were included: "Peau d'âne" ("Donkey-Skin"), "Les souhaits ridicules" ("The Foolish Wishes"), and "Griselidis" ("Patient Griselda"). The frontispiece of the volume bore the subtitle *Contes de Ma Mère l'Oye (Tales by Mother Goose)* and a dedication to Elizabeth Charlotte d'Orleans, the King's niece. The work was purported to have been written by Pierre d'Armancouer, Perrault's youngest son, who was nineteen at the time. This ascription has led to much speculation as to the true authorship of the stories. Some believe that Perrault heard the stories from his son and that the two coauthored them. Others believe that, wishing to avoid ridicule for having written apparently childish stories, Perrault placed his son's name in the volume.

The tales became very popular and were often imitated. In fact, Perrault had great influence on the eighteenth-century fashion of writing fairy tales. The first English edition, translated by Robert Samber, appeared in 1729, and since then the stories have been translated into many languages. The *Contes* have been illustrated by such notable artists as Gustav Doré and William Heath Robinson. Individual tales have been illustrated by Marcia Brown, whose version of *Cinderella* (1954) was awarded a Caldecott Medal; William Stobbs (*Little Red Ridinghood*, 1972); and Paul Galdone (*Puss in Boots*, 1976), among others. As the Perrault retellings of the stories circulated in Europe in the eighteenth century, many of them returned to the oral tradition. For example, it is believed that the version of "Little Red-Cap" collected by the Brothers Grimm descended from Perrault's tale. In Perrault's stories kindness or goodness is the most important virtue. Because he is kind to a cat, the human hero of "Puss in Boots" is aided by his pet and marries a beautiful princess. Cinderella forgives her sisters and gives them a place at court. The kind sister in "The Fairies" is rewarded with roses and diamonds. Although in "Bluebeard" and "Patient Griselda" marriage can bring unhappiness, it is generally seen as the greatest bliss in life. Cinderella, the cat's master, the Sleeping Beauty, and Donkey-Skin find happiness with their royal mates. Beauty is generally a reflection of inner goodness, although, in order to see this beauty and goodness, it is sometimes necessary to look beneath appearances. Four of the stories embody one of the most common folktale motifs, the triumph of the youngest child; as Perrault stated in the moral to "Hop o' My Thumb," "Often the runt of the litter ends up making the family fortune."

The stories are not without violence and threats of death. The most violent is "Bluebeard," in which the young bride discovers the corpses of her husband's previous brides and is only just rescued by her brothers. One of the most frequent forms of death is by being devoured. Little Red Riding Hood is gobbled up by the wolf, and is not rescued as she is in other versions. The mother-in-law of the Sleeping Beauty wishes to eat her granchildren. Only Hop o' My Thumb's quick thinking saves him and his brothers from becoming the ogre's dinner.

Perrault's most interesting additions to his traditional materials are the morals he appended to the stories. Most of the morals were straightforward, as in "Bluebeard": "Curiosity is a charming passion, but can only be satisfied at the price of a thousand regrets," or "Puss in Boots": "A great inheritance may be a fine thing; but hard work and ingenuity will take a young man further than his father's money." At times, however, the morals are satiric, as in the alternate moral for Cinderella: "However great may be your god-given store, they will never help you to get on in the world unless you have a godfather or a godmother to put them to work for you."

There are other satiric elements unobtrusively interspersed in the stories. In "Puss in Boots," the brothers in dividing their inheritance do not hire lawyers, for "if they had done so, they would have been stripped quite bare, of course." When the hero meets the princess, the king, impressed with the youth's wealth, offers his daughter in marriage, "after his fifth or sixth glass of wine." In "The Sleeping Beauty," the courtiers are not interested in the prince or princess: "Since none of them were in love, they were all dying of hunger."

TIPS FOR PARENTS AND TEACHERS: All of Perrault's stories make good reading, particularly in the middle elementary grades. His versions of "Cinderella," "The Sleeping Beauty," and "Little Red Riding Hood" can be compared to those of the Brothers Grimm. Students in the upper elementary grades can discuss Perrault's morals and can make up their own morals for the various stories.

Petersham, Miska *(1888 – 1960), and* Petersham, Maud *(1890 – 1971)*
American

Born in a small village near Budapest, Hungary, Miska Petersham studied art in Italy, and moved to America in 1912, quickly finding work. While he was employed at the International Arts Service in New York, he met Maud Fuller, whom he tutored and later married. During the 1930s, the Petershams illustrated textbooks and works by such authors as Carl Sandburg (*Rootabaga Stories*, 1922; *Rootabaga Pigeons*, 1923), Charles Lamb (*Tales from Shakespeare*, 1923), Johanna Spyri (*Heidi*, 1932), and Collodi (*Pinocchio*, 1932). *Miki*, the first book they wrote and illustrated themelves, appeared in 1929.

The Petershams' books can be divided into three categories: Bible stories, books about American history and culture, and their own original stories. Included in the first group are *The Ark of Father Noah and Mother Noah* (1930), *The Christ Child* (1931), *David* (1938), *Joseph and His Brothers* (1938), *Moses* (1938), *Ruth* (1938), and *The Shepherd Psalm* (1962). The text for each of these volumes was based on the King James Version of the Bible and the pictures on sketches done on the Petershams' trips to the Near East. Many of the Petershams' stories were based on the authors' own backgrounds. *Miki* tells of an American boy's visit to Hungary and draws on Miska Petersham's boyhood. *Auntie and Celia Jane and Miki* (1932) tells of Maud Petersham's childhood with her aunt and of son Miki's joyful times when the aunt lived in their house. In *Miki and Mary: Their Search for Treasures* (1934), Miki is joined by a cousin on a trip to Europe.

The Petershams are best-known for their books dealing with American history and customs: *An American ABC* (1941), *The Rooster Crows* (1945), a Caldecott Medal book, *The History of One Hundred Years of U.S. Postage Stamps* (1947), *A Bird in the Hand: Sayings from Poor Richard's Almanac* (1951), *The Story of the Presidents of the United States of America* (1953), and *The Silver Mace: a Story of Williamsburg* (1956). Miska Petersham explained the significance of these books: "In these books we make I am happy when we can picture some of those wonderful things American children can claim as their heritage. . . . We are trying to put before the children of this country those things which are theirs for the taking." Maud Petersham remarked, "We long to make children understand the courage, faith, and hard work it took to build America."

TIPS FOR PARENTS AND TEACHERS: The poems from *The Rooster Crows* can be used along with traditional nursery rhymes for children of all ages. Works relating to American history should be grouped with similar works by other authors, thus giving readers in the upper elementary grades a variety of interpretations.

Picture Books and Illustration

The visual and literary arts have been closely related since earliest times. Wall paintings, found in caves around the world, are believed to be simple narrations of important events and religious stories of primitive peoples. The elaborate masks which have been developed by many societies were often used to enhance dramatizations of major stories. Not surprisingly, books for children began to include illustrations from an early date, it being the belief of adults that visual accompaniments to words helped young readers to understand more fully the materials they were reading. The earliest picture book for children dates back to 1659, when the Moravian bishop Comenius published *Orbis Pictus*, an educational volume which was republished in many European countries. One of the most important early American picture books was *The New England Primer*, believed to have been first published in 1691.

The illustrations for early children's books were generally very crude wood blocks, and the resultant pictures were generally extremely awkward. However, as the process of steel engraving developed in the later eighteenth century, illustrations became more refined. Two of the first major children's illustrators were Thomas Bewick (1753–1828), whose best-known work appeared in such books as *Fables of Aesop and Others* (1774), and George Cruikshank (1792–1878), who illustrated the *Fairy Library* (1853) and *Grimms' German Popular Stories* (1823 and 1826).

The first great flowering of the picture book took place in England in the 1860s and 1870s, at which time three artists of great talent, Randolph Caldecott, Walter Crane, and Kate Greenaway, collaborated with Edmund Evans, the foremost color engraver of the day, to produce what are considered now to be among the finest picture books of all times. Until this period, limitations of the printing processes made it virtually impossible to recreate both the grace and movement of line and the variety of color found in most narrative art. However, Evans, using box wood for his plates and often using several plates to reproduce the subtle gradations of color, was able to print pictures which were very close to the originals. Crane, with his concern for quality illustration and his sense of page design, revealed the artistic possibilities of the picture book; Caldecott showed how to make pictures extensions of, rather than mere illustrations of the meaning of the text; while Greenaway made delicate color and exquisite detail integral aspects of illustration for children.

During this period, several of the greatest illustrators of longer works also published. In England, John Tenniel created illustrations for Lewis Carroll's Alice books (1865, 1871) which have never been equalled. In the United States, Howard Pyle entered the new field of magazine illustration, contributing to such periodicals as the famous *St. Nicholas* magazine. Pyle was one of the first major artists to illustrate in full color and taught such well-known later illustrators as N.C. Wyeth.

Another major flowering of picture book artistry occurred in the early decades of the twentieth century. Beatrix Potter, drawing on her detailed knowledge of English plants and animals, created a series of minute classics with books like *The Tale of Peter Rabbit* (1902) and *The Tale of Squirrel Nutkin* (1903). L. Leslie Brook not only illustrated well-known fairy-tales and nursery rhymes, but also, in *Johnny Crow's Garden* (1903), *Johnny Crow's Party* (1907), and *Johnny Crow's New Garden* (1935), combined few words with a richly humorous series of illustrations to create three humorous classics which retain their humor and vibrancy today. Arthur Rackham illustrated dozens of picture books, using watercolors, silhouettes, and other media to enhance the mood of the various stories he dealt with. In the 1920s, Ernest Shepard illustrated A.A. Milne's well-known Winnie-the-Pooh books with such success that, like Tenniel's with Carroll's, his name is almost synonymous with that of Milne.

For the past fify years, the picture book has been the dominant form of children's literature in both England and the United States. In America, the publication of Wanda Gág's *Millions of Cats* in 1928 is said to mark the beginning of the modern picture book, integrating pictures and text in such a way that the total impact of the story comes from the combination of both elements. During the 1930s, Robert Lawson, Ingri and Edgar Perrin d'Aulaire, and Virginia Lee Burton furthered the development of the form, and in 1938 the American Library Association first awarded the Caldecott Medal for the most distinguished American picture book for children.

Since the conclusion of World War II, the picture book has flourished, with a variety of artists expanding the characteristics of the form. Choosing media suited to the tone and culture of the stories she was considering, Marcia Brown created a series of distinguished single volume retellings of folktales from around the world; Robert McCloskey mixed realistic settings with humorous incidents in a group of stories located in the areas in which he had lived; Ezra Jack Keats used collages to depict the lives of small children living in inner cities; and Maurice Sendak explored the inner worlds of the small child. In England, Brian Wildsmith used brilliant colors in an impressionistic way as he retold simple fables and wrote short tales of his own; Charles Keeping, like Keats, depicted the life of the inner-city, employing styles which reflected the child's impression of the realities he experienced.

Artists have used a variety of media, carefully choosing materials and techniques which best express their themes. Certain artists have become associated with one form of art: for example, Keats, as noted above, and Leo Lionni have used collage. However, other artists have experimented with styles and media. Barbara Cooney, twice winner of the Caldecott Medal, has borrowed from Medieval, Renaissance, and American primitive styles. Gail Haley, the only person to have won both the Caldecott (American) and the Greenaway (English) medals, approximated the texture of medieval tapestries in *The Green Man* (1979) and African designs in *A Story, a Story*. Gerald McDermott, who has retold and illustrated folktales from around the world, incorporates the design elements of the appropriate cultures into his own art. This technique is best seen in *Arrow to the Sun* (1974), in which patterns from Pueblo pottery and wall paintings blend with his modern graphic design qualities to communicate theme and character development.

In "reading" a picture book, one must carefully notice all the visual elements of the volume and discover how these are made part of the total book. For example, cover page, end-papers, title page, and dedication page often act as a kind of "overture," presenting images, color patterns, and designs which will be important in the main body of the story. A case in point is Virginia Lee Burton's *The Little House* (1942), in which the cover not only depicts the main character, but also introduces the circle motif which will be important later; the endpapers are like old-fashioned wallpaper, reinforcing the nostalgic elements of the story, and the pictures on the endpapers ironically present the progress of transportation. The title page, in addition to employing natural colors which later will symbolize the happy times of the house, also employ old-fashioned sampler-like lettering for the title, again emphasizing the nostalgia. The dedication page reintroduces the circle motif, this time in the form of a circle of daisies, flowers that will be related to the house's happy times in the country.

Within the body of the story, the pictures make use of several significant elements; small details can reveal elements about characters. Max, in Sendak's *Where the Wild Things Are*, has drawn a picture of what looks like one of the creatures he later meets in the dream journey. Peter, in Keat's *Whistle for Willie*, slouches disconsolately against a lamp-post, at the edge of the picture, an indication of his feelings of inadequacy. In Leo Lionni's *Frederick*, the color gradually disappears from the pictures as the winterbound mice become more bored and depressed.

In addition to carefully studying individual pictures, the "reader" should notice the relationships between pages. In *Where the Wild Things Are*, the illustrations become bigger and bigger as Max moves into his dream world. In *The Little House*, the circular lines which dominated the pictures of the house's happy times in the country are replaced by sharper angular lines as it is engulfed by the spreading city.

TIPS FOR PARENTS AND TEACHERS: In choosing picture books for children, adults should look first for quality illustrations — the art work should not be inferior; and second for illustrations which enhance the verbal elements, adding new dimensions to the words. By reading a number of books which have won the Caldecott and Greenaway Medals, adults will become aware of both the qualities which make some books better than others and the variety of artistic styles to be found in picture books. In working with younger children, adults should encourage children to look carefully at individual pages, including covers, endpapers, and title pages, spotting details, colors, and designs. By becoming an attentive viewer, the child will get more out of each book he or she experiences and will, in most cases, become a more careful reader when the attention is turned to words. It should not be thought that picture books are only for preschoolers or children in the early elementary grades. Students of the upper elementary and junior high grades will enjoy studying illustrated versions of folktales and myths from around the world and will enjoy such complex picture books as Jean Jacques Loup's *The Architect* (1977), Guy Billout's *Number 24* (1973), and Jörg Steiner and Jörg Muller's *Rabbit Island* (1977).

Poetry

Of all types of literature, poetry is probably the most ancient. The religious and ceremonial chants of primitive people constituted the earliest poems; in cultures with written languages, major poets have generally appeared before major prose writers; and children's earliest vocal reponses are often rhythmic and singsong. But, although poetry seems to be a basic aspect of human life, it is not easy to define. William Wordsworth called it "the spontaneous overflow of powerful feelings," while Alexander Pope praised poetry because it contained "what oft was thought but ne'er so well expressed." For Robert Frost, poetry was language used to provide "a momentary stay against confusion." If poetry in general is difficult to define, children's poetry is equally so. Perhaps the best that can be said is that children's poetry is that poetry which can be understood and enjoyed by the children reading or listening to it. It does not have to be specifically written for them; indeed, some of the worst so-called children's poetry was consciously created for a young audience. Poetry which is dull and confusing for girls and boys is certainly not children's poetry.

One of the most distinguishing features of poetry is its use of what educators Joan L. Glaser and Gurney Williams have called "hard-working words." The sounds and rhythms of words and their connotative as well as denotative meanings are used to convey the intellectual or emotional content of a poem. Rhyme, the repetition of similar sounds, is one of the most easily recognized elements of poetic language, although not all poems rhyme. The skillful writer can use rhyming words to emphasize points and to create pleasing musical patterns; the incompetent writer is often a slave to rhyme and the results are often heavy-handed and monotonous. While not all poems use rhyme, nearly all poems employ some kind of rhythm, in which mixtures of stressed and unstressed syllables create patterns. Regular rhythm is generally referred to as *meter*, in which accented and unaccented syllables are found. Like rhyme, a rigid metric pattern, carried on line after line, can become monotonous; however, with subtle variation, metric patterns enhance mood and message. Free verse does not use a regular meter or line length, but uses other devices to create a sense of rhythm. Irregular rhythmic patterns may consist of repetition of similar phrases at the beginnings of lines, or the repetition of initial consonants (alliteration). In addition to alliteration and rhyme, poets employ other sound patterns to develop their poems. One of the most important of these is onomatopoeia, the use of sounds which reflect the sense of the words (the phrase "sizzling bacon" is a favorite example).

More than is the case in prose, poetry uses words to create vivid, specific pictures and to suggest a variety of connotations. *Imagery* is the term used to describe those words which evoke sense perceptions; the good poet is able to choose exactly the right word or phrase to create the physical picture he wishes. Unlike most prose, where the word means very specifically what it says, poets use language connotatively, bringing into a poem a number of related ideas or emotions. In reading poems, one should pause over individual words, allowing them to create the emotions, pictures, or ideas the poet intended. Poetry should not be skimmed; it is not for the fast or superficial reader, but for the contemplative reader who wishes to savor rather than gulp.

A final element of poetry, one which many poets use to give their works an overall shape or form, is the stanza, a group of lines which has a definite pattern, usually determined by the rhyme scheme, length and metric pattern of the lines, and the number of lines. For example, the ballad stanza consists of four lines, the first and third contain four strong beats while the second and fourth contain three; there is also a set rhyme scheme which is consistent within each ballad. Two favorite stanza patterns with children in the middle elementary grades are the limerick and the haiku. The former, used generally for humorous subjects, has five lines, the first, second, and fifth of which are the same length and rhyme, while the third and fourth are shorter and rhyme with each other. The haiku, a major form of Japanese poetry, consists of a total of seventeen syllables, five in the first line, seven in the second, and five in the third.

Until the later part of the eighteenth century, there was virtually no poetry written for children. However, children probably enjoyed ballads, the short poems now known as nursery rhymes, and those poems for adults which were within their range of understanding. Four of the earliest writers who created poetry specifically for chilaren were Isaac Watts, whose religious poetry was collected in *Divine Songs* (1715), William Blake, who captured the joys and terrors of childhood in *Songs of Innocence* (1789) and *Songs of Experience* (1794), and Jane and Ann Taylor, who emphasize correct moral and social conduct in *Poems for Infant Minds* (1804–5). In the United States, early poetry was either heavily religious, or copied the patterns of the above-mentioned English writers, especially Watts and the Taylors. What is now considered the first major American children's poem, Clement Moore's *A Visit from St. Nicholas*, appeared in 1823.

The mid- and late nineteenth century marked the first great flowering of poetry for children. Interestingly, the most important poets created nonsense verses, poems which presented foolish, often eccentric characters, absurd situations, and humorous language. These authors realized that poetry for children need not be moralistic or religiously edifying; they understood that children enjoyed ridiculous situations and language and believed that catering to these tastes was in itself a worthwhile goal of poetry. In England, Edward Lear perfected the limerick to create a portrait gallery of strange and funny characters, while Lewis Carroll's Alice books parodied the dull poetry which had until then provided the main poetic fare for children. In the United States, Laura Richards began publishing her nonsense poetry in the new children's magazine *St. Nicholas*. Nonsense poetry became immediately popular with children and has maintained its popularity into the twentieth century. Some of the major writers in the tradition established by Lear, Carroll, and Richards are Hilaire Belloc, John Ciardi, and Dennis Lee.

Another important tradition which developed in the late nineteenth and early twentieth centuries was that of exploring the thoughts and perceptions of the young child, seeing the world from his, rather than an adult's point of view. The greatest of these writers, Robert Louis Stevenson, created in *A Child's Garden of Verses* (1885) a group of poems which celebrate the imaginative world of the solitary young child and which recognize the terrors as well as the joyous moments in that world. Walter de la Mare, in numerous volumes published in the early decades of this century, looked carefully at the worlds of nature and the imagination, and presented them in sensitive and subtle poetic language. During the 1920s, A.A. Milne created two small volumes dealing with the world of the young child, *When We Were Very Young* (1924) and *Now We Are Six* (1927). Written for his son, Christopher Robin, they are excellent reflections of the egocentric view of the world taken by a preschooler.

The range of modern poetry for children is so great that we can note here only a few of the major trends and important writers. Recognizing that children respond most fully to poetry to which they can relate, authors have first sought to deal with the world familiar to children and then to introduce them to new, yet still important elements they may not yet know. The inner world of the child, his emotions, sense of self, and reactions to his ever-expanding environment have been sensitively portrayed by such poets as Myra Cohn Livingston, David McCord, and Karla Kuskin. Harry Behn, Carl Sandburg, and Robert Frost have described the world of nature. As urbanization has progressed and the city experience has become the dominant one for most children, city poems have been included in such anthologies as Nancy Larrick's *I Heard a Scream in the Street* (1970). The life of minority groups have provided the basis for collections by James Houston (*Songs of the Dream People: Chants of the Indians and Eskimos*, 1972), and Nikki Giovanni (*Spin a Soft Black Song*, 1971).

Another recent trend in the publishing of poetry is the gathering of poems dealing with the same subject into anthologies, thus giving children a variety of approaches by a variety of authors. Among the many fine anthologies are Arnold Adoff's *I Am the Darker Brother* (1968), William Cole's *A Book of Animal Poems* (1973), Mary Downie and Barbara Robertson's *The Wind Has Wings: Poems from Canada* (1968), Lee Bennett Hopkins' *City Talk* (1970), Myra Cohn Livingston's *Callooh! Callay! Holiday Poems for Young Readers* (1978), Lillian Morrison's *The Sidewalk Racer and Other Poems of Sports and Motion* (1977), and Helen Plotz's *Imagination's Other Place: Poems of Science and Mathematics* (1955). There are several excellent general anthologies, including *A Time for Poetry* (edited by May Hill Arbuthnot and Sheldon Root, 1968), *Piping Down the Valleys Wild* (edited by Nancy Larrick, 1968), and *The Oxford Book of Children's Verse* (edited by Iona and Peter Opie, 1973).

TIPS FOR PARENTS AND TEACHERS: Children can be started on poetry at a very early age. Even though they may not understand the words, children of one or two years old enjoy the music and rhythm of poetry. In fact, parents should regularly read aloud the poetry they themselves enjoy. The nursery rhymes can be introduced at an early age, with the children being encouraged to clap to the rhythm of the words and to recite poems when they are able to. In choosing poetry for preschoolers and children in the early elementary grades, it is important to find material to which they can relate; generally this means including a generous sampling of poems about objects, animals, and people they are familiar with, and several nonsense poems. Poems about silly situations seem to be favorites of children of all ages. Children in the middle elementary grades enjoy narrative poetry, while children in the upper elementary and junior high grades are able to respond to poems dealing with the less happy elements of life. It is important to avoid poems which are didactic, sentimental, and condescending; poems which talk about childhood rather than to children tend to turn children off poetry. The teacher should make poetry an integral part of the school day. In addition to having a special time in which the teacher and student can share poems that are particular favorites, poetry can be introduced at any time which seems appropriate: for example, when a child tells the class about something special that has happened in his or her life, or when an aspect of a science or social studies lesson reminds the teacher of a related poem. Memorization and over-analysis are areas of poetry study which should be avoided with children. Remember: poetry was meant to be read aloud—practice the poems you like so that you can read them more effectively to children.

The Tale of Peter Rabbit, by Beatrix Potter, Frederick Warne & Co., London, 1902. Potter's delicate water colors catch the excitement of the chase as Peter runs for his life.

Potter, Beatrix *(1866 – 1943)*
English

Born in South Kensington of an independently wealthy family, Beatrix Potter spent a quiet childhood with her younger brother and her authoritarian parents. The highlights of her childhood were the long vacations the family spent in Scotland and the Lake District of England. She was interested in reading, drawing, and natural history and sketched her pets and the scenery and wild animals of these regions.

In 1893, Beatrix Potter's career as a storybook writer-illustrator began. In a letter to five-year-old Noel Moore, the son of a former governess, she included the sketches and story of Peter Rabbit. Several years later, noticing the vogue for small-format children's books, she tried unsuccessfully to have it published and, this failing, had a privately printed edition of 250 brought out at a cost to her of eleven pounds. When publisher Frederick Warne noticed its modest success, he invited her to resubmit the story, which appeared in 1902 in an edition of 6000 and became an instant success. It was the first of a series of books which was to make Beatrix Potter one of the best-known writers in the English language. It has been translated into twelve languages.

In 1903, Warne published *The Tailor of Gloucester,* the author's personal favorite, a story she had heard years earlier, and one which was also first published privately. In the next ten years, beginning with *The Tale of Squirrel Nutkin* in 1903 and ending with *The Tale of Pigling Bland* in 1913, Beatrix published eighteen books with Warne. Not all were originally issued in the now familiar size of 4½" x 5". *The Pie and the Patty Pan* (1905), *The Roly-Poly Pudding* (1908), and *Ginger and Pickles* (1909) appeared in large format; and *The Story of a Fierce Bad Rabbit* (1906) and *The Story of Miss Moppet* (1906) first appeared in panoramic form. So successful were her books that they quickly went into second and third printings. In 1906, with her royalties and money from an inheritance, she was able to purchase Hilltop Farm near Sawrey in the Lake District. In 1913, she married William Heelis of nearby Ambleside. Although she wrote six new books, concluding in 1930 with *The Tale of Little Pig Robinson*, also based on a story letter, Beatrix Potter's interest in story writing seems to have been replaced by her concern for farming.

Surveying Beatrix Potter's complete works, one is aware of an overall pattern or vision which, although based on her love and knowledge of the English countryside and its animals, has a unique quality. In a letter to Bertha Mahoney Miller she wrote, "I do not remember a time when I did not try to invent pictures and make for myself a fairyland amongst the wild-flowers, the animals, fungi, mosses, woods and streams, all the thousand objects of the countryside; that pleasant unchanging world of realism and romance, which in our northern clime is stiffened by hard weather, a tough ancestry, and the strength that comes from the hills." It is, she wrote in her journal, the vision of childhood tempered by the common sense and knowl-edge of adulthood. She presents a rural world free of the influences of the modern technology of her time, and populated by a number of animals who live in a generally harmonious and interrelated way. The almost evanescent quality of her watercolors and the clothing and homes of the animals have the effect of moving her settings one step from the ordinary world of the author and her readers.

The adventures of her characters are related in a prose style which, at its best, is the perfect vehicle for the material. Beatrix Potter was a demanding and disciplined writer, as she explained in *The Horn Book*: "I think I write carefully because I enjoy my writing, and enjoy taking pains over it . . . . My usual way of writing is to scribble, and cut out, and write it again and again. The shorter and plainer the better. And I read the Bible (*unrevised* version and Old Testament) if I feel my style wants chastening."

Her plots are most successful when they focus on one or two major adventures of one or two characters. Peter Rabbit has a narrow escape in Mr. McGregor's garden; Squirrel Nutkin's impudence leads to the loss of his tail; Jemima Puddle-Duck's silliness and ignorance nearly result in her becoming a dinner for Mr. Fox. Her less successful stories, such as *The Tale of Mrs.*

Tittlemouse (1910), *Ginger and Pickles*, and *The Tale of Little Pig Robinson*, lack this focus and are loose and often rambling. Throughout her works, Beatrix Potter views honestly the foolishness, vanity, ignorance, and indiscretion of her characters, revealing her common sense attitude to their weaknesses. Although she satirizes, she does so with a gentle humor and good nature.

Reading all the stories, one notices many recurring motifs. Chief of these are clothing, food, and home. Making clothing is the tailor of Gloucester's livelihood and without his occupation he is in danger of starving; Peter Rabbit's loss of his shoes and clothing results from his indiscretion and gluttony. Peter, the Flopsy Bunnies, and Pig Robinson find themselves in dangerous situations because of overeating and they find themselves potential dinners for others. Often the stories conclude with the central character's return to his dwelling, safe and presumably wiser for his adventures. Home represents security in an often dangerous world, a world which Beatrix Potter views without the sentimentality so often found in animal fantasy. She believed that "Nature, though never consciously wicked, has always been ruthless." Thus, the predatory activities of the fox and badger in *The Tale of Mr. Tod* (1912), although terrifying, are also seen as part of Nature's ways. Only Mr. McGregor, who captures the six sleeping children of Benjamin Bunny, and the cook and captain in *Little Pig Robinson* are sharply criticized and even then, with her common sense, Beatrix Potter draws attention to the follies of Benjamin's life-style and Little Pig Robinson's naiveté.

The greatest triumph of the Beatrix Potter tales is the perfect blend of the text and the art. This art is a mixture of the realism and romance noted above. Many of the characters, including the hedgehog Mrs. Tiggy-Winkle and the mice and rabbits, were based on the pets she had as a child and young woman and on the animals of Hilltop Farm. The backgrounds are similarly painted from actual scenes: Cumberland in *The Tale of Peter Rabbit*, Derwentwater in *The Tale of Squirrel Nutkin*, Hilltop in *The Tale of Jemima Puddle-Duck* (1908). Her careful observations of interiors and furniture are seen in *The Tailor of Gloucester* and *The Tale of Tom Kitten* (1907). However, this realism is transformed in the stories. The backgrounds never dominate and the animals assume unique personalities. As is seen best in *The Tale of Jeremy Fisher* (1906), they are generally dressed in clothes which do not distort their animal anatomies and their homes are scaled down to their appropriate sizes. Only in stories like *The Tale of Pigling Bland* and *The Tale of Little Pig Robinson*, where animals and people converse and interact freely, is the credibility of the Beatrix Potter world weakened.

TIPS FOR PARENTS AND TEACHERS: Even though only some of the stories will be widely read, school libraries should have the complete set of

Potter works. In the early elementary grades, children can examine how the characters of the various animals are the direct causes of their adventures. Peter Rabbit can be compared to such other fictional rabbits as Br'er Rabbit, and those in Robert Lawson's *Rabbit Hill*.

❧Provensen, Martin *(1916 –)*, *and* Provensen, Alice *(1918 –)*
American

Although both Martin and Alice Provensen were born in Chicago and decided early in their lives to become illustrators, they did not meet until the 1940s. While working on a film for the United States Navy, Martin met Alice Twitchell, who had worked for the Walt Disney Studios. They were married in 1944 and a year later they moved to New York. Although their first picture book, *The Golden Mother Goose*, appeared in 1948, it was not until they illustrated *The New Testament* (1953) and *Iliad and Odyssey* (1956), using material gathered on trips to Israel and Greece, that they attracted wide attention. In the 1960s, two of their books, *Karen's Curiosity* and *Karen's Opposites* (both 1963), were based on their daughter. Their illustrations for Louis Untermeyer's *Aesop's Fables* (1965) reflected their ability to combine humorous illustrations and innovative page designs to cast new light on old stories.

In 1950, they bought a farm in New York State and have lived and worked there since. Maple Hill Farm has provided the models for many of animals they have drawn and is the setting for such books as *Our Animal Friends* (1974), *The Year at Maple Hill Farm* (1978), *A Horse, a Hound, and a Gander* (1979), and *An Owl and Three Pussycats* (1981). The books contain a number of two-page spreads, each one depicting a different month and containing an almost Brueghelesque proliferation of detail suggestive of the vitality and variety of the farm.

During the 1970s, the Provensens have used a variety of artistic styles to communicate their ideas. Examples are seen in two books which adapt traditional materials: *The Mother Goose Book* (1976) and *A Peaceable Kingdom: The Shaker Abecedarius* (1978). In the former, they gather together on a single- or double-page spread a number of similar rhymes, and create an illustration or design pattern which unites the rhymes and offers visual interpretation. In the latter, they use a parchment-like background to depict humorously the one hundred and four animals listed in the Shaker Manifesto of 1882. In

1981, they illustrated *A Visit to William Blake's Inn*, a collection of poems by Nancy Willard which won the Newbery Medal and was named a Caldecott Honor Book.

TIPS FOR PARENTS AND TEACHERS: These books are excellent for preschool and elementary aged children. Parents should help children to see how details in each page are integrated to create a complete design.

The Merry Adventures of Robin Hood, Scribner's, New York, 1946. Pyle's sturdy drawings reflect his love of depicting vigorous, masculine heroes.

THE MERRY FRIAR CARRIETH ROBIN ACROSS THE WATER

❦Pyle, Howard *(1853 – 1911)*
❦ *American*

Born of Quaker parents in Wilmington, Delaware, where he was to reside most of his life, Howard Pyle during his childhood was a relatively solitary daydreamer who enjoyed the rural countryside and who, with his mother's encouragement, became interested in art and literature.

In 1876, *Scribner's Monthly* accepted his article "Chincoteague: The Island of Horses," based on his trip to the Virginia coast. Encouraged, he moved to New York to work as an illustrator and writer in the rapidly expanding magazine industry. Several of his stories, poems, and illustrations appeared in the new children's magazines of the period, including Harper's *Young People*, *The Youth's Companion*, and the renowned *St. Nicholas* magazine, whose editor, Mary Mapes Dodge, encourged Pyle in his beginning years as an illustrator.

The Merry Adventures of Robin Hood, his first book, was published in 1883.

Pyle worked hard at the volume, incorporating into it not only his love of the old ballads, but also a wealth of historical research. In addition, he provided the dozens of pen and ink illustrations and chapter headings and directed the overall design of the book, choosing type styles, paper types, and seeing it through the press. The book enjoyed a steady, although not immediately spectacular success and gradually assumed the position of a classic. Many critics consider it Pyle's finest children's book.

In 1886, Pyle published *Pepper and Salt*, a series of short tales for children based on standard folk themes and character types. In 1888, a similar volume, *The Wonder Clock*, appeared. Pyle later wrote two other books in the folktale/fairy story style: *The Garden Behind the Moon: A Real Story of the Moon Angel* (1895), and *Twilight Land* (1895), a collection of oriental-style tales.

Pyle's first novel for children, *Otto of the Silver Hand*, was published in 1888. It is set in Germany during the Middle Ages, a time referred to by the author as "a great black gulf in human history, a gulf of ignorance, of superstition, of cruelty, and of wickedness." Otto, the young hero, is the son of a robber baron and becomes a pawn in the violent struggles. A gentle spirit, he represents Pyle's ideal of a hope for better times. In 1892, *Men of Iron*, Pyle's second medieval novel for young readers, appeared. The hero, Myles Falworth, who lives during the reign of England's Henry IV, becomes a knight and avenges wrongs done to his father. One of Pyle's most interesting publications during the last ten years of the nineteenth century was *The Story of Jack Ballister's Fortunes* (1895), which drew on the author's interest in Colonial history and the legends and tales of pirate adventure along the Atlantic coast during the eighteenth century.

Pyle returned to the Middle Ages for his last great works for children. Over a seven-year period beginning in 1903, he researched, wrote, and illustrated four volumes on the life and death of King Arthur and the adventures of the Knights of the Round Table. In the first volume, *The Story of King Arthur and His Knights* (1903), he wrote, "when, in pursuing this history, I have come to consider the high nobility of spirit that moved these excellent men to act as they did, I have felt that they have afforded such a perfect example of courage and humility that anyone might do exceedingly well to follow after their manner of behavior in such measures as he is able to do." *The Story of the Champions of the Round Table* appeared in 1905; *The Story of Sir Lancelot and His Companions*, in 1907; and *The Story of the Grail and the Passing of Arthur*, in 1910.

With the exception of his folk-like stories, Pyle's tales are those of high adventure and are filled with heroes. It is not a gentle world but filled with violence and evil, a fact which some readers have considered unusual in the light of Pyle's Quaker upbringing. However, as he explained in writing about the pirates Captain Kidd and Blackbeard, "He who chooses may read between the lines of history this great truth: Evil itself is an instrument toward the shaping of good. Therefore the history of evil as well as of good should be read, considered, and digested." This attitude explains his interest in the Middle Ages and the buccaneer era of the eighteenth century. Placed in violent and evil settings, his heroes must face great challenges, internal and external, before they can prove their worth. King Arthur is the greatest hero, being for Pyle "the most honorable, gentle Knight who ever lived in all the world." Using his physical courage and his high ideals, he works to achieve order in a chaotic land. Another aspect of Arthur appeals to Pyle: his emergence into greatness from apparently humble origins. As an American, Pyle was attracted to an aristocracy of merit rather than title.

TIPS FOR PARENTS AND TEACHERS: In the middle elementary grades, *The Merry Adventures of Robin Hood* is still an excellent introduction to Pyle's stories. Readers should notice not only the heroic deeds of Robin, but his complex character: he is both brave and cunning, loyal and audacious. The folktales can be compared to the works of the Grimms, Hans Christian Andersen, and George MacDonald. The Arthurian stories are at times heavy going, but can be enjoyed by good readers in the upper elementary and junior high grades.

Tales from Times Past, ed. by Bryan Holme, Viking, New York, 1977. Rackham's silhouettes for "Cinderella" capture the grace and elegance of the French court.

Rackham, Arthur *(1867 – 1939)*
English

Born in London, Arthur Rackham, like so many famous illustrators, began drawing as a child. During the 1880s, he had several of his illustrations accepted by English magazines; however, recognizing that improvements in the technique of printing photographs would lessen the demand for magazine illustrators, he turned his attention in the 1890s to book illustration. In

1899, Rackham contributed a colored frontispiece and eleven black and white illustrations to Mary Lamb's classic, *Tales from Shakespeare*. The illustrations for "A Midsummer Night's Dream" possess the sense of enchantment, the contorted trees, and the subdued colors which characterize his best work.

Rackham's reputation as a major illustrator was established with the publication of *Fairy Tales of the Brothers Grimm* in 1900 and Washington Irving's *Rip Van Winkle* in 1905. Rackham remarked that his childhood love of the Grimms had remained strong in adulthood. The stories appealed to his gothic interests, and his settings depicted well the gloomy, tangled forests and the haunted places and creatures often found in the tales. Irving's *Rip Van Winkle* also contained scenes of enchantment. Also, the title character and the townspeople were individuals well able to call forth Rackham's interest in human nature and his satiric bent.

During the first two decades of this century, Rackham's activity continued unabated and included illustrations for stories about King Arthur (1910, 1917), for J.M. Barrie's *Peter Pan at Kensington Gardens* (1906, 1912), *Alice's Adventures in Wonderland* (1907), *Aesop's Fables* (1912), and Charles Dickens' *A Christmas Carol* (1915).

In 1919 and 1920 respectively, Rackham illustrated C.S. Evans' retellings of *Cinderella* and *The Sleeping Beauty*, companion volumes which many critics consider his best books. Each of the texts is longer than the traditional versions, and the expanded form gives Rackham the opportunity to develop his graphic designs over a large area and to indicate the changing moods of each tale. The dominant art form in both is the silhouette, an appropriate vehicle for indicating the movement and body language of the characters. In each book there are three double-page, three-color silhouettes presenting major scenes. While the silhouettes are markedly different in style from Rackham's usual illustrations, they do create the sense of enchantment associated with the stories, and the grace and elegance of the French court in which they were first told.

During the 1930s, Rackham illustrated, among other works, Clement Moore's *The Night Before Christmas* (1931), John Ruskin's *King of the Golden River* (1932), Christina Rossetti's *Goblin Market* (1933), and Kenneth Grahame's *The Wind in the Willows* (1939).

During his lifetime, Rackham illustrated over thirty children's books. His contribution is more than just a series of pictures, for he has created a vision of a special, enchanted world. This world, as many commentators have noted, is a mixture of the magic and the material, of the otherworldly and the ordinary. For example, his trees, with their contorted limbs and gnarled, face-like surfaces were, at least from the 1920s on, modelled on trees growing on his own property. His characters, as critic Selma Lanes has noted, may be supernatural creatures, but often they are shown engaged in mundane activities. In *Rip Van Winkle*, the eerie scenes from the Catskill Mountains contrast the solid, realistically portrayed life of the town. Even in the strangest, most haunted of his settings, Rackham provides a solidity to the surfaces he depicts, be they trees, rocks, fabrics, or furniture. Rackham's pictures are more than just illustrations from a given text. He himself maintained that the illustrator performed an independent function and referred to himself as a "partner, not servant" of the author. Thus, while he is faithful to the text, he is able to give it added dimensions.

TIPS FOR PARENTS AND TEACHERS: In reading well-known tales to children of various ages, it is useful to have copies of Rackham's illustrations which can be compared to those of other artists. The Cinderella illustrations can be carefully studied in the middle elementary grades so that students can see how they add to the elegant mood of the story in style, as well as content.

Raskin, Ellen *(1928 –   )*
American

Born in Milwaukee, Ellen Raskin wanted, as a child, to be a musician, but studied art at the University of Wisconsin and travelled to New York where she became a free-lance artist, illustrating, among others, works by William Blake (*Songs of Innocence*, 1966), Bill and Vera Cleaver (*Ellen Grae*, 1967, and *Lady Ellen Grae*, 1968), and Rebecca Caudill (*Come Along*, 1969). Tiring of "interpreting other writers' ideas, never my own," she wrote and illustrated *Nothing Ever Happens on My Block* (1966), the first of over a dozen books of her own. Among the best-known of her picture books are *Nothing Ever Happens on My Block*, *Spectacles* (1968), *And It Rained* (1969), and *Twenty-Two, Twenty-Three* (1976). She has also written four novels, *The Mysterious Disappearance of Leon (I Mean Noel)* (1971), *Figgs and Phantoms* (1974), *The Tattooed Potato and Other Clues* (1975), and *The Westing Game* (1978), winner of the Newbery Medal.

Raskin's picture books, which reflect her training as a graphic designer, deal with unusual events in the lives of relatively ordinary children. In *Nothing Ever Happens on My Block*, a bored young boy is oblivious to the exciting events surrounding him. The text embodies his lament, while the illustrations are all filled with details which portray a world of excitement and adventure of which he is unaware. In *Franklin Stein* (1972), the hero works in his attic making a large robot-like creature that wins the neighborhood pet show. Each of her picture books challenges the reader to notice the details which contradict the simplicity of the text.

Like the picture books, the novels also challenge the reader. Each is a puzzle book, containing hints and clues which the careful reader can use to uncover the mysteries. The best-known of these books, *The Westing Game*, gathers together sixteen heirs to the Westing fortune and gives them the clues they need to claim the great wealth. As in her illustrated works, Raskin uses words to puzzle and to create humor.

TIPS FOR PARENTS AND TEACHERS: In the early elementary grades, children reading *Nothing Ever Happens on My Block* can be asked to discuss all the things Chester does not notice and can then consider what kind of a boy he is. Upper elementary and junior high readers can, at various stages of reading the novels, try to guess the outcome of the stories.

Realistic Fiction

Of all the forms of story, realistic fiction has been the most recent to develop. Traditional folktales, legends, and myths, making use, as they generally do, of magic and supernatural beings and occurrences, were the dominant forms of story until the eighteenth century. However, as the novel developed in England, realistic stories became more dominant until, for many people, the term fiction has become synonymous with realistic fiction as distinct from fantasy. One of the earliest realistic novels, and one which in abridged forms became a favorite with children, was Daniel Defoe's *Robinson Crusoe* (1719), the story of the Englishman who lived for several years on a deserted tropical island. Although the story was fictitious, being only loosely based on an actual event, Defoe meticulously described setting and the day-to-day activities of his hero, giving the story the appearance of a direct account. That children enjoyed the story very much is attested to by the large numbers of editions prepared for young readers which appeared over the next hundred or more years.

During the early nineteenth century, realistic fiction received the approval of many critics who believed that fantasy was escapist and that only pictures of life as it was could be morally valuable for children. The results, however, were generally not good literature; rather, children were often forced to read dull, moralistic tracts which, under the guise of realistic fiction, sought to instruct them in correct moral and social behavior.

The last half of the nineteenth century marked what many critics have called the Golden Age in realistic fiction for children. The two major forms of realistic fiction to flower in that period were the adventure story and the family story. In England, three writers are generally associated with the adventure story: R.M. Ballantyne (1825–1894), G.A. Henty (1832–1902), and Frederick Marryat (1792–1848). Drawing on the interest generated by accounts of the dangers and excitement of exploration on the high seas and of the strange and peril-filled lives of people in the new colonies, these writers loaded their stories with fast-paced action and incidents of nobility and courage. Ballantyne's best-known novels were *The Young Fur Trader* (1856) and *The Coral Island* (1857); Henty wrote nearly one hundred adventure stories including *With Wolfe in Canada; or, The Winning of a Continent* (1886) and *The Bravest of the Brave; or, With Peterborough in Spain* (1886); Marryat is remembered for such stories as *Mr. Midshipman Easy* (1836) and *The Phantom Ship* (1839). While often set in unfamiliar settings, places which would be considered exotic to the readers, these novels presented characters who lived up to the ideals held by the predominantly British readers: courage, nobility, and the belief in the rightness of the British cause. The influence of these three authors was great during the rest of the nineteenth century and well into the twentieth century. Robert Louis Stevenson, who in the introductory poem to *Treasure Island* paid tribute to Ballantyne, made use of the conventions developed by that writer to create what many critics consider the greatest adventure story ever written, *Treasure Island* (1883). J.M. Barrie, in *Peter and Wendy* (1911), affectionately parodies many of the dominant features of adventure stories.

The family story had its first great flowering in the United States. Louisa May Alcott's *Little Women* (1868–9) and its many sequels portrayed the daily lives of children and young adults with sensitivity and honesty, generally avoiding the sentimentality found in the works of lesser writers. Along with English writer Edith Nesbit's stories about the Bastable children (*The Story of the Treasure Seekers*, 1899, *The Wouldbegoods*, 1901, and *The New Treasure Seekers*, 1904), Alcott's books are considered among the finest family stories ever written.

During the nineteenth century, two other major American writers created classics of realistic fiction. In *The Adventures of Tom Sawyer* (1876), Samuel Clemens (Mark Twain) combined the daily play of young boys with the real violence of frontier America, and, in *The Adventures of Huckleberry Finn* (1884), he took his central character through the center of America where he experiences the darkest elements of the American character. Howard Pyle, who is best remembered for his retelling of the Robin Hood and King Arthur legends, turned to the Middle Ages as the subject for two historical adventures: *Otto of the Silver Hand* (1888) and *Men of Iron* (1892).

Another important type of nineteenth-century realistic fiction was the school story. During this period, English private schools developed as an important element of society, the forming ground for future citizens. Writers, seeking both to create books with materials familiar to their young readers and to inculcate the values of upper- and middle-class British society, produced large numbers of these novels. One of the most important of these was Thomas Hughes' *Tom Brown's School Days* (1857), which was set around the famous Rugby School, and which showed the young hero developing, after many struggles, into a mature, capable adult. Other important works in this genre were Frederick Farrar's *Eric* (1858) and Rudyard Kipling's *Stalky and Co.* (1899).

During the twentieth century, as the number of readers grew rapidly and the costs of printing and distribution lessened, many American companies began publishing series books, that is, a number of volumes all about the same character. While late nineteenth-century writer Gilbert Patten's stories about Frank Merriwell made series books popular, it was not until Edward Stratemeyer began publishing at the turn of the century that they really became big business. Before he died, Stratemeyer had inaugurated nearly one hundred series and had written over two hundred books himself. Among the best-known of his titles were those about Tom Swift, the Bobbsey Twins, the Hardy Boys, and Nancy Drew. For a large number of the books, Stratemeyer hired "ghost writers" who filled in the plot outlines he supplied them. The completed works were published under the names of such fictitious authors as Laura Lee Hope, Fenton W. Dixon, and Carolyn Keene. Soon after they were published, large numbers of educators and librarians criticized their literary merit, noting that they had trite plots and stereotyped characters. However, the books have maintained their popularity to the present, a fact which is due in part to their easy reading levels and in part to the fact that, since the 1950s, earlier titles in the various series have been modernized, making them more accessible to newer readers.

The most important realistic children's fiction of this century fits into two categories: historical and contemporary realism. Much of the historical fiction includes elements of the adventure story, as young heroes and heroines confront dangerous situations in times past. Esther Forbes' *Johnny Tremain* (1943) places the young hero in the midst of Revolutionary Boston; the novels of Rosemary Sutcliff are often set in the era of Roman and Anglo-Saxon Britain; Hester Burton is often interested in the period of the French Revolution. Each of these writers combines three elements: exciting action, the personal development of the central character, and the sweep of large historical events in which the character finds him or herself involved. In addition to facing the challenges of all writers of fiction, the telling of a consistent, well-structured, and engaging story, the author of the historical novel must also maintain historical accuracy. Not only must major events and characters, as well as social conditions, be correctly depicted, but the central characters must not be anachronisms. That is, they must think the way individuals of the historical period would, not the way someone in the twentieth century would react.

In the United States, another type of historical fiction has dealt with the relatively routine lives of people who lived in earlier ages. The pioneer experience has formed the basis of the famous Little House books of Laura Ingalls Wilder and Carol Brink's *Caddie Woodlawn* (1935). While there is both danger and excitement in these books, it is not of the cataclysmic nature found in historical novels relating to major events. These stories capture the point-of-view of the central figure, a young child who is learning about the life around her. As this character learns about the world around and about the means of gathering food, cooking, sewing, and other such activities, the young reader learns as well. *A Gathering of Days* (1979), by Joan Blos, describes a nineteenth-century New England girl who is in her teens.

In addition to Esther Forbes' *Johnny Tremain*, there are many excellent novels dealing with various periods of American history. Among these are Elizabeth Speare's *The Witch of Blackbird Pond* (1958) and Walter Edmond's *The Matchlock Gun* (1941), both about colonial times; James Lincoln and Christopher Collier's *My Brother Sam is Dead* (1974), set during the Revolutionary War; Paula Fox's *The Slave Dancer* (1973), a depiction of the horrors of the slave trade; and Irene Hunt's *Across Five Aprils* (1964), which is set in the Civil War era.

Stories dealing with contemporary life, that is, with the lives of boys and girls living in the time in which the book was written, have remained popular throughout the twentieth century. Many of these books present family situations not unlike those which the reader may have experienced. In them, the young characters undergo the relatively normal crises attendant upon growing up. Eleanor Estes, in her series of books about the Moffat family, presents the children of a widow experiencing the first day of school, the acquisition of a library card, the sale of a house, and the marriage of the eldest sibling. Judy Blume, in *Blubber* (1974) and *Superfudge* (1980), portrays the problems a boy has coping with a younger brother, while Betty Greene, in *Philip Hall Likes Me, I Reckon Maybe* (1974), portrays the life of a rural southern girl as she copes with school and a boy she doesn't think she is really interested in.

By far the most dominant type of modern realistic novel for children is what has been called the novel of social realism or the problem novel. During the last twenty years, such taboo subjects as alcoholism, sex, and divorce have been treated with frankness and honesty. While some of these works have been merely sociological texts with dialogue and others have been somewhat moralistic approaches to the subjects, there have been a group of writers who do not treat their characters as mere symbols embodying a particular problem. M.E. Kerr in such works as *Dinky Hocker Shoots Smack* (1972) and *Is That You, Miss Blue?* (1975), Norma Klein in *Mom, the Wolfman, and Me* (1972), Judy Blume in *Are You There God? It's Me, Margaret* (1970), and Paul Zindel in *The Pig Man* (1968) all show their characters convincingly confronting situations which have developed in part because of the troubled, unsettled, modern times in which they live.

TIPS FOR PARENTS AND TEACHERS: Like all good fiction, good realistic stories present consistently built plots, believable characters, and honestly examined themes. Whether they are dealing with humorous or serious situations, with contemporary or historical times, the authors of such works respect both their stories and their readers, believing that the former are worth telling well and honestly and that the latter are worth being both entertained and enlightened, not preached at or pandered to. In reading historical fiction, one should look not only for factual accuracy, but also for cultural accuracy; characters should respond to the events of the story the way they would have in the time and place in which the story is set. Writers of stories dealing with contemporary situations should avoid both sensational and clichéd subjects; if they are dealing with problems faced by modern children, they should try to understand how children would react to these problems and they should present each problem fairly, not with a preconceived moral view.

Realistic fiction can be read by children of all ages. Picture books such as those by Ezra Jack Keats will present situations similar to those experienced by preschool and early aged children. Books like Brinton Turkle's *Thy Friend Obadiah* (1969) will provide an introduction to other times and places for early elementary aged children. Historical novels can be introduced in the upper elementary and junior high school grades, when readers are better able to understand the larger forces which shaped events and lives. Stories of social realism should be appropriate to the level of understanding of the reader; in-depth studies of the problems of sex, divorce, and drugs, for example, are probably best understood by children in the upper elementary and junior high grades.

Richards, Laura *(1850 – 1943)*
American

Born in Boston, the daughter of Samuel Gridley Howe, a pioneer in the education of the blind, and Julia Ward Howe, composer of "The Battle Hymn of the Republic," Laura Richards was introduced to poetry at a very early age. She remarked in her autobiography, *Stepping Westward* (1931), "I would rather read poetry than eat my dinner any day. It has been so all my life." "The hurdy gurdy," she said about her poetic impulses, "turned ever faster and faster, each new baby requiring a new output of jingles." At times, she would use the back of one of her babies as a writing table. Beginning in the 1870s, many of her poems appeared in *St. Nicholas* magazine, and, in 1880, she published *Five Mice in a Mouse-Trap*, the first of over ninety volumes of fiction, poetry, drama, biography, and autobiography she was to write before her death in 1943.

Laura Richards is now remembered for her songs, lyrics, and nonsense verse. However, during her lifetime, her fiction for young readers was very popular. Her most popular novel, virtually unread today, was *Captain January*, which was made into a silent movie starring Baby Peggy in 1924, and in 1936, into a talking picture with Shirley Temple. Laura Richards wrote several biographies about such prominent women as Florence Nightingale, Joan of Arc, and Abigail Adams.

During her lifetime, her children's poetry earned Laura Richards the unofficial title, "America's Poet Laureate of Nonsense." She wrote hundreds of poems which appeared in nine volumes: *Sketches and Scraps* (1881), *In My Nursery* (1890), *Sun Down Songs* (1899), *The Hurdy-Gurdy* (1902), *The Piccolo* (1906), *Jolly Jingles* (1912), *Tirra Lirra* (1932), *Merry-Go-Round* (1935), and *I Have a Song to Sing to You* (1938). Not surprisingly, some of the poems are dated, dealing with everyday objects of the nineteenth-century child; unfortunately, some of them, especially those dealing with American Indians, are what would now be called racist, often presenting unflattering stereotypes. However, at their best, Laura Richards' poems maintain their freshness decades after their writing, combining a ludicrous content with strong rhythms and rhymes.

Many of her poems contain two odd individuals who make even odder companions. A mameluke and a hospidar wander together in search of words to rhyme with their names; Mrs. Snipkin and Mrs. Wobblechin are women of different sizes; a Phrog and a Snayle love each other, but neither will live in the other's element. Her interest in portraying odd couples may reflect the influence on her writing of Edward Lear, one of her favorite authors.

Sometimes the poems are about the difficulty of writing poetry, as the poet creates linguistic situations in which the completion of a rhyme scheme, rhythmic pattern, or stanza form seems almost impossible. One time she has a haddock feed on shaddock, quite simply, she states, because "There's no other food that will rhyme!" Often she uses words as "Okeefinokee," or "hottentot" for the sheer delight of finding words which can be made to rhyme, even if they must be invented. In "Jeremi and Josephine," the poet lets the reader complete the rhyme of each fourth line, commenting, "This simple tale is thus, you see,/ Divided fair, 'twixt you and me." In "Eletelephony," one of her best-known pieces, the poem is as much about the narrator's difficulties in untangling her tongue as it is about the elephant's problems with the telephone.

Laura Richards is not a subtle poet; but she is dexterous at her craft, knowing well how to manipulate words, rhythms, and stanzas to create the desired nonsense effects. She delights in rhythmic, but strange sounding names: Little John Bottlejohn, Whopsy Whitlesey Whanko Whee, Cato Theophilus Jones. Her rhythms are basic, generally trochaic, carrying the reader swiftly through the nonsense material.

TIPS FOR PARENTS AND TEACHERS: Richards' poems are meant to be read aloud. Both sounds and situations delight children of all ages. In the early elementary grades, children can draw pictures of the ridiculous characters; in the middle and upper elementary grades, children can imitate her poems, writing about cartoon or comic book characters or creations of their own imaginations.

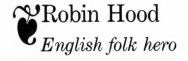

Robin Hood
English folk hero

Probably no character in English folklore and literature is more widely known than Robin Hood. Dressed in Lincoln green; a superior archer, leader of men, and savior of the poor; surrounded by such loyal friends as Little John, Friar Tuck, and Will Scarlet; and constantly threatened by enemies like the Sheriff of Nottingham, the Bishop of Hereford, and Guy of Gisborne, the outlaw hero has been a favorite subject of ballads and stories for over six hundred years.

"Modern" interest in Robin Hood dates from the late eighteenth and early nineteenth centuries. Scholars and poets were then rediscovering the Middle Ages and the ballad forms of that era. Moreover, the Romantic writers, who were concerned with the common man and the rebel against tyranny, found in Robin Hood a congenial subject.

Although children have probably always enjoyed Robin Hood stories, it is not until the nineteenth century that versions specifically for children appeared. This is not surprising for, as a folk hero, Robin Hood appeared in stories designed for a general audience and the idea of writing and publishing stories designed for the entertainment of a young audience did not emerge until the nineteenth century. In 1883, Howard Pyle, the American author-illustrator, published *The Merry Adventures of Robin Hood*, a work which quickly established itself as a classic. Pyle's writing is noted for its use of detail, its depth of characterization, and its formal, storytelling style.

Several twentieth-century authors and illustrators have successfully approached the subject. Ian Serraillier, has published modernizations of old ballads in *Robin and His Merry Men* (1969). Caldecott Medal-winning illustrator Virginia Lee Burton joined with Anne Malcolmson and Grace Castagnetta to produce *Song of Robin Hood* (1947), modernizations of eighteen traditional ballads. Designed in the style of medieval manuscripts, the book includes musical scores, many of them the original tunes which accompanied the ballads. Roger Lancelyn Green and Rosemary Sutcliff, Carnegie Medal-winning historical novelist, have also written significant prose versions of Robin Hood. Green's *The Adventures of Robin Hood* (1956) recounts the birth, death, and twenty-four adventures of the hero. Rosemary Sutcliff's *The Chronicles of Robin Hood* (1950) traces Robin's career from the time of his becoming an outlaw to his death at Kirkless Nunnery.

In spite of the continued popularity of the Robin Hood stories, very little is known about how, when, and where they originated. Several scholars have tried to show that Robin was an actual person living some time before the fourteenth century. Others have suggested that his character and adventures are based on lives of many people. Outlaws, it is pointed out, were numerous in the later Middle Ages and many were the subjects of legends. It is argued that these legends gradually fused and were focused on one character, Robin Hood. Whatever the origin of the stories, one thing is certain: by the time Robin Hood emerges as a major folk figure in the late fifteenth century, he is a yeoman hero. In fact, as several scholars have stated, he is to the common man what King Arthur was to the nobility: the ideal hero. Moreover, he was an Anglo-Saxon and, as such, in opposition to the hated Norman invaders.

However, more important to Robin's heroic stature than his sociocultural background are the traits of his character. A handsome man, he is renowned for his skill in hand-to-hand combat and archery. But more significantly, he is both courageous and intelligent. While he does not back away from confrontations, he uses his wits to overcome superior numbers and to escape from dangerous situations. He is, at times, daring to the point of audacity, often placing himself in difficult situations for the pure joy of the encounters. Generally, however, Robin's actions are undertaken to fulfill his sworn mission to help his people against tyrannical and dishonest secular and ecclesiastical leaders.

The forest, be it Sherwood or Barnesdale, is symbolically important. Although the forest was the king's property as were the deer in it, it was also the refuge of outlaws, who found sanctuary in its pathless wilderness. As the Robin Hood stories became more popular, the forest also came to be seen as the site of a simpler, purer way of life, one free from the complexities of urban life. Hunting, seeking adventure, and working under the lightly imposed authority of Robin Hood, the Merry Men were regarded as pursuing an ideal existence close to nature. The simplicity and adventure of this life may account for the popularity of the Robin Hood stories with younger readers. Not only are the tales easy to follow and filled with heroic and physical adventure, they also present characters who are free of imposed authority. With the exception of Marian and Alan-a-Dale's wife, Alice, there are no women in the forest. The Merry Men are like little boys who have run away from their mothers and who can come and go as they please, enjoying the fellowship of like-minded individuals and engaging in adventures without the fretting of parents.

TIPS FOR PARENTS AND TEACHERS: The Robin Hood legends can be introduced in the middle elementary grades. It is wise to read the stories from a variety of versions, giving students an awareness of a variety of styles. Robin can be compared to such other trickster figures as Anansi (West African), Br'er Rabbit (black American), and Glooscap (American Indian). In the upper elementary grades, the phases of Robin's life and his heroic characteristics can be related to those of other major cultural heroes like Beowulf (British), Nanabozho (American Indian), and Maui (Hawaiian).

Scarry, Richard *(1919 –   )*
American

Born in Boston, Richard Scarry attended the Boston Museum of Fine Arts School before serving in World War II as an art director in the Army. In 1946, he began a career as illustrator for Golden Books, illustrating for such authors as Margaret Wise Brown (*Boss of the Barnyard*, 1946, and *Two Little Miners*, 1949), Kathryn Jackson (*Let's Go Fishing*, 1949, and *The Golden Bedtime Book*, 1955), and Leah Gale (*The Animals of Farmer Jones*, 1953). He has also illustrated three books written by his wife, Patricia. The first book Scarry wrote and illustrated himself, *The Great Big Car and Truck Book*, appeared in 1951. However, it was not until 1963, with the publication of *The Best Wordbook*

Ever, that his work became widely known. He has written and illustrated over sixty books.

The central characters in most of Scarry's books are humanized animals, it being his belief that younger children can better identify with animals than with human beings. Each of his books is crammed with details. Exploring the pages, which may appear cluttered but are actually carefully designed, the young child is given a chance to discover new items. He can also learn about the world in which he lives, for, although the characters are animals, the activities they engage in are close to those of the readers. Some of Scarry's most popular stories are mysteries, including *The Great Pie Robbery* (1969) and *The Supermarket Mystery* (1969).

TIPS FOR PARENTS AND TEACHERS: The preschooler who is encouraged to look attentively at the details on one of Scarry's pages will be better prepared to understand the significant details of more complex picture books. A young child should not be limited to Scarry books, but should experience a wide variety of artistic styles.

Where the Wild Things Are, by Maurice Sendak, Harper & Row, New York, 1963. In the wordless two-page spreads in the center of *Where the Wild Things Are*, Sendak communicates the rhythms of dance and music.

Sendak, Maurice *(1928 –)*
American

Born in Brooklyn, New York, Maurice Sendak remembers how, as a child, he listened to his father tell stories about his own childhood in Poland, from which he had emigrated just before World War I. These stories, which Sendak says instilled him with an "Old World feeling," combined with his own drawing and his writing stories with his brother Jack, laid the foundation for his later work. As a child, he suffered long periods of illness and found time to dream and imagine. He began his career as a professional artist adapting "Mutt and Jeff" comic strips for comic books, studied at the Art Students League in New York, and worked as a store window designer.

Sendak first attracted notice in the early 1950s as an illustrator of others' works. In 1951, he began a long-standing collaboration with author Ruth Krauss. *A Hole is to Dig* (1952) was named by *The New York Times* as one of the best illustrated books of the year, and *A Very Special House* (1953) earned Sendak the first of his eight Caldecott Honor Medals. Two other important collaborations of this period were with Meindert De Jong and Else Minerak. Between 1953 and 1962, Sendak illustrated seven of De Jong's novels. For Else Minerak, Sendak illustrated six "Little Bear" books, part of the Harper "I Can Read" series. The illustrations anticipate Sendak's work in the 1960s, making extensive use of crosshatching and presenting figures of considerable solidity. His page design is in harmony with the concept of the easy reader, illustrations clearly relate to text, and there are no superfluous, distracting details. *Little Bear's Visit* (1961), the fifth of the series, was a 1962 Caldecott Honor Book.

In 1956, Sendak published *Kenny's Window*, the first book he wrote and illustrated himself. The loosely organized plot focuses on Kenny's attempt to find answers to seven questions a four-legged rooster had asked him in a dream. In finding the answers, the boy learns about such emotions as friendship, love, and trust, and realizes that he wishes to live at home rather than in the magic garden of his dream. *Kenney's Window* is illustrated with pen and ink sketches covered by either brown or grey washes which suggest the quality of a dream.

Sendak's next two books, *Very Far Away* (1957) and *The Sign on Rosie's Door* (1960), continue the theme of the relationships between the child's fantasy and real worlds. Martin, hero of *Very Far Away*, is also the first of Sendak's characters who decide to run away because they are dissatisfied with home conditions. *The Sign on Rosie's Door* is based on Sendak's teenage memories of a little girl who used to hold forth on the street below his window. Rosie moves freely into her fantasy world and invites her playmates to join her, generally with success. This story, which is unusual among his books in that it deals with the interactions of several children, served as the basis for an animated television special, *Really Rosie*, aired in 1975.

During the 1960s, Sendak produced the books which led to his being recognized as the foremost living children's illustrator. He continued his work as an illustrator, winning Caldecott Honor Medals for *Little Bear's Visit* (1961), and Charlotte Zolotow's *Mr. Rabbit and the Lovely Present* (1962), in which his impressionistic use of color anticipates the use of color in *Where the Wild Things Are*. In addition, he created a series of superb pen and ink drawings for works by American poet-critic Randall Jarrell (*The Bat Poet* in 1964 and *The Animal Family* in 1965), Nobel Prize winner Isaac Bashevis Singer

(*Zlateh the Goat*, 1966), and nineteenth-century fantasist George MacDonald (*The Golden Key* in 1967 and *The Light Princess* in 1969).

In 1963, Sendak published *Where the Wild Things Are*, his best-known book and winner of the Caldecott Medal. A classic presentation of the solitary child who escapes from an unpleasant reality into a world of his own imagining, the book is a perfect blend of design, illustration, and text. While critical response was generally enthusiastic, there was controversy. Some librarians maintained that the pictures of the monsters would scare children, while psychologist Bruno Bettelheim criticized it as being an inaccurate presentation of a child's method of dealing with conflict. The book has since been translated into many languages and made into an animated film and an opera.

Sendak's *The Nutshell Library*, a boxed set of four 2 ⅜ × 3 ⅜" books, was also published in 1964. *Alligators All Around* and *One was Johnny* are alphabet and counting books, respectively; *Chicken Soup with Rice* is about the months; and *Pierre* is a cautionary tale. These books are in the tradition of "little books," which were made so famous by Beatrix Potter.

Hector Protector, and As I Went Over the Water (1965) and *Higglety Pigglety Pop! or There Must be More to Life* (1967) are both based on traditional nursery rhymes. The first book uses the technique of Randolph Caldecott, who made his pictures suggest meanings not contained in the words. *Higglety, Pigglety, Pop!* is the story of Jennie, a Sealyham terrier who, although having everything in life, feels discontented and leaves home to seek a place as leading lady in The World Mother Goose Theatre. This is an unusual book in which the heroine is placed in many situations, the dreamlike qualities of which are reminiscent of *Alice in Wonderland*. Critics have interpreted the book as a parable on the differences between contentment and fulfillment and as an allegory of the journey into death. Sendak's illustrations, all in pen and ink, enhance the quality of strangeness created by the text. The fine crosshatching gives a darkness to each of the scenes, but in each there is a mysterious luminescence. The overall impression the book creates is not unlike the impressions created by much late nineteenth-century fantasy.

In 1970, Sendak won his seventh Caldecott Honor Medal for *In the Night Kitchen*, a story which returns to the fantasies of a solitary child. Awakening in the middle of the night, Mickey falls out of his bedroom and his pajamas into the night kitchen, where three bakers inadvertently mix him into their cake batter. Escaping, Mickey fashions a dough airplane and flies to the top of a giant bottle of milk, where he gets the milk the bakers need for their cake. His task accomplished, he returns to bed and sleeps contentedly. Some critics have complained that the plot line is ephemeral. However, it is an important analysis of a child's assertion of his own identity and self-worth.

Artistically, the book introduces new features of Sendak's art. He uses the design techniques of comic books, mixing the sizes, shapes, and numbers of panels on each page. This technique is no mere gimmick, for it helps to create a sense of movement as Mickey floats and flies from bedroom to bakery to milk bottle and back to bedroom. Narrative is enclosed in captions, and dialogue in balloons, thus lessening the division between words and text that exists in most picture books. Sendak also uses elements of pop art, having Mickey fall into a city composed of giant cartons of baking ingredients.

During the 1970s, Sendak's artistic pace has decreased. In 1973, he provided the pen and ink drawings for *The Juniper Tree*, a retelling by Lori Segal and Randall Jarrell of tales of the Grimm Brothers. The illustrations reflect the earthiness and also the frequent terror and grotesqueness of the stories. Sendak also illustrated another Grimm Brothers story in 1973, *King Grisley-Beard*. In 1976, in *Some Swell Pup; or Are You Sure You Want a Dog?*, an instruction book coauthored by Matthew Margolis, Sendak experimented with colors brighter than those of his earlier books. *Outside Over There*, the third book of a trilogy which started with *Where the Wild Things Are* and continued with *In the Night Kitchen*, appeared in 1981 and was named a Caldecott Honor Book. It tells how Ada must rescue her sister who has been stolen and taken to the land of goblins.

Sendak's great achievement, so far as it can be analyzed, results from his ability to adapt his style to the needs of a specific work and from his sensitive depiction of the inner nature of childhood. "Style," he remarked, "is purely the means to an end, and the more styles you have, the better." In his great work in the 1960s, he moves from an impressionistic rendering of landscape in *Mr. Rabbit and the Lovely Present*, to the dark cross-hatching and water colors of *Where the Wild Things Are*, to the comic book style of *In the Night Kitchen*. Even illustrating two different works of one author, he shows flexibility. For George MacDonald's *The Golden Key* and *The Light Princess*, Sendak uses pen and ink; but in the former book he creates effects of strangeness and mystery through the subtle use of light spaces, while in *The Light Princess*, humor and satire are introduced by giving solidity and exaggeration to the figures and incidents depicted.

Sendak succeeds admirably in presenting the child's world from the child's point of view. "I do seem," he told Virginia Haviland, "to have the knack of recalling the emotional quality of childhood." The child's world is not always a pleasant one and his experiences can be terrifying. However, "children enjoy a little anxiety and heart failure as long as they know that all will end alright." In the adventures, the child moves into a fantasy world in which his play helps him to adapt better to the real world to which he returns. Sendak asserts that adults and children see the world differently: "There are those very infinitesimal fragmentary seconds of time in a child's life when something extraordinary can happen, but it's so quiet that the grownups around don't see it happening . . . . It's like a child being in one world and the mother being in another, and they both don't know they're in a different world and yet they're sitting on the same bed." A major aspect of the child's view is his seeing adults as large and often ugly and threatening; often Sendak's pictures of adults are presented as such.

TIPS FOR PARENTS AND TEACHERS: Like all great works of art, Sendak's major books can be read by people of many ages and can unfold new meanings with each rereading. Preschoolers can discuss the meanings of the pictures in *Hector Protector*. In the early elementary grades, students can notice the facial expressions of Max and the relationships between his waking and dream worlds in *Where the Wild Things Are*. In the middle and upper elementary grades, the reasons for Max's behavior can be considered. In the upper elementary grades, the appropriateness of the illustrations for the Grimm Brothers and George MacDonald stories can be debated.

The Cat in the Hat, by Dr. Seuss, Random House, New York, 1957. The depiction of the cat's balancing act reflects the chaos found throughout Dr. Seuss' story.

❦Seuss, Dr.: pseudonym of ❦Theodor Seuss Geisel *(1904 –   )*
American

Born in Springfield, Massachusetts, Theodor Geisel worked as the editor of the Dartmouth humor magazine. After graduating from

Dartmouth College, he went to Oxford University, intending to earn a doctorate in English. However, he returned to the United States after a year, married author Helen Palmer, and began a career as a cartoonist and commercial artist. His cartoons, many of them signed "Dr. Seuss," appeared in *Life, Vanity Fair, The Saturday Evening Post,* and other magazines.

In 1937, after having been rejected twenty times, Geisel's first children's book, *And to Think That I Saw It on Mulberry Street,* appeared. It was published, as nearly all of his children's books have been, under the pseudonym Dr. Seuss. The idea for the story came to him when, sailing home after a visit in Europe, he began making up verses to fit the rhythm of the ship's engines. A small boy, warned by his father to "stop telling such outlandish tales," notices a horse and wagon as he walks home and, in his imagination, transforms them into wondrous creatures and conveyances. His second book, *The 500 Hats of Bartholomew Cubbins* (1938), is a folk-like story about a boy who takes his hat off before the king and discovers another one on his head. Only after removing five hundred hats and facing the threat of execution, does the boy find himself bareheaded. *The King's Stilts* (1939) tells what happens when the stilts on which the king walks around his kingdom mysteriously disappear. In *Horton Hatches the Egg* (1940), the author's favorite book, an elephant is hoodwinked into sitting in a tree warming the egg of a vacationing bird.

During World War II, Geisel worked as a political cartoonist and as a filmmaker for the Army. One of his films, *Your Job in Germany,* was rereleased as *Hitler Lives* and, in 1946, won an Academy Award as the best documentary short. After the war, Geisel continued his filmmaking and won two more Academy Awards, one in 1947 for the script of *Design for Death,* about the Japanese, and another in 1951 for the cartoon *Gerald McBoing-Boing.*

Geisel continued writing children's books, publishing seven in the decade after the war, three of them winners of Caldecott Honor Medals: *McElligot's Pool* (1947), *Bartholomew and the Oobleck* (1949), and *If I Ran the Zoo* (1950). In each of these, youthful heroes face absurd situations and come up with their own solutions. Another popular book he wrote at this time is *Horton Hears a Who!* (1954), in which the elephant helps save a microscopic civilization.

In 1957, Geisel published *The Cat in the Hat,* a story which was to have a major influence on books for beginning readers. During the 1950s, important educators had drawn attention to the decreasing reading skills of children, and novelist John Hersey had suggested that imaginative writers like Geisel should create beginning readers to supplant the dull texts available. For a year Geisel worked with a controlled vocabulary list and produced a book which has since become one of the all-time best-selling children's books. In 1957, Geisel became president and editor of Beginner's

Books, a company which published easy readers in which short sentences, strong rhymes and rhythms, and nonsense words and situations were used. He has written several of the volumes in the series, some of them under the pseudonym of Theo Le Seig (Geisel spelled backwards).

Geisel has written several other stories, the best-known being *How the Grinch Stole Christmas* (1957), the story of a creature who, having "a heart two sizes too small," decides to rob a village of its holiday; *Yertle the Turtle* (1958), a satire on Hitler; and *The Lorax* (1971), an ecological fable. He has also been involved in the production of eight television specials based on his books.

Although his friend Clifton Fadiman has stated that the Dr. Seuss books have no hidden meaning, having been written only to entertain, it is possible to find many recurrent themes in Geisel's stories. The dominant ingredient in his stories is nonsense, or "logical insanity" as the author has termed it. Seuss has been compared to nonsense writers Edward Lear and Lewis Carroll and has been placed within the tradition of the American tall tale. In his books, as critic Margery Fisher has noted, "fantasy and reason are shown on a collision course." Hats mysteriously appear on a child's head; an elephant sits in a tree incubating an egg; a cat creates chaos in a normal household.

Critic Selma Lanes has suggested that there may be a serious concern underlying the chaos and nonsense. In the plots, the situations create increasing anxiety which is resolved at the last possible moment: the cat miraculously cleans things up as the children's mother walks in the door; the final hat is removed as Bartholomew faces execution. Lanes concludes, "The anxiety in Seuss's books always arises from the flouting of authority, parental or societal."

Many of Geisel's books are moral fables, although, as the author remarked, "When we have a moral, we try to tell it sideways." In *Horton Hears a Who!* the importance of all beings, no matter how small, is stressed. At the end of *How the Grinch Stole Christmas*, the characters come to understand the nonmaterialistic joys of Christmas. *The Lorax* stresses the dangers of misusing the environment.

Geisel has often written about his lack of formal art training and, in explaining the reason for his creating such strange characters, has stated, "My animals look the way they do because I never learned to draw." However, his illustrations are appropriate representations for the chaos and nonsense of the narratives. As a writer, he has attempted to practice a lesson he learned during his advertising career: "Eliminate the unnecessary." He works for up to a year on the texts for each of his books, going through many revisions, striving to find the rhythms and strange-sounding words which best suit specific stories.

The Dr. Seuss books have been very popular, over fifty million having been sold. Although he has been criticized, several reviewers feeling that the books of the last twenty-five years fit too easily into predictable narrative, linguistic, and artistic patterns, he is more often praised. Barbara Bader has summarized, "Piper, prophet, magician, priest—these are the words for Dr. Seuss; and for Geisel, entertainer-in-chief." Selma Lanes wrote that Geisel is important because "in a day when children's books are almost unrelievedly beautiful and elevating, his are intentionally rough-drawn, tough-talking, and almost downright ugly."

TIPS FOR PARENTS AND TEACHERS: The Seuss books are justifiably regarded as American classics and all children should be given the opportunity of knowing them. However, because they are all similar in linguistic and artistic styles, they should be supplemented with books by other authors and illustrators, thus giving young children exposure to a variety of narrative and pictoral techniques.

When We Were Very Young, by A.A. Milne, illus. by Ernest H. Shepard, McClelland and Stewart, Toronto, 1925. In the frontispiece to A.A. Milne's *When We Were Very Young*, Shepard depicts the solitary, imaginative boy who is the focus of the poems to follow.

HALFWAY DOWN

Shepard, Ernest *(1879 – 1976)*
English

Born in London, the son of an architect, Ernest Shepard as a boy illustrated stories told him by his sister: "I made a point of trying to draw everything, and would illustrate some of the more exciting passages . . . . I always had several odds and ends of paper stuffed inside my sailor tunic." His father felt sure he would become an artist, although Ernest would then have preferred a more exciting career. In 1907, after completing his art training, Shepard began to draw for *Punch* magazine, for which he worked until 1959.

During his lifetime, Shepard illustrated over one hundred children's books. His most famous collaborations was with A.A. Milne. *When We Were Very Young* appeared in 1924, followed by *Winnie-the-Pooh* in 1926, *Now We Are Six* in 1927, and *The House at Pooh Corner* in 1928. In later years, Shepard illustrated over two dozen books which were adaptations of or spin-offs from the first four.

Shepard's illustrations were so important that they have become almost inseparable from the stories and poems themselves. While working on the pen and ink drawings, he frequently consulted with Milne. The pictures of the solitary child, Christopher Robin, were based on Shepard's own son, Graham, and show the boy engaged in play, watching the world around him, and standing or sitting contemplatively. When he is with adults or visiting the city, the boy looks very small. The animals, Pooh, Piglet, and his friends, are fully realized as characters. Backgrounds generally suggest the English countryside and villages of the period.

Next to the Winnie-the-Pooh books, Shepard's best-known illustrations are those he did for Kenneth Grahame's *The Wind in the Willows* (1931). In *The Horn Book* magazine, Shepard later described his meeting with Grahame: "'I love these little people,' the author remarked of his characters, 'be kind to them.'" After spending an afternoon sketching scenes and animals near Grahame's home, Shepard showed his work to the author, who stated, "I'm glad you've made them real." His prefatory map, illustrating the major scenes of *The Wind in the Willows*, indicates how completely he envisioned the world of Grahame's story.

TIPS FOR PARENTS AND TEACHERS: Unfortunately many young children are familiar only with the Walt Disney illustrations for the Winnie-the-Pooh stories. While they are similar to Shepard's, they lack the sensitivity of Shepard's. Children should be introduced to the originals.

Shulevitz, Uri *(1935 –   )*
American

Born in Warsaw, Poland, Shulevitz fled with his family when that city was bombed in 1939. In Paris, Shulevitz developed a love for films and, with a friend, created a comic strip. At twelve, he won first prize in a drawing contest for the school children of his section of Paris. In 1949, the family moved to Israel, where Shulevitz studied at the Art Institute of Tel Aviv and served as the art director of a magazine for teenagers.

In 1959, Shulevitz came to New York where, after studying at the Brooklyn Museum Art School, he began writing and illustrating children's books. His first published work, *The Moon in My Room* (1963), tells of the fantasy worlds discovered by a small boy sitting in his bedroom. After illustrating several books by other writers, he wrote and illustrated *One Monday Morning* (1967), a cumulative story which he has called a "confrontation between fantasy and reality." For six days, a king, queen, prince, and their ever-increasing entourage visit the walkup apartment of a small boy, only to find him out; on Sunday, he is at home. In the final pages, the pictures reveal that the colorful royal visitors are really a pack of cards with which the child is playing in his drab apartment.

Shulevitz won the Caldecott Medal for his illustrations for Arthur Ransome's version of *The Fool of the World and the Flying Ship* (1968). In his acceptance speech, Shulevitz spoke of the Fool's refusal "to be bound by the generally accepted opinion of himself," and of his ability to break down false distinctions as he marries the Czar's daughter.

Shulevitz's next work, *Rain Rain Rivers* (1969), was the first of his books in which a simple text and an impressionistic use of color were employed to describe a phenomenon of nature. Using pale green, blue, and yellow washes to color the ink sketches, Shulevitz presents a little girl's reactions to the coming of a spring rain. In *Dawn* (1974), Shulevitz keeps his text to an absolute minimum, using first dark blues and later the colors of sunrise to evoke the mood of early morning on a lake.

During the 1970s, Shulevitz continued to illustrate traditional stories. Among the best known are *Soldier and Tsar in the Forest* (1972), a Russian tale translated by Richard Lourie; *The Magician* (1973), which Shulevitz translated from the Yiddish of J.R. Peretz; and *The Treasure* (1979), another Russian folktale, for which he was awarded a Caldecott Honor Medal. In 1973, he illustrated Isaac Bashevis Singer's *The Fools of Chelm and Their History*.

Discussing his illustrations, Shulevitz has remarked, "Having a visual approach, I sometimes conceive of a book like a movie, using words only when something cannot be said in pictures. Mostly . . . I try to suggest and evoke." His cinematographic technique can best be seen in *The Fool of the World*, in which the movement from page to page suggests the hero's physical journey toward the palace and spiritual journey toward fulfillment. Shulevitz has also stated, "I don't believe in imposing one style on different stories, but rather 'listen' and let the story guide the style and technique. As a result, my books have taken a variety of visual expressions."

TIPS FOR PARENTS AND TEACHERS: Preschool children can be encouraged to feel the emotions communicated by the colors in *Dawn* and *Rain Rain Rivers*. Early elementary aged children should notice how the illustrations in *The Fool of the World* reflect changes in the hero's emotions and social status.

❦The Sleeping Beauty
Folktale

Although different retellings include different incidents, in all its versions "The Story of the Sleeping Beauty" follows a basic plot outline: at her christening, the long-awaited child of a king and queen is cursed with early death by a fairy who had not been invited to the festivities. This doom is softened to a one-hundred-year sleep by one of the other fairies, and, despite all the precautions taken by the king, the daughter, during her fifteenth year, pricks her finger on a spindle and falls into a deep sleep. A century later, she is awakened by a young prince who marries her.

As is the case with many of the widely retold European folktales, the best known versions of "The Sleeping Beauty" are those of Charles Perrault ("La Belle au bois dormant," 1697), and the Brothers Grimm ("Briar-Rose," 1812). While both relate the basic plot outlined above, there are significant differences. Perrault adds an episode which follows the prince's marriage to the girl. He does not take her home, but keeps her existence a secret from his father and his mother, the latter, we learn, a child-eating ogre. When he ascends the throne, he brings his wife and two children to his castle. However, while he is away at the wars, his mother orders the servants to kill and cook the wife and children. Through the agency of a kind servant, they are spared and, at the conclusion, the mother plunges into and perishes in the boiling vat she had prepared for the Sleeping Beauty. This episode is not included in the Brothers Grimm version.

"The Sleeping Beauty" contains many motifs found in folktales around the world, the most important of these being the long-awaited child, the curse of the vengeful fairy, the ineffective parents, the long sleep, and the awakening through love. The underlying significance of these motifs gives the story a power which has made it one of the most popular children's stories of the last two centuries. Having waited so long for their child, the parents tend to be over-protective; in ordering the destruction of all spindles, they have tried to shield their daughter from, rather than to warn her about, the dangers she must face. The long sleep has been interpreted by psychologist Bruno Bettelheim as "the long, quiet concentration on oneself that is . . . needed [as one matures]." Author-critic P. L. Travers has related the story to traditional initiation rites: "There are elements of a secret and forbidding ritual in the theme, reminders of initiation ceremonies where the neophyte dies — or sleeps — on one level and awakens on another." The sleeper's awakening before the eyes of the admiring prince symbolizes her emergence into mature womanhood. In his retelling of the event, twentieth-century author Walter de la Mare used floral imagery which emphasized this point: "It was as if from being as it were a bud upon its stalk, she had become suddenly a flower, and they smiled each at the other."

TIPS FOR PARENTS AND TEACHERS: In the middle elementary grades, children can discuss the role of the girl's parents in the story and can consider how responsible they are for their daughter's fate. In the upper elementary grades, the behavior of the prince in Perrault's version can be analyzed. How mature is he in his relations with his wife and mother?

Snow White
Folktale

Collected by the Brothers Grimm early in the nineteenth century, this story of the beautiful young maiden threatened by a jealous stepmother has been one of the most favorite of the European folktales, particularly since 1938, when Walt Disney made it into his first full-length animated motion picture.

The appeal of the story is apparent. The princess without her natural mother must face the stepmother, who possesses great power. This power is motivated by her jealousy. As many critics have noted, the woman's constant questioning of her mirror reflects both her vanity and insecurity. When the girl is of sufficient age to be a direct threat to her self-concept, the queen must destroy her. The Grimms note that "envy and pride grew higher and higher in her heart like a weed, so that she had no peace day or night." Not only is the queen's death justifiable within the framework of the plot, but also it is symbolic of how her hatred has ultimately destroyed her.

During the story, Snow White is extremely vulnerable, being rescued successively by the hunter, the dwarfs, and the prince. However, as psychologist Bruno Bettelheim has argued, the story traces the progress of her development into a mature woman. He notes that, "It is the years Snow White spends with the dwarfs which stand for her time of troubles, of working through problems, her period of growth." They cannot finally protect her, and she must fall to the temptations represented by the apple, symbol of "love and sex, in both its benevolent and its dangerous aspect." The eating marks the end of her innocence, the sleep a kind of death leading to her rebirth into mature love.

TIPS FOR PARENTS AND TEACHERS: In the middle and upper elementary grades, children can discuss the nature of Snow White's innocence and the stepmother's jealousy. The forest, a symbol of the isolation and fear the girl experiences, can be compared to the forest in "Hansel and Gretel" and "Little Red Riding Hood."

Sperry, Armstrong *(1897 – 1976)*
American

Born in New Haven, Connecticut, Armstrong Sperry spent much of his youth drawing and writing, reading the South Seas adventure stories of Jack London, Herman Melville, and Robert Louis Stevenson, and listening to yarns spun by his great-grandfather, a one-time sailor. In 1925, he accepted a position as assistant ethnologist on an expedition to the South Seas. He spent a year on Bora Bora, learning the language, studying the customs, listening to the legends, and sketching, and his experiences formed the basis for many of the books he was later to write.

In 1940, Sperry published the book for which he is remembered today: *Call it Courage*. It is the story of Mafatu, a chief's son, whose fear of the sea which had drowned his mother and nearly taken him makes him an outcast in the village and a great disappointment to his father. Determined to overcome this fear, the boy, accompanied by his dog and pet albatross, paddles a canoe to a distant island, and after surviving against the sea, the elements, a shark, and cannibals, returns to his home a courageous, respected hero. In recounting the story, Sperry uses the style of the oral story teller, capturing the ritual quality of a traditional legend. His illustrations, in aqua, have a simple, block-like quality which harmonizes with the language of the story. *Call It Courage* was awarded the Newbery Medal in 1941.

TIPS FOR PARENTS AND TEACHERS: In the middle elementary

grades, students can carefully examine the successive stag█ of Mafatu's circular journey, noticing how his character develops to the point where he is able to return home with pride.

Spier, Peter *(1927 –   )*
American

Born in Amsterdam, the Netherlands, Peter Spier grew up in Broek, a small village used by Mary Mapes Dodge as the setting for *Hans Brinker, or the Silver Skates* (1865). His artistic interests were encouraged by his illustrator-journalist father, Jo Spier. After studying art in Amsterdam and serving in the Royal Netherlands Navy, he worked for a weekly newspaper. He was sent by the paper to Houston, Texas, in 1952 and a year later moved to New York, where he now lives. Spier began illustrating books in the early 1950s and has illustrated over sixty titles, including Mary Mapes Dodge's *Hans Brinker* (1958). However, he is best known for his own picture stories and his adaptations of well-known songs.

In his illustrating of songs, Spier is in the tradition of Randolph Caldecott, whom he read as a child, and Maurice Sendak, both of whose visual presentations gave new dimensions to familiar words. *The Fox Went Out on a Chilly Night* (1961), winner of a Caldecott Honor Medal, uses a New England setting. In *The Star-Spangled Banner* (1973), Spier's paintings portray the circumstances which the anthem originally depicted and then gives contemporary relevance to the words, showing the Supreme Court, racially mixed school children, and the first moon landing. For his collections of nursery rhymes, Spier not only visited the locations depicted, he also engaged in extensive historical research, a summary of which is contained in notes at the end of each book. *To Market! To Market!* (1967) portrays life on an eighteenth-century market day in Delaware.

Spier had long contemplated a pictoral rendition of the story of Noah and the great flood. However, when he discovered that there were twenty children's versions in print, he realized that he would need a new angle. He felt that the other versions presented a "joyous, sun-filled Caribbean cruise. . . . None of them showed Noah shovelling manure." Using a sixteenth-century Dutch poem by Jacob Revins as a point of departure, he portrayed a more realistic version of the events. Loading the Ark, Noah had to contend with a stubborn donkey, his wife's fear of mice, and a swarm of bees, all of whom wished entry. During the deluge, dirt and dung accumulated, a cat raided the hen's nest, and boredom set in. And when it came time to disembark, Noah discovered that the cat had had a litter of kittens. *Noah's Ark* (1977) received the Caldecott Medal.

The initial impression that one has on looking at Spier's picture books is of clutter and even chaos. However, the dozens of pen-sketched details on every page portray the vitality which Spier sees in the world. People are seen either curiously watching the major events depicted, or, as in the pictures of seventeenth-century Dutch painter Bruegel, going about their daily activities.

TIPS FOR PARENTS AND TEACHERS: Preschoolers should be encouraged to notice and discuss the dozens of details found on nearly every page of a Spier book. In the early and middle elementary grades, students can suggest why Spier included the details he did. The implications of the pictures in the song books can be the subject of a writing assignment in the middle elementary grades.

Sylvester and the Magic Pebble, by William Steig, Simon and Schuster, New York, 1969. Old-fashioned furniture reinforces the feelings of coziness and security which dominate the conclusion of *Sylvester and the Magic Pebble*.

Steig, William *(1907–   )*
American

Born in New York City, the son of two painters, William Steig began reading and drawing at an early age. From 1925 to 1929, he studied at the National School of Design in New York and in 1930 began a career as a magazine illustrator, contributing to such publications as *Life*, *The New Yorker*, and *Colliers*. Steig did not publish his first children's book until he was sixty-one years old. *Roland, the Minstrel Pig* (1968) is the story of a musician who sets out into the world, escapes from a devious fox, and finds a place in the royal court. Steig earned national attention with his next book, *Sylvester and the Magic Pebble* (1969), about a young donkey who collects pebbles, discovers a wishing stone, is transformed into a rock, and spends a winter separated from his distraught parents. The book won the Caldecott Medal.

Steig's later picture books include *Amos and Boris* (1971), a parable about the friendship between a mouse and a whale; *Farmer Palmer's Wagon Ride* (1974), a slapstick description of a farmer's return to his home; *The Amazing Bone* (1976), a Caldecott Honor Book, the account of Pearl the Pig's discovery of a magic object; *Caleb and Kate* (1977), a folk-like story about a husband who, after a quarrel with his wife, is changed into a dog; and *Tiffky Doofky* (1978), the tale of a garbage-collecting dog's search for a true love. *Gorky Rises* (1980) recounts the adventures of a frog who discovers a formula for weightlessness.

Steig has also written three longer children's stories, each illustrated with his own sketches. *Dominic* (1972) is about a dog who sets out to see the world and ends up freeing an enchanted princess from her hundred-year sleep. *The Real Thief* (1973) is a study in guilt. After his friend Gawain the Goose is unjustly accused of stealing the king's treasure, Derek the mouse undergoes the remorse of the undiscovered thief. *Abel's Island* (1976), winner of a Newbery Honor Medal, describes how Abel, a wealthy dandy of a mouse, survives for a year on a wilderness island onto which he has been cast during a storm.

During the course of his adventures, each of Steig's characters comes to know himself better, to appreciate the value of love and friendship. Roland and Dominic, restive in their family lives, seek new worlds and set out on the open road, experiencing dangers, but ultimately finding fulfillment. On his deserted island, Abel discovers his vocation: wood carving. However, the characters need companionship. Abel, alone, is desolate. Turning into stone, Sylvester sinks into a long, numb sleep. The discovery of a true love, as in *Dominic* and *Tiffky Doofky*, or the reunion with loved ones, as in *Sylvester and the Magic Pebble*, *Abel's Island*, and *Caleb and Kate*, is a kind of ultimate fulfillment.

With the exception of *Caleb and Kate*, the central figures in Steig's stories are animals: dogs, pigs, donkeys, and mice. In the tradition of Kenneth Grahame and E.B. White, Steig makes his animals convincing as individuals in their own right and also uses them as vehicles with which to satirize human nature. Steig's stories also make extensive use of folklore conventions. Three of them are like traditional stories: *Amos and Boris* resembles Aesop's "Lion and the Mouse," *Roland, the Minstrel Pig* is a variation of

"Henny-Penny," and *The Amazing Bone* has parallels to "Little Red Riding Hood." The conclusion of *Dominic* parallels "The Sleeping Beauty." Witches play important roles in several stories and, in *Sylvester and the Magic Pebble* and *Caleb and Kate*, the traditional motif of transformation is used.

For the artistry of his picture books, Steig has achieved wide renown. His pictures, generally in watercolors, capture the satire, humor, and tenderness of his narratives. His animal figures, while anatomically accurate, are also humanized through the clothing they wear and their facial expressions.

TIPS FOR PARENTS AND TEACHERS: Steig's picture books can be studied in the early elementary grades. Children can notice the emotions conveyed by the pictures and can discuss the reasons for the characters' being in such awkward situations. In the middle and upper grades, readers can notice how Steig's novels parody traditional literary forms (enchanted princesses and deserted islands) and can discuss how the parodies also contain serious themes.

Stevenson, Robert Louis *(1850 – 1894)*
Scottish

Born in Edinburgh, Scotland, the only son of Thomas and Margaret Stevenson, Robert Louis Stevenson spent much of his childhood confined indoors suffering illnesses caused by weak lungs. His almost constant companion was his nurse, Alison Cummings, "Cummy" as she was affectionately called, to whom, many years later, Stevenson was to dedicate *A Child's Garden of Verses*. She read him Bible stories and poetry and, when he was older, Stevenson himself devoured adventure stories by the popular writers James Fenimore Cooper, Robert Ballantyne, and Frederick Marryat. When he was fifteen, he published his first book, an historical pamphlet printed at his father's expense. Thus began a nearly thirty-year career which saw him write twenty books of fiction, eight plays, critical essays, many travel books, four famous boys' adventure stories, and one of the best-loved of all collections of children's poems.

In 1883, Stevenson published the book for which he is best remembered and which earned him the status of one of the greatest children's writers of all times: *Treasure Island*. Originally read to his father and stepson and then serialized in *Young Folks' Magazine*, it quickly sold five thousand copies and has not been out of print since. It is the story of young Jim Hawkins, who discovers a treasure map in the trunk of a dead seaman. The boy is made cabin boy on a ship sent to recover the treasure and, when the piratical crew, led by one-legged Long John Silver, turns on the captain and Jim's friends, he becomes instrumental in saving the ship and recovering the fortune.

Because he had to support himself and his family by writing, Stevenson did not rest on his laurels and in the next few years published sixteen books, three of which were for children. *A Child's Garden of Verses* (1885) included poems which had first appeared in *Penny Whistles*, privately printed in 1883. In 1886, he published *Kidnapped: Being Memoirs of the Adventures of David Balfour in the Year 1715*, an adventure story set during a period in which Jacobite Scots had rebelled against England. The central figure is seventeen-year-old David Balfour, who is kidnapped and put aboard a ship bound for the colonies. During the passage, the ship runs down a small craft whose only survivor is Alan Breck Stewart, a Highlander and Jacobite who lives a life constantly on the run. Alan and David survive a shipwreck and travel across country together, in grave danger after they witness and are suspected of the murder of a much-hated government official. At the conclusion of the novel, David has returned home to claim his inheritance and Alan prepares to flee to the continent.

Written earlier, but not published in book form until 1888, *Black Arrow* is an adventure story set in fifteenth-century England during the Wars of the Roses. Initially more popular than *Treasure Island*, *Black Arrow* is now the least-read of Stevenson's adventure stories. Stevenson's last great adventure story for boys, *Catriona* (published in the United States as *David Balfour*), a sequel to *Kidnapped*, appeared in 1893.

In the introduction to *Kidnapped*, Stevenson wrote, "This is no furniture for the scholar's library but a book for the winter evening school room when the tasks are over and the hour of bed draws near; [with] no more desperate purpose than to steal some young gentleman's attention from his Ovid, carry him for a while into the Highlands and the last century, and pack him to bed with some engaging images to mingle with his dreams." Unlike so many nineteenth-century writers, he did not believe that literature for children should have a moral purpose.

The hero of each novel is a boy or young man who must make his way in a violent, treacherous world. This character is not exceptional; in fact he is often very ordinary, thus allowing the reader more easily to identify with him. He is also often incredibly naïve, not understanding the nature of the adult world, and Stevenson often seems to laugh at the hero's simplicity. However, he is staunchly moral, an admirable characteristic which, nonetheless, makes his dealings with others, particularly his close friends, difficult. He often has an adult companion whose different code of life he finds difficult to accept or to understand. Throughout, the young hero's emotions and reactions are consistent with his ingenuous nature.

To create the poems for *A Child's Garden of Verses* Stevenson turned back to his childhood, recapturing his own youthful perceptions of the world, but drawing only lightly on the long illnesses he suffered or the frequent nightmares he endured. Virtually all of the sixty-four poems are spoken by a child who gives the reader his subjective responses to his worlds, real and imaginary. Literally, this world extends from his bedroom, down the stairs to the rest of the house, out into the garden, and occasionally into the fields and woods beyond. However, through the powers of his imagination, the child is able to transform the objects in that world so that it is much larger. His imagination is busiest at night, and many of the poems in *A Child's Garden of Verses* depict the most personal and often most lonely time in a child's life. Going to bed at night is a significant, often frightening, experience. However, in the morning, the child awakens to the happiness of home.

TIPS FOR PARENTS AND TEACHERS: Of all of Stevenson's adventure novels, only *Treasure Island* is still widely read. In the upper elementary grades students can consider how well Jim Hawkins reacts to the moral dilemmas he faces. The poems from *A Child's Garden* which deal with the powers of the child's imagination make an interesting complement to a story like Sendak's *Where the Wild Things Are*.

Sutcliff, Rosemary *(1920 –   )*
English

Rosemary Sutcliff was born in West Clanden, Surrey, England, and her childhood years were marked by travel, illness, painting, and reading. Her father was in the navy and the family moved about frequently until, when Rosemary was ten, he retired and the family settled in Devonshire. As a young child, she was stricken with Still's disease, a crippling ailment which left her permanently handicapped. In 1950 she published her first book, *The Chronicles of Robin Hood*. Sutcliff's next three works focused on Renaissance England. *The Queen Elizabeth Story* (1950) uses a little girl's longing to see the great ruler as a framework for a series of descriptions of daily life in a small Elizabethan town. *The Armourer's House* (1951) uses a similar technique to describe London life. In *Brother Dusty-Feet* (1952), the adventures of a boy who joins a group of strolling players provides Sutcliff with the opportunity to portray a variety of scenes. After publishing *Simon* (1953), an English Civil War story centering on two friends, one a Cavalier, the other a Roundhead, Rosemary Sutcliff began work on what were to become her best known books, a series dealing with Roman Britain. The first of these stories, *Eagle of the Ninth* (1954), is about Marcus Flavius Aquila who, with his friend and former slave Esca, decides to travel into the dangerous lands beyond the Roman Wall to recover the Eagle standard, which could become a powerful rallying symbol for the northern tribes should they attack Roman Britain. The second novel of the sequence, *The Silver Branch* (1957), takes place several generations later. Justin, a young surgeon newly arrived in Britain, meets his cousin Flavius, a descendant of Marcus. When the two discover a plot against the British Emperor Carausius, they flee their posts and later, under the symbol of the rediscovered Eagle, lead a band of outlaws against the new emperor Allectus and his invading Saxon cohorts.

By the time depicted in the third novel, *The Lantern Bearers* (1959), the Roman presence in Britain, which had long been crumbling, has disappeared. Aquila, another descendant of Marcus, deserts as the last legion departs Britain. As the ships sail, he lights the beacon for the last time, an act symbolic of his attempt to keep the light of hope glowing in the times of Saxon invasion. Later he escapes to the mountains, where he becomes a lieutenant to Ambrosius who fights to keep the Saxon invaders at bay. *The Lantern Bearers* received the Carnegie Medal as the outstanding British children's book of 1959.

Roman Britain and the period just after provided the setting of several other of Sutcliff's historical novels. *The Outcast* (1955) is the story of a young orphan boy who, washed ashore in Britain and later made a galley slave, finally earns a home. *Dawn Wind* (1961) deals with the coming of Christianity after the last Saxon raids. In *Mark of the Horse Lord* (1965), Phaedrus, a former slave and gladiator, finds a new life in Britain. *Capricorn Bracelet* (1973) uses the bracelet to provide continuity for stories about a family of Roman solidiers living in Britain from 61 AD to 383 AD. Other periods have provided the settings for further of Sutcliff's historical novels: the Bronze Age in *Warrior Scarlet* (1958), and the period of the Norman Conquest in *Shield Ring* (1956) and *Knight's Fee* (1960). In 1961, Rosemary Sutcliff again adapted a traditional legend, *Beowulf* (reprinted in 1966 as *Dragon Slayer*), the story of the hero who as a young man killed the monster Grendel and his mother and many years later died fighting a dragon. In its prose style, the work is distinguished by its ability to capture the rhythms and kennings of the original Anglo-Saxon, while at the same time being intelligible to younger readers. Other legends she has since retold include *The Hound of Ulster* (1963) and *The High Deeds of Finn MacCool* (1967) from Ireland, and *Tristan and Iseult* (1971), part of the Arthurian saga.

The central character of most of Sutcliff's novels is a boy or young man growing into adulthood. At the beginning of or early in the story, he is made an outcast. However, he is not completely alone and is usually given the chance of friendship with an individual who is not of his class or culture. The different and often long quest for self-fulfillment is best seen in *Eagle of the Ninth* and *The Lantern Bearers*. In the former, Marcus, a young and somewhat insecure centurion, sees his old world destroyed when he is lamed. However, he develops new understanding and maturity when he discovers and is able to accept the fact that the Ninth Legion was a corrupt and disintegrating band of men. In addition to escaping the Saxons and leading Ambrosius' forces against them, Aquilas, in *The Lantern Bearers*, engages in deep personal struggles. When his legion, the last in Britain, departs, he must choose between loyalties; when he sees his house burned and his father murdered, he is haunted by nightmares; and when he discovers his sister married to a Saxon, he loses his faith in humanity. The extent of his personal anguish and bitterness is revealed in his treatment of his wife, whom he generally ignores. His final victory is over more than Saxons; it is over himself. He can again love and care.

The major goal of the quest of the Sutcliff heroes is double: self-fulfill-ment and a sense of belonging within a community. Coming from a variety of locations and cultures, and living in a different time, they come to share a common quality, their love of Britain.

TIPS FOR PARENTS AND TEACHERS: Sutcliff's novels are best suited for the upper elementary and junior high grades, at which time students can better understand the clash of historical forces and the often difficult pro-gress of the heroes toward a sense of fulfillment.

❦Taylor, Mildred *(1948? –   )*
American

Born in Jackson, Mississippi and raised in Toledo, Ohio, Mildred Taylor grew up learning about her Southern roots: "By the fireside in our northern home or in the South where I was born, I learned a history not written in books but one passed from generation to generation on the steps of moonlit porches and beside dying fires in one-room houses, a history of great-grandparents and of slavery and of the days following slavery; of those who lived still not free, yet who would not let their spirits be enslaved." In her teens she became very aware of the discrepancy between the history taught in white textbooks and that she had learned from her family, and she determined to write about "people who had done nothing more spectacular than survive in a society designed for their destruction." After graduating from the University of Toledo, working for the Peace Corps in Ethiopia, and taking graduate work at the University of Colorado, she began writing about "people [who] were graced with a simple dignity that elevated them from the ordinary to the heroic." Drawing on her family's history, she wrote three books about the Logan family, telling about their defense of their dignity and their land in a racially hostile south. *Song of the Trees* (1975) describes the Logans' fight to save their land from lumbering interests which wish to possess it. In *Roll of Thunder, Hear My Cry* (1976), winner of the Newbery Medal, the Logans, standing up for their rights, find themselves the victims of increasing racial hostility. *Let the Circle Be Unbroken* (1981), set in 1935, deals with the Logans' struggles during the Depression.

In addition to providing, as Taylor wrote, "heroes missing from the schoolbooks of my childhood," the novels about the Logan family provide vivid, moving pictures about the 1930s in the rural South, a time and a place unfamiliar to most young readers, black or white. *Roll of Thunder* is, in addition, a treatment of a universal theme: a young girl's painful growth to maturity. Narrated by nine-year-old Cassie Logan, it presents the sorrow, fear, and anger she experiences as she becomes aware of the violence and hatred in the world that surrounds her. As her father tells her: "Baby, you had to grow up a little today. . . . It happened and you have to accept the fact that in the world outside this house, things are not always as we would have them be."

TIPS FOR PARENTS AND TEACHERS: For students in the upper elementary and junior high grades, all Taylor's novels make excellent reading, not only as introductions to an historical period and to racial hatred, but also as moving portraits of basic human emotions. Students should notice the complexity of the world in which the Logans live and should understand that Cassie's often simple responses are not always adequate for coping with the confusing world of which she is becoming aware.

Alice's Adventures in Wonderland, ed. by Donald Rackin Wadsworth, Belmont, California, 1969. Tenniel's illustrations of the "Alice" books are the classic depictions of the frustrations felt by the heroine during her adventures.

♥Tenniel, Sir John *(1820 – 1914)*
English

Born in London, John Tenniel was largely self-taught as an artist, having left the Royal Academy School when he became dissatisfied with the instruction. He illustrated his first book, *Aesop's Fables*, in 1848, and, in 1851, began a fifty-one-year association with *Punch* magazine, where he distinguished himself as an editorial cartoonist.

When Charles Lutwidge Dodgson was looking for someone to provide more professional illustrations than his own for his story *Alice's Adventures in Wonderland*, he turned to Tenniel. In letters to friends, Tenniel reported that Dodgson was extremely fussy, often demanding that minute changes be made in details. However, when the first edition was printed in 1865, Tenniel himself was fussy, objecting to the poor quality of the printing. On his advice, Dodgson withdrew the first printing and a second, better-produced edition appeared in November, 1865.

Tenniel reluctantly agreed to illustrate *Through the Looking-Glass*. However, he played an active role in the final form of the book, suggesting that Dodgson omit an episode about a wasp in a wig. In a famous letter to Dodgson, he wrote, "Don't think me brutal, but I am bound to say that the *'wasp'* chapter doesn't interest me in the least, & I can't see my way to a picture. If you want to shorten the book, I can't help thinking — with all submission — that *there* is your opportunity." *Through the Looking-Glass* appeared in 1871. *The Wasp in a Wig* was not published until 1977.

In spite of the problems he experienced working with Dodgson, Tenniel, who was knighted in 1893, produced the illustrations which have always been most closely associated with the Alice books. This is perhaps because of the closeness of their collaboration; Tenniel produced the images Dodgson desired. The illustrations are neither pleasant nor cute. Darkened by a great deal of crosshatching, they reflect the frustrations and anxieties Alice experiences during her adventures. Alice herself is never pictured as smiling as she confronts the unreasonable characters in her dream or in the looking-glass world. The adults and animals, with the exception of the Cheshire Cat, scowl or look worried or bewildered.

TIPS FOR PARENTS AND TEACHERS: Although younger children may be frightened by the illustrations for the Alice books, those in the upper elementary and junior high grades can see how they reflect Alice's frustrations and the ridiculousness of the adults. Tenniel's illustrations can be compared to those of other artists.

The Three Bears
English folktale

Although this well-known story did not appear in print until 1837, in Robert Southey's anonymously published collection *The Doctor,* it seems to have enjoyed considerable popularity in the early part of the nineteenth century. In its early nineteenth-century form, the story appears as a typical cautionary tale in which an intruder — depicted as an old woman, not a young girl — violates the sanctity of private property and is punished. An 1831 manuscript version, written in verse and illustrated in watercolors by Eleanor Mure for the birthday of her four-year-old nephew, tells of three bears who, being tired of living in the forest, decide to buy an elegant city mansion. When an old woman calls on them and is rebuffed, she decides to enter their house unbidden and, doing so, drinks the milk and breaks the chair and bed of the smallest bear. When the occupants discover her "long they debate what, in justice, should be their old enemy's fate." Failing to drown or burn her, they place her on top of the church steeple of St. Paul's, where, we are told, she may still be.

During the nineteenth century, the story underwent two major changes. First, the old woman became a young girl, first called "Silverhair," later "Goldenhair," and finally "Goldilocks," the name by which she is best known today. John Cundall, who introduced the first change in 1849, explained that "there are so many other stories of old women." That the change should have proved so popular is probably due to the fact that younger readers could relate to a child more easily than to an old woman. The second major alteration was the transformation of the bears from merely large, medium, and small, to a father, mother, and baby. This change had two results. It made the house seem even more private property; it belonged to a very close family. Accordingly Goldilocks, the single human invader, seemed more alien in the setting and her intrusion was obvious.

The story has remained very popular during the twentieth century and has been adapted to meet the needs of a changing society. Generally, the attitude toward Goldilocks has softened; she is often presented as a lost little girl who is hungry, tired, and, at worst, inquisitive. As a cautionary tale, it is now often told to warn children of the dangers of becoming lost in the wilderness,and the bears, rather than the little girl, become the threatening force. The tale has been used by various cultures, one of the most interesting adaptations coming from Canada's Northwest Territories. In "Little Miss Eider Duck and the Three Nanooks," a duck seeks shelter in the igloo of three polar bears who have gone for a stroll while their seal meat cools. In the end, the bears invite the duck to remain with them, for "this was the Friendly North and you may enter anywhere in a storm."

TIPS FOR PARENTS AND TEACHERS: After having had the story read to them in the early elementary grades, the children can examine different illustrated versions, noticing which ones best depict the girl's personality and the surprise of the characters at the final confrontation. Brinton Turkle's *Deep in the Forest* (1976) is an interesting reversal of the traditional story.

Tolkien, J.R.R. *(1892 – 1973)*
English

J.R.R. Tolkien wrote, remembering his childhood, "I desired dragons with a profound desire. Of course, I in my timid body did not wish to have them in the neighborhood, intruding into my relatively safe world, in which it was, for instance, poossible to read stories in peace of mind, free from fear. But the world that contained even the imagination of Fafnir was richer and more beautiful, at whatever the cost of peril." Although born in South Africa, Tolkien spent his childhood near Birmingham. A good student, he often used to create imaginary languages and to write stories about the characters who spoke them.

After studying English at Oxford University, Tolkien married his childhood sweetheart Edith Bratt in 1916, and shortly after served in France during the First World War. Sent home with "trench fever," he began writing the mythological stories for which he was to become famous. In 1920, he joined the faculty of the University of Leeds, and in 1925 he returned to Oxford, where he taught until 1959. While establishing a reputation as one of England's foremost literary scholars, Tolkien continued to write fantasies, all of them drawing on his vast learning in the languages and literatures of Northern Europe.

The idea for his most famous children's story, *The Hobbit*, came in the 1930s while he was marking student examinations. "One of the candidates had mercifully left one of the pages with no writing on it . . . and I wrote on it: *'In a hole in the ground there lived a hobbit.'* Names always generate a story in my mind. Eventually I thought I'd better find out what hobbits were like." Susan Dagnall of the publishing firm of Allen and Unwin saw the manuscript of the resulting stories he wrote for his children and suggested that they be printed. The publisher's young son, Rayner Unwin, read and heartily approved of the adventures, and they appeared in 1937 as *The Hobbit*.

The Hobbit quickly became a success. It was enthusiastically reviewed by, among others, C.S. Lewis, and the American edition, published in 1938 by Houghton Mifflin, was named the best children's book in the *New York Herald Tribune's* Spring Book Festival. Since then, its popularity has remained consistently high and, in 1977, it was made into an animated television special.

The hero of *The Hobbit* is Bilbo Baggins, a middle-aged, comfortable, and ordinary individual; he is shaken from his lethargy by the arrival of Gandalf, a wizard who makes it virtually impossible for Bilbo not to join with thirteen dwarves who wish to reclaim a treasure held by the dragon Smaug. The rest of the story describes not only Bilbo's adventures, but also his inner growth as an individual.

Throughout all his experiences, Bilbo is what critic Diana Waggoner has called a "low-mimetic hero," an ordinary person who rises to the occasion when necessary. Tolkien's biographer, Humphrey Carpenter, has said that the hobbits, especially Bilbo, represented what the author admired about the English: their ability to shake themselves from their average life when they had to. At the end of the novel, when Bilbo has returned to his home, the wizard Gandalf does not allow him to become too proud: "You are only quite a little fellow in a wide world after all!"

Although *The Hobbit* is told for children, in a style that Tolkien later grew to dislike, it also has serious undertones. Tolkien himself remarked, "Mr. Baggins began as a comic tale among conventional and inconsistent Grimm's fairy-tale dwarves, and got drawn into the edge of it — so that even Sauron the Terrible [the evil figure of *The Lord of the Rings*] peeped over the edge. And what more can hobbits do? They can be comic, but their comedy is suburban unless it is set against things more elemental."

The Hobbit proved so popular that the publishers requested a sequel. Tolkien offered several children's stories which were rejected as being of insufficient magnitude to cash in on the earlier work's success. He then began to work on what was to become *The Lord of the Rings*. However, he was unsure of the direction the story would take. After many delays, extensive revisions, and much quarrelling with his publishers, who were reluctant to bring out his still fragmentary *Silmarillion* (posthumously published in 1977), the book appeared in three volumes, in 1954 and 1955: *The Fellowship of the Ring*, *The Two Towers*, and *The Return of the King*. An American edition appeared shortly after and since then, *The Lord of the Rings* has been translated into a dozen languages. It has been estimated that by 1970 over three million paperback copies had been sold.

The Lord of the Rings is only loosely a sequel to *The Hobbit*. Although it includes Bilbo Baggins, Gollum, and Gandalf, as well as the ring of invisibility Bilbo discovered in Gollum's cave, its focus and purpose are much larger. When it is discovered that the ring is evil, possessing the soul of anyone who wears it too long, and that it is sought by Sauron, the evil Lord of Mordor, Bilbo's nephew Frodo and several companions begin a long quest to take the ring to the cracks of doom, where it can be destroyed. Frodo is only one of a very large cast of characters, but becomes deeply involved in the clashes between the forces of good and evil.

While working on *The Lord of the Rings*, Tolkien published *Farmer Giles of Ham* (1949), the story of a reluctant hero who is ordered to kill a dragon. Other children's stories he wrote were *The Adventures of Tom Bombadil* (1962), a collection of poems about one of the minor characters from *The Lord of the Rings*; *Smith of Wooton Major* (1967), about a boy who is transported to fairy land; and *The Father Christmas Letters* (1976). In 1977, four years after his father's death, Christopher Tolkien published *Silmarillion*, the mythological book Tolkien had been working on for over fifty years.

While Tolkien is remembered and respected for his literary and linguistic scholarship, his fame rests on *The Hobbit*, *The Lord of the Rings*, and, to a much lesser extent, his smaller children's stories. The sources of his great works were Norse, Celtic, and Germanic legends, myths, and sagas, and his Roman Catholic beliefs. However, even though one can find echoes of many works in his stories, Tolkien's stories are original. *The Lord of the Rings* has been called the only great epic of the twentieth century and has been compared in scope to Edmund Spenser's Renaissance epic, *The Faerie Queene*.

In discussing his type of writing in the essay "On Fairy-Stories," Tolkien referred to the "sub-creator," one who created a world through his words in a manner parallel but inferior to the act of divine creation. The result was a secondary world, complete with geography, living creatures, language, and history. Tolkien wrote that his own stories originated from his interest in inventing languages: "The 'stories' were made . . . to provide a world for the languages." When successfully written, stories evoke in the reader a sense of "literary belief," an ability to accept the fictional worlds on their own basis. "It is," he wrote, "essential to a genuine fairy-story . . . that it should be presented as 'true.'" When a story works, "we stand outside our own time, outside Time itself, maybe." He also wrote that "the peculiar quality of 'joy' in successful fantasy can thus be explained as a sudden glimpse of the underlying reality or truth."

Although in *The Silmarillion* and elsewhere, Tolkien describes the earlier eras of his world of Middle Earth, it is the Third Age, the time of *The Hobbit* and *The Lord of the Rings*, that he most fully explores. It is filled with a wide range of creatures: elves, dwarves, goblins, ents or tree people, evil orcs, human beings, and others. The best-known creatures are the hobbits, short, stout creatures with large, furry feet. Generally, they live quiet, contented, uneventful lives in the Shire. They are, in many ways, like average Englishmen. Tolkien wrote, "The Hobbits are just rustic English people, made small in size because it reflects the generally small reach of their imagination — not the small reach of their courage or latent power." This courage is seen in Bilbo, Frodo, and Sam Gamgee, who become heroes almost in spite of themselves.

TIPS FOR PARENTS AND TEACHERS: In the middle elementary grades *Farmer Giles of Ham* can be compared to E. Nesbit's *The Last of the Dragons* and Kenneth Grahame's "The Reluctant Dragon." *The Hobbit* is better understood by upper elementary students who have an awareness of the characteristics of the folklore creatures Bilbo meets. In reading the novel, they should notice the steps by which Bilbo develops into a hero. For middle and upper elementary aged readers, *The Father Christmas Letters* make a refreshing change from the typical, clichéd Christmas stories.

❤Tudor, Tasha *(1915 –   )*
American

Born in Boston, Tasha Tudor grew up in rural Connecticut, where she enjoyed drawing and reading, especially the books of Beatrix Potter. Since the publication of her first book, *Pumpkin Moonshine,* in 1938, Tasha Tudor has celebrated a simple nineteenth-century life style. *New England Butt'ry Shelf Cookbook* (1965) and *Tasha Tudor's Old Fashioned Christmas Book* (1979) reflect her love of traditional crafts. She has also illustrated such nineteenth- and early twentieth-century classics as *Fairy Tales from Hans Christian Andersen* (1945), Clement Moore's *The Night Before Christmas* (1962), Frances Hodgson Burnett's *The Secret Garden* (1962), and Kenneth Grahame's *The Wind in the Willows* (1966). In two books illustrated for her daughter Efner Tudor Holmes, *Amy's Goose* (1977) and *Carrie's Gift* (1978), she sensitively portrayed the New England countryside. Her *Mother Goose* (1944) was named a Caldecott Honor Book.

TIPS FOR PARENTS AND TEACHERS: In the early and middle elementary grades, Tudor's books provide an introduction to a vanished way of American life. They can be related to *Ox-Cart Man* (Barbara Cooney and Donald Hall) and *A Gathering of Days* (Joan Blos).

Turkle, Brinton *(1915 –   )*
American

Born and raised in Alliance, Ohio, Brinton Turkle studied theatre at Carnegie Tech and art at the Boston Museum of Art School. He has illustrated over fifty books, including works by such authors as Elizabeth Coatsworth (*You Say You Saw a Camel,* 1959), Ann McGovern (*If You Lived in Colonial Times,* 1964), Eve Merriam (*The Story of Ben Franklin,* 1965), and F.N. Monjo (*Poor Richard in France,* 1973).

Turkle is best known for his stories about Obadiah, a small Quaker boy living in nineetenth-century Nantucket. In *Obadiah, the Bold* (1965), the hero wants to become a sea captain. *Thy Friend Obadiah* (1969), a Caldecott Honor Book, describes his relationship with a sea gull; in *The Adventures of Obadiah* (1972), he becomes involved in a sheep shearing festival; and in *Rachel and Obadiah* (1978), he meets his match. The illustrations realistically depict the background of Nantucket and portray the liveliness of the young boy. Turkle's other books include *The Magic of Millicent Musgrave* (1967), *The Fiddler of High Lonesome* (1968), and *Deep in the Forest* (1976). The last is a wordless picture book in which the traditional story of Goldilocks is reversed.

TIPS FOR PARENTS AND TEACHERS: In the middle elementary

grades, the Obadiah stories can introduce an aspect of nineteenth-century life, and *Rachel and Obadiah* can humorously introduce a female hero. In studying *Deep in the Forest*, students can notice parallels to the traditional story of Goldilocks and can create dialogue for the little bear.

Twain, Mark: pseudonym of Samuel Clemens *(1835 – 1910)*

American

Like his famous characters Tom Sawyer and Huckleberry Finn, Samuel Clemens spent his boyhood close to the Mississippi River. Born in Florida, Missouri, he moved with his family to Hannibal when he was three years old. In many ways, his childhood in this pioneer river town was idyllic, although he did witness much of the violence common to the frontier: murder, beating of slaves, and drunkenness. He was brought up in the Calvinist tradition and many of his biographers have suggested that this upbringing contributed to the senses of guilt and pessimism he felt in his adult years.

In 1847, Clemens began over twenty years travelling and working at various jobs. He lived in St. Louis, New York, Philadelphia, Cincinnati, Virginia City (Nevada), and San Francisco, and travelled to Hawaii, Europe, and Palestine, while working as a printer, reporter, public lecturer, and riverboat pilot. While in Virginia City, he first used his famous pen name, Mark Twain (from a riverboat expression signifying safe passage in shallow water), and wrote a story which brought him national recognition, a tall tale, "The Celebrated Jumping Frog of Calaveras County." His travels to Palestine were described in his humorous book *The Innocents Abroad* (1869).

In 1870, he married Olivia Langdon and moved to Connecticut. This move marked a major break with his past. For the rest of his life, Twain lived among the literary establishment of the East, and his writings about the West took on a nostalgic tinge, as if, separated from the West by time and geography, he were almost looking back, like Kenneth Grahame, on golden days.

In 1876, Twain published his most famous children's novel, *The Adventures of Tom Sawyer*, in which he drew on memories of his own childhood to tell the story of a boy who enjoys fantasizing that he is Robin Hood or a pirate, engages in escapades which annoy his Aunt Polly, and falls in love with Becky Thatcher, the new girl in town. However, the novel contains real danger as well as boyish adventures. Tom, along with his friend Huckleberry Finn, witnesses a brutal murder, and when an innocent man is accused, courageously testifies on his behalf. At the novel's climax, Tom and Becky become lost in the unexplored parts of McDougal's caves and are nearly discovered by the murderer, Indian Joe.

Shortly after he had completed *The Adventures of Tom Sawyer*, Clemens began writing a story about Tom's friend Huckleberry Finn. However, work proceeded slowly; the story was shelved for some time and was not published until 1884, as *The Adventures of Huckleberry Finn*. In the interim, he published two of his better-known works, *The Prince and the Pauper* (1881), a novel set in England in the time of Henry VIII, in which two look-alikes, the king's son and a commoner, exchange places, and *Life on the Mississippi* (1883), descriptions based on his boyhood years and his times as a river-boat pilot.

The Adventures of Huckleberry Finn is more than a sequel to *The Adventures of Tom Sawyer*. Told in the first person, it is the story of Huck's voyage down the Mississippi with the escaped slave Jim. Huck, who is escaping from the civilized ways of the Widow Douglas, with whom he had gone to live at the end of *The Adventures of Tom Sawyer*, and from his violent and drunken father, confronts the evil and hypocrisy of the various river-bank societies he encounters. He must also face the troubles of his own conscience. Thoroughly conventional in his notions about black people and slavery, he gradually realizes that Jim is a human being and a loyal friend, and he courageously decides to risk eternal damnation rather than turn his friend in to the authorities.

The concluding third of the book has generated a great deal of critical controversy. Many people have found it excessively long and tedious. Huck's giving in to Tom's plans is seen as reflecting an inconsistency in characterization. Others have said that the reintroduction of Tom is unnecessary to the resolution of the conflicts.

While *The Adventures of Huckleberry Finn* is in many ways a boys' adventure story, it also contains a great deal of satire and many complex themes which can only be fully understood by adult readers. In fact, it is a major component of American literature courses in universities and has been analyzed in hundreds of critical articles. Among the book's strongest supporters have been the poet T.S. Eliot and the novelist Ernest Hemingway, who said that modern American literature began with the publication of *The Adventures of Huckleberry Finn*.

No other of Twain's books has achieved the lasting reputation of *The Adventures of Tom Sawyer* or *The Adventures of Huckleberry Finn*. Among the best-known of his later books are *A Connecticut Yankee in King Arthur's Court* (1889), the story of a man who is transported back to an earlier era, and *The Man That Corrupted Hadleyburg* (1900), a bitter and ironic satire. He also published two seldom-read sequels to his Tom Sawyer stories: *Tom Sawyer Abroad* (1894) and *Tom Sawyer Detective* (1896), neither of which possesses the depth of the earlier stories.

During the last years of his life, Clemens became increasingly pessimistic. His wife died in 1904, and one of his daughters in 1909. One of the few happy occasions of his later years was his acceptance of an honorary doctorate from Oxford University in 1907. He died in 1910.

As a writer for children, Clemens is one of the first modern masters of realism. Technically, as Ernest Hemingway recognized, he handled dialogue with great skill. He also was able to depict scenery with great accuracy and to make his descriptions contribute to the mood of a particular moment in a narrative. Perhaps because he remembered his own childhood so well, Clemens portrays his youthful characters with great honesty. On the one hand, he captures their sense of fun and carefree happiness; on the other, he shows their terror at the violence which can suddenly erupt into their world. He also knows that children often view adults as tyrannical and arbitrary. He sees children as complex beings, often struggling with their developing consciences.

In the field of adventure fiction, Clemens struck out in new directions. As critic John Rowe Townsend has written, "These books showed that adventure did not have to be sought at the other side of the world; it was as near as your backyard. Adventure did not happen only to stiff-upper-lipped heroes of superior social status; it could happen to ordinary people, even to inferiors . . . and chattels."

TIPS FOR PARENTS AND TEACHERS: In studying *Tom Sawyer*, junior high readers should notice the alternations between make-believe and actual situations. Does Tom behave the same way at play as he does in dangerous moments, or does he have to change his notions of acceptable conduct? In reading *Huckleberry Finn*, students can analyze the hypocrisy of the adults Huck meets.

The Beast of Monsieur Racine, by Tomi Ungerer, Farrar, Straus, & Giroux, New York, 1971. Ungerer's blend of tenderness and urbane satire are embodied in this scene from *The Beast of Monsieur Racine*.

Ungerer, Tomi *(1931 –   )*
American

Born in Strasbourg, France, Tomi Ungerer moved to New York in 1956 and began a career as an illustrator. In the mid 1970s, he moved to Ireland.

Ungerer's first children's book, *The Mellops Go Flying*, the story of an adventurous family of pigs, was published in 1957. Their later adventures were described in *The Mellops Go Diving for Treasure* (1957), *The Mellops Strike Oil* (1958), and *The Mellops Go Spelunking* (1963). In 1958, he published *Crictor*, the first of several stories about unusual animals and their human friends. Crictor is a boa constrictor. *Adelaide* (1959) is about a winged kangaroo; *Emile* (1960), an octopus; *Rufus* (1961), a bat; and *Orlando* (1966), a vulture.

In *The Three Robbers* (1962), an account of evil men won over to goodness by a little girl, Ungerer began to focus his attention on people. *Moon Man* (1967) describes the unhappy results of a Man-in-the-Moon's desire to visit Earth so that he can dance. In *Zeralda's Ogre* (1967), a child-eating monster is tamed by the cooking abilities of a little girl whom he later marries. In *The Beast of Monsieur Racine* (1971), Ungerer's best known and most popular book, a retired tax collector discovers a monster eating his prize pears and befriends it, only to discover that it is really two children in a costume.

Ungerer's most recent stories, *No Kiss for Mother* (1973) and *Allumette: A*

Fable with Due Respect to Hans Christian Andersen, the Grimm Brothers, and the Honorable Ambrose Bierce (1974) are the most emotionally intense of his stories. In the former, Piper Paw, a young cat, feels hostility to the adults in his world. In the latter, a poor girl's wishes come true and she gives her new wealth to the poor.

The success of Ungerer's narratives depends on the reader's acceptance of an absurd premise. Once it is accepted, each story follows a logical pattern, grotesque or ridiculous though it may be, and presents several serious themes. One of these is the value of true friendship. After Monsieur Racine befriends the beast, he philosophically remarks, "I lost my pears but found a companion." The very unusual nature of many of these friendships, people and snakes, bats, vultures, or beasts, helps to emphasize their depth: the friends care less for social conventions than for true relationships.

From *Moon Man* onward, Ungerer's stories have become increasingly more critical of society. Among those rushing to look at the newly landed Moon Man is an ice cream man who "hurried to set up his stand for the spectators." In *The Beast of Monsieur Racine*, crowds riot, attacking each other and performing "unspeakable acts." Ungerer's stories often present a dark view of human nature. He has said, "I depict awful things in order to destroy them . . . . Actually, the world is as cruel now as it has always been, except that people know more about it because of the vast expansion of communication."

Much of the meaning of Ungerer's stories is communicated through the illustrations. In the earlier books, the illustrations, generally simple sketches using limited color, help to create a gentle humor. However, in later books, they communicate more darkly satiric messages. In *Moon Man*, a photographer and a farmer armed with a pitchfork stand side by side. In *The Beast of Monsieur Racine*, a tramp walks by, a bloody foot protruding from his pack; a gendarme assaults a lady; a maid empties a chamberpot on a passerby. In *Allumette*, a derelict sprawls in a wrecked car; nearby, a poor girl roots through a garbage can as huge rats look on.

TIPS FOR PARENTS AND TEACHERS: Because of the sophistication of their themes, Ungerer's picture books are best used in the upper elementary grades. After noticing the absurd, often grotesque humor, students can consider the serious social themes Ungerer is presenting.

The *Biggest Bear*, by Lynd Ward, Houghton Mifflin, Boston, 1952. Ward's illustrations for *The Biggest Bear* depict emotions not described in the text.

Ward, Lynd *(1905 –)*
American

Born in Chicago, Lynd Ward spent his childhood in Evanston, Illinois, Newton Centre, Massachusetts, and Englewood, New Jersey. During the many summers spent in Lonely Lake in Ontario's north woods, he developed the deep love of nature seen in his books. Ward studied art at Columbia University's Teachers College, and after his marriage to May McNeer, studied at the National Academy of Fine Arts in Leipzig, Germany.

Ward has illustrated over one hundred books. Many of them, including *Beowulf* (1939) and Robert Louis Stevenson's *Kidnapped* (1948), have been limited edition gift books and, in 1954, he was awarded the Silver Medal of the Limited Editions Club for his outstanding work over a twenty-five year period. For his illustrations for Stuart Holbrook's *America's Ethan Allan* (1949), Ward received a Caldecott Honor Medal.

In the books he has illustrated and written himself, Ward considers himself not "a writer but rather an artist whose stories sometimes need some words." He has noted that "the artist is able to tell a story in which the usual relation of much text to little picture is exactly reversed and the greatest part of the story is told by the pictures themselves." He recalls that as a child he would often not read the words of the illustrated books he perused, allowing the continuity between the pictures to create the story.

Not surprisingly, in the three children's books entirely by Ward, *The*

Biggest Bear (1952), *Nic of the Woods* (1965), and *The Silver Pony* (1973), the pictures are more important than the text.

For *The Biggest Bear*, winner of the Caldecott Medal, Ward drew on his memories of Canada's north woods to tell the story of Johnny Orchard, a little boy who feels humiliated because his family's is the only barn without a bearskin on it. Striding into the woods determined to shoot a bear, Johnny finds a small cub which he brings back to the farm. Most of the humor of the story is conveyed by Ward's black and brown watercolors. The depiction of the havoc wreaked by the growing bear provides an example of Ward's belief in the artist's "power to control a succession of images in time, so that the cumulative effect upon the viewer is a result of not only what images are thrown at him, but the order in which they come." Four pictures reveal the damage; however, the bear is seen in none of them. It dominates the fifth picture, sitting upright, drinking from a bottle of maple syrup. The contrast between the earlier pictures and this one shocks the viewer into realizing the tremendous growth of the animal.

Nic of the Woods is the story of a young dog's first summer in the north woods. Using blues and blacks, Ward portrays the beauty and desolation of the Ontario wilderness. In *The Silver Pony*, Ward's third children's book, there are no words. Eighty-one full-page illustrations in black watercolors tell the story of a young farm boy who discovers a winged pony which he rides to the four points of the compass. In the variation of light and dark shades in the individual pictures and through the development of a continuity between the illustrations, Ward delicately communicates the many emotions of the story.

TIPS FOR PARENTS AND TEACHERS: Ward's books reveal that shading can be as important as full color in creating theme, mood, and character. Students in the middle elementary grades can notice the series of ironic surprises set up by the pictures in *The Biggest Bear*. In the upper elementary grades students can discuss the relationship between the boy's imaginative and physical worlds in *The Silver Pony*.

White, E(lwyn) B(rooks) *(1899 –   )*
American

Born in Mount Vernon, New York, E.B. White began writing at an early age. After serving in World War I, he returned to university, graduating from

Cornell in 1921, spent two years as a reporter, and worked his passage on a boat to Alaska. In 1927, he began his long and distinguished career with the *New Yorker* magazine. In 1938, White and his wife bought a farm in Brooklin, Maine, and White's observations of life on the farm influenced many of the scenes in *Charlotte's Web*. In 1945, *Stuart Little*, the first of his three children's books, was published, followed by *Charlotte's Web* in 1952 and *The Trumpet of the Swan* in 1970. In 1963, he received the presidential Medal of Freedom, and in 1970, the Laura Ingalls Wilder Award for his "substantial and lasting contribution to literature for children."

When *Stuart Little* appeared in 1945, White was generally regarded as one of American's finest essayists. He had not considered himself a children's writer, and the writing and publishing of *Stuart Little* was itself somewhat of an accident. He reports having had a dream about Stuart and writing it down the following day for possible use in a story for a young niece. However, the story kept getting shelved for more pressing duties and was only completed twelve years later.

The focus of each of the three children's novels is on a character who is born with a deficiency which makes a normal life difficult. Stuart, second son of the Frederick C. Littles, is only two inches tall and looks like a mouse; Wilbur the pig is the runt of a spring litter and in danger of being destroyed; Louis the trumpeter swan is born mute and thus cannot give mating calls. During the course of each story, the central character must confront his problem and either overcome it or adapt himself so that he can live with it.

The problems of Stuart Little are both physical and existential. Being only two inches tall, he must face the inconveniences and dangers of living in a normal-sized world. As the only human being existing in mouse form, he is, as several critics have noted, an outcast or misfit, alone in a world that can never really understand him. As he himself poignantly remarks, "I'm not tall enough to be noticed — yet I'm tall enough to want to go to Seventy-second Street." The hopelessness of his situation becomes most evident when he falls in love with Margalo, a bird rescued by Mrs. Little. Obviously they are incompatible, and when Stuart leaves home to search for her in the vast north, he is like the narrator of Herman Melville's *Mardi*, engaging in an unending quest for ideal beauty.

Wilbur must, after he has escaped the fate of a runt pig, learn to overcome his feelings of inadequacy. However, unlike Stuart, who is almost completely on his own, Wilbur receives considerable help from his barnyard friends. First, he is rescued from Mr. Arable's axe by eight-year-old Fern, who protests against the injustice of destroying runts. However, when he is moved to Zuckerman's barnyard and learns from one of the sheep that he is being fattened for fall slaughter, he reacts in panic and terror. Through the efforts of his spider friend Charlotte A. Cavatica and the other barnyard animals, Wilbur achieves fame and thus salvation from slaughter. More important, he overcomes his own feelings of inferiority and through Charlotte's help, he understands the meaning of friendship and the significance of death in the cycles of nature.

Louis, the mute swan of *The Trumpet of the Swan*, decides he must learn to write and goes to school where, with the aid of a slate and pencil, he learns to communicate with his human friends. However, because without a voice Louis cannot court his love Serena, his father steals a trumpet from a Billings, Montana, music store. Although thrilled with the instrument, Louis realizes he must earn money to pay his father's debt before he can court Serena and begins an odyssey which sees him playing his trumpet at a summer camp in Ontario, in the Boston Public Gardens, and at a night club in Philadelphia. His talent earns him fame and wealth, but loyalty to his father and love for Serena are his only concerns, and, returning to his family, he gives his father all his money, weds his lady, and lives a happy life in the wilderness. White referred to this book as a love story; it could also be called his version of "The Ugly Duckling," the story of a handicap overcome.

While his children's stories are based on absurd situations, White is able to make the reader accept the situations, and he then uses them as the basis of stories that are humorous, moving, and often very profound. He achieves his successes by skillfully convincing the reader of his fantasy worlds, by fully developing major characters and surrounding them with important secondary characters, by clearly delineating the settings in which his characters move, by subtly intimating the themes of his stories, and by delicately varying his style to suit the tone and mood of the specified moment.

The animal characters are described in such a way as to make them true to both their animal natures and elements of human nature. Not only did White carefully study the animals to be used in his stories, but he introduced factual details into the narratives in ways which enhance the moods of the stories. The explanation of how swans become airborne is placed in the mouth of Louis' pedantic and wordy father; Charlotte recounts the trapping of a victim in the manner of a boxing announcer, thus lessening the horror; and the author describes the building of a spider web in a manner which conveys both the intricacy and marvelousness of the procedure. In addition, each of the central characters in undergoing their conflicts experiences such human emotions as fear, love, despair, hope, grief, and fulfillment, all described without the sentimentality often found in animal fantasies.

White's secondary characters, both human and animal, provide the author with the opportunity of satirizing human nature. Snowball, the Littles' cat, embodies cruelty; Templeton, the barnyard rat, complete self-centeredness; and Louis' father, inflated self-importance. Dr. Carey, Stuart's dentist friend, is the adult who loves to play with children's toys; Mr.

Zuckerman, basking in Wilbur's glory, is the individual who considers others' accomplishments important only as they reflect well upon himself; and Mr. Bickle, the head camp counselor who invites Louis to be a bugler, the adult who uses his own status to appear important before children. Two of the children in White's stories, Fern in *Charlotte's Web* and Sam Beaver in *The Trumpet of the Swan*, are used to illustrate a major theme: growth and change. Fern progresses from a little girl playing with dolls, to one listening to the conversations of animals, and finally to one interested in boys. She has matured during the summer. Sam Beaver had written in his diary, "I wonder what I'm going to be when I grow up?" In the course of his friendship with Louis the trumpeter swan, he discovers his vocation, that of a zookeeper.

Although there are occasional lapses in his writing, White's success as a storyteller owes a great deal to his masterful style, which he makes suit his many purposes. His skillful use of dialogue conveys the emotions of his characters, and his descriptions of actions capture such moods as the humor of barnyard chases, the sadness of Charlotte's lonely death, and the pathos of Stuart's northward journey. He is very successful in his descriptions of nature, which, in addition to being accurate, are also lyrically evocative. At intervals in *Charlotte's Web* are descriptions which capture the moods of the changing seasons. Throughout the stories are epigrammatic statements which, although they are about his characters, satirize human nature. Preparing to journey in search of Margalo, Stuart Little outfits himself at a tailor shop: "He charged everything and was well pleased with his purchases." Mr. Bickle introduces the swan to his campers. "Louis is a musician. Like most musicians, he is in need of money."

TIPS FOR PARENTS AND TEACHERS: White's children's novels are classics which should be read to, or by, all middle elementary aged children. *Charlotte's Web* is an excellent story for introducing children to the idea of death as a fact of life. It is also an excellent study of the differences between egotism and self-worth. Both *Stuart Little* and *The Trumpet of the Swan* can probably best be studied by upper elementary aged children. *Stuart Little* stresses the uncertainties of life; *The Trumpet*, the need for struggle and hard work in the search for happiness.

White, T(erence) H(anbury) *(1906 – 1964)*
English

Born in Bombay, India, T.H. White had a very unhappy childhood which, he later recalled, led him to strive for excellence in all his endeavors.

After graduation from Cambridge, he taught school and began publishing novels and books of poetry. In 1936, he retired from teaching to write full time, and for the next twenty years devoted his major energies to retelling the legends of King Arthur and his knights. In 1957, he was to say, "It sounds preposterous to say so, but on a great subject, which is the epic of Britain, you have to write downright badly to make a mess of it."

The Sword in the Stone, the story of Arthur's boyhood, appeared in England in 1938 and a year later in the United States. *The Witch in the Wood* was published in 1939, the year White moved to Ireland, where he lived until 1946. *The Ill-Made Knight* appeared in 1940, and these three volumes were combined with *The Candle in the Wind* to form *The Once and Future King* (1958). *The Book of Merlyn*, an account of Arthur's meeting with Merlyn the night before the king's defeat by Mordred, was published posthumously (1977). Considered by many critics to be the most important twentieth-century retelling of the Arthurian legends, *The Once and Future King* served as the major source for the Broadway musical "Camelot." In 1946, White published *Mistress Masham's Repose*, a children's novel about a lonely girl who meets a race of tiny people descended from the Lilliputians discovered by Lemuel Gulliver in Jonathan Swift's eighteenth-century satire *Gulliver's Travels*.

White's reputation in children's literature is based on two books, *The Sword in the Stone* and *Mistress Masham's Repose*. While superficially very different, they are fundamentally similar: both show two dispossessed individuals growing in wisdom as they move toward acquiring their rightful inheritances. Arthur, nicknamed Wart, lives under the shadow of his foster-brother Kay and believes that he will never become a knight. Under the guidance of the sometimes befuddled Merlyn, he learns to think for himself and about other people. Maria, a ten-year-old orphan controlled by her villainous guardians, discovers tiny people on an island in the ruinous estate she is to inherit. Her mentor is an absent-minded professor who teaches her that she must respect the individuality of the little people whom she is sometimes tempted to treat as playthings.

Both children have exciting adventures. Arthur, with Kay, aids Robin Wood (Hood) in a daring rescue of prisoners from Morgan the Fay's castle, and at various times is transformed by Merlyn into different types of animals. Maria is imprisoned by her evil guardians, but is courageous in her defense of her new-found friends. While both have adult helpers, they must take on their most dangerous quests alone. It is then that their inner strengths are most fully developed.

A significant theme found in both books deals with the misuses of power. Arthur's strength arises from the fact that he is kind and truly wants to help others. Maria is told by the professor, "People must not tyrannize, nor try to be great because they are little. My dear, you are a great person yourself, in any case, and you do not need to lord it over others, in order to prove your greatness."

TIPS FOR PARENTS AND TEACHERS: The Sword in the Stone is best read by junior high students who are familiar with the basic legends. They should notice White's use of anachronisms to make many of his points. For upper elementary students who have enjoyed Mary Norton's *The Borrowers, Mistress Masham's Repose* is a good follow-up. Students should consider the moral dilemmas faced by Maria.

Wilder, Laura Ingalls *(1867 – 1957)*
American

Born near Lake Pepin, Wisconsin, the second of four children, all girls, Laura Ingalls spent her first six years in the wilderness of the Wisconsin forests. Of her childhood, she was later to recall, "The mind of a child is peculiarly attuned to the beauties of nature and the voices of the wildwood and the impression they made was deep." When she was seven, the family travelled by covered wagon to the Missouri Territory where they lived for a year before being dispossessed by the United States Government. They then moved east to Minnesota, where Mary, the eldest daughter, went blind after contracting scarlet fever. Ingalls suffered successive crop failures and the family relocated in South Dakota where Laura attended school, taught, and met Almanzo Wilder, whom she married in 1885. These years of her life provided the basis for the famous Little House books.

Bad luck struck the Wilders in the early years of their marriage. Laura Ingalls Wilder wrote, "We experienced complete destruction of our crops by hailstorms; the loss of our little house by fire; the loss of Almanzo's health from a stroke of paralysis, and then the drought years of 1892–93–94." The family decided to move, and set out in 1894 to Missouri, settling near Mansfield, Missouri. Rocky Ridge Farm was their home for the rest of Wilder's life. Although she did not incorporate elements of her life there in any of her stories, Rocky Ridge Farm was the place she liked best. Of the area she wrote, "There is no other country like the Ozarks in the world."

Although in *These Happy Golden Years* (1943) Wilder describes having written a school composition which was highly praised by her teacher, she did not seriously think of becoming a writer until she was middle-aged. The idea for a series of children's books based on her childhood emerged during the 1920s. According to critic Rosa Ann Moore, Wilder, working closely with her daughter, prepared a book tentatively titled, "When Grandma Was a Little Girl." It was turned down by Alfred A. Knopf before being published by Harper and Row in 1932 as *The Little House in the Big Woods*. It was extremely popular and was awarded a Newbery Honor Medal. A sequel was requested and six were written. With the exceptions of *Farmer Boy* (1933) and *The Little House on the Prairie* (1935), each was named a Newbery Honor Book.

Taken as a group, the Little House books present a chronicle of Laura's life from a small child to a married woman and are an intimate history of the development of areas of the American West in the later part of the nineteenth century. In *The Little House in the Big Woods*, Laura is five years old, living with her mother and father and two sisters in a small log cabin in the Wisconsin wilderness. *The Little House on the Prairie* (1935) opens with the Ingalls making the first of their many moves. The family perseveres and, within a year, they have planted their crop and built a cabin. However, when the government declares their presence illegal, Pa quickly decides to move rather than be evicted by soldiers. In *On the Banks of Plum Creek* (1937), the family has settled in Minnesota. Ma is happy to be closer to civilization and Pa is sure that they can make a good living on the land. However, a plague of grasshoppers wipes out their crop. The Ingalls struggle courageously and the book ends with Pa, who has been lost four days in a blizzard, coming home in time to celebrate Christmas.

However, the Ingalls' misfortunes continue. Mary becomes blind and, at the beginning of *By the Shores of Silver Lake* (1939), they are ready to move again. Pa goes west to work on the railroad being built through South Dakota and to stake a land claim. The final four books of the series are set in and around DeSmet, South Dakota. In *By the Shores of Silver Lake*, Pa establishes his claim, to which the family moves at the end of the book. *The Long Winter* (1940) describes the family's struggles to survive when the town is isolated by continuous blizzards and fuel and food run dangerously low. Almanzo Wilder, who with his brother Royal has moved west to stake a claim, courageously drives through the bitter cold to procure supplies for the village. The last two books focus on Laura's growth to maturity. In *The Little Town on the Prairie* (1941), the family has saved enough money to send Mary to a school for the blind, Laura attends school and becomes involved in the social activities of the town, and, at the book's conclusion, earns a teaching certificate. In *These Happy Golden Years* (1943), she succeeds in her first teaching job, completes her own schooling, marries Almanzo, and moves with him to the "Little Gray Home in the West."

The popularity of the "Little House" books was so great that Harper and Row, the publishers, decided to issue a uniform edition, illustrated by Garth Williams, in 1953. It is estimated that over ten million copies of the individual titles in this edition have been sold. In 1954, Wilder was named the first recipient of the Laura Ingalls Wilder Award, presented every five years by the American Library Association "in recognition of an author or illustrator whose books, published in the United States, have over a period of years made a substantial and lasting contribution to literature for children." The popularity of the books continues unabated in the 1980s, and they formed the basis of an NBC television series starring Michael Landon as Pa.

The focus of the books is on Pa and Laura, and to a lesser extent Ma, Mary, and Almanzo. Pa, restless and hard working, mixing common sense with vision, and exhibiting high moral standards, provides the stability of the family. When he is at home playing his fiddle, the others feel secure, in spite of the howls of nearby wolves, the threat of Indian attacks, or the ravages of winter. When, in *The Long Winter*, he cannot play his fiddle because of the numbing cold, the others realize how desperate their situation is. When he is away from home, the family feels lonely and insecure. Although fiercely independent, he realizes the value of neighborliness: "I've never been beholden to any man yet, and I never will be. But neighborliness is another matter." He becomes, by virtue of his strong character, a leader in the emerging town of DeSmet. As he appears in the series, he symbolizes the frontier spirit.

Laura, a little girl at the opening of the first book, and a married young woman at the conclusion of the last, is very much like her father. She, too, is restless for open spaces. She "liked the High Prairie best. The prairie was so wide and sweet and clear." Although small in stature, she is feisty and determined. Often her high spirits get her in trouble: visiting Lake Pepin for the first time, she rips her pocket while greedily stuffing it with stones; she often fights with her more demure sister Mary; exploring Plum Creek against her father's orders, she nearly drowns; and she implicitly supports a class mutiny against an unfair teacher. However, her feisty determination helps her: she thrives in the wilderness environment, succeeds as a teacher, and proves a good companion to the equally fiery Almanzo.

In a way, Laura's growth to maturity can been seen as a realistic fairy tale. *The Little House in the Big Woods* begins with the sentence: "Once upon a time, sixty years ago, a little girl lived in the Big Woods of Wisconsin, in a little gray house made of logs." Several years later, challenges faced and obstacles conquered, the "princess" marries her "prince" and the series closes with her entering a little gray house on the prairie.

Not only are the Little House books about an actual girl who lived in the late nineteenth century, but also they are a symbolic portrayal of the qualities which led to the settlement of the American West. In this respect, Wilder is within a tradition of American children's literature of the 1930s and 1940s. At a time when depression and later world war threatened the spirit of the

American republic, writers like Carol Brink in *Caddie Woodlawn* and Robert Lawson, James Daugherty, and Edgar and Ingri d'Aulaire in their biographies of frontiersmen and early statesmen celebrated the pioneer spirit of America.

Although in the later books the elements of progress become more evident, the emphasis in the series is on the farm as the basis of the expanding country. In a sense, the books are a celebration of the agrarian ideal: the belief prevalent in the nineteenth century that the strength of the Republic rested with farms and the people who ran them. In *Farmer Boy*, Almanzo's father tells him, "A farmer depends on himself and the land and the weather. You work hard, but you work as you please, and no man can tell you to go or come. You'll be free and independent, son, on a farm." Struggling against blizzards and droughts, prairie fires, plagues of grasshoppers and blackbirds, and the whims of a distant government, the characters in the Little House books eventually emerge triumphant. Their ideals are focused in the frequent Fourth of July celebrations described in the stories. Attending one, Laura hears an orator recite the Declaration of Independence and realizes what they are fighting for.

The Little House books are not without their faults. Ma's horror and disgust of Indians can be seen as racist. At times, the moral tone is rather heavy-handed. Pa's stories about his father's escapades and the recounting of Laura's misdeeds often sound like the cautionary tales Laura read in her Sunday School papers. The books seldom present inner psychological conflicts. Ma, seen as a traditional lady, often appears as a two-dimensinal character. However, in their realistic portrayal of frontier life, their delineation of the growing to maturity of Laura, and their elevation of the characters, events, and landscapes to symbolic levels, the Little House books have justly achieved their status as classics of American children's literature.

TIPS FOR PARENTS AND TEACHERS: The Little House books can be read progressively in the middle and upper elementary grades; as readers mature, so does Laura. In reading *The Little House in the Big Woods*, students can notice that Laura's trips from home become longer as she grows. In the upper elementary grades, the spirit of frontier people can be discussed and the type of character required to survive and thrive analysed.

Wildsmith, Brian *(1930 –)*
English

Born in Penistone, a small mining town in northern England, Brian Wildsmith had originally intended to become a chemist. However, as a teenager he suddenly "discovered" art and enrolled in the Barnsley School of Art and later the University of London's Slade School of Art. In 1957, he began a career as a free-lance artist, creating colored book covers and illustrating books, and in 1961, received his first major commission and provided fourteen color plates for an Oxford University Press edition of *The Arabian Nights*.

Although his work for the book was not favorably reviewed, the Oxford University Press stood by him, and his second book, *Brian Wildsmith's ABC* (1962), was awarded the Kate Greenaway Medal. He has since illustrated over two dozen books, sixteen of which he also wrote. Three were named runners-up for the Kate Greenaway Medal: *The Lion and the Rat* (1963), *The Oxford Book of Poetry for Children* (1963), and *Brian Wildsmith's Birds* (1967).

Wildsmith's books can be divided into five categories: concept books, animal books, poetry books, retellings of traditional stories, and original stories. *Brian Wildsmith's ABC* and *Brian Wildsmith's 1, 2, 3s* (1965), which the author says is his favorite book, set the pattern for many of his books. In the former, a variety of brightly and often impressionistically painted animals and objects — a butterfly, a unicorn, and a violin, to name but three — are placed against flat-colored backgrounds. In the latter, three basic shapes — rectangles, circles, and triangles — are formed into colorful designs.

Wildsmith has created three books about various types of animals: *Brian Wildsmith's Wild Animals* (1967), *Brian Wildsmith's Birds*, and *Brian Wildsmith's Fishes* (1968). The organizing principle behind each of these books is an examination of the collective names of animals. Thus in *Birds* the artist presents "a wedge of swans," "a nye of pheasants," "a fall of woodcock," and others. The illustrations are both accurate and impressionistic, as the artist uses lavish colors, particularly on the background.

Wildsmith's collections of poetry, *The Oxford Book of Poetry*, *Brian Wildsmith's Mother Goose* (1964), and *A Child's Garden of Verses* (1966), are all illustrated in his characteristic style. In *Mother Goose*, harlequin designs are used frequently. The illustrations to Stevenson's *Child's Garden of Verses* render the child's viewpoint through an impressionistic use of color, but they do not capture the notes of fear that creep into some of the nighttime poems.

The seventeenth-century French fabulist La Fontaine is a favorite author of Wildsmith, as his stories present universal themes which can be appreciated by children of many cultures. Wildsmith has retold and illustrated five of them: *The Lion and the Rat* (1963), *The North Wind and the Sun* (1964), *The Rich Man and the Shoemaker* (1965), *The Hare and the Tortoise* (1967), and *The Miller, the Boy, and the Donkey* (1969). He has also adapted Bible stories in *Brian Wildsmith's Illustrated Bible Stories* (1968) and retold a medieval religious legend, *The True Cross* (1977).

Two of Wildsmith's original stories, *The Little Wood Duck* (1972) and *The Lazy Bear* (1973), resemble traditional fables. *Python's Party* (1974) is the story of a snake who tries unsuccessfully to trick other animals into becoming his supper. In these stories, text is minimal, with the illustrations providing mood and conflict. This characteristic is seen best in *Brian Wildsmith's Circus* (1970) which contains only two lines of text: the words "The circus comes to town . . . ," on the first page, and " . . . the circus goes on to the next town," on the last. Between them, a series of double-page spreads show the continuity of movement from the circus parade, through animal and acrobatic acts, to the departure.

In describing Wildsmith's illustrations, critics have used such terms as "exuberant," "kaleidoscopic," and "harlequinesque." While a viewer's initial impression may be one of the vividness of the pictures, the illustrations are embodiments of Wildsmith's theory of the picture book. Noting that the artist must approach each subject differently, just as a musician must approach each composer differently, Wildsmith wrote: "Illustrating books should rather be like playing the piano. . . . Each book should have its own appearance which makes it different from any other book." A painting should seek to express the essence of what is represented and, in illustrating a story, the artist should "enlarge on the text to create a pictorial form that is at one with the text and yet is a thing to itself." For Wildsmith, the form and color of a painting are important, particularly as these are elements to which children respond strongly.

Wildsmith's artistry, while it has received much praise, has also received strong criticism. Often it is said that the pictures become their own reasons for being and do not really augment the text. Writing about *Brian Wildsmith's Mother Goose*, Maurice Sendak commented, "The decorator-color images grossly underestimate the poetry by grossly overshooting the mark." A major question asked by critics is whether Wildsmith creates picture books or collections of vivid pictures. Many believe that the latter is the case and that instead of developing a continuity from page to page, individual pictures become isolated objects.

TIPS FOR PARENTS AND TEACHERS: In sharing Wildsmith's books with preschoolers, adults are advised to consider pictures individually rather than in sequence. Small children enjoy discussing each picture at length, commenting on colors and details. *Wildsmith's ABC* is an excellent introduction to the letters, to the objects depicted, and to various colors.

Charlotte's Web, by E.B. White, illus. by Garth Williams, Harper & Row, New York, 1952. Williams combines animal and human features to depict Wilbur's emotions in *Charlotte's Web*.

❦ Williams, Garth *(1912 –   )*
American

Although he was born in New York, Garth Williams grew up and studied in England. After returning to the United States after World War II, he began working for the *New Yorker* magazine, where he met E.B. White. White invited him to illustrate his first children's book, *Stuart Little* (1945), and since then Williams has devoted his time almost exclusively to the illustrating of children's books. Of the more than sixty works he has illustrated, he is best known for his work with Golden Books in the years after World War II, for his illustrations of E.B. White's two classics, *Stuart Little* and *Charlotte's Web* (1952), and for the pictures in the 1953 reissue of Laura Ingalls Wilder's "Little House" books.

Williams' best works for Golden Books, which included *Baby Farm Animals* (1953) and *The Big Golden Animal ABC* (1957), were full-color picture books containing personified animals. Discussing his technique of depicting animals, Williams wrote, "I start with the real animal, working over and over until I can get the effect of human qualities and expressions and poses. I redesign animals as it were." His greatest portrayals of animals are found in *Charlotte's Web*. The illustrations have become as closely linked to White's story as Sir John Tenniel's are with Lewis Carroll's Alice books, or Ernest Shepard's with A.A. Milne's Winnie-the-Pooh stories.

In the late 1940s, Ursula Nordstrom of Harper and Row invited Williams to illustrate a proposed reissue of Laura Ingalls Wilder's semi-autobiographical stories. Writing later in *The Horn Book,* he remembered his initial reaction: "My knowledge of the West at that time was almost zero and I could not see myself undertaking the work happily until I had seen the country that formed the background of the stories. And so I decided to visit Mrs. Wilder in Mansfield, Missouri, where she still lives; and then follow the route which the Ingalls family took in their covered wagon." He also engaged in extensive research about the locales and times of the stories.

TIPS FOR PARENTS AND TEACHERS: In the early and middle elementary grades, Williams' illustrations to *Charlotte's Web* can be used to introduce readers to the personalities of the major characters. The illustrations for the "Little House" books can be carefully examined to give students a better sense of the physical aspects of nineteenth-century pioneer life.

Yashima, Taro: pseudonym of Jun Atsushi Iwamatsu *(1908 –   )*
American

Born Jun Atsushi Iwamatsu, in the southern country village of Kagoshima, Japan, the youngest of three sons, Yashima was early exposed to art by his father, a country doctor who collected Oriental art masterpieces. As a student, Yashima belonged to an underground movement and was several times jailed. Political pressure, along with a belief that he could only revive a flagging inspiration by studying Western art led Yashima and his wife Mitsui to leave temporarily their young son and travel to New York City. While working for the United States Army during World War II, Yashima adopted, for security reasons, his pen name, one which, he says, symbolized his homesickness: "Taro" meaning "healthy boy," and "Yashima" standing for the eight islands of old Japan.

Yashima did not begin writing and illustrating children's books until the early 1950s, when he told his young daughter stories. Finding the traditional Japanese stories somewhat dull and emotionless, he described his own happy childhood in *The Village Tree* (1953) and *Plenty to Watch* (1954), the latter created with his wife.

In 1955, Yashima published his best-known story, *Crow Boy*, the first of three of his books to win a Caldecott Honor Medal. Set in Japan, it is the story of a small boy who, on entering school, is treated as an outcast by the other children and is mockingly named "Chibi," or tiny boy. When, on the day of the annual talent show, Chibi prepares to imitate the voices of crows, the children are at first scornful, but when they hear the boy they are deeply moved and realize their cruelty to him. He is given a new name, "Crow Boy," in recognition of his talents. The story is remarkable for Yashima's deep understanding and sensitive portrayal of both the lonely child and his peers. This is achieved not only through the simple but poetic text, but also through Yashima's crayon and ink drawings. They accurately present the landscape, buildings, and clothing of the story, and communicate impressionistically the loneliness and later fulfillment of Crow Boy.

Umbrella (1958) is the first of three Yashima stories in which his daughter Momo is a central character. Designed as a present for her eighth birthday and winner of a Caldecott Honor Medal, it describes how the two-year-old child was given her first new umbrella and rain shoes and then had to wait impatiently for rain. Set in New York City, the book once again demonstrates Yashima's ability to see life from the child's point of view. *Momo's Kitten* (1961) and *Youngest One* (1962) are about the girl as she grows older.

During the 1960s, Yashima returned to Japan and after his visit wrote *Seashore Story* (1967), winner of his third Caldecott Honor Medal. A group of Japanese children playing in the sand remember the ancient story of Urashima, who had returned to his home after a long sea journey to a beautiful palace to find that everything had changed, that no one remembered him, and that he was very old.

The dominant theme of Yashima's picture books is the need for the child to grow and to understand a wider range of experience. *The Village Tree* and *Plenty to Watch* introduce a little girl living in New York City to Japanese village life of earlier years. In *Crow Boy*, Chibi in his long walks to school comes to understand nature, and later his schoolmates understand him. The children of *Seashore Story*, visiting a familiar setting and hearing an old, well-known story, learn a new lesson: the dangers of forgetting loved ones.

TIPS FOR PARENTS AND TEACHERS: In studying *Crow Boy*, early elementary aged children can notice how large white spaces in the illustrations indicate Chibi's isolation, while his central positioning in later illustrations reveals his new status. In the middle elementary grades, the theme of forgetting one's past presented in *Seashore Story* can be discussed.

Yolen, Jane *(1939 –   )*
American

Born in New York City, Jane Yolen received a bachelor's degree from Smith College before working as assistant juvenile editor for Alfred A. Knopf. In 1963, David McKay published *Pirates in Petticoats*, the first of her over thirty books for children. She has received several literary honors, including the Golden Kite Award presented by the Society of Children's Book Writers for *The Girl Who Cried Flowers* (1974). *The Girl Who Loved the Wind* (1972) was presented the Lewis Carroll Shelf Award, while *The Emperor and the Kite* (1967), illustrated by Ed Young, was a Caldecott Honor Book. She now lives in rural Connecticut with her husband and three children and has completed a Ph.D. in children's literature at the University of Massachuetts.

Jane Yolen is chiefly known as a teller of literary fairy tales. A student of folklore and mythology, the function of which she sees as "explaining and giving ways of dealing with reality," her own works are replete with character types, situations, and settings similar to those of traditional stories. Four recurring character types in her stories are the rejected child (*The Boy Who Had Wings*, 1974, and *The Emperor and the Kite),* the child hero (*Greyling*, 1968), the mysterious lover ("The Girl Who Cried Flowers" and *The Little Spotted Fish*, 1975), and the adult who cannot accept the imperfections of life (*The Sultan's Perfect Tree*, 1977). Within this variety, a common theme emerges: transformation, the changing of character. A dominant folkloristic motif, this process of character growth is achieved through self-awareness of inner worth (*The Boy Who Had Wings* and *Greyling*), or through the achievement of a loving relationship with another (*The Little Spotted Fish* or "The Promise"). A variation of the Beauty and the Beast theme, the external change from a woman to a dove ("The Hundredth Dove"), or from a seal to a maiden ("The White Seal Maid"), is a metaphor for internal change.

TIPS FOR PARENTS AND TEACHERS: As Yolen has remarked, her stories are for older children (middle and upper elementary grades) who can better understand the psychological themes embodied in her works.

Duffy and the Devil, by Harve and Margot Zemach, Farrar, Straus & Giroux, New York, 1973. The humorous conclusion of *Duffy and the Devil* is enhanced by this illustration with its contrast between the nude squire and his surroundings.

Zemach, Harve *(1933 – 1974), and* Zemach, Margot *(1931 –   )*
American

Born in Los Angeles, Margot Zemach grew up in Oklahoma City, New York City, and Los Angeles. A lonely child, she spent much of her time reading and drawing illustrations for fairy tales. She reported, "I believed wholeheartedly in the existence of fairies and used to sit outside on the stairs waiting for them to appear." She studied at the Los Angeles County Art Institute, the Jepson Institute of Art, the Chounard Institute of Art, and the Vienna Academy of Fine Arts, where she met Harve Fischtrom, a graduate student of history, whom she married in 1957. The couple returned to Boston and, as Harve and Margot Zemach, published their first children's book, *Small Boy is Listening*, in 1958.

The couple collaborated on ten more books, Harve writing the text and often helping with overall design and layout and Margot providing the illustrations. Many of the stories, among them *Nail Soup* (1964), *Salt* (1965), and *A Penny a Look* (1971), are based on traditional tales. For her illustrations of their adaptation of *Duffy and the Devil* (1973), an old Cornish tale, Margot Zemach was awarded the Caldecott Medal. Harve Zemach's original stories include *The Judge* (1969), a Caldecott Honor Book; *Awake and Dreaming* (1970); and *The Princess and the Froggie* (1975).

In adapting stories or writing his own, Harve Zemach chose plots which allowed him to portray comic situations, satirize human nature, and develop humorous language patterns. For Zemach, the act of writing and telling stories is "an extension of being a parent . . . . It can be a civilizing moment, a boost to the child's dignity and self-regard, a chance for an older person to help a younger one form his taste and clarify his ideas."

In addition to creating stories with her husband, Margot Zemach has illustrated works by such writers as Isaac Bashevis Singer (*Mazel and Shlemazel*, 1967, and *When Shlemiel Went to Warsaw and Other Stories*, 1968), and Lloyd Alexander (*The Foundling*, 1973). Since her husband's death, she has adapted or written three books on her own: *Hush Little Baby* (1976); *It Could be Worse* (1976), a Caldecott Honor Book; and *To Hilda for Helping* (1977). Margot Zemach seeks to capture the humor and the sense of the absurd in the stories through her line drawings and use of colors, usually washes, "that will strengthen rather than negate the drawing." In *Duffy and the Devil*, faces and human figures reveal greed, vanity, and laziness. In *Hush Little Baby*, the words of the peaceful lullaby contrast the illustrations in which a child cries, a cat tries to catch a bird, and a huge dog, after stealing food from the stove, stretches out on a double bed.

TIPS FOR PARENTS AND TEACHERS: Zemach's illustrations reveal characters possessed of a wide variety of emotions. Preschool and early elementary children can discuss these emotions after looking carefully at the facial expressions.

An Expanding Six-Foot Reference Shelf on Children's Literature: A Bibliographic Essay

During the last ten years, there has been a knowledge explosion in the field of children's literature. Specialists in many fields have realized that children's reading is important and that it is necessary for adults to have a thorough understanding of the field in order to give children a good grounding in literature. The books discussed below are not the only studies available for the interested adult, but they certainly will provide access to the basic information and clues to where other materials can be found. They are also the books which I have found most useful in writing *Children's Literature from A to Z*. Interested readers can put together a basic six-foot reference shelf on children's literature by selecting some of the books described here and then can gradually expand the shelf to suit their own needs.

One of the most useful aspects of background information for the adult reader of children's literature is material about the author of a specific book. What are the facts of the person's life? What books did she or he read? What are the characteristics of this author's writing: themes, styles, subject matter? What have critics written about his or her works? Fortunately there is no shortage of reference books in this area. Brian Doyle's collection entitled *The Who's Who of Children's Literature* (New York: Schocken Books, 1968) is somewhat dated, but contains good, brief articles about major British, American, and continental writers. It is particularly useful for its coverage of pre-World War I writers and illustrators. Lee Bennett Hopkins has created interesting profiles of over 150 contemporary writers and illustrators in *Books Are by People* (New York: Citation Press, 1969) and *More Books by More People* (New York: Citation Press, 1974). Hopkins visited each of the people he writes about, and the results are lively and entertaining. In *Pied Pipers* (New York: Paddington Press, 1975), Justin Wintle reprints transcripts of interviews conducted with contemporary writers. Designed for both older children and adults, the books in Junior Authors series—*The Junior Book of Authors* (1951), *More Junior Authors* (1963), *The Third Book of Junior Authors* (1972), and *The Fourth Book of Junior Authors and Illustrators* (1978)—published by H. W. Wilson (New York) contain brief essays about authors, past and present, from around the world. Where possible, the authors and illustrators themselves have contributed essays about their own lives.

Among other, more technical books and series about authors, *Twentieth Century Children's Writers*, edited by D. L. Kirkpatrick (New York: St. Martin's Press, 1978), contains over 1500 pages of biographical facts, publications lists, and brief critical essays on hundreds of authors who have written in English. A short appendix discusses nineteenth-century writers. *Something about the Author* (Detroit: Gale Research, 1971–   ) was, at last count, up to its thirty-second volume. Each volume covers about forty authors, listing basic facts and publications and excerpting interesting things about the subjects' lives from biographies and from their own statements. Each entry is illustrated with photographs of the authors and of places associated with their lives, as well as with illustrations from the books. Gale Research also put out the two-volume set *Yesterday's Authors of Books for Children* (1977, 1978), which follows the format of *Something about the Author*, except that the entries are longer. This series has been discontinued and entries on noncontemporary writers have been included in *Something about the Author* beginning with volume 16. Another Gale series, *Children's Literature Review* (1976–   ) now in its fifth volume, reprints reviews of major books by and excerpts from critical articles and books and about authors and illustrators. Each volume includes material on approximately twenty authors. This series is a valuable reference tool for use in detailed research on a specific writer. *A Dictionary of Literary Biography—Volume 22: American Writers for Children, 1900–1960* (Gale, 1983), edited by John Cech, contains detailed critical essays on the careers of forty-three American children's writers. Subsequent volumes in this series are planned to include contemporary and early American and English authors and illustrators. The works listed in this paragraph are all valuable, but inclusion of many of them will certainly expand the reference shelf far beyond six feet.

Illustrators past and present have been thoroughly treated in five books published by Horn Book (Boston). Four of these—*Illustrators of Children's Books 1744–1945* (1947), compiled by Bertha E. Mahony, Louise P. Latimer, Beulah Folmsbee; *Illustrators of Children's Books: 1946–1956* (1958), compiled by Bertha Mahony Miller, Ruth Hill Viguers, and Marcia Dalphin; *Illustrators of Children's Books: 1957–1966* (1968), compiled by Lee Kingman, Joanna Foster, and Ruth Giles Lontoft; and *Illustrators of Children's Books: 1967–1976* (1978), compiled by Lee Kingman, Grace Allen Hogarth, and Harriet Quimbly—contain chapters outlining major subjects for the various historical eras and biographical statements and bibliographical summaries for the major and many minor illustrators of the period covered. *The Illustrator's Notebook*, edited by Lee Kingman (1978), is a lavishly illustrated compilation of articles which have appeared over the years in the prestigious American journal *Horn Book Magazine.*

A major history of children's literature has still to be written; however there are two very useful one-volume surveys and several books dealing with specific eras. The revised edition of *A Critical History of Children's Literature*, edited by Cornelia Meigs (New York: Macmillan, 1969), is divided into four sections, each written by a specialist: "Roots in the Past up to 1840," "Widening Horizons 1840–1890," "A Rightful Heritage 1890–1920," and "Golden Years and Time of Tumult 1920–1967." John Rowe Townsend's book *Written for Children* (Philadelphia: Lippincott, 1974) is recommended as a short, good, easily read introduction to children's literature. Among the many interesting books dealing with specific trends and historical periods are: Gillian Avery, *Childhood's Pattern: A Study of the Heroes and Heroines of Children's Fiction, 1770–1950* (London: Hodder and Stoughton, 1975); Marcus Crouch, *Treasure Seekers and Borrowers: Children's Books in Britain, 1900–1960* (London: Library Association, 1962); F. J. H. Darton, *Children's Books in England: Five Centuries of Social Life* (Cambridge: Cambridge University Press, 1958); Sheila Egoff, *Thursday's Child: Trends and Patterns in Contemporary Children's Literature* (Chicago: American Library Association, 1981); Monica Kiefer, *American Children through Their Books* (Philadelphia: University of Pennsylvania Press, 1970); Anne Scott MacLeod, *A Moral Tale: Children's Fiction and American Culture 1820–1860* (New York: Archon, 1975); and Samuel F. Pickering, Jr., *John Locke and Children's Books in Eighteenth-Century England* (Knoxville: University of Tennessee Press, 1981).

Many significant pieces of writing about children's literature have appeared in periodicals and other less easy to find places. Fortunately, many of these essays have been gathered together into collections. One or two of these collections would certainly make an excellent addition to the six-foot shelf. *The Signal Approach to Children's Books*, edited by Nancy Chambers (Harmondsworth, England: Kestrel Books, 1980), contains twenty-five essays originally published in the small but influential British journal *Signal*. The second edition of *Only Connect: Readings on Children's Literature*, edited by Sheila Egoff, G. T. Stubbs, and L. F. Ashley (Toronto: Oxford University Press, 1980), includes essays by well-known people in the field, such as Roger Lancelyn Green, J. R. R. Tolkien, P. L. Travers, and Clifton Fadiman. Another omnibus collection is *Children's Literature: Views and Reviews*, edited by Virginia Haviland (Glenview, Ill.: Scott, Foresman, 1972), which includes "Of Classics and Golden Ages," "Children: Their Reading Interests and Needs," and "Folk Literature and Fantasy." *Crosscurrents of Criticism: Horn Book Essays 1968–1977*, edited by Paul Heins (Boston: Horn Book, 1977), reprints essays from *Horn Book Magazine*. A book which will be of particular interest to teachers is *The Cool Web: The Pattern of Children's Reading*, edited by Aidan Warlow, Margaret Meek, and

Griselda Barton (London: The Bodley Head, 1977); it includes the essays "The Reader," "What the Author Tells Us," and "Approaches to Criticism."

Several authors have recently compiled their own books of essays, each one providing interesting and often provocative insights into children's literature. Bruno Bettelheim's book *The Uses of Enchantment: The Meaning and Importance of Fairy Tales* (New York: Random House, 1976) is a controversial psychoanalytic approach to the best-known European folktales. In *The Green and Burning Tree: On the Writing and Enjoyment of Children's Books* (Boston: Little Brown, 1969), Eleanor Cameron, writer of many children's novels, includes the essays "Fantasy," "Writing Itself," and "The Child and the Book." Selma G. Lanes' book *Down the Rabbit Hole: Adventures and Misadventures in the Realm of Children's Literature* (New York: Atheneum, 1971) includes essays on authors and illustrators such as Kate Greenaway, Arthur Rackham, Maurice Sendak, and Dr. Seuss. *Fairy Tales and After: From Snow White to E. B. White* by Roger Sale (Cambridge, Mass.: Harvard University Press, 1978) treats classic writers such as Lewis Carroll, Beatrix Potter, Kenneth Grahame, and L. Frank Baum. Lillian H. Smith's book *The Unreluctant Years: A Critical Approach to Children's Literature* (New York: Viking, 1967) is a brief but very thoughtful discussion of the major genres of children's literature. In *A Sounding of Storytellers* (Philadelphia: Lippincott, 1979), John Rowe Townsend discusses fourteen contemporary writers, giving critical overviews of their works.

A large number of books, many of them originally intended as texts for university courses, have been written with the intention of showing adults how to bring children and literature together. Of these, the most useful are: May Hill Arbuthnot, *Children's Reading in the Home* (Glenview, Ill.: Scott Foresman, 1969); Dorothy Butler, *Babies Need Books* (London: The Bodley Head, 1980); Joan I. Glazer and Gurney Williams III, *Introduction to Children's Literature* (New York: McGraw-Hill, 1979); Charlotte S. Huck, *Children's Literature in the Elementary School* (3d ed. updated, New York: Holt, Rinehart, and Winston, 1979); and Zena Sutherland, Dianne L. Monson, and May Hill Arbuthnot, *Children and Books* (6th ed., Glenview, Ill.: Scott Foresman, 1981). The last three of these volumes deal with similar subject matter, and any one would suffice as a beginning entry for the six-foot shelf.

Finally, for people who wish to keep up to date on children's literature, we note several journals and two professional associations: *Children's Literature*, an annual publication of Yale University Press (New Haven, Conn.), contains scholarly articles and reviews. *Children's Literature Association Quarterly* publishes articles and reviews as well as announcements of current interest. (Subscription information may be obtained from Alethea

Helbig, English Department, Eastern Michigan University, Ypsilanti, Michigan.) *Children's Literature in Education*, published quarterly, presents not only scholarly articles, but also essays on the teaching of literature to children. (Subscription information may be obtained from Agathon Press, 15 East 26th Street, New York, New York.) *Horn Book Magazine*, the most influential publication in the field, appears six times a year and includes articles by contemporary authors and illustrators, as well as reviews of new books. (Subscription information may be obtained from The Horn Book, 31 St. James Avenue, Boston, Massachusetts.) *Signal: Approaches to Children's Books* is published three times a year by The Thimble Press, Lockwood, Station Road, South Woodchester, Stroud, Gloucester GL5 5EQ, England. This journal describes children's literature from a variety of angles, all interesting.

The Children's Literature Association, formed in 1973 to promote serious scholarly study of the field, in addition to publishing the *Quarterly* described above, holds an annual conference featuring papers, panels, and keynote addresses by major authors and illustrators. (Membership infor-mation may be obtained from Alethea Helbig, English Department, Eastern Michigan University, Ypsilanti, Michigan.) The Children's Literature Assembly, a division of the National Council of Teachers of English (NCTE), publishes a quarterly newsletter and sponsors special meetings at the NCTE conventions. (Membership information may be obtained from NCTE, 1111 Kenyon Road, Urbana, Illinois.)

Index of Titles

About the Author

Now professor of English at the University of Alberta, Edmonton, Canada, Jon C. Stott earned his Ph.D. degree at the University of Toronto. He first began teaching children's literature while a member of the faculty of Western Michigan University. His numerous articles on children's literature have appeared in British, American, and Canadian journals, and he has conducted workshops on the teaching of literature to children in over fifty cities in the United States and Canada.

Professor Stott is active in many professional organizations and is a member of the founding Board of Directors of the Children's Literature Association, of which he was also the first president. At present, he is working on a study of native peoples in children's literature.